HISTORY OF AMERICAN

THOUGHT AND CULTURE

Paul S. Boyer

General Editor

Universities and the Capitalist State

*Corporate Liberalism and the
Reconstruction of American
Higher Education, 1894–1928*

CLYDE W. BARROW

The University of Wisconsin Press

The University of Wisconsin Press
114 North Murray Street
Madison, Wisconsin 53715

3 Henrietta Street
London   WC2E 8LU, England

5   4   3   2   1

Printed in the United States of America

Library of Congress Cataloging-in-Publication Data
Barrow, Clyde W.
   Universities and the Capitalist State/Clyde W. Barrow.
   350 pp.   cm. — (History of American thought and culture)
   Includes bibliographical references.
   1. Intellectuals—United States. 2. Higher education and state—United States.
3. Industry and education—United States. 4. Social classes—United States.
I. Title. II. Series.
HM213.B34   1990
305.5'52'0973—dc20   89-39217
ISBN 0-299-12400-2   CIP
ISBN 0-299-12404-5 (pbk.)

To my mother,
Wanda R. Barrow

Contents

Figures

Tables

Acknowledgments

THE INDUSTRIAL character of contemporary university work is never more readily apparent than when one acknowledges the many people who have contributed their labor to the production of those commodities we call books. The intellectual labor process is now a socialized and genuinely collective effort that takes place on a national and even global scale. It requires many kinds of labor, occupational skills, clerical support, and administrative services by persons who are often invisible to the university professor. Many anonymous people should therefore be recognized at the outset as an integral component of the production process which resulted in this book.

Of course, I also owe many special debts to people whose names I do know. Two current members and one former member of the UCLA Department of Political Science deserve special mention. Professor Richard Ashcraft's 1981 seminar on Mannheim's *Ideology and Utopia* was the original inspiration for the present work. In this and a subsequent seminar on twentieth-century Marxism, I produced a series of small papers in which I examined the problem of ideology in Marx, the theory of organic intellectuals in Gramsci, and their relation to Mannheim's sociology of knowledge. These papers drew heavily on Mannheim in translating the problem of ideology from an abstract epistemological question into a concrete political problem that centered on the institutional relationship between intellectuals, social structures, and the state. I concluded these papers with the development of a dissertation research design that required me to work out a political economy of class formation for American intellectuals. Professor Ashcraft subsequently supervised the work that was first completed as a political science dissertation in 1984. Karen Orren, an original reader of my dissertation, also contributed her substantial knowledge of American political development and institutional political economy. Her critical advice was important to any practical success I may have had in integrating a theoretical approach to the state with historical and institutional analysis. Questions posed in a seminar on the role of executive politics in American institutional development offered by Stephen Skowronek in 1982 have influenced my conceptualization of the state.

During two years in the political science department at Texas A&M University, I was also the beneficiary of its members' current focus on the problems of political leadership. Thus, I am indebted to Ed Portis and Charles Wiggins for bringing me to TAMU. I must thank Bryan D. Jones for making the full resources of that growing department available to a visiting junior faculty member. It proved to be a populist island in which the current work took on much of its present shape. Paul S. Boyer and Michael W. Apple subsequently read a revised version of the original manuscript. They both offered critical suggestions that resulted in a substantially improved final product.

I must also thank several individuals who were generous enough to do tedious research for a stranger. This industrial army of archivists (from whom I have extracted a bit of surplus value in the form of unpaid labor) supplied me with often obscure biographical information that made it possible to complete Chapter 3. These include Barbara S. Meloni, Curatorial Associate, Harvard University Archives; Mary Allegrini, Library Assistant for the New Jersey Historical Society; Jody Hansen, Rutgers University Archives; Ann Preston, Archivist, Drexel University; Dr. Thomas Verich, University Archivist, University of Mississippi; Charles R. Schultz, University Archivist, Texas A&M University; Cynthia J. Beeman, Research Assistant, Archives, Texas State Library; Caroline F. Ziemke, Archival Associate, Indiana University Archives; Andrew F. Johnson, Librarian, Pacific Northwest Collection, University of Washington; Lisa Browar, Curator of Rare Books and Manuscripts, Vassar College; D. Cheryl Collins, Archivist, and Jean C. Dallas, Director, Riley County (Kansas) Historical Society; Martin B. Steffenson, Head of Reference, South Dakota State University; Dayton W. Canaday, Director, Historical Resource Center, Pierre, South Dakota; Karen Laughlin, Librarian, State Historical Society of Iowa; Terry Abraham, Archivist, Washington State University Library; Michael F. Milewski, Archives Assistant, University of Massachusetts at Amherst; and some still anonymous individuals at the Chicago Historical Society, Nevada Historical Society, and Kansas State University Archives.

Shonnie Finnegan, Director of the SUNY—Buffalo University Archives, was gracious and efficient in making the Capen Papers available to me on short notice when I could afford very little time to examine them. Paige Gibbs and Charlie McNeil have been extremely helpful in finding materials that were necessary to completing the final version of the manuscript. I thank Claire Suen for the advance work that made my research trip to the National Archives an efficient one. Julie Vaccaro was exceptionally cooperative in lending her technical assistance. Her efforts facilitated the retooling of my academic capital with more recent technical innovations. She also rescued vital portions of the final text from a binomial limbo where it might otherwise have been lost forever.

Financial support for travel to the National Archives came from a 1983 institutional research grant to the UCLA Department of Political Science. Professor Richard Sisson, then chair of the department, is to be thanked for making those funds available at an opportune time. These funds were supplemented by two grants from the University of California Chancellor's Patent Fund in the winter of 1983 and fall of 1984. A travel grant from the Southeastern Massachusetts University Research Committee allowed me to examine the Capen Papers in October of 1987. Each of these grants has contributed substantially to my accumulation of the archival materials which constitute the core of Chapters 5 and 6.

Finally, I must thank my wife, Trini, who understood the peculiar demands of my work. Her interest and support in this project was vital to its completion. There are of course many friends and colleagues who have contributed in their own way.

Abbreviations

AAUP	American Association of University Professors
ACE	American Council on Education
AEA	American Economic Association
AFL	American Federation of Labor
AFT	American Federation of Teachers
APSA	American Political Science Association
ASS	American Sociological Society
AAC	Association of American Colleges
BLS	Bureau of Labor Statistics
BMR	Bureau of Municipal Research
CFAT	Carnegie Foundation for the Advancement of Teaching
CCP	Committee on Classification of Personnel
CEST	Committee on Education and Special Training
CEE	Committee on Engineering Education
COPI	Committee on Public Information
CND	Council of National Defense
ECE	Emergency Council on Education
GEB	General Education Board
ILL	Intercollegiate Liberal League
ISS	Intercollegiate Socialist Society
LID	League for Industrial Democracy
NAS	National Academy of Sciences
NA	National Archives
NDA	National Defense Act of 1916
NEA	National Education Association
NHSB	National Historical Service Board
NRC	National Research Council
NSL	National Security League
NPL	Non-Partisan League
ROTC	Reserve Officer Training Corps
SSRC	Social Science Research Council

SEB   Southern Education Board
SPEE   Society for the Promotion of Engineering Education
SATC   Student Army Training Corps
USBE   United States Bureau of Education
USDA   United States Department of Agriculture
USDW   United States Department of War

UNIVERSITIES AND THE

CAPITALIST STATE

Introduction

THERE IS an emerging consensus among Marxist theorists of the state that political development in the advanced capitalist societies is explained by continuing efforts to reconcile the contradictory demands of capitalism and democracy.[1] On the one hand, state policies that promote economic development within the framework of a capitalist economy must continually defer to the market rules of private capital accumulation. The division of labor between politics and markets thus facilitates a natural alliance between state elites and capitalists.[2] Where capital remains a private asset, state elites must necessarily grant a privileged position to the preferences of the capitalist class, if growth strategies are to succeed. The political consequence, particularly in the age of the modern corporation, is a capitalist class which rules even when it does not directly govern.[3] On the other hand, the reemergence of democratic movements during the late nineteenth and early twentieth centuries has equally compelled the state to simultaneously pursue other contradictory strategies of egalitarian redistribution. The latter have become necessary to the maintenance of its claims to democratic, popular legitimacy. The contradictory policies associated with this balance of social power have for several decades established an unstable consensus that is institutionalized as the liberal state.

However, the persistence of periodic economic crises has continually challenged the ability of state elites to effectively reconcile these contradictory demands. The suspension of these demands in a progressive political consensus has relied and still depends upon a coordinated strategy of regulated economic growth. Economic growth must be sufficient simultaneously to sustain private capital accumulation (i.e., profits and corporate reinvestment), and permit redistributive policies that promote a continual rise in general standards of living for most citizens. Consequently, cyclical accumulation crises, which still periodically reappear in capitalist economies, present a continuing and

3

ever-present spectre of class struggle even in the advanced capitalist societies.

The institutional outcome of this struggle has been a gradual displacement of underlying economic crises onto the state through a variety of economic and social policies aimed at managing class conflict. The liberal state has paradoxically been able to promote the requisite levels of private (i.e., corporate) accumulation only by socializing various costs of production, primarily through fiscal policies and spending programs that are justified as social investments. Yet, actual decisions about the deployment of capital, its utilization, and its long-term consequences for society have remained in the private sector. Thus, democratic states must also meet citizen demands for redressing the social and environmental effects of these decisions, while leaving intact the institution of private property. It is in these two occurrences—crisis displacement and regulation—that we find an explanation for the political development of capitalist states during the last century.[4] In both instances, the progressive strategy of political development has been chiefly characterized by increasingly interventionist policies of bureaucratic social and economic control that have resulted in escalating fiscal and political strains within the state. A democratic political resolution of these conflicting demands has thus required a constant expansion of the state's ability to extract resources from society, the enhancement of its bureaucratic and administrative capacities, and a strengthening of the institutions for social control.[5]

Therefore, conceptually the state and political power can no longer be identified merely with classical definitions of government.[6] The state has become a social-industrial complex of overlapping public (and even nominally private) associations that formulate policy, exercise regulatory authority, and assist in social control from a variety of independent institutional centers. This matrix now encompasses an array of relatively autonomous institutions that include civil administration; the legal system; professional police, military, and intelligence forces; interest groups; parties; professional associations; public corporations; educational institutions; and the mass media. Moreover, the growing complexity and relative autonomy of these diverse centers increasingly requires that a concrete understanding of political development must adopt a more focused institutional approach to the analysis of specific institutions and related policy formation.

The claim for such an approach is being strengthened by current comparative studies which clearly demonstrate that actual rates and forms of social investment, as well as the extent and type of bureaucratic regulation, are largely determined by the need to sustain reinvestment, redistribution, and neighborhood effects at levels which are politically determined by the existing development of actual class conflict and state power.[7] As a result, it is evident that the strategic consensus-building policies adopted by individual states, and by the related institutions within those states, cannot be adequately explained if they are approached as abstract and automatically functioning components in the capitalist mode of production, any more than they could previously be understood simply as uncontested instruments in the hands of a governing elite.[8] There in fact seem to be three analytic problems in a Marxist theory of the state which can be resolved only through specific institutional studies. These are the political relation between state and capital, the actual impact of class conflict on political development, and the organizational capacities of a particular state's power. The way in which these three phenomena are historically and institutionally related will explain the particular paths of political development identified with individual capitalist states.

This suggests that the natural alliance between state and capital must henceforth be identified with a degree of empirical and institutional precision that cannot be deduced from any *a priori* model of the capitalist mode of production. In the first place, the capitalist class— broadly designated as the owners of the means of production—is clearly by no means a fixed or historically unchanging social formation. The particular way in which it is organized or disorganized will greatly influence its own political capacities in relation to the state and to other classes that are contesting state power.[9] Political hegemony, while structured within a natural alliance, remains contingent upon a historical ability to develop coherent conceptions of class interest, to articulate these as concrete issues or policies, and to build political institutions which enable that class to assume leadership in wider coalitions. Class hegemony is therefore an institutional *balance of power* between state, capital, and popular classes that is crucially mediated by independent problems of historical class formation and political organization. The contingency of these events means that analytic and structural theorizing cannot substitute for the kind of research that is necessary to a documentation of their role in state-building and political development.[10]

Similarly, it is therefore impossible to deduce the historical character of class struggles from any general model of capitalist development. General models of economic and social structure may be adequate to diagnose the general crises and conflicts which states must resolve in particular modes of production. However, the real social forces of historical class formation that shape political development will influence the severity with which economic crises are experienced as consciously organized political and ideological struggles and, hence, the ability of state elites to manage those crises.[11] Actual levels of organized class conflict will consequently widen or narrow the political space available for individual statesmanship and political initiative, as well as the range of feasible policy options open to state elites, parties, and the ruling class. In other words, the strength of class organization in each particular capitalist society is an important determinant of a state's relative autonomy or heteronomy and cannot be conceptually presumed as part of a theoretical framework.

Likewise, states are also constructed and reconstructed to better manage critical change and to institutionalize shifts in the balance of class hegemony within and between social classes.[12] These periods of institutional reform are usually accompanied by changes in the type of personnel who occupy their authoritative positions. Such alterations will facilitate the development of a particular class hegemony, but for that hegemony to become effective, the class must remain mobilized and promote a real agenda. Moreover, as I will subsequently argue, the class conflict associated with these reforms frequently occurs with an amazingly high degree of conscious planning and long-range political vision that encounters equally conscious resistance from those adversely affected by institutional transformations of state power.[13]

This observation goes directly to the problem of state power. As specifiable institutional networks, all capitalist states display historically different, even if comparable, patterns of organization which either centralize or diffuse state power in relation to society. This directly affects their political capacities to extract resources legitimately through taxation, to administer policies through bureaucracies, and to control or directly regulate group conflicts through courts, regulatory agencies, police, armies, and schools. As a result, political structures also "powerfully shape and limit state interventions in the economy, and they determine ways in which class interests and conflicts get organized into (and out of) politics in a given time and place."[14] An adequate account of the state must therefore incorporate this institutional specificity into its explanations, because individual states have "their own structures, their own history, and their own patterns of conflict" which "impact upon class relations and economic development."[15] Many theorists are therefore beginning to recognize the necessity of undertaking specific historical analyses of states that are situated in their own irreducible paths of class formation and institutional development.[16]

It is this understanding of the state and the methodological conclusions derived from it that guide the historical analysis which follows. It is my basic contention that the class formation of a modern intellectual stratum in the United States has been decisively shaped by the contradictory imperatives that emerged from attempts to reconcile the rise of corporate capitalism with the claims of political democracy. The American intellectuals' modern historical formation is a consequence not only of their professionalization and migration into the university, but also of class conflicts which emerged around efforts to construct an "ideological state apparatus" that was centered on the university.[17]

These developments were part of the much larger social and political struggle that accompanied the building of a corporate-liberal state in America.[18] This new phase of American political development began essentially with the Populist uprising and ended with its consolidation in the New Deal, a period we often call "the age of reform."[19] The new state constructed during this period was substantially different from the mercantilist state founded in 1789 and the laissez-faire industrial state reconstructed in the decade from 1861 to 1870.[20] The new political problem confronted by reformers was one of balancing conflicting demands for social equality and economic efficiency.[21]

The consensual solution to this problem lay in a nominal bifurcation of politics and administration that has been called "the corporate ideal."[22] The major goal of institutional reform was to separate administration from politics by making the former "scientific." This occurred through the managerial rationalization of institutional structures, which were simultaneously staffed by expert personnel. These executive structures were then to be accountable to the democratic public for the results of their actions.

The age of reform was therefore dedicated to the administrative reconstruction of American institutions as diverse as the judiciary, civil service, military, parties, municipal government, schools, and universities. Each in turn was reorganized, expanded, and staffed with newly professionalized personnel. These personnel were expected to maintain a commitment to the professional ideals of autonomous scientific neutrality and specialized expertise, but were also expected to perform a public service.

This dual goal was a political contradiction that in the case of the intellectuals was clarified in two simple questions: autonomous from whom and accountable to whom? The answers to these questions yielded radically different conceptions of what objectivity and public service meant in a society structured by class conflict. Moreover, the issues raised in these disputes were only tentatively resolved on the contested terrain of professional associations, legislative assemblies, colleges, and universities.[23]

These are not merely analytic questions posed by the contemporary theorist. They were consciously articulated by intellectuals, state officials, corporate executives, farmers, and workers who were all concerned with defining the relation between schooling, social class, and the state. Many clearly understood exactly what was at stake in this formative period. A class war to conquer the intellectuals appeared as part of the wider conflicts engendered by the rise of corporate capitalism and the construction of a new American state.

One consequence of this formative struggle is that many of the stresses and contradictions of advanced capitalism were displaced onto the universities and concurrently onto contemporary intellectuals. Contemporary theorists of the ideological state apparatus have generally suggested that its economic displacement is identifiable in the successful socialization of two costs of private production. These are manpower training and the provision of a scientific-technical infrastructure to support modern industry and national defense.[24]

The traditional American college was not readily adaptable to an "instrumental order" designed to pursue these missions, nor did college intellectuals and the democratic movements readily accept these missions as legitimate.[25] At least two axes of stress and contradiction reappeared within the university that continue to fragment American intellectuals. The institutionalization of a corporate ideal in the university achieved legitimacy in the wider democratic community only to the extent that it was accompanied by the development of an "expressive order" which has recently been called the "culture of aspiration."[26] The socially efficient integration of curriculum and research with the personnel and technical requirements of corporate capitalism has been perceived as legitimate only to the extent that the state has promoted a meritocratic ideal of individual achievement and advancement through the schools and universities.[27] The corporate ideal of administrative rationality in education was reconciled with demands for educational democracy through an expressive myth of universal equal opportunity that opened the university to wider and wider segments of the population. This democratization of knowledge actually creates the myth that success and failure are solely the consequence of talent, intelligence, merit, ambition, and hard work.[28]

Yet, in fact we now know that when standardized measurements of performance are applied to an unequal system of schools and universities, individuals are generally sorted out in the system by class. The educational system thus merely mediates the reallocation of individuals to occupational positions that reproduce the existing class structure through vocational and professional certification (i.e., manpower training) while shifting the costs of training onto the state. Furthermore, the mediation of class structure by education infuses it with a cultural-ideological image in which the haves and the have-nots are perceived (even by themselves) as the talented and the untalented, the intelligent and the incompetent. The intellectuals' own commitment to an expressive order of democratic meritocracy periodically places them in conflict not only with the existing class structure and its elite, but also with the instrumental order of an educational system that empirically violates its own expressive order.[29]

A second axis of conflict centers on the intellectuals' ideal of professional objectivity and autonomy. The imperatives of the corporate ideal, regardless of whether they emanate directly from the corporation or come through the state, are fundamentally mission-directed. The role of an ideological state apparatus is to focus research (both basic and applied) and to coordinate vocational-professional manpower training with labor and capital markets. This goal often conflicts with the intellectuals' own cultural or scientific intentions which rest on a traditional claim to autonomy, that is, to collective self-management.

Nevertheless, along both axes, class struggles over the intellectual labor process have led to an incomplete and still unstable reconstruction of the American intelligentsia under the rationalizing influence of a bureaucratic corporate ideal.[30] What radical scholars must therefore rediscover is not merely that intellectuals play a significant role in the reproduction of capitalism and the capitalist state, but that education has been and remains every bit as much a contested terrain as the shop floor, the party caucus, and the halls of legislative assemblies.[31]

The social and institutional forces currently converging on American colleges and universities are in fact the continuation of conscious, long-term political strategies that are pushed forward with each fiscal crisis of the university. Colleges and universities are once again in the midst of a continuing cycle of integrative policies designed to bring them and their personnel ever closer to the exploitative requirements of capital and the adventurism of state elites.[32] The American college and university is continually pressured by business and state to adopt further modifications in its curriculum and research that emulate a corporate ideal first proposed more than three-quarters of a century ago. This contemporary background makes the present work political, even polemical in its goals.

It is written with two objectives in mind. It is first intended as a contribution to current theoretical debates on political development and the role of the state in advanced capitalist society. This aim is pursued through a historical analysis of the ideological state apparatus that treats it as a comparative case study in political institution-building. I believe the chief theoretical contribution on this point is to shift the examination of ideological state apparatuses away from an in-put/out-put systems analysis of structural causation by looking inside the so-called black box where intellectuals appear concretely as teachers, researchers, and political actors. This historical framework also provides a theoretical reference for the more important task of developing an ideology critique of the contemporary class consciousness of American intellectuals. The educational processes and conflicts set in motion during the age of reform remain important because this period established the basic institutional contours that shape the practical class consciousness of contemporary American intellectuals. The unstable institutional and ideological structure that developed during the original period of class formation has changed very little over the last several decades. The institutionalized self-image through which American intellectuals now understand themselves was itself a historically contingent political accommodation of this period that has been carried forward into contemporary social theory as a form of intellectual false consciousness.[33]

The analysis which emerges suggests that it is no accident that similar works are now appearing from several quarters of American academe.[34] This book is firmly situated in a critical American genre that traces its origins to Thorstein Veblen. Books of this type appear cyclically in twentieth-century American history whenever higher education is required to assume a larger role in sustaining capital accumulation and the American ideology with each successive economic or legitimation crisis. In this respect, it is important to recognize the corporate ideal as a political program that can be opposed constructively with practical pedagogical and institutional alternatives, but only if intellectuals once again assume that responsibility.[35] The unstable accommodation between intellectuals, capitalism, and the state has, after all, long been referred to as "the problem of the intellectuals."[36] Thus, the current educational crisis is partly a question of whether or not the intelligentsia can live up to its own historical mission. This piece is an adventure in that still-unfinished story.

The subsequent chapters of this enterprise have been organized by a simple plan. Chapter 1 starts with a hypothesis grounded in Marxist theory that leads to an analysis of the economic origins of the corporate ideal. This supplies the empirical-historical framework for a comparative analysis of the social composition of university governing boards in Chapter 2. The framework is developed further in Chapters 3–5, where I discuss the historical efforts by American businessmen to build an ideological state apparatus around the universities by coordinating their activities with the functional and organizational imperatives of an advanced capitalist society, namely, efficiency, functional division of labor, tangible returns on investment, and employer-employee relations.

In Chapters 6–8, I examine the impact of these developments on the intellectuals and their organizational reactions to them. Attempts to reject the corporate ideal through an alliance with the working class have failed to materialize except in scattered instances. Most intellectuals have chosen to negotiate an opportunistic historical accommodation with business interests and the state by accepting the new organizational structure of university life in exchange for limited procedural guarantees of personal security, which, I argue, has not included academic freedom.

1

Economic Origins of the Corporate Ideal

THE UNIVERSITY has traditionally been described as a corporation of learning. Veblen defines it as a "body of mature scholars and scientists, the faculty—with whatever plant and other equipment may incidentally serve as appliances for their work."[1] Its generally accepted ideal is the pursuit of knowledge for its own sake.[2] Thus, it is conceived of as a sanctuary for scholarship working to no ulterior end because it is "controlled by no consideration of expediency beyond its own works."[3]

However, the emergence of intellectuals as a professional social type has, more than ever before, meant that the full-time pursuit of science is conditioned by the use of scarce material resources.[4] Personal income, advanced degrees, libraries, classrooms, attendance at scholarly meetings, research funds, research assistance, publication, and other factors all constitute practical limitations that economically condition the possibility of engaging in full-time teaching and research. Hence, even though it is considered incidental to the philosophical ideal of a university, an organizational capacity to acquire these resources and convert them into a practical capability for conducting teaching and research make this property central to any empirical-historical definition of the university.[5]

Instrumental order among intellectuals is always historically contingent upon their possession of some instruments of production. Marx called these tools the "material means of mental production".[6] The particular conditions and specific form in which these instruments are utilized define the intellectuals' labor process. It is the intellectual labor process that constitutes what legitimately counts as teaching and scientific thinking in any society as opposed, for instance, to propaganda, ideology, or opinion. The modern university, in licensing and

12

employing those claiming to be intellectuals, certifies them as competent to engage in social practices which are presumed to yield objective knowledge. It thereby bestows upon certain intellectuals the normative image of "scientists." It does this by granting, denying, or revoking the certification and employment of specific individuals or groups of intellectuals. This effectively allows or withholds access to the social practices conditioned by the use of its physical property.[7] In this respect, the ideal of the university asserts that it guarantees "academic freedom" exactly insofar as it enables intellectuals to organize their labor process independent of any extraneous controls on the access, use, and distribution of their material means of production. Self-management of the labor process is the professional ideal of a university.[8]

In contrast to this professional ideal, however, laws regulating the property relations of American capitalism have never regarded universities as corporations of learning identified with the tenured faculty. Instead, legal custodianship of university property has typically been vested by the state in an external board of directors whose members are variously designated as trustees, regents, overseers, visitors, or governors. Governing boards are what legally constitute universities as corporations, corporations which, since the Dartmouth College Case, are fundamentally the same as any other business enterprise. Governors are vested with the proprietary right to regulate the disposition of university property, subject only to the legal constraints of corporate charters, the obligation of contract, and other statutory or judicial provisions which define the meaning and rights of property in American law.[9] One must therefore draw an empirical distinction between physical "possession" of the means of mental production by faculties and the legal "ownership" of these tools by public and private governing boards.[10]

The separation of professional claims to autonomy from proprietary rights in the university thus, at least in principle, mediates the conversion of material resources into the practical capability for teaching and research. Moreover, since modern intellectuals rarely own any substantial means of production, their institutional existence is in general dependent on the patronage of these public or private benefactors. It is therefore more likely, I will argue, that under normal circumstances "the class which has the means of material production at its disposal has control at the same time over the means of mental production."[11] The existing property relations which constitute the foundations of capitalist society—particularly as they structure the internal development of American universities—erect historical limits on the possible autonomy of intellectuals. Proprietary control and institutional regulation of the means of mental production are the organizational relations by which social classes exercise a controlling influence on the intellectual labor process. I shall call this social relationship "ideological power."[12]

The thrust of this work is to argue that the corporate ideal as applied to the university was actually a class-political program designed to conquer ideological power. The program was directly and precisely linked to the emergence of modern corporations through the property connection established in the material means of mental production. In this respect, the emergence of American universities is best understood as a cultural component of the Industrial Revolution, related transformations of class structure, and the culmination of these upheavals in the social rationalization movements of the progressive era.[13]

THE TRANSFORMATION OF AMERICAN
ECONOMIC STRUCTURE, 1861–1929

Capitalist development in the United States has occurred as a continuing series of long waves.[14] Each wave has been fueled by the introduction and eventual exhaustion of what Baran and Sweezy call an "epoch-making innovation." These innovations are clearly evident in their profound influence on both the economic location of industrial activity and the composition of product output.[15] Rationalization has been primarily concerned with attempts to maintain efficiency in industry (i.e., profit and capital accumulation) and to routinize the control of "human resources" within relations of production that promote the accumulation of capital and private property.[16]

The epoch-making innovation which actually ignited an industrial revolution in America was the construction of a national railway system from 1861 to 1907. Railroad mileage quintupled between 1865 and 1893.[17] Decennial data on the growth of U.S. industrial assets "suggest that from 1850 to 1900 investment in the railroads exceeded investment in all manufacturing industries combined."[18] Construction of the railway system simultaneously stimulated other manufacturing and mining industries, such as iron, steel, coal, industrial machinery, and machine tools. The automobile played a similar role as the new epoch-making innovation after 1907.

The concurrent relative decline in agriculture is evident in any number of simple statistical measurements. The proportion of value added to the U.S. domestic economy by agriculture declined from approximately 54 percent in 1859 to 33 percent in 1899. The proportion of value added by manufacturing surged from almost 32 percent to more than 53 percent during the same period, while mining activity tripled according to the same measurement.[19] Similarly, whereas farming accounted for over 35 percent of total U.S. gross domestic product between 1869 and 1878, it fell to less than eleven percent by 1930.[20]

Labor also migrated into the factories, mines, and railroad centers along with other forms of capital. In 1860, over eighty percent of the total U.S. population lived in rural areas, while probably well over one-half actually lived on farms. The United States, as a whole, technically became an urban nation for the first time with the census of 1920, which found over 51 percent of the population residing in urban areas and only slightly less than one-quarter of the population still living on farms.[21]

Railroads were an epoch-making innovation in another sense as well. Their development produced changes in the *structure* of industrial and mercantile activity and not just in the composition or location of productive output. Railroad transportation connected previously isolated local and regional markets into a national network of economic exchange and promoted the emergence of a national market structure. Raw materials and agricultural products could be transported to distant manufacturing centers, while new markets for manufactured goods were opened to firms that had previously produced only for their own local markets. Firms which had previously enjoyed local monopolies were now subject to national competition. The construction of a national railroad system, along with other postbellum internal improvements, thus initiated an era unparalleled for its unrestrained competition within industries where markets were being restructured by the invasion of national firms and enterprises.[22]

National markets were closely related to the internal development of modern business organization. Most manufacturing was still concentrated in small shops and factories as late as 1860. There were only limited opportunities for expansion, since most enterprises produced for local markets where increases in demand depended upon population growth. Moreover, most of this manufacturing was concentrated in light industries such as textiles, clothing, leather, shoes, and furs. Manufacturing establishments were generally small-scale enterprises owned and managed by a single individual, family, or partnership. Estimates suggest that before the Civil War not more than 6 to 8 percent of U.S. manufacturing activity even took place in corporations.

Following the construction of the railroads, there were new possibilities for growth in individual companies as major new markets were opened to aggressive competitors. Industrial establishments grew as the more successful competitors captured larger and larger proportions of a national market. Small businesses and the larger joint-stock companies were rapidly displaced by the emergence of the modern corporation as the basic unit of business organization. Close to two-thirds of manufacturing output was produced in corporations by 1900.[23]

The largest of the new industrial enterprises often grew to include operations, functions, and establishments situated throughout the nation. Their efficiency and control ultimately required totally new methods of management that set in motion a movement toward industrial rationalization. The rationalization of management was pioneered once again by the railroads from about 1850 through the 1870s.

Rationalization of internal organization was a three-part process. It began with the separation of administration from operations, and the reorganization of operational functions into separate geographical divisions. Each of the geographical units was then internally departmentalized according to specialized function. Finally, functional departments were coordinated through centralized decision-making in a hierarchical authority pyramid. Authority was concentrated in administration and flowed from the top to the bottom of an organization. This pattern, according to Chandler, established the precedent for corporate organization-building in the 1890s and afterward, when large-scale businesses became increasingly common. By the end of World War I, most large industrial companies in the United States "were administered through much the same type of organization—the centralized, functionally departmentalized structure."[24]

Concentration and rationalization of production were not confined to the internal operation of individual corporations within industries, but also gradually extended to relationships between corporations within entire industries. From the 1870s through the 1890s—a long-wave accumulation crisis then known by businessmen as the "Great Depression"—the new competitive pressure on prices, labor shortages, and the necessity of adjusting to constant technological innovation created a long-term tendency for the rate of profits to fall.[25] A further result of this new market structure was that businessmen, rhetoric to the contrary, developed a profound contempt for unrestrained competition and its damaging effect on profits. Consequently, as soon as the free market was triumphant in America, business undertook persistent efforts to abolish it.[26]

Various techniques were attempted to achieve this goal. Business competitors in the same industry made informal "gentlemen's agreements" to not cut prices in an industry. These always failed when one of the "gentlemen" sought the short-term competitive advantage of being the first to secretly cut prices. Businessmen then turned to industrial profit pools and later to trusts as efforts were made to link the profits of individual businesses to the profitability of the industry as a whole. Yet, few of these succeeded because competitors maintained their separate corporate identities and again constantly sought the slight advantage to profits of being the first to breach agreements. Eventually, it was the merger which succeeded in rationalizing industrial production in concentrated centers of control.[27]

Railroads again provided the model for the merger movement that dominated the industrial history of the 1890s. Competition between parallel lines (separate railways that competed on the same route) was ended by simply buying out or merging competing railroad companies. As early as the 1880s, however, railroad companies had reached such enormous sizes that their consolidation and purchase required far more capital than individual entrepreneurs or even entire corporations could generate from their personal or internal cash reserves. The merger movement frequently required even the largest corporations to seek assistance from the new investment banks, which could generate new supplies of capital by floating bonds, underwriting new stock issues, or extending long-term corporate loans.

Most domestic capital in the United States was already absorbed by the industrial revolution. Therefore, the American merger movement increasingly relied on the few banks with consistent access to the large surpluses of European capital that were searching out opportunities for foreign investment during the rise of European imperialism. These avenues were already heavily monopolized by a very few large investment banks in New York City and the industrial Northeast. J. P. Morgan and Company was the main avenue for channeling British capital into American industry. Kuhn, Loeb, and Company was nearly unchallenged in underwriting American railroad bonds in Germany.

By the turn of the century, northeastern investment bankers and other financiers held massive amounts of long-term corporate loans, bonds, and stocks. The holdings of a single bank were often in different companies competing against one another in the same industry. Consequently, investment bankers developed a long-term interest in planning the profitability and strength of the industry as a whole, rather than in stressing the short-term advantage of one company over its competitors. This was particularly true to the extent that investment banks adopted policies which enabled them to deliver specialized financial services to particular industries. These policies led them to focus increasingly on delivering capital and other financial services to only one or a few major industries such as steel, railroads, oil, or heavy machinery.[28]

The dependence of industrial establishments on these specialized financial institutions increased as corporations continued to grow in size and assets. All nonfinancial corporations obtained from 40 to 45 percent of their total capital requirements from external sources (i.e., borrowing, bonds, securities) by the turn of the century. Large manufacturing establishments derived at least 30 percent of their capital from outside sources.[29]

This strategic control of capital enabled a new fraction of financiers to eventually emerge as a dominant group in directing the course of American industry. Financiers pressured companies into mergers and often forced involuntary mergers to protect their capital interest in various industries. Indeed, the first wave in the merger movement began in the late 1880s, when J. P. Morgan pressured several major railroads to form cartels. In his own words, his intention was to rationalize the railroad industry by avoiding "wasteful rivalry."[30]

These early efforts accelerated during the 1890s. The Panic of 1893 and its ensuing depression caused most of the large railroads, already weakened by decades of rate wars and overbuilding, to declare bankruptcy. Practically the entire industry was placed in receivership by the courts. This allowed J. P. Morgan and Kuhn, Loeb to take direct control of the reorganization and administration of the railroads as the representatives of creditors, lenders, and bondholders. These financiers, in turn, used this authority to further consolidate, concentrate, and rationalize the railway system.[31]

Following this successful venture, major financiers "fostered and financed mergers among the major competing firms in one industry after another, " culminating in 1899, when over 1,200 mergers took place in one year.[32] Even an industrialist as powerful as Andrew Carnegie found that he was no match for a J. P. Morgan when he tried to resist the merger which created U.S. Steel. The structural tendency toward consolidation continued at a lower rate of activity until after World War I, when the merger movement reached its next apex in 1929 (see Fig. 1.1).

The concentration and rationalization of entire industries under the direction of finance capitalists significantly increased the tendency

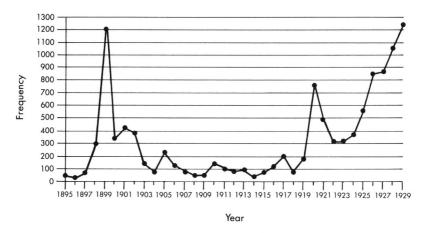

Fig. 1.1. Mergers from 1895 to 1929

Sources: Data from 1895 to 1919 from Ralph L. Nelson, *Merger Movements in American Industry, 1895–1956* (Princeton: Princeton University Press, 1959). Data from 1920 to 1929 from Temporary National Economic Committee, *Investigation of Concentration of Economic Power* (Washington, D.C.: GPO, 1941).

toward monopolization of manufacturing, mining, and transportation. In less than a decade, from 1897 to 1905, more than 5,300 industrial firms were merged into only 318 corporations such as Standard Oil, U.S. Steel, and International Harvester. By 1904 there were twenty-six major "trusts," each accounting for 80 percent or more of production in its respective field of industry. Most of these trusts were concentrated in heavy manufacturing, mining, and utilities. Smaller and more competitive enterprises remained predominant only in light industry, trade, and merchandising, although even in these sectors such giants as United Fruit, R. C. Macey, and Sears were emerging. The net result was that by 1929, the 200 largest nonfinancial corporations owned 48 percent of the assets of all nonfinancial businesses in the United States.[33]

The process of concentration initiated and directed by investment financiers was accompanied by a simultaneous centralization of the industrial economy. Continuous mergers financed by the large investment banks, coupled to the banks' specialization in specific industries, led to the appearance of distinct "financial groups." Financial groups became dominant forces in the American economy during the opening decades of the twentieth century. Financial groups were first clearly identified in 1912 by an investigation of the U.S. House Banking Committee.[34]

The typical financial group always included a major investment bank as its core. This bank was usually supported in its capital generation by several commercial banks and insurance companies. The latter were linked directly to the investment bank and often directly to each other through a network of interlocking directors. Their common interest in certain client companies or industries was structured by shared investments and underwriting of these companies or industries.[35]

Hence, every financial group was surrounded by client satellites in a particular industry or industries, such as heavy manufacturing, mineral extraction, railroads, or utilities. Since the patron banks and financiers usually held large blocks of outstanding stock in these companies, they could always elect some of their own institutional representatives as directors of their client companies. They could maintain a direct presence on the decision-making bodies of the client corporations in addition to indirectly structuring the parameters of corporate policy-making by attaching specific conditions to loans, bonds, and securities underwriting.[36]

It would be unnecessary and tedious to outline these financial groups in detail. Nevertheless, it is important to my subsequent arguments to note the major groups which structured the U.S. industrial economy during the late nineteenth and early twentieth centuries. Table 1.1 provides a partial listing of these groups as defined by Gardiner C. Means in a study for the National Resources Committee in 1935. Eight major groups can be identified: (1) the Morgan–First National (New York City), (2) Kuhn, Loeb (New York), (3) Rockefeller (New York), (4) Boston, (5) Mellon (Pittsburgh), (6) Chicago, (7) Cleveland, and (8) Du Pont (Detroit).

These groups and their client members were all among the 250 largest corporations in the United States. Among the 200 largest non-financial corporations in the United States, at least 88 (44%) could be positively identified as members of financial groups. These, in turn, were clustered around 17 of the nation's 50 largest financial institutions. The vast majority of the remaining 112 largest nonfinancial corporations tended to have some ties, such as loans and interlocking directors, to the financial groups. However, Means did not classify these as group members because they were too loosely associated with the patron financial institutions to be technically classified as members according to Means's strict criteria or because no single center of control could be ascertained.

As the table also makes evident, the geographic center for the eight financial groups was the industrial Northeast, particularly New York City, where three of the most powerful and extensive groups were

Table 1.1. Major Financial Groups and Corporations among the Two Hundred Largest
       Nonfinancial Corporations Identifiable as Group Members, 1912–1935

Morgan/First National

Banks
    J. P. Morgan and Co. (N.Y.)
    Drexel and Co. (Philadelphia)
    First National Bank of N.Y.
    New York Trust Co.
    Guaranty Trust Co. of N.Y.
    Bankers' Trust Co. of N.Y.
Railroads and Related Co.'s
    N.Y. Central RR
    Atchison, Topeka & Santa Fe Ry
    Northern Pacific Ry
    Delaware, Lackawanna, & West Ry
    Western Pacific Ry Co.
    Southern Ry Co.
    Missouri Pacific Ry Co.
    Denver & Rio Grande West RR Co.
    Chicago & Eastern Illinois Ry Co.
    Pullman, Inc.
    Baldwin Locomotive Works
Utilities and Related Co.'s
    International Telephone & Telegraph
    American Telephone & Telegraph
    Electric Power & Light Co.
    Consolidated Edison of N.Y.
    Public Service Corp of N.J.
    American Power & Light Co.
    National Power & Light Co.
    American Gas & Electric Co.
    Columbia Gas & Electric Co.
    General Electric Co.
    United Gas Improvement Co.
    American Radiator & Sanitary Corp.
Natural Resources
    U.S. Steel Corp.
    Allegheny Corp.
    Kennecott Copper Co.
    Phelps-Dodge Corp.
    Continental Oil Co.
    Glen Alden Coal Co.
    Philadelphia & Reading Coal & Iron
    St. Regis Paper Co.
Other
    National Biscuit Co.
    Montgomery Ward Co., Inc.
    Commonwealth and Southern Corp.

(continued on the following page)

Table 1.1. Major Financial Groups and Corporations among the Two Hundred Largest
          Nonfinancial Corporations Identifiable as Group Members, 1912–1935
          (*continued*)

Kuhn, Loeb & Co.

Bank
  Bank of the Manhattan Co. (N.Y.)
Railroads
  Pennsylvania RR Co.
  Union Pacific RR
  Southern Pacific RR
  New York, New Haven, & Hartford RR Co.
  Lehigh Valley RR
  Illinois Central RR
  Wabash Ry Co.
  Chicago, Milwaukee, St. Paul & Pacific RR Co.
  Delaware and Hudson Co.
  Boston & Maine RR Co.
  Chicago & Northwestern Ry Co.
  Norfolk & Western Ry Co.
  Missouri-Texas-Kansas RR Co.
Utility
  Western Union Telegraph Co.

Rockefeller

Bank
  Chase National Bank
Oil
  Standard Oil Co. of Indiana
  Standard Oil Co. of New Jersey
  Standard Oil Co. of California
  Ohio Oil Co.
  Socony Vacuum Oil Co., Inc.
  Atlantic Refining Co.

Boston

Bank
  First National Bank of Boston
Light Industry
  United Fruit Co.
  United Shoe Machinery
  American Woolen Co.
Other
  Stone & Webster, Inc.
  U.S. Smelting & Refining Co.
  Edison Electric Illuminating Co. of Boston

Mellon

Banks
  Mellon National Bank (Pittsburgh)
  Union Trust Co. (Pittsburgh)
Natural Resources and Refining
  Aluminum Co. of America (Alcoa)
  Crucible Steel Co. of America
  Jones & Laughlin Steel Co.
  American Rolling Mill Co.
  Pittsburgh Coal Co.
  Gulf Oil
  Koppers Co.
Utilities and Related Co.'s
  Brooklyn Union Gas Co.
  United Light & Power Co.
  Westinghouse Electric & Mfg. Co.
Other
  Pittsburgh Plate Glass Co.

Chicago

Banks
  Continental Illinois National Bank & Trust Co.
  First National Bank (Chicago)
  Northern Trust Co.
  Harris Trust & Savings Bank (Chicago)
Utilities
  Commonwealth Edison Co.
  Peoples' Gas Light & Coke Co.
  Public Service Co. of Northern Illinois
Other
  Armour & Co.
  International Harvester Co.
  Marshall Field & Co.
  Wilson & Co.

Cleveland

Bank
  Cleveland Trust Co.
Steel
  Republic Steel Co.
  Inland Steel Co.
  Cleveland-Cliffs Iron Co.
  Wheeling Steel Corp.
  Youngstown Sheet & Tube Co.
Other
  Goodyear Tire & Rubber Co.

(continued on the following page)

Table 1.1. Major Financial Groups and Corporations among the Two Hundred Largest
Nonfinancial Corporations Identifiable as Group Members, 1912–1935
(*continued*)

Du Pont
Bank
National Bank of Detroit
Automobiles and Related Co.'s
General Motors Corp.
U.S. Rubber Co.
E. I. Du Pont de Nemours & Co.

Source: Gardiner C. Means, *The Structure of the American Economy* (Washington, D.C.:
GPO, 1939), pp. 162–63.

based (Morgan; Kuhn, Loeb; and Rockefeller). These three groups had
financial associations and industrial holdings throughout the United
States. The other five were generally regional clusters located around
the Great Lakes, in New England, or in the Mid-Atlantic area.[37] The
Morgan group was easily the largest and economically the most powerful. In fact, at least 35 of the 200 largest nonfinancial corporations in the
United States were members of the Morgan group.

A sense of the centralized economic structure institutionalized by
these groups can be gleaned from a few examples. For instance, utility
companies within the Morgan group produced 37 percent of the total
electrical generating capacity in the United States by 1935. The Morgan
railroad cluster owned 26 percent of all rail mileage in the country. The
Kuhn, Loeb, railroad cluster controlled 22 percent of all U.S. railroad
mileage.[38]

THE TRANSFORMATION OF AMERICAN
CLASS STRUCTURE, 1861–1929

The social and legal framework defined by private ownership of wealth
in the means of production meant that the transformation of American
economic structure was duplicated by a similar concentration and centralization of class structure. Richard Hofstadter notes that "up to about
1870 the United States was a nation with a rather broad diffusion of
wealth, status, and power, in which the man of moderate means, especially in the many small communities, could command much deference and exert much influence."[39] The large number of small family
farmers, as well as the small size of business enterprises, reproduced a
social structure in which wealth had a relatively wide distribution. There
were unquestionably significant inequalities between classes, but these

Table 1.2. Proletarianization of the U.S. Labor Force: Percentages of Workers, Entrepreneurs, and Administrators

Year	Wage and salaried Employees[a]	Self-employed entrepreneurs[b]	Managers and officials	Total
1780[c]	20.0	80.0	—	100.0
1880	62.0	36.9	1.1	100.0
1890	65.0	33.8	1.2	100.0
1900	67.9	30.8	1.3	100.0
1910	71.9	26.3	1.8	100.0
1920	73.9	23.5	2.6	100.0
1930	76.8	20.3	2.9	100.0

Sources: Table from Michael Reich, "The Evolution of the United States Labor Force," in Richard C. Edwards, ed., *The Capitalist System*, 1st ed. (Englewood Cliffs, N.Y.: Prentice-Hall, 1972), p. 175. The Figures Reich uses for 1780 are from Jackson Turner Main, *The Social Structure of Revolutionary America* (Princeton: Princeton University Press, 1965).

Note: The labor force here is defined as all income recipients who participated directly in economic activity; unpaid family workers have been excluded.

[a]Excluding salaried managers and officials.

[b]Business entrepreneurs, professional practitioners, farmers, and other property owners.

[c]Figures for 1780 are rough estimates. Slaves, who constituted one-fifth of the population, are excluded; indentured servants are included in the wage and salaried employees category.

differences paled in comparison to those which emerged after 1870, when the character of class conflict shifted from one between property-owning classes (i.e., capital and agriculture) to one between capital and labor.

The proportion of the U.S. population self-employed in business or farming provides an indication of this development (see Table 1.2). Although figures for the period before 1880 are still incomplete, an extrapolation from estimates by Jackson T. Main to those available for 1880 suggests that Hofstadter's description of preindustrial American social structure is fairly accurate. The period of heavy industrialization after 1880 is accompanied by a growing concentration of wealth and a parallel proletarianization of the general population.

Yet not only did the property-owning classes shrink as a proportion of the population, but an equally dramatic centralization of power occurred within the capitalist class. Hofstadter observes that before the American industrial revolution, "the small merchant or manufacturer, the distinguished lawyer, editor, or preacher was a person of local eminence in an age in which local eminence mattered a great deal," especially in the "absence of very many nationwide sources of power and prestige." It has been estimated, for instance, that "during the 1840s there were not twenty millionaires in the entire country."[40]

Table 1.3. Share of Personal-Sector Assets and Liabilities Held by
Top 1 Percent of Adults, 1922 and 1929 (percentages)

Type of property	1922	1929
Real estate	18.0	17.3
U.S. government bonds	45.0	100.0
State and local bonds	88.0	100.0
Other bonds	69.2	82.0
Corporate stock	61.5	65.6
Cash, mortgages, and notes	31.0	34.0
Pension and retirement funds	8.0	8.0
Insurance	35.3	27.0
Miscellaneous property	23.2	29.0

Source: Table from Robert J. Lampman, *The Share of Top Wealth-Holders in National Wealth* (Princeton: Princeton University Press, 1962), p. 209.

The emergence of the corporation as a dominant form of industrial organization altered the broad distribution of power and prestige within the capitalist class. By 1893, a U.S. Census Bureau statistician reported that only 9 percent of American families owned 71 percent of all wealth in the country.[41] Robert Lampman's estimates for the U.S. Bureau of Economic Research indicate that by 1922, following the merger movement, the private concentration and centralization of wealth had become even more pronounced (see Table 1.3). Centralization was greatest in the area of securities ownership, where only 1 percent of the population owned nearly two-thirds of all outstanding corporate stocks and bonds.[42]

However, the transformation and polarization of class structure was an uneven process that radiated outward from the regional centers occupied by the major financial groups. For instance, regional figures on urbanization show that most of the country was a generation behind the Northeast in patterns of economic and social development, while the South lagged behind by at least two generations (see Table 1.4). In fact, except for the Northeast, every region remained predominantly rural and agricultural until 1920. Only later do economic and class structures begin to even out across the nation into a genuinely national social structure. Even then, the South still trailed behind the rest of the nation. Consequently, figures on the distribution of the remaining U.S. farm population from 1890 to 1930 show that farmers were concentrated overwhelmingly in the South and the Midwest, where they often formed "concurrent majorities" of the electorate (Table 1.5).[43]

Uneven development clearly resulted in regional variations in class structure and local or concurrent patterns of political hegemony within

Table 1.4. Percentage of U.S. and U.S. Regional Population Living in Urban Areas, 1860–1930

	1860	1870	1880	1890	1900	1910	1920	1930
United States	19.7	25.7	28.2	35.1	39.7	45.7	51.2	56.2
Northeast	35.8	44.3	50.8	59.0	66.1	71.8	75.5	77.6
North Central	13.9	20.8	24.2	33.1	38.6	45.1	52.3	57.9
South	16.0	25.8	30.2	37.1	39.9	47.9	51.8	58.4
West	9.6	12.2	12.2	16.3	18.0	22.5	28.1	34.1

Source: Compiled and tabulated from U.S. Bureau of the Census, *Historical Statistics of the United States: From Colonial Times to 1970* (Washington, D.C.: GPO, 1972), pp. 11–12, 22.

the wider structure of national class relationships. This is significant, as I will later suggest, to an explanation of regional variations among American colleges and universities. Subsequent data will demonstrate that the composition of college and university governing boards was extremely sensitive to regional and local variations in economic and class structure even after the nationalization of the American political economy. Whether state, local, or private institutions, their governing boards were generally directed by the concerns of locally dominant elites.

Many of the local institutional rivalries and national conflicts which disrupted higher education in the age of reform can be traced to the antagonistic social forces struggling for ideological supremacy.[44] The most deep-seated of these conflicts were the perennial party battles between American farmers and urban elites and also between capital and labor.[45] Farmers were generally waging a defensive struggle against their deteriorating position in an industrial society. Labor was attempting to establish its identity as a subordinate but rising class within an emergent industrial democracy.

However, there were significant regional differences even within the

Table 1.5. Regional Distribution of Total U.S. Farm Population, 1890–1930 (percentages)

	1890	1900	1910	1920	1930
Northeast	12.9	11.3	9.0	7.9	7.5
North Central	40.3	37.1	33.4	31.8	31.4
South	43.3	47.6	51.9	53.4	53.6
West	3.5	4.0	5.6	6.9	7.5
Total	100.0	100.0	100.0	100.0	100.0

Source: U.S. Bureau of the Census, *Historical Statistics of the United States: From Colonial Times to 1970* (Washington, D.C.: GPO, 1972), p. 458.

Table 1.6. Average Acreage of Farms by U.S. Region, 1860–1930

	1860	1870	1880	1890	1900	1910	1920	1930
Northeast	111	104	98	97	97	96	99	85
North Central	140	124	135	133	145	157	172	181
South	336	214	153	140	138	114	109	110
West	363	339	312	324	394	300	364	434

Source: Figures tabulated from data in U.S. Bureau of the Census, *Historical Statistics of the United States: From Colonial Times to 1970* (Washington, D.C.: GPO, 1972), pp. 459–60.

rural class structure. Major regional distinctions are evident in the average size of farms (see Table 1.6). The Northeast, and especially the Midwest, remained regional strongholds of the traditional family farm. In the South, figures deceptively suggest *prima facie* that large plantations were broken up during Reconstruction and replaced with small freeholds, but these figures obscure what was actually a steadily expanding landlord-tenant and sharecropping system. U.S. Census figures on farm acreage for this period did not reflect ownership, but only

Table 1.7. Distribution of Land Ownership, Management, and Tenancy among U.S. and Southern Farmers, 1900–1930 (percentage of total number of farmers)

	1900	1910	1920	1930
United States				
Full owner	55.8	52.7	52.2	46.3
Part owner	7.9	9.3	8.7	10.4
Manager	1.0	1.0	1.1	1.0
Tenant	35.3	37.0	38.1	42.4
	100.0	100.0	100.0	100.0
South				
Full owner	47.2	42.9	43.8	36.9
Part owner	5.1	7.0	6.0	7.0
Manager	0.7	0.5	0.6	0.5
Tenant	47.0	49.6	49.6	55.6
	100.0	100.0	100.0	100.0
% of all U.S. tenant farmers living in the South	60.8	65.2	64.7	67.1
% of all U.S. sharecroppers living in the South	—	—	100.0	100.0

Source: U.S. Bureau of the Census, *Historical Statistics of the United States: From Colonial Times to 1970* (Washington, D.C.: GPO, 1971), p. 465.

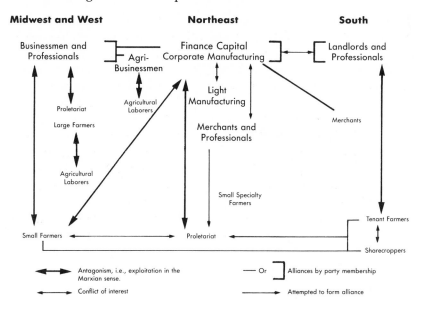

Fig. 1.2. Structure of Class Conflict in the United States, circa 1890
   Note: On antagonism and conflict of interest, see Etienne Balibar, *Reading Capital* (London: New Left Books, 1970), pp. 203, 290.

the average size of each farm actually worked by a different family. Consequently, the continuing concentration of land ownership in the South was disguised by then-current statistical measures.

The data in Table 1.7 on farm ownership reveals that whereas most American farmers either owned or partly owned (i.e., mortgaged as nominal owner) their land, most tenant farmers and all sharecroppers were consistently concentrated in the South. About 45 percent of all tenants and sharecroppers in the South were black, or conversely, nearly all blacks in southern agriculture were tenants and sharecroppers.[46] In the Far West, especially in California, farms and ranches were already operated as large-scale agribusinesses.

Figure 1.2 provides a visual illustration of patterns in the American class structure around 1890.

This description is clearly not aimed at supplying an exhaustive account of American capitalist development. I have emphasized specific patterns in that development which are theoretically significant to the emergence of the American university and which constitute the recurring themes of subsequent chapters. The first of these is the rise of the corporation during the late nineteenth and early twentieth century. Its consolidation under groups of national finance capitalists established the model of organization we call the corporate ideal.

Moreover, the economic origins of the corporate ideal were not value-neutral. The corporate ideal was adopted as a strategic solution to the global accumulation crisis in capitalism that occurred from 1870 to 1896 and which reappeared between 1917 and 1948. Its primary orientation was the profitable utilization of material and human resources. Furthermore, the corporate ideal was itself merely one component in the development of a social structure where the ownership and control of those resources was already increasingly centralized. Thus, patterns of rationalization must be understood against the backdrop of a national accumulation crisis in which rising conflict between labor and capital, between farmers and capital, and within capital linked the problems of resource efficiency to the problem of human organizational control.[47]

2

Who Owns the Universities? Class Structure and the Material Means of Mental Production

THE MODERNIZATION of American universities, as well as the emergence of the professional academic intellectual, coincided with the industrial revolution in America. The structural patterns associated with capitalist development reappear in a series of quite similar events that also revolutionized the American college and its labor process. The transformation of the traditional American college into the modern university followed the same patterns of institutional change: concentration of the means of mental production, centralization and bureaucratization of administrative control, the construction of national academic markets, and the rationalization of market relations between competing institutions.

It is true that scattered and unrelated events had established some institutional precedents for these changes as early as the 1870s and 1880s. However, the pace of change "accelerated abruptly in the 1890s" and continued at an accelerated rate until the end of World War I. By the end of the postwar decade, the American university had permanently "assumed something like its present form" with "patterns of structure, intellectual organization, and financing that are still recognizable today."[1]

Contemporary historians have explained this transformation primarily in terms of internal structural imperatives that emerged out of more diffuse changes in American culture. For instance, Bledstein notes that enrollments in American colleges and universities increased as a culture of professionalism gained ascendancy in the middle-class occupations. The rise of professionalism made university certification the institutional foundation for a new urban middle class whose claim to exclusivity and market privileges rested on its educational credentials. The path to individual social mobility was thus shifted from the frontier to higher education during the late nineteenth and early twentieth centuries. Likewise, David O. Levine concludes that a second boom in academic enrollments after World War I can be traced to the culture of aspiration generated among the middle classes by the progressive movement.[2]

In this context, Geiger argues that rising academic enrollments led to institutional competition for prestige, since prestige made it easier to secure the resources necessary for continued growth. Successful growth, in turn, required new forms of internal organization to administer and direct these "human resources," as well as certain curricular concessions to the vocational mentality of students motivated by a meritocratic culture.[3] Veysey concludes that in the midst of this academic boom centralized bureaucratic procedures became essential if universities were to avoid "confusion and drift."[4]

Certainly these tendencies were present, but the explanations which rely upon them fail to address the way in which institutional competition for resources was shaped by the problem of who controlled those resources in American society. This property nexus was in fact a crucial determinant of what eventually came to count as institutional prestige. Moreover, it thereby decisively influenced the kind of internal organization that was adopted for university governance, and influenced the specific form in which a vocational mentality was integrated into the American college and university.

There were bitter political contests over how modern universities would fulfill their changing historical mission by responding to the needs of an industrial democracy. There were disputes over the structure and content of these changes that were closely tied to their implications for different groups in American society. It is my contention that participants understood the possible outcome of these contests as a consequence of struggles to control the material means of mental production and with them the intellectual labor process. The emergence of the modern college and university in America was a class struggle for ideological power. Consequently, a central and consciously articulated point of contention was always the question, Who owned the universities?

Thorstein Veblen found that even as late as 1918, "within the memory of men still living, it was a nearly unbroken rule that the governing boards of these higher American schools were drawn largely from the

Table 2.1. Vocations of Trustees in Fifteen Private Institutions of Higher Education, Selected Years, 1860–1930 (percentages)

	1860–1861	1870–1871	1880–1881	1890–1891	1900–1901	1910–1911	1920–1921	1930–1931
No. of cases	281	323	354	355	374	388	394	429
Clergyman	39.1	34.4	33.3	28.5	23.0	16.5	10.4	7.2
Businessman	22.8	25.4	25.4	24.8	25.7	25.0	27.2	31.9
Banker	4.6	8.4	8.8	11.5	12.8	17.8	16.0	20.3
Lawyer	20.6	19.8	21.8	23.7	25.7	25.5	26.9	21.4
Educator	5.0	6.8	6.2	7.6	8.0	9.3	11.4	10.0
Physician	4.6	3.1	2.3	3.1	3.2	3.1	4.3	4.4
Engineer	0.7	0.6	0.6	0	1.1	1.8	2.3	3.5
Farmer	2.1	1.2	0.8	0.6	0.5	1.0	0.5	0.2
Housewife	0	0	0.8	0.3	0	0	1.0	0.9
Unknown	0.4	0.3	0	0	0	0	0	0
Total[a]	99.9	100.0	100.0	100.0	100.0	100.0	100.0	100.0
Total businessmen and bankers	27.4	33.8	34.2	36.3	38.5	42.8	43.2	52.2
Total businessmen, bankers, and lawyers	48.0	53.6	56.0	60.0	64.2	68.3	70.1	73.6

Source: Table from Earl J. McGrath, "The Control of Higher Education in America," *Educational Record* 17 (April 1936): 264.

Note: Institutions included here are Williams, Amherst, Lafayette, Wesleyan, Hamilton, Lawrence, Carleton, Beloit, Wabash, Knox, Yale, Pennsylvania, Cornell, Princeton, and Dartmouth.

[a]Totals may not equal 100% because of rounding.

clergy and were also guided mainly by ecclesiastical, or at least devotional, notions of what was right and needful in matters of learning."[5] He found it significant to an explanation of contemporary changes that for "a generation past," American colleges and universities had been coming under the governance of businessmen and politicians—which, he wryly concluded, "amounts to saying that it is a substitution of businessmen."[6] Earl J. McGrath's empirical survey of the social composition of college and university governing boards from 1860 to 1930 confirmed Veblen's observation.[7]

McGrath reported that bankers and businessmen on university governing boards increased from approximately one-fourth of total membership in 1860 to about one-half in 1930. Lawyers were the next largest occupational group, but individual biographical data indicated that attorneys sitting on university governing boards were increasingly engaged in corporate law and were often officers or directors for various business enterprises. Consequently, McGrath argued that one

Table 2.2. Vocations of Trustees in Five State Institutions of Higher Education, Selected
    Years, 1860–1930 (percentages)

	1860–1861	1870–1871	1880–1881	1890–1891	1900–1901	1910–1911	1920–1921	1930–1931
No. of cases	46	62	46	48	48	45	44	46
Businessman	23.9	22.6	28.3	20.8	27.1	35.6	34.1	23.9
Lawyer	39.1	33.9	28.3	39.6	37.5	24.4	27.3	30.4
Banker	4.4	3.2	13.0	12.5	12.5	22.2	18.2	13.0
Farmer	15.2	6.5	4.3	6.3	0	2.2	4.6	8.7
Educator	8.7	16.1	13.0	14.6	12.5	6.7	6.8	4.4
Physician	2.1	6.5	8.7	6.3	2.1	8.9	9.1	10.9
Clergyman	4.4	11.3	4.3	0	6.3	0	0	2.2
Housewife	0	0	0	0	0	0	0	6.5
Engineer	2.2	0	0	0	2.1	0	0	0
Total[a]	100.0	100.1	99.9	100.1	100.1	100.1	100.1	100.0
Total businessmen and bankers	28.3	25.8	41.3	33.3	39.6	57.8	52.3	36.9
Total businessmen, bankers, and lawyers	67.4	59.7	69.6	72.9	77.1	82.2	79.6	67.3

Source: McGrath, "The Control of Higher Education," p. 265.
Note: Institutions included are the Universities of Nebraska, Missouri, Minnesota,
Iowa, and Michigan.
[a]Totals may not equal 100% because of rounding.

could justifiably classify the two occupations as a single interest group
which controlled from two-thirds to three-quarters of all positions on
university governing boards by 1930 (see Tables 2.1 and 2.2).

McGrath's survey distinguished between public and privately
owned universities, yet found that "the controlling bodies of higher
education have been selected from the same classes regardless of the
manner of selection." As a result, it seems necessary in the case of
public universities to introduce a further distinction in relations to
production between *de jure* public "ownership" and the *de facto* character of class "control." Furthermore, subsequent studies have repli-
cated these findings with sufficient regularity over the last fifty years to
indicate that "plutocratic" patterns of class control are, from a historical
perspective, a structural feature of the university in capitalist society.[8]

As important as these findings have been in confirming Veblen's
impressionistic hypothesis, there is a sense in which they are equally
ambiguous in defining the relationship between university modernization and the academic culture of a business civilization. Consequently, I
undertook a further historical survey aimed at deriving a more precise

relationship between the development of American social structure and university governance, particularly with reference to the historical framework elaborated in the previous chapter. The survey, which is analyzed in this chapter, included thirty-three colleges and universities in twenty-one states from 1861 to 1929. The sample was chosen to collect representative examples of institutions reflecting variations in geographic region, type of legal control (public and private), size, and institutional type. The general results of the survey are recorded in Tables 2.3 and 2.4.

My survey results closely resembled McGrath's earlier findings, despite some differences in the use of occupational categories. The one major difference is my conclusion that McGrath's findings underestimated the proportion of farmers and other agriculturalists (e.g., ranchers, horticulturalists, millers) on the early governing boards of public universities.[9] In addition, I found that despite a general historical tendency toward uniformity in the social control of higher institutions, different institutional types diverged from this pattern in degrees that seem theoretically significant to an explanation of the conflicts which took place in universities during this time.

College and university governing boards were highly sensitive to local and regional distributions of economic and political power. I have subdivided my discussion of the larger sample into five institutional types to illustrate this point: (1) major private universities and technical institutes in the Northeast, (2) private liberal arts and denominational colleges, (3) public universities in the South, (4) public universities in the Midwest and the West, and (5) land-grant colleges.

MAJOR PRIVATE UNIVERSITIES AND TECHNICAL INSTITUTES IN THE NORTHEAST

Table 2.5 shows the social composition of governing boards at major private universities and technical institutes in the Northeast between 1861 and 1929. It is indicative of the historical origins of these schools that Protestant clergy were still the single largest interest group represented on these governing boards (22.5%) as late as a decade after the Civil War. Private governing boards were self-perpetuating corporations which generally elected their own successors, and hence, the clergy was able to temporarily maintain its control against internal and external pressures toward the secularization of institutional culture.

Thus, well into the 1890s, the educational mission of these institutions was still largely guided by the classical emphasis on communicat-

Table 2.3. Vocations of Trustees at Private Colleges, Universities, and Technical Institutes, 1861–1929 (percentages)

	1861–1880	1881–1900	1901–1920	1921–1929
No. of cases	147	150	179	144
No. with vocation unidentified	21	21	10	11
Professionals				
Clergyman	40.8	18.0	15.1	9.0
Physician	7.5	10.0	5.6	6.3
Educator[a]	4.8	4.0	5.0	6.9
Lawyer	11.6	24.7	21.2	14.6
Judge[b]	6.8	5.3	3.4	1.4
Subtotal	71.5	62.0	50.3	38.2
Businessmen				
Journalist[c]	0.7	1.3	1.1	2.1
Merchant/commerce	12.2	6.0	4.5	9.7
Mfg./mining	3.4	4.7	9.5	13.9
Railroad man	0.7	7.3	6.2	4.2
Engineer	0.7	2.0	1.1	2.1
Banking/finance	1.4	8.7	15.6	19.4
Subtotal	19.1	30.0	38.0	51.4
Agriculturalist	0	0	0	0
Government officials				
Federal	1.4	3.3	3.9	2.8
State/local	4.1	1.3	2.2	0.7
Military	2.0	2.0	0.6	1.4
Subtotal	7.5	6.6	6.7	4.9
Other	2.0	1.3	5.0	5.6
Total[d]	100.1	99.9	100.0	100.1
Total businessmen and lawyers	31.6	54.7	59.2	66.0

Sources: See Tables 2.5 and 2.8.

Note: Institutions included are Dickinson, Oberlin, Vassar, Lafayette, Williams, Harvard, Rutgers (until 1915), Columbia, the University of Pennsylvania, Johns Hopkins, Chicago, and Drexel Institute of Technology.

[a]Most persons reported as educators in this and all subsequent tables were university presidents, professional foundation executives, and state superintendents of public instruction. Only a very few were professors, teachers, or scientists.

[b]Includes only state and local judges or magistrates. Federal judges are reported as federal government officials.

[c]Most persons listed as journalists were publishers or editors and are hence classified as businessmen.

[d]Totals may not equal 100% because of rounding.

Table 2.4. Vocations of Trustees at Public Colleges and Universities, 1861–1929
          (percentages)

	1861–1880	1881–1900	1901–1920	1921–1929
No. of cases	231	146	139	109
No. with vocation unidentified	9	18	21	3
Professionals				
Clergyman	9.1	2.1	1.4	0.9
Physician	4.3	1.4	2.9	0.9
Educator	7.4	6.9	9.4	4.6
Lawyer	23.4	24.7	25.2	20.2
Judge	4.3	4.1	2.2	0.9
Subtotal	48.5	39.2	41.1	27.5
Businessmen				
Journalist	2.6	4.1	3.6	9.0
Merchant/commerce	4.8	4.8	5.0	2.8
Mfg./mining	3.9	5.5	5.8	11.0
Railroad man	2.2	2.7	4.3	0.9
Engineer	0.9	1.4	2.9	2.8
Banking/finance	5.6	11.6	18.0	20.2
Subtotal	20.0	30.1	39.6	46.7
Agriculturalist	20.8	19.2	13.0	16.5
Government officials				
Federal	2.2	1.4	1.4	0
State/local	6.5	6.2	2.9	2.8
Military	1.7	1.4	0	0
Subtotal	10.4	9.4	4.3	2.8
Other	0.4	2.6	2.1	6.4
Total[a]	100.1	100.1	100.1	99.9
Total businessmen and lawyers	43.4	54.8	64.8	66.9

Sources: See Tables 2.11, 2.13, 2.15.

Note: Institutions included are the Universities of South Carolina, Mississippi, Arkansas, Kansas, Nebraska, Wyoming, Nevada, California, Washington, Indiana, Illinois, and Massachusetts; and the College of Charleston, Louisiana State University, Texas A&M University, Pennsylvania State College, Ohio State University, Iowa State College of Agriculture and Mechanic Arts, Kansas State College of Agriculture and Applied Science, South Dakota State College, and the State College of Washington.

[a]Totals may not equal to 100% because of rounding.

Table 2.5. Vocations of Trustees at Major Private Universities and Technical Institutes in the Northeast, 1861–1929 (percentages)

	1861–1880	1881–1900	1901–1920	1921–1929
No. of cases	40	100	108	73
No. with vocation unidentified	8	6	0	0
Professionals				
Clergyman	22.5	10.0	4.6	2.7
Physician	12.5	10.0	5.6	8.2
Educator	5.0	6.0	5.6	6.8
Lawyer	10.0	25.0	16.7	11.0
Judge	10.0	3.0	3.7	0
Subtotal	60.0	54.0	36.2	28.7
Businessmen				
Journalist	0	2.0	1.9	1.4
Merchant/commerce	17.5	9.0	6.5	9.6
Mfg./mining	0	4.0	10.2	13.7
Railroad man	2.5	8.0	6.5	4.1
Engineer	0	3.0	0	2.7
Banking/finance	5.0	9.0	19.4	21.9
Subtotal	25.0	35.0	44.5	53.4
Agriculturalist	0	0	0	0
Government officials				
Federal	2.5	5.0	6.5	4.1
State/local	12.5	2.0	3.7	1.4
Military	0	2.0	0.9	1.4
Subtotal	15.0	9.0	11.1	6.9
Other	0	2.0	8.3	11.0
Total	100.0	100.0	100.1	100.0
Total businessmen and lawyers	35.0	60.0	61.2	64.5

Sources: The occupational information is drawn from *Who Was Who in America*, 5 vols. (Chicago: Marquis Publications, 1963); *Historical Register of Harvard University* (Cambridge: Harvard University Press, 1937), pp. 35–42; William H. S. Demarest, *A History of Rutgers College, 1776–1924* (New Brunswick: Rutgers College Press, 1924); Columbia University, *Handbook of Information, 1890–1891* (New York: Columbia University Press, 1891), p. ix; Lightner Witmer, *The Nearing Case* (New York: B. W. Huebsch, 1915), pp. 103–6; *Johns Hopkins Half Century Directory, 1876–1926* (Baltimore: Johns Hopkins Press, 1926); Thomas Wakefield Goodspeed, *The Story of the University of Chicago* (Chicago: University of Chicago Press, 1925), pp. vii–viii; Floyd W. Reeves, *Organization and Administration* (Chicago: University of Chicago Press, 1933), pp. 132–33; Moses Kirkland, *History of Chicago*, 2 vols. (Chicago: Mensell and Co., 1895), 1:349, 476; 2:28, 117, 305; Thomas Wakefield Goodspeed, *The University of Chicago Biographical Sketches* (Chicago: University of Chicago Press, 1922), 1:101–22; Edward D. McDonald and Edward M. Hinton, *Drexel Institute of Technology, 1891–1941* (Philadelphia: Drexel Institute of Technology, 1942).

Note: The sample includes Harvard, Rutgers (until 1915), Columbia, the University of Pennsylvania, Johns Hopkins University, the University of Chicago, and the Drexel Institute of Technology.

ing a coherent Protestant ethic. Education was aimed at shaping moral character through the development of mental discipline. Students were guided through a fixed curriculum that was thought to achieve this educational mission. That curriculum consisted primarily of biblical languages (Hebrew, Greek, Latin), the trivium (grammar, logic, rhetoric), and the quadrivium (arithmetic, geometry, astronomy, music).

The curriculum was important not so much as a substantive body of knowledge, as for its role in transmitting a coherent corporate identity in which graduates thought of themselves as the hiers of a cultural tradition that defined them as "gentlemen," "college men," members of a "learned profession" or members of an "educated class." Henry Adams, reflecting on the time, concluded that as a consequence of their common education, "lawyers, physicians, professors, merchants, were classes, and acted not as individuals, but as though they were clergymen and each profession were a church."[10] This view lent some historical plausibility to the ideal of an autonomous corporation of learning, insofar as governing boards shared an identity with the university as the common reference point constituting an educated class whose values they generally shared with the academic community.

It is also against this background that one can identify the educated class with a professional-mercantile elite that was led and influenced by the clergy in its understanding of the university's historical mission. The political bloc associated with this northeastern standing order controlled over three-quarters of the positions on governing boards at major private universities during this time, just as it had done for the last two hundred years. It remained a significant social force in major universities until the turn of the century. Businessmen, such as modern bankers or industrial manufacturers, were virtually absent from these boards and do not appear in significant numbers until the early twentieth century.

After this time, lawyers gradually displaced clergymen as the leading professional group on these boards, while heavy-industrial corporate interests (i.e., railroad men, engineers, manufacturers) replaced local merchant capitalists. Railroad men constituted about 53 percent of the heavy industrialists by 1900, a phenomenon which suggests a close and timely adjustment of governing board personnel to the shifting social location of economic resources in the Northeast. The combined tendencies of the early twentieth century indicate that the northeastern standing order, in which Protestant clergy served as the organic intelligentsia for a mercantile elite, was being overturned by a new alliance of heavy industrialists for whom engineers and lawyers assumed the leading role as an organic intelligentsia.[11] By 1920, however, sizeable numbers of bankers and financiers appear on these boards to complete the consolidation of corporate finance capital as a hegemonic political bloc in the major northeastern private universities.

A further specification of these shifting internal alliances yields some interesting results that define an institutional linkage to the social structure with even greater theoretical precision. Businessmen on the governing boards of major universities came increasingly from dominant positions within the northeastern industrial and financial establishment. In the two decades from 1901 to 1920, almost 45 percent of all board members classified as either lawyers or businessmen were attached, either as an officer or a director, to at least one company affiliated with a northeastern financial group. Sixty percent of these had their group affiliation through one of the core investment or commercial banks within the respective group. The Morgan–First National group was predominant in terms of the total number of positions (i.e., executive offices and directorships) among this group of trustees. Table 2.6 shows the proportional distribution of these positions among those financial groups represented on the governing boards in 1915.

The same pattern was even more pronounced during the 1920s. Sixty-two percent of trustees classified as lawyers or businessmen held positions in at least one financial or industrial enterprise associated with a major financial group. Evidence also reveals that among this group of governors, the holding of multiple or interlocking positions on different companies within the same group was fairly common by 1920. Among all trustees listed as lawyers or businessmen during this decade, each held an average of two corporate positions among the top 250 industrial and financial institutions in the United States. Those who sat as representatives of a financial group each held an average of two positions in different companies within that group. The Morgan group remained the single most visible presence. However, the emergence of a Cleveland group, and the relative decline of Kuhn, Loeb, and Company, all roughly parallel the shift in epoch-making innovation from railroads to automobiles (see Table 2.6).

Furthermore, empirical patterns of multiple position–holding among bankers, lawyers, railroad men, engineers, and other heavy industrialists justifies their classification as a single interest group to be designated as corporate finance capital. Indeed, these occupational categories are so intermeshed by the 1920s that any attempt to separate them is more often than not an exercise in futility. Table 2.7 shows the percentage of persons classified as lawyers or businessmen who simul-

Table 2.6. Business Positions of Trustees Attached to Financial Groups: Major Private Universities in the Northeast, 1915 and 1929 (percentages)

Financial group	Trustees' industrial location			All positions
	Banking	Mfg/Utilities	Railroads	
		1915		
Morgan	57	42	38	48
Chicago	29	29	0	21
Kuhn-Loeb	0	0	62	17
Boston	14	29	0	14
Total	100	100	100	100
		1929		
Morgan	39	43	0	37
Cleveland	15	29	0	21
Chicago	23	19	0	18
Boston	23	9	0	13
Kuhn-Loeb	0	0	100	11
Total	100	100	100	100

Note: The table includes trustees who were officers or directors of companies affiliated with a financial group. Each executive office and directorship is counted as a separate business position. The table emphasizes, first, the industry (e.g., banking) in which business positions were occupied and, second, the distribution of those positions among the financial groups (e.g., Morgan). For example, in 1915, 57% of all the banking positions occupied by trustees attached to financial groups were held in banks affiliated with the Morgan group. In the same year, 48% of all business positions occupied by trustees attached to financial groups were held in companies affiliated with the Morgan group.

taneously held positions in both banking and manufacturing establishments between 1861 and 1929. By the 1920s, over 53 percent of the persons listed in these two groups were holding positions simultaneously in banking and manufacturing.

Similarly, lawyers were so well integrated into this interest group that they not only practiced corporate law but held corporate executive offices and directorships. The percentage of lawyers and businessmen who held a law degree and at least one business position is shown in Table 2.7. Insofar as I could determine, roughly a quarter of these two occupational groups could be cross-listed by 1921–29 (and I suspect these measurements are substantial underestimates). The figure does not include attorneys engaged in the independent practice of corporate law, but only those who actually held official positions as business executives or directors. Nevertheless, the historical tendency toward lawyers' integration into corporate structures is evident. It is further confirmed by Hubert Park Beck's findings regarding the same phe-

Table 2.7. Multiple Position-Holding among Trustees Classified as Lawyers or Businessmen: Major Private Universities in the Northeast, 1861–1929

Years	% in both finance and manufacturing	% of lawyers in business/ businessmen with law degrees
1861–1880	14.3	7.1
1881–1900	14.0	10.5
1901–1920	48.5	16.7
1921–1929	53.3	24.4

nomenon in 1934–35. Beck found that by that time about 50 percent of
all professionals serving on university governing boards were either
officers or directors in a business enterprise.[12]

There is a strong empirical presumption for the claim that during the
first three decades of this century, governing boards at major private
universities in the Northeast came firmly under the direction of corporate officials attached to the dominant financial groups. Even more
detailed information on individual universities (not included here)
further reveals an imperfect regional division of educational clients
among the patron financial groups.[13] For instance, representatives of
the Cleveland and Chicago groups were most heavily concentrated in
the University of Chicago. The Boston group appears most closely
associated with universities in New England such as Harvard. The
Morgan and Rockefeller groups appear most frequently on the governing boards of institutions in the New York and Mid-Atlantic region
such as Rutgers, Columbia, and the University of Pennsylvania. Perhaps because railroads were far more extensive in the geographic reach
of their corporate organization, Kuhn-Loeb representatives were generally scattered throughout the country.[14]

Any itemized list of the financial holdings and business associations
of the trustees of major private universities during this time indicates
that despite the natural regional division of clients, their business
interests extended literally from coast to coast and could be found in
every region of the country. It was this association with the national
interests of finance capital, I will later argue, that was central to the
accumulation of the material means of mental production by these
universities, to their leadership in the rationalization of the higher
educational system, and, to that extent, their ability to act as national
beacons defining the meaning of university excellence.

Nevertheless, identifying this parallel between the development of
class structure and the changing composition of university governing
boards is one task; explaining it is something different. Veblen notes

that the social role of university governing boards was historically associated with the original religious mission of higher education. On the one hand, they were:

an aimless survival from the days of clerical rule, when they were presumably of some effect in enforcing conformity to orthodox opinions and observances among the academic staff. At the same time, when means for the maintenance of denominational colleges commonly had to be procured by an appeal to impecunious congregations, it fell to these bodies of churchmen to do service as sturdy beggars for funds with which to meet current expenses.[15]

Modern governing boards inherited this dual responsibility for regulating the orthodoxy of academic staff and curriculum and for acting as the primary institutional mechanism through which the university lays claim to socially scarce material resources that can be converted into the material means of mental production. Veblen seems to explain correctly the rise of businessmen on university governing boards as primarily a consequence of their importance in executing the latter role, which is called patronage.

During the nineteenth and early twentieth centuries, wealthy benefactors held a crucial position in the distribution of financial patronage to American colleges and universities. In 1872, 47 percent of all funds for higher education (public and private) was derived from private benefactions.[16] Private benefactions were still the single largest source of funding for colleges and universities as late as 1905, when contributions accounted for 33 percent of total income for all U.S. institutions of higher education.[17] The figure was obviously much higher for private colleges and universities. Consequently, Veblen found, it was "held to be expedient in case of emergency to have several wealthy men identified with the governing board, and such men of wealth are also commonly businessmen. It is apparently believed . . . that in case of emergency the wealthy members of the boards may be counted on to spend their substance in behalf of the university".[18]

With industrialization and the increasing concentration of wealth, northeastern universities necessarily turned to those sources of patronage which were most likely to control their society's scarce material resources. By 1890, these sources were mainly manufacturers, railroad men, and financiers. The first generation of new millionaires were often persuaded to make large contributions to higher institutions in exchange for positions on university governing boards. This patronage relationship was still believed compatible with the university's transcendental mission, because it was anticipated that few, if any, of these businessmen would actually attend board meetings.[19] There was a silent understanding that any position as a fiduciary trustee was an honorary recognition conferring prestige and social status on its possessor, but not one that would materially alter the balance of power on governing boards or their orientation to educational policy.

For a while, this assumption corresponded with actual practice. Businessmen at first viewed association with a college or university as a source of personal or community prestige; prior to the latter 1880s, they "were not much interested in what was taught, and widely regarded any course other than engineering as a waste of time."[20] In fact, a comparison of the social composition of the governing boards of major private technical institutes (e.g., Drexel) with other institutional types not surprisingly reveals that bankers and manufacturers consistently constituted a much larger percentage of trustees at a much earlier time. Yet, by the 1890s, this attitude was changing; and as prudent investors, capitalists assumed their positions on governing boards and started to exercise their formal powers.

There were several reasons for this change that theoretically can be related to a matrix of new economic, political, and ideological problems confronting the emerging corporate establishment. The immediate and directly economic interest was tied to industrial needs for manpower training and basic research to support industrial development. Political concerns were primarily the outgrowth of problems created by the emergence of progressive democracy. Finally, the cultural image of businessmen (as robber barons), as well as generalized ideological hostility to the business corporation (in support for antitrust, public ownership, and regulation), undermined the national consensus on free enterprise that had supported the growth of the modern corporation.

In the economic field, technical and professional manpower needs were already outstripping the supply of labor well before the turn of the century. One empirical survey of the technical labor force indicates that growth in demand for engineers and scientists during this time was exponential.[21] A Carnegie Foundation study found that as technical and engineering problems became routinely associated with underlying questions of industrial organization, about half of all businessmen started consciously to employ professional engineers graduated from engineering colleges in preference to men trained mainly through practical experience. This percentage was much higher among executives in heavy industry.[22] Following World War I, there was another explosion in demand for trained scientists, along with increasing demands for universities to undertake the kinds of basic research that would provide a steady, directed, and predictable flow of knowledge into industrial laboratories for application and development.[23]

Although technical and scientific institutes were being founded as fast as philanthropists could endow them, they were simply unable to produce the large numbers of engineers, technicians, and scientists required by the industrial revolution. In addition, most of the federally endowed agricultural and mechanical colleges were either too weak in technical fields or too far removed from the geographic centers of industrial activity to be useful until the end of the 1920s. Consequently, businessmen (especially those in the major financial groups) turned to the rapid transformation of traditional higher institutions as a solution to the problem. For instance, in 1862 there were only six general scientific and/or engineering schools attached to the major private universities, by 1917 sixty-four (51%) of all such schools were attached to colleges or universities. The proportion of formally educated practicing engineers rose from 12 percent in 1870 to 50 percent in 1917.[24]

However, the business interest in higher education must also be situated relative to broader concerns with politics and culture. The rise of populist and progressive democracy subjected corporate establishments to greater political scrutiny, legislative restriction, administrative regulation, litigation, and the challenge of organized labor. International trade imposed new intellectual and political demands on business, especially after 1914. As a consequence, business executives had an equal need for knowledge in political science and government, international relations, foreign languages, law, industrial psychology, and economics. Yet, in adapting this knowledge to their own needs, they introduced a corporate ideal of social efficiency and rationalization into the universities which redefined these fields in terms of the same instrumental logic that supplied the organizational norms for the modern corporation.

The new corporate establishment had a vested interest in higher institutions that could produce broadly educated professional executives and related service personnel, but on a different model than that offered by the traditional college. Indeed, throughout this period, an increasing proportion of corporate executives were receiving liberal arts and professional college degrees.[25] In fact, one 1909 survey of business attitudes toward higher education revealed that while the ordinary American businessman was an "anti-intellectual," executives associated with major East Coast corporate establishments such as steel, railroads, mining, utilities, and banking preferred a "liberally educated" executive over a so-called "man of experience."[26]

This points toward a reassessment of the specific ideological meaning of claims by scholars such as Veblen and Hofstadter that place "business in the vanguard of anti-intellectualism in our culture."[27] Generalized claims about the incompatability of the businessman's practical orientation with the intellectuals' transcendental orientation cannot sufficiently explain the peculiarly political character of business anti-intellectualism during the formation of the modern American university.[28]

The political contest between business and the intellectuals was specifically related to corporate perceptions of the widespread ideological hostility to capitalism in twentieth-century American life. However true or false these perceptions may be, as Stanley Herman observes, a rightest segment of American businessmen have always been critical of intellectuals because they trace the dangerous influence of labor disturbances, popular rebellion, reds, pinks, and fellow travelers to "a few fuzzy-minded but still harmful college professors." A liberal wing of the corporate establishment, if less overtly repressive in its approach to this problem, has been equally concerned with regulating social science as a way of correcting what it considers widespread misperceptions about business.[29] It is not so much that businessmen have been anti-intellectual as against certain kinds of intellectuals.

PRIVATE LIBERAL ARTS AND DENOMINATIONAL COLLEGES

Small private liberal arts and denominational colleges were linked directly to this same structure of class power through their governing boards, although at a lower level in the emerging hierarchy within the capitalist class (see Table 2.8). Governing boards at these institutions also consistently retained a much higher proportion of clergymen, with clergymen remaining the single largest group of trustees even as late as 1920. Although secular liberal arts colleges showed a greater proportion of merchants and lawyers on their early governing boards than did strictly denominational colleges, they are classed as a single group because widespread secularization tended to transform the latter into liberal arts colleges by 1929. In these institutions, the traditional mission of moral education was carried forward in modern concepts of liberal and humanistic education.

The transition towards governing boards controlled by bankers, corporate lawyers, and heavy industrialists proceeded at a much slower pace than at the major private universities. Furthermore, the representation of finance capital (i.e., those lawyers and businessmen who simultaneously sat as officials of both banking and manufacturing

Table 2.8. Vocations of Trustees at Private Denominational and Liberal Arts Colleges, 1861–1929 (percentages)

	1861–1880	1881–1900	1901–1920	1921–1929
No. of cases	107	50	71	71
No. with vocation unidentified	13	15	10	11
Professionals				
Clergyman	47.7	34.0	31.0	15.5
Physician	5.6	10.0	5.6	4.2
Educator	4.7	0	4.2	7.0
Lawyer	12.2	24.0	28.2	18.3
Judge	5.6	10.0	2.8	2.8
Subtotal	75.8	78.0	71.8	47.8
Businessmen				
Journalist	0.9	0	0	2.8
Merchant/commerce	10.3	0	1.4	9.9
Mfg./mining	4.7	6.0	8.5	14.1
Railroad man	0	6.0	5.6	4.2
Engineer	0.9	0	2.8	1.4
Banking/finance	0	8.0	9.9	16.9
Subtotal	16.8	20.0	28.2	49.3
Agriculturalist	0	0	0	0
Government officials				
Federal	0.9	0	0	1.4
State/local	0.9	0	0	0
Military	2.8	2.0	0	1.4
Subtotal	4.6	2.0	0	2.8
Other	2.8	0	0	0
Total	100.0	100.0	100.0	99.9
Total businessmen and lawyers	29.0	44.0	56.4	67.6

Sources: *Who Was Who in America*; James Monroe Taylor and Elizabeth Hazelton Haight, *Vassar* (New York: Oxford University Press, 1915); Charles Coleman Sellers, *Dickinson College: A History* (Middletown: Wesleyan University Press, 1973), pp. 492–501; David Bishop Skillman, *The Biography of a College: Being the History of the First Century of the Life of Lafayette College*, 2 vols. (Easton, Pa.: Lafayette College, 1932), 1:194, 340, 377–78, 2:118, 227, 253, 316–24; John W. Leonard, ed., *Who's Who in Pennsylvania* (New York: L. R. Hammersley and Co., 1908); John Barnard, *From Evangelicalism to Progressivism at Oberlin College, 1866–1917* (Columbus: Ohio State University Press, 1969), pp. 10–11, 110–11; Calvin Durfee, *Williams Biographical Annals* (Boston: Lee and Shephard Publishers, 1871), ch. 3.

Note: The sample includes Vassar, Dickinson, Lafayette, Oberlin, and Williams colleges.

Table 2.9. Multiple Position–Holding among Trustees Classified as Lawyers or Businessmen: Private Denominational and Liberal Arts Colleges, 1861–1929

Years	% in both finance and manufacturing	% of lawyers in business/ businessmen with law degrees
1861–1880	0	10.0
1881–1900	4.6	4.6
1901–1920	5.3	10.5
1921–1929	8.5	12.8

establishments) was much smaller. As the figures in Table 2.9 indicate,
even by 1929 less than 9 percent of the lawyers and businessmen on
these governing boards represented finance capital.

Consequently, a much smaller proportion of these occupational categories can be located as members of the major financial groups. The
information collected for this survey suggests that between 1900 and
1929, no more than 10 to 20 percent of lawyers and businessmen could,
at any time, be linked to the financial groups. Those attached to a
financial group were usually directors or officers for subordinate railroad or heavy industrial establishments. I could not identify a single
one who held a position in any of the core financial institutions at the
center of these groups. Among the small proportion who could be tied
to a subordinate industrial element in the financial groups, 62 percent
of the offices held from 1901 to 1920 were in the Morgan group. This
proportion later fell to 50 percent. The remainder in both cases were
held in the Kuhn group. Another significant difference is that lawyers
on these governing boards seemed to exhibit greater structural distance or autonomy from business. Table 2.9 indicates that after 1880 the
proportion of lawyer-businessmen (i.e., those persons with law
degrees holding directorships or offices in a business establishment)
on boards of private liberal arts and denominational colleges was only
about half the percentage found in the major private universities at
comparable times.

Similarly, bank officials on the governing boards of small liberal arts
and denominational colleges came overwhelmingly from locally based
financial institutions. Manufacturers on the boards were either engaged in light industry or owned small to medium-sized manufacturing establishments. Instead of serving as counsel for corporate
establishments, lawyers on the boards were more likely to turn to local
and state politics as an avenue for advancement and prestige.

Like the colleges which they governed, most of the trustees were
inhabitants of technically urban but still small-town America. Many of
these areas were close enough to the center of industrialization to be

profoundly affected by its consequences and yet also remain on its social and economic periphery. In New England, for instance, some two-thirds of all students in these colleges came from families that can be described as rural or small-town middle class.[30] Even to the extent that college governors associated themselves with an image of entrepreneurial capitalism or the new urban professional, they did not necessarily identify themselves with the interests of the emerging corporate establishment.

It was precisely this group that was most threatened by the status revolution. It was a group caught between the power of corporate capital and the demands of a rising working class. Hence, elements of these classes frequently became local leaders of the Progressive movement.[31] Progressivism provided a uniquely "conservative" program of reform that on the one hand improved labor's material condition and regulated business practices, and yet preserved the basic economic framework of private property, free markets, and the emphasis on individual achievement. Meanwhile, it introduced a conception of democracy in which professional middle-class experts assumed leading roles as social engineers, reformers, legislators, and technical advisors to business, government, and labor.[32]

The idea of a liberal education infused progressive ideology with a moral and humanistic critique of conditions within capitalism without indicting the basic structure of capitalist society. In his study of New England colleges, George E. Peterson found that liberal arts and denominational colleges emphasized this mission in the ideal of a harmonious moral or Christian community as opposed to the divisiveness of class conflict and unregulated markets. Ultimately, this moral vision, given certain reforms, was not incompatible with corporate concepts of functional integration and scientific rationalization, which were equally designed to achieve social harmony as social efficiency.[33]

In this connection, governing boards defined linkages to important structures of political power for both major universities and small liberal arts or denominational colleges. Table 2.10 indicates the proportion of trustees not already listed as full-time government officials who served in public office during, or sometime prior to, their affiliation with a governing board. The highest office held by a given individual (proceeding from local to federal) is used as the basis for classification. Because of the great difficulty of securing more detailed information on many of the trustees, I must caution readers that the figures in this table should be interpreted as evidence of general trends rather than as anything approximating a definitive measurement of actual proportions.

These figures indicate that prior to 1880, trustees holding public

Table 2.10. Percentage of Trustees Who Served in Public Office: Major
Private Universities and Private Denominational and Liberal
Arts Colleges, 1861–1929

	Federal office	State or local office
Universities		
1861–1880	2.5	35.0
1881–1900	11.0	6.0
1901–1920	8.3	11.1
1921–1929	12.3	6.9
Colleges		
1861–1880	8.4	12.2
1881–1900	12.0	4.6
1901–1920	1.5	5.6
1921–1929	7.0	4.2

office in both types of institutions were largely state legislators, governors, and other state or local officials. Their primary political orientation and party attachments were to a local constituency. After 1880, the
relative preponderance of public-office holders shifts toward national
government for both types of institutions. Nevertheless, there is a
distinct difference in their points of linkage with national political
power. From 1881 to 1929, 78 percent of the trustees holding federal
office on the boards of small liberal arts and denominational colleges
were elected as congressmen from their local districts. Local political
attachments were merely redefined in relation to the process of national political development. In contrast, 100 percent of those on the
boards of major private universities who held federal office held appointive offices in the executive or judicial branches of national government. Most often they were U.S. Supreme Court justices or executive
appointees in the Departments of State, War, or Treasury. This difference appears at precisely that time when the national executive
branch and courts were assuming dominance in the direction of policy,
while congressional and local governmental authority was on the wane.

PUBLIC UNIVERSITIES IN THE SOUTH

State ownership of universities first emerged as the dominant institutional type outside the industrialized Northeast and only gradually
assumed national importance during the twentieth century. In the
South, where state universities were first established before the Civil
War, governing boards consistently retained a close relationship with

traditional landed elites and their conservative political allies in state and local government. Consequently, Southern institutions, despite their nominal public ownership, were typically aristocratic (and even martial) in their educational orientation and governance. As Table 2.11 indicates, there was remarkable stability in the social composition of these governing boards relative to what one finds elsewhere in the country.

The South's traditionally rural cast is readily captured in the sparse distribution of businessmen on governing boards, even in the few urban universities. From 1861 to 1920, these boards were easily controlled by large plantation owners, landlords, and lawyers or political bosses who carried forward the ideology of the Old South. The agriculturalists listed in this sample were all plantation owners or, later, rentier landlords whose chief source of income was derived from agricultural rents paid by tenants and sharecroppers or from agricultural royalties (e.g., timber). Nearly all the lawyers were state and local political leaders who usually held positions in the state legislatures.

Table 2.12 shows the proportion of trustees who held public office prior to, or during, their tenure on a southern university governing board. Most of them pursued professional politics in addition to (or aside from) their regular occupations. In no other region of the country did universities maintain as close and direct a linkage to political or state elites as one finds in the South. In another striking contrast, what little attachment these institutions had to national political development disappears at precisely that time when private universities and colleges were assuming a closer relationship to the federal government. Interesting in this respect is the finding that former Confederate army officers at or above the rank of major increased on these boards from 15 percent in 1861–80 to at least 31 percent between 1881 and 1900. Over one-half of the latter had been generals in the Confederate armies.

Practically every effort to redefine the class and racial structure of higher education in the South came from outside the region.[34] When Reconstruction succeeded only in substantially reconstructing the Old South, northern churches responded by establishing several Negro denominational colleges in the region. There were thirty-one such institutions by 1928. Generally, these institutions were poorly governed and poorly funded by white clergymen and absentee church boards in the North which had little direct contact with the black institutions under their control. Eventually, seventeen black denominational colleges controlled by black churches were founded, but the

Table 2.11. Vocations of Trustees at Public Universities in the South, 1861–1920
(percentages)

	1861–1880	1881–1900	1901–1920
No. of cases	61	26	21
No. with vocation unidentified	5	4	5
Professionals			
Clergyman	1.6	3.8	0
Physician	4.9	0	4.8
Educator	9.8	7.7	9.5
Lawyer	32.8	42.3	42.9
Judge	9.8	11.5	9.5
Subtotal	58.9	65.3	66.7
Businessmen			
Journalist	1.6	3.8	0
Merchant/commerce	4.9	0	4.8
Mfg./mining	0	0	4.8
Railroad man	0	0	0
Engineer	1.6	0	0
Banking/finance	1.6	7.7	9.5
Subtotal	9.7	11.5	19.1
Agriculturalists	16.4	7.7	9.5
Government officials			
Federal	3.3	3.8	4.8
State/local	6.6	7.7	0
Military	3.3	3.8	0
Subtotal	13.2	15.3	4.8
Other	1.6	0	0
Total	99.8	99.8	100.1
Total agriculturalists and lawyers	49.2	50.0	52.4

Sources: *Who Was Who in America;* Allen Cabaniss, *The University of Mississippi: Its First Hundred Years* (Hattiesburg: University and College Press of Mississippi, 1971); Dunbar Rowland, *History of Mississippi*, 2 vols. (Jackson: S. J. Clarke Publishing Co., 1925); *Historical Catalogue of the University of Mississippi, 1849–1909* (Nashville: Marshall and Bruce, 1910), pp. 81–83; John Hugh Reynolds and David Yancey Thomas, *History of the University of Arkansas* (Fayetteville: University of Arkansas Press, 1910); Walter L. Fleming, *Louisiana State University* (Baton Rouge: Louisiana State University Press, 1936); *Soard's New Orleans Directory for 1878* (New Orleans: L. Soard's and Co., 1878); J. H. Easterby, *A History of the College of Charleston, Founded 1770* (Charleston: Scribner Press, 1935), pp. 262–65; *Charleston Directory, 1866; Cyclopedia of Eminent and Representative Men of the Carolinas of the Nineteenth Century*, 2 vols. (Madison, Wis.: Brant and Fuller, 1892), 1:69, 245, 286, 610–11, 661–63, 673; Daniel Walker Hollis, *University of South Carolina*, 2 vols. (Columbia: University of South Carolina Press, 1956); George Sessions Perry, *The Story of Texas A&M* (New York: McGraw-Hill Book Co., 1951).

Note: The sample includes the Universities of Mississippi and Arkansas, Louisiana State University, the College of Charleston, the University of South Carolina, and Texas A&M University.

Table 2.12. Percentage of Trustees Who Served in Public Office: Public
Universities in the South, 1861–1920

Years	Federal office	State or local office
1861–1880	4.3	38.0
1881–1900	0	54.0
1901–1920	0	67.0

continuing poverty of southern black populations kept these schools weak and poorly funded.

The national government attempted to legislate black colleges into existence with the Second Morrill Act of 1890. This legislation required any state which maintained separate public colleges for blacks and whites, and which accepted Morrill funds, to divide the funds equally between a white and black college. The legislation resulted in the establishment of a subordinate tier of public arts and industry colleges (A&Is) for blacks in the South. However, these were always controlled quite unsympathetically by the same traditional classes that dominated the rest of public higher education in the South.

The greatest successes in black higher education were the nine independent private Negro colleges, such as Howard University, Tuskegee Institute, and Hampton Institute, institutions essentially supported (and strongly influenced) by northeastern industrialists and the many charitable foundations established by this group. Educational foundations such as the General Education Board, the Slater Fund, the Anna T. Jeannes Fund, the Peabody Fund, and the Phelps-Stokes Fund spent millions of dollars on these colleges mainly as technical institutes for the development of a black middle class of schoolteachers, ministers, skilled workers, and farmers.[35] They were unquestionably the most successful black institutions in securing an external social patron financially strong enough to support them in an otherwise hostile environment.[36]

STATE UNIVERSITIES AND LAND-GRANT COLLEGES IN THE MIDWEST AND THE WEST

In the remaining regions of the country, primarily the Midwest and the West, essentially two types of public institutions battled one another for supremacy. These were the land-grant colleges and the state universities. The first Morrill Act of 1862 provided the initial impetus for establishing public institutions for higher education in these regions. The legislation was intended to promote the creation of land-grant colleges for the "liberal education of the agricultural and industrial classes." Revenues derived from the sale of federal land-grants provided permanent endowments for the construction and support of these colleges.

Some states—such as Wisconsin, California, and Massachusetts— designated their federal land-grant college as the official state university. But, the more common method of organizing state higher education in these regions was to found a state university and a land-grant college in competition with one another for prestige and very limited public funds. Since the land-grant colleges were generally located in the heart of rural agricultural areas, pork-barrel politics in the state legislatures usually necessitated the concurrent chartering of a state university in a major urban area, often the state capital. The latter developed professional and informational resources for a growing urban area and for the conduct of state government.

By and large, these state universities shared the same educational orientation as major private universities in the Northeast, and indeed, were often consciously modelled on those institutions. Moreover, the patterns of development one finds in the social composition of their governing boards parallel the eastern counterparts in nearly every respect (see Table 2.13). By the turn of the century, state universities were generally governed by a political bloc of bankers, heavy industrialists, and corporate attorneys. Similarly, although to a lesser degree than one finds in the major private universities, this political bloc increasingly crystallized around a distinct group of finance capitalists. This is evident again in the steadily emerging occupational interface between bankers, manufacturers, and lawyers (see Table 2.14).

However, the direct presence of northeastern financial groups was relatively weak even among finance capitalists sitting on the governing boards of state universities in these regions. In 1915, only slightly more than 5 percent of the lawyers and businessmen on these governing boards were directly associated with member companies of the major financial groups. In 1929, that figure was still just less than 6 percent. In the recorded cases, these few were all railroad men associated with national trunk lines such as the Southern Pacific, Union Pacific, Northern Pacific, Central Pacific, or Atchison, Topeka, and Santa Fe.

Another significant feature of these boards is that about one-half of those listed as agriculturalists can be consistently identified as agribusinessmen. This term is used not simply to designate large farmers

Table 2.13. Vocations of Trustees at State Universities in the Midwest and West, 1861–1929 (percentages)

	1861–1880	1881–1900	1901–1920	1921–1929
No. of cases	91	53	60	53
No. with vocation unidentified	0	1	2	1
Professionals				
Clergyman	19.8	3.8	3.3	1.9
Physician	6.6	3.8	3.3	1.9
Educator	4.4	7.5	10.0	5.7
Lawyer	22.0	18.9	26.7	24.5
Judge	4.4	3.8	1.7	1.9
Subtotal	57.2	37.8	45.0	35.9
Businessmen				
Journalist	2.2	3.8	1.7	9.4
Merchant/commerce	7.7	5.7	3.3	1.9
Mfg./mining	6.6	11.3	3.3	5.7
Railroad man	3.3	7.5	6.7	1.9
Engineer	0	0	0	0
Banking/finance	7.7	13.2	21.7	20.8
Subtotal	27.5	41.5	36.7	39.7
Agriculturalists	6.6	9.4	11.7	11.3
Government officials				
Federal	1.1	1.9	1.7	0
State/local	5.5	7.5	1.7	1.9
Military	2.2	0	0	0
Subtotal	8.8	9.4	3.4	1.9
Other	0	1.9	3.3	11.3
Total	100.1	100.0	100.1	100.1
Total businessmen and lawyers	49.5	60.4	63.4	64.2

Sources: *Who Was Who in America;* Clifford S. Griffin, *The University of Kansas: A History* (Lawrence: University Press of Kansas, 1974); Burton Dorr Myers, *Trustees and Officers of Indiana University, 1820–1950* (Bloomington: Indiana University Press, 1951); Samuel Bradford Doten, *An Illustrated History of the University of Nevada* (Reno: University of Nevada Press, 1924); Verne A. Stadtman, ed., *The Centennial Record of the University of California, 1868–1968* (Berkeley and Los Angeles: University of California Press, 1968), pp. 407–29; Robert N. Manley, *Centennial History of the University of Nebraska,* 2 vols. (Lincoln: University of Nebraska Press, 1969), 1:16–18, 107, 142, 176, 314; J. Sterling Morton, *Illustrated History of Nebraska,* 2 vols. (Lincoln: Jacob North and Co., 1905), 1:523, 2:467; Arthur C. Wakely, *Omaha,* 2 vols. (Chicago: S. J. Clarke Publishing Co., 1917), 2:50, 120; Wilson O. Clough, *A History of the University of Wyoming, 1887–1964* (Laramie, 1965), pp. 14, 103, 322–26; Charles M. Gates, *The First Century at the University of Washington* (Seattle: University of Washington Press, 1961); Cornelius H. Hanford, *Seattle and Environs* (Seattle: Pioneer Historical Publishing Co., 1924), pp. 342–45; Clinton A. Snowden, *History of Washington,* 4 vols. (New York: Century History Co., 1909).

Note: the sample includes the University of Kansas, Indiana University, and the Universities of Nevada, California, Nebraska, Wyoming, and Washington.

Table 2.14. Multiple Position–Holding among Trustees Classified as Lawyers, Businessmen, or Agriculturalists: State Universities in the Midwest and West, 1861–1929

| Years | Lawyers and businessmen | | Agriculturalists |
	% in both finance and manufacturing	% of lawyers in business/business-men with law degrees	% also in business
1861–1880	2.2	4.4	50.0
1881–1900	15.6	6.3	40.0
1901–1920	13.2	18.4	43.0
1921–1929	17.7	20.6	50.0

or ranchers but also to identify those agriculturalists who held positions in (or owned) a separate business or bank (see Table 2.14). This peculiar pattern of agricultural representation suggests that the more powerful agricultural elites were already integrated into the general structure of regional capitalist economies.

On the other hand, the governing boards of land-grant colleges originally maintained stronger associations with a more traditional farmer-agrarian interest (see Table 2.15). Until approximately 1880, many of the trustees were farmers of relatively modest social standing, especially in states where the agrarian interest was effectively organized.[37] Yet, soon thereafter, the institutions began slipping from their control. As elsewhere in the country, lawyers, bankers, and manufacturers assumed ever greater prominence on these governing boards.

By the 1920s, when the political power of agriculture was on the wane, even these institutions were being governed by businessmen. Furthermore, the proportion of agribusinessmen increased from 19 percent between 1860 and 1880 to at least 33 percent in 1900. An interesting characteristic of all these businessmen was their position on the industrial periphery, where they maintained an essentially local and populistic conception of community interests. This is evident in their minimal ties to even the lowest tiers of finance capital. Those who did reveal such linkages were confined almost exclusively to the boards of a very few eastern land-grant colleges, such as Cornell and MIT, which, for all practical purposes, were really part of the northeastern system of major private universities and technical institutes.

The one significant breach in this trend occurred during the Populist revolt. Like state legislatures and governorships, public university governing boards also came under the control of Populists. It is difficult to assess the precise extent of Populist influence. However, from 1860

Table 2.15. Vocations of Trustees at Land-Grant Colleges, 1861–1929 (percentages)

	1861–1880	1881–1900	1901–1920	1921–1929
No. of cases	79	67	58	56
No. with vocation unidentified	4	13	14	2
Professionals				
Clergyman	2.5	0	0	0
Physician	1.3	0	1.7	0
Educator	8.9	6.0	8.6	3.6
Lawyer	17.7	22.4	17.2	16.1
Judge	0	1.5	0	0
Subtotal	30.4	29.9	27.5	19.7
Businessmen				
Journalist	3.8	4.5	6.9	8.9
Merchant/commerce	1.3	6.0	6.9	3.6
Mfg./mining	3.8	3.0	8.6	16.1
Railroad man	2.5	0	3.5	0
Engineer	1.3	3.0	6.9	5.4
Banking/finance	6.3	11.9	17.2	19.6
Subtotal	19.0	28.4	50.0	53.6
Agriculturalists	40.5	31.3	15.5	21.4
Government officials				
Federal	2.5	0	0	0
State/local	7.6	4.5	5.2	3.6
Military	0	1.5	0	0
Subtotal	10.1	6.0	5.2	3.6
Other	0	4.5	1.7	1.8
Total	100.0	100.1	99.9	100.1
Total businessmen and lawyers	36.7	50.8	67.2	69.7

Sources: *Who Was Who in America;* Julius Terras Willard, *History of the Kansas State College of Agriculture and Applied Science* (Manhattan, Kans.: Kansas State College Press, 1940); William H. Powers, *A History of South Dakota State College* (Brookings: South Dakota State College Press, 1931); Earl D. Ross, *A History of the Iowa State College of Agriculture and Mechanic Arts* (Ames: Iowa State College Press, 1942); William J. Petersen, *The Story of Iowa,* 4 vols. (New York: Lewis Historical Publishing Co., 1952); Enoch Albert Bryan, *Historical Sketches of the State College of Washington, 1890–1925* (Spokane: Inland American Printing Co., 1928); Herbert Hunt, *Tacoma: Its History and Its Builders,* 3 vols. (Chicago: S. J. Clarke Publishing Co., 1916); N. W. Durham, *History of the City of Spokane and Spokane County,* 3 vols. (Chicago: S. J. Clarke Publishing Co., 1912); James E. Pollard, *History of the Ohio State University* (Columbus: Ohio State University Press, 1952), pp. 419–22; J. Fletcher Brennan, ed., *A Biographical Cyclopedia and Portrait Gallery of Distinguished Men, With an Historical Sketch of the State of Ohio* (Cincinnati: John C. Yorston and Co., 1879), p. 302; Wayland Fuller Dunaway, *History of the Pennsylvania State*

to 1880 only 6 percent of agriculturalists on land-grant college governing boards were officers in a Grange or other agricultural society.
During the rise of the Farmers' Alliance and the Populist Party (1881–
1900), the proportion increased almost fivefold to about 29 percent.
After the collapse of organized agrarianism, the percentage again fell,
to just 11 percent. Where information is available from individual
college histories, evidence indicates that Populists temporarily won
substantial majorities on governing boards at the Universities of Washington and Missouri and Kansas State College. There was a Fusionist
majority at the University of Nebraska and a Silver party victory at the
University of Nevada. There were much later victories (1916–21) by the
Non-Partisan League at the University of Montana, the University of
North Dakota, and Oklahoma State. However, these were all brief
storms of resistance against the larger general trend toward business
control.

Figure 2.1 illustrates the theoretical structure just outlined for the
period around 1880–90. It reveals a curious anomaly which requires
one final comment. A phenomenon equally as significant as who *did* sit
on these governing boards is the question of who did not wield any
authority. During a period when industrial workers were emerging as
the largest social class in America, not a single representative of industrial labor that I could identify served on any of the governing boards.
This finding was duplicated in at least two earlier studies, conducted in
1917 and 1920.[38] Similarly, Hubert Park Beck's survey of thirty leading
American colleges and universities in 1934–35 found that even then,
less than one-half of one percent of trustees represented organized
labor during a period of massive and militant labor mobilization.[39]

  Such data provide a prima facie justification for asking to what extent
modern universities can be described as an "ideological apparatus."

College (Lancaster: Pennsylvania State College, 1946): Leonard, *Who's Who in Pennsylvania*, 1904 and 1908 editions; *Encyclopedia of Pennsylvania Biography: Portrait and Biographical Record of Lancaster County, Pennsylvania* (Chicago: Chapman Publishing Co., 1894),
p. 291; Winton U. Solberg, *The University of Illinois, 1867–1894* (Chicago: University of
Illinois Press, 1968), pp. 81–82; *Twenty-Eighth Report of the Board of Trustees of the Univer-
sity of Illinois* (Springfield: Illinois State Journal Co., 1916), p. 5; *Thirty-Fifth Report of the
Board of Trustees of the University of Illinois* (Urbana: University of Illinois Press, 1930),
p. v; Harold Whiting Cary, *The University of Massachusetts* (Amherst: University of
Massachusetts Press, 1962).
  Note: the sample includes Kansas State College of Agriculture and Applied Science,
South Dakota State College, Iowa State College of Agriculture and Mechanic Arts, the
State College of Washington, Ohio State University, Pennsylvania State College, the
University of Illinois, and the University of Massachusetts.

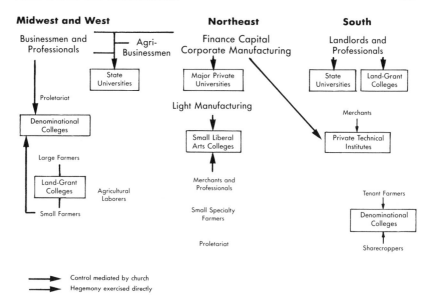

Fig. 2.1. Relative Social Location of Colleges and Universities in the Class Structure, circa 1890

For governing boards can at least influence "the broad framework, the long-run goals, and the general atmosphere of the university."[40] Certainly, as Miliband observes, the actual control entailed by this dominance "greatly varies, and may well in normal circumstances be of a formal kind."[41] It is for this reason that one cannot theoretically impute the role of an ideological apparatus to universities in capitalist society merely from a positional analysis of governing boards. However, historical circumstances often tend not to be normal in universities, particularly during periods of wider social upheaval and political change. Moreover, it is during these periods that the structures which regulate and define normal behavior are established for succeeding generations as the outcome of those conflicts associated with political and institutional development.

In this respect, the appearance of businessmen of governing boards merely opened the doors of American universities to a political movement for institutional rationalization that Weinstein describes as the corporate ideal. The rationalization of American universities also initiated a class conflict between business and university intellectuals. The concrete balance of institutional power that has been established between business and intellectuals as a consequence of this conflict is what I argue can be understood as the process of constructing an ideological apparatus.

3

Corporate Power and Social Efficiency: The Industrialization of American Universities

I HAVE pointed to a parallel between three historical developments: the rising prominence of corporate capitalists on university governing boards, the institutional modernization of American universities, and the academic development of a professional intellectual type. The theoretical shortcomings of instrumental and positional critiques of state elites are old territory, so it is not my intention to argue that the social composition of governing boards is in itself sufficient to account for the other developments. Yet, I would suggest with Miliband that there is still "reason for attaching considerable importance to the social composition of the state elite in advanced capitalist countries." That reason is the strong presumption created "as to the general outlook, ideological dispositions and political bias" of those groups which wield the organs of legitimate political authority within the state.[1]

The changing social composition of governing boards signals a shift in the class relations of intellectual production. This shift constituted an opening through which businessmen acquired an institutional capacity to reconstitute dramatically the intellectual labor process with modernizing policies. However, it was in the class struggles engendered by this process that American intellectuals were actually reconstituted as a social group.

Moreover, the problems of political organization and class formation were surmounted only in the development of a new kind of educational institution. This institution was the private educational foundation.[2] It was the educational foundation which first linked general

60

conceptions of class structure and class interest to the disparate actions of university administrations that were otherwise acting independent of one another.[3] The Carnegie Foundation for the Advancement of Teaching (CFAT) and the General Education Board (GEB) were particularly significant among these for their role in the formation of a coherent ideological conception of corporate class interests in higher education. They played a decisive role in promoting organized class action and, thus, were "the key mediating institutions" through which the needs of monopoly capital were "systematically built into the structure of higher education during the early years of the century."[4]

EDUCATIONAL FOUNDATIONS AND FINANCE CAPITALISM

The ideas which led to the endowment of the Carnegie Foundation germinated at a White House luncheon held by Theodore Roosevelt in the summer of 1904. Henry S. Pritchett, president of MIT, is reported to have been "bursting with ideas about the organization of higher education in America."[5] These ideas so impressed Andrew Carnegie that two years later he endowed the foundation with a grant of ten million dollars and Carnegie appointed Pritchett as the foundation's first president.

The Carnegie Foundation was nominally governed by a board of trustees which always included a large majority of prominent university presidents from throughout the United States. However, the full board rarely met more than once or twice a year, and then primarily to consider proposals brought to it by the foundation's executive committee and full-time professional staff. As a result, the executive committee, with the foundation president as its ex-officio presiding officer, quickly emerged as the real center of policy formation.

The original executive committee was constructed around a rather unique nucleus of what might be called organic "corporate intellectuals." For instance, Pritchett was not only a former president of MIT, but a professional engineer who also sat on the board of directors of the Atchison, Topeka, and Santa Fe Railroad. Among the committee's other six members was Nicholas Murray Butler, president of Columbia University and a director for New York Life Insurance Company. Charles C. Harrison, provost for the University of Pennsylvania, had been a manufacturer from 1863 to 1892, before retiring to assume his role as an educational administrator. Alexander C. Humphreys, the president of Stevens Institute of Technology, had a long history in the utility industry as an officer and engineer for Bayonne and Greenville Gas Light

Company (1872–81), Pintsch Lighting Company (1881–85), and United Gas Improvement Company (1885–94). He remained a senior partner in Humphreys and Glasgow of London. In addition, the original executive committee included Frank A. Vanderlip, the vice-president of National City Bank, and Robert A. Franks, president of Home Trust Company.

Pritchett, Butler, Vanderlip, and Franks remained on the executive committee as a stabilizing nucleus for more than twenty years. The intellectual type which they represented was rather common on the executive committee. From 1906 to 1929, 80 percent of the members of the CFAT executive committee maintained some direct connection with a major business or financial corporation either as directors or executive officers. Thirty percent of the executive committee members were attached to companies with membership in either the Morgan–First National group (which had absorbed Carnegie Steel) or the Rockefeller group, both based in New York City.

The General Education Board was similarly chartered by John D. Rockefeller in 1903. Frederick T. Gates, a young Baptist clergyman, was appointed president of the foundation in 1907. Gates was Rockefeller's personal business representative and his "most important counsellor" in other matters as well. Dr. Wallace Buttrick, a former president of the Peabody Education Fund, and Gates's college friend, had already been appointed secretary and executive officer four years earlier.[6] These two men supplied the cornerstone of executive leadership to the GEB for approximately twenty years. The larger social composition of the board is indicated in Table 3.1. Among the businessmen on this board between 1903 and 1929 were some of the nation's most prominent bankers and industrialists, including Andrew Carnegie and John D. Rockefeller, Jr. The latter, according to one board official, "in a sense represented" his father.[7]

Three-quarters of the lawyers who served on the board were also corporate officers or directors. Thus, a single bloc of corporate interests directly controlled almost 60 percent of the positions on this board. At least 45 percent of the members of this bloc sat as officers or directors at banks or industrial corporations which were also members of the major New York City financial groups. Among such members, 44 percent belonged to the Morgan group, 44 percent to the Rockefeller group, and 12 percent to the Kuhn-Loeb group. Both foundations provided a forum in which representatives of the largest financial groups in the United States could sit together and organize their class consciousness

Table 3.1. Occupations of GEB Members, 1902–1929

Occupation	Number	Percentage
Businessman	16	48.6
Lawyer	4	12.1
Educator	11	33.3
Minister	2	6.0
Total	33	100.0

Sources: Data compiled from list of officers and members in
The General Education Board: An Account of Its Activities (New
York: GEB, 1915) and GEB, *Annual Report* for years 1914–1915
through 1928–1929; *Who Was Who in America.*

relative to the university in cooperation with prominent educators and
university presidents.[8]

The cohesion of this educational network was facilitated by a complex system of interlocking directors with other educational foundations that was analogous to that found in the financial groups. Among
the GEB members listed as "educators," approximately one-third were
full-time professional administrators for other foundations. The rest
were university presidents. Table 3.2 lists some other major foundations and indicates the number of GEB members sitting as trustees for
these foundations; if a GEB member served as a major executive officer
of these other foundations, that fact is also noted in the table.

The presence of so many members and officers from other foundations on the GEB enabled it to coordinate and centralize the activities of
nearly all other major private educational foundations, each of which
was merely a smaller version of GEB. The existence of interlocking
trustees between the Southern Education Board, the Peabody Fund,
and Slater Fund was actually the result of explicit agreements between
GEB and these other organizations designed to secure "harmony of
purpose and unity."[9] Abraham Flexner, a prominent GEB staff member, reports that letters between the various boards informing each
other of projects, field visits, private conversations, and meetings were
"frequent" and "enthusiastic." Members of the various boards also
regularly discussed their problems at one another's meetings.[10]

In effect, GEB was the coordinating mechanism in a complex and
sophisticated network of conscious class action (see Fig. 3.1). This
network was further consolidated when GEB reached a formal agreement with CFAT to share and exchange information in 1908. The
agreement occurred shortly after Charles Eliot, president of Harvard

Table 3.2. Interlocking Foundation Directors: GEB Members Serving on Other Major
Foundations, 1902–1929

Foundation	No. of GEB members	Offices held on other foundation
Rockefeller Foundation	10	president
Southern Education Board	5	
Slater Education Fund	4	president treasurer
Peabody Education Fund	2	presidents (2)
Carnegie Foundation	2	founder secretary
Jeannes Fund	1	president
Southern Educational Foundation	1	
Sage Foundation	1	

Sources: See Table 3.1.

University, resigned as president of the CFAT board of trustees to become a member of GEB. Andrew Carnegie was already a member of GEB. Furthermore, the two foundations negotiated an informal division of labor in which GEB increasingly focused its efforts on the South (also the main focus of Peabody, Slater, and Jeannes), while CFAT concentrated its resources in the Northeast and elsewhere to a lesser degree.

FOUNDATION POLICY AND THE PROBLEM OF ADMINISTRATIVE CONTROL

The Carnegie Foundation was ostensibly established to endow a national pension fund for professors teaching in private nondenominational colleges and universities. Nevertheless, its charter also authorized activities perceived by its trustees as incidental, but necessary to the administration of the pension fund.[11] Pritchett clearly understood from the outset that these "incidental" activities could become a way of influencing the development of American universities at a crucial juncture in their history, as he indicated in reflections some years later:

I had naturally given more attention to the matter [of the potential of the incidental activities] than other members of the group, since I had been concerned with the project for some months. In the discussion of this small group I put forward the suggestion, that while the primary purpose of Mr. Carnegie's gift was the establishment of a pension system, there would be involved in the administration of this gift a scrutiny of education which would not only be desirable in the granting of pensions, but would go far to resolve the confusion that then existed in American higher education.[12]

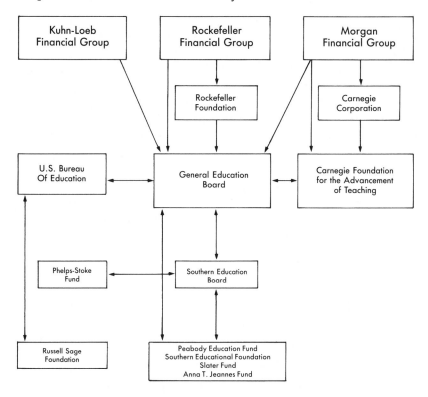

Fig. 3.1. Interlocking Network of Financial Groups and Educational Foundations

Note: This figure is a simplification of the real network. Thus, the diagram is drawn from a perspective which identifies GEB and CFAT as power centers, with subordinate relationships of dominance and hegemony articulated around these centers; however, because of limited space, the figure does not indicate the many direct ties between the subordinate foundations and the financial groups.

The "scrutiny of education" to which Pritchett referred was an outgrowth of procedures developed for distributing the foundation's money. In deciding which institutions were eligible to receive CFAT assistance, the foundation had first to define what constituted a "professor," a "college," a "university," "private" versus "public" institutions, and "denominational" as opposed to independent institutions. Both CFAT and GEB undertook extensive institutional surveys to formulate specific empirical definitions that could "scientifically" designate the meanings imputed to each of these terms. As Hollis notes, "Much was made of the fact that these scientific studies would take philanthropy out of the realm of whim and sentiment and put it on the impersonal factual basis of private business corporations."[13]

In fact, some months before the executive committee's first meetings, Pritchett was already at work reformulating the concept of the university in an article which asked "Shall the University Become a Business Corporation?"[14] In this early study, Pritchett compared the six largest private and public American universities with the six largest European universities in terms of the efficiency ratio between educational expenditures and forms of college administration. Pritchett observed that the American university was already tending "more and more to conform in its administration to the methods of the business corporation."[15] He pointed to the analogy between university governing boards and corporate boards of directors, under whom there was a president and various departments, each with its own managerial head as an example of this claim. He noted, on the other hand, that the European university was a "free association of scholars and teachers." He acknowledged that as a consequence European professors enjoyed a level of self-determination in politics and scholarship that one could not find in the United States.[16]

Yet, puzzling from the standpoint of "educational efficiency" was his finding that European universities were also economically more efficient and cost-effective than their American counterparts. Pritchett concluded that a "very large part" of this difference was "due to differences in administrative ideals." Thus, even from a business standpoint, the study forced him to pose an obvious question: "Would the American university . . . be bettered if its administration were turned over to the faculty instead of being vested, as now, in a board of trustees?" Despite what seemed the obvious answer, Pritchett replied, "With certainty . . . a radical change of this sort would work harm." Like most businessmen of his day, Pritchett argued (even against his own evidence) that businessmen were unequivocally superior administrators and that "no type of man has been developed who is a wiser councilor than the businessman of large sympathy and of real interest in intellectual problems."[17] A twist of logic, made plausible only by an unyielding faith in the abilities of American businessmen, led Pritchett to the conclusion that American universities were less efficient than European institutions because their emerging corporate structure was still too underdeveloped to yield its full advantages. The solution to educational efficiency thus lay in bringing universities under stronger control by businessmen and into greater conformity with corporate models of business organization. This was a view shared publicly by other important members of his executive committee.[18]

Pritchett turned to none other than Frederick Taylor, the father of scientific management, for assistance in developing his corporate ideal of the university. In March of 1909, Pritchett wrote to Taylor explaining his ambition for "an economic study of education" to be sponsored by the Carnegie Foundation. Taylor recommended Morris L. Cooke for the study. Cooke, a young mechanical engineer, was a well-known protégé and personal friend of Taylor's.[19] He was a leading figure among the generation of corporate reformers often referred to as the progressive engineers. Cooke already had a long history of political activism as an advocate of social engineering based on the use of scientific data and technical processes in political and government decision-making. His ideal for the American nation was that it would some day be organized as one vast "socially efficient" production unit in which all aspects of social life—industry, government, family, and culture—would be coordinated toward the single goal of national prosperity.[20]

Cooke's study, *Academic and Industrial Efficiency,* was published by CFAT the following year with an introduction by Pritchett. Pritchett described the study as a response to "the criticisms of American colleges and universities made during the past few years by businessmen."[21] The report's central aim was to develop conceptual tools for making "an estimate of the cost and the output both in teaching and research."[22] In this pathbreaking theoretical work, Cooke did successfully develop a calculus by which to measure the efficiency and productivity of educational institutions in a manner similar to that being employed in industrial factories. He also noted that demand for this calculus originated with "men of means who have money which they are willing to devote to educational purposes". As he pointed out to his readers: "everyone likes to feel that the money which he devotes to educational and charitable and philanthropic purposes is well expended; and other things being equal that university or that department, which has an organization making possible the highest efficiency will in the long-run receive the greatest consideration from such public benefactors."[23]

The report found that two different systems of college administration currently prevailed in the United States. In both cases, governing boards were peripheral to university administration, being mainly preoccupied with the fiduciary trust of investing endowments or other fund-raising activities. Cooke's findings thus indicated that Pritchett (as well as contemporary historians) had actually overemphasized the immediate applicability of the corporate analogy to the academic world. While academic institutions did have a board, a president, and department heads, this analogy was somewhat deceptive when compared to the traditional practices and customs which actually governed university life.

Local custom or outright indifference by governing boards had usually left the actual governance and administration of a university to either faculty committees or benevolent but autocratic presidents. Cooke's report found that "committee management" under the leadership of a charismatic president was the typical scheme characterizing most universities. There was apparently little hierarchical differentiation within the institution, even at this rather advanced period in the history of American universities. In fact, both presidents and deans at this time were usually prominent faculty members still actively engaged in undergraduate teaching, research, and academic professional meetings. They received only a nominal addition to their salary for the extra administrative tasks they performed.

Although governing boards supposedly wielded the final authority in all fiduciary, educational, and personnel matters, meetings of the trustees were usually dominated by the university or college president. However, even the most autocratic presidents at least formulated policies in consultation with faculty committees. The college president assumed the day-to-day administration of the institution, usually with the assistance of a small executive committee of local regents and influential faculty members. Governing boards were inclined to accept the recommendations of this committee on appropriations, educational policy, curriculum, faculty appointments, and promotions. Close ties to the faculty and the absence of a strong governing board made it likely that in practice presidents would look to the campus community for legitimation of their policies. These factors promoted an institution that was administered within the shared orientation of individual academic communities.

Internal control over university policy, research, and curriculum was strengthened by the existing budget system. Appropriations by boards and legislatures were usually made in lump sums for the university or department. The internal distribution of this money was strictly a university or departmental concern. The practice of "post-auditing" the expenditures of individual professors and departments was virtually nonexistent. There was rarely any prior determination by others of the worthiness or scholarly interest of a professor's research. There was little, if any, external direction to the conduct of scientific inquiry. The laissez-faire approach to research was supported by a promotion system frequently based on seniority or the general reputation of faculty members within the local campus community. For the same reason, disputes within the academic community over proper subjects of inquiry, methodology, or what counted as interesting work stood less chance of emerging as an obstacle to individual professional advancement (and, one suspects, made unnecessary the production of the vast quantities of unread and also generally uninteresting paperwork now found in educational bureaucracies).[24]

Likewise, the concept of a "department" or a "field" was still very weak and not defined with nearly the same bureaucratic precision that one could find in corporations. An individual was usually appointed to something like a chair of moral philosophy, as a lecturer in history and political science, or as assistant professor of political economy, social economy, or moral economy. The definition of what that meant was left largely to the individual professor, who could independently decide what courses would be offered, when they would be offered, and what topics belonged within this general designation. A natural scientist might just as readily pursue metaphysics as chemistry.

Cooke and Pritchett both found this ambiguity in university organization a problem "from the viewpoint of one outside college work." Cooke considered Taylor's newly published *Principles of Scientific Management* "more or less applicable in the college field," so he adopted the implicit assumption that "one best way" could be found for organizing the material means of mental production.[25] A scientific determination of this best way required access to detailed accounting and time-use information that was comparable (i.e., standardized) across time and between units of analysis. Yet again, contrary to the corporate ideal, Cooke found that of the eight major northeastern universities he surveyed, only two or three had administrative organizations and accounting routines "at all comparable with what goes on in the everyday business world."[26]

The chief difficulty in establishing an accounting and administrative system for the university lay precisely in how it most differed from business. In business, profits and the rate of return on capital investment could always provide a bottom line for the measurement of industrial efficiency. The maximization of profits could thus be used as an absolute gauge for determining what method of organizing work was best within the existing social relations of capitalist production. In education, however, there was no absolute measure of efficiency, because universities were not organized to produce a profit for their owners.

Cooke argued that the next best measure would be a standardized statistical concept by which departments and universities could be compared for efficiency relative to an empirically derived average. A social average of efficiency could be established as the norm for making organizational and administrative judgments once enough data was collected throughout the nation. The key unit of measurement in this new calculus was called the "student-hour." A student-hour was "one hour of lectures, of laboratory work, or recitation room work, for a single pupil."[27] It was possible with this conceptual tool to calculate relative faculty workloads, the cost of instruction per student-hour, and ultimately the rate of educational efficiency for individual professors, courses, fields, departments, and universities.

The theoretical effect of this new measurement was to focus attention on professors as mental workers for the first time in their history. If the university was conceptualized as an economic unit of production, the role of the professor as its chief producer was altered as well. The religious mentality that promoted university life as a unique and special "calling" was discarded by Cooke for an industrial conception of intellectual "labor."

Cooke pointed out that "the industrial world is coming more and more to feel that all work is done under certain broad principles, and that the application of these principles to one industry is little different from their application to any other."[28] The problem of academic efficiency was in principle no different from that of industrial efficiency because "all large and continuing causes rest upon formal organization and upon some assured machinery of administration."[29] Organization was primarily an engineering problem. Administering this organization was the function of management.

Therefore, organizational efficiency demanded that a worker not "produce any longer by his own initiative," but "execute punctiliously" the orders given by management, "down to their minutest details."[30] From this perspective, Cooke attacked the professor's traditional belief that teaching and scholarship were so "radically different" from other kinds of labor that one could not "apply the same standards of criticism to his work as obtain generally thoughout other departments of life." Cooke insisted, on the contrary, that professors "must be governed and measured by the same general standards that generally obtain in other occupations."[31]

The theoretical justification for, as well as the precise methods of, proletarianizing the intellectuals were elaborated by Cooke in considerable detail. The first alteration was that increased academic productivity required that professors be "relieved" of all administrative and governing roles in the university. The first principle of scientific management was specialization and functional differentiation of tasks within the division of labor. In later policy statements on university governance, CFAT continually reiterated "a clear line of differentiation between the function of . . . a [governing] body and that of the teaching staff."[32]

Once the roles of governance, administration, and productive labor were defined, the practical task was to break down the traditional guild that still prevailed in the college, because it restricted the introduction of a free competitive market in intellectual labor. The twin pillars of the academic guild were faculty inbreeding and tenure. The master-apprentice relationship between advanced students and professors sustained patterns of inbreeding in which the graduates of a university were often immediately hired to fill new vacancies or to replace their aging mentors.[33] Tenure protected unproductive labor and hence reduced the social average of academic efficiency below real productive capacity. Cooke's recommendation to administrators was clear on this point: "If the same standards of efficiency are to be applied to college teachers as are applied elsewhere, it will mean that when a man has ceased to be efficient he must be retired."[34]

A free market in intellectual labor would allow higher institutions to abolish salary schedules based on length of service, tenure, and professorial rank in favor of adjustable wage schedules structured around quantifiable measures of individual productivity. This would also require that foundations, governors, administrators, and professional associations create and actively promote the development of a national market for intellectual labor. Hence, Cooke encouraged administrators to conduct national searches through placement advertising and the distribution of employment bulletins by professional organizations. This would encourage competition for positions among faculty and promote national horizontal mobility that would break up regional differences and inbred schools of thought. Cooke pointed out that once a free market was established, its structural features would pressure professors into adopting a more competitive outlook on individual productivity.

There were two other measures that could be adopted to further raise productivity. One was to increase the amount of labor time. Another was to increase the efficiency of that labor time. The key to efficiency in the industrial world was that "a good workman is considered apart from the appliances and tools which may be necessary for the pursuit of his occupation." The labor process and the means of production can therefore be reorganized by owners and management at will to realize gains in efficiency. Cooke anticipated that a primary obstacle to academic efficiency would be the professor's attitude "that the lectures he gives and his pedagogical mechanisms are his own property."[35]

Another crucial element in the productivity of the industrial factory was individual specialization and the standardized interchangeability of parts. A capacity for repetition increased the productivity of the individual worker. Standardization facilitated mass production, an easier introduction of technical innovations, and the replacement of depreciated capital. Cooke therefore recommended greater research and teaching specialization by faculty as a condition for promoting more intensive mass production.

If adopted in conjunction with the new student "elective system," faculty specialization meant that courses could also become standardized, interchangeable parts with precise and predetermined specifications with which students could be assembled. Their interchangeability would facilitate rapid adjustment to changes in demand for particular products (i.e., majors or informational fields). Cooke went so far as to recommend the creation of a central "file of drawers in which were placed the lecture notes for all the different courses, written in a rather uniform style and all on standardized cards." This would reduce unnecessary duplication of start-up costs, since each professor would no longer have to organize his own set of notes. Instead, as new notes were added or updated, "the value of this part of the departmental equipment was constantly appreciating."[36] He even developed specialized accounting techniques for measuring faculty time use and the proportion of faculty salaries expended on the performance of specific tasks.[37]

Accompanying this increase in the productivity of variable capital (i.e., labor costs) was a call for greater efficiency in the utilization of constant or fixed capital (i.e., plant and equipment). To exemplify the problem, Cooke also conducted plant utilization surveys at Williams College and Columbia University. Classrooms were used an average of 2.83 hours per day at Williams and 3.45 hours per day at Columbia. Cooke could find "no insuperable reason why rooms cannot be used more economically."[38] Not only were low rates of plant utilization wasteful, but these also indicated a general excess of academic plant capacity throughout the country. He encouraged foundations to concentrate educational resources only on the most efficient institutions in order to promote the realization of economies of scale.

Cooke attributed the inefficiencies in plant utilization to the fact that departments tended to "own" buildings and classrooms within universities. The remedy he recommended was that "the management of all buildings should be in the hands of some central authority and operated under as complete rules as can be established: the same rules, of course, applying to all buildings no matter what the purposes for which they are used." A careful accounting of building expenses and plant maintenance would then allow a central accounting office to charge departments proportionately for plant costs relative to use by the various departments. The costs of fixed capital could be similarly integrated into measurements of efficiency for individual courses and professors. Cooke's report provided detailed forms and procedures for administrators who wished to accept his advice.[39]

A careful accounting of time use by professors combined with figures on course enrollment and plant utilization would finally enable administrators to calculate the costs per student-hour for different fields, courses, and professors. Cooke acknowledged that with the adoption of these administrative standards, "it will undoubtedly follow that certain institutions will drop certain lines of work which are done at too high a relative expense."[40] In fact, with detailed statistics, it would be possible to identify not only the particular operations to be discontinued, but particular courses to be eliminated, or even faculty to be dismissed.

Cooke was equally dismayed that research was "being done with the minimum of inspection and control." He argued against the practice of undirected research and lamented that there were no means "of controlling the amount of research work done in the various departments except through the general departmental appropriations." So long as departments were left in charge of their own resources, however, this autonomy was an inevitable result. He suggested the elimination of lump-sum allocations to departments as a solution to this problem. Cooke proposed instead that trustees should specifically earmark research appropriations in advance, while establishing a "general research board whose duty it would be to organize the general policy of the institution in the matter of research." This board would also allocate individual research topics to faculty based on their relevance to a general research agenda designated as appropriate for the university and approved by the trustees. Expenditures could subsequently be post-audited against the original earmarked appropriations. He emphasized that "nothing can be done which will have a greater or more immediate effect in minimizing departmental autonomy than keeping a close watch on departmental expenses."[41]

The importance of adopting these financial and administrative procedures was emphasized by Pritchett in another CFAT publication released the same year. He insisted that it was "the duty of every college . . . to make annually a report to the public of its financial operations. . . . No college which refuses to do this deserves to be entrusted with money."[42] Pritchett knew well that a desire for access to the CFAT pension fund provided a financial incentive for higher institutions to make the organizational changes recommended by Cooke. Regulating access to the fund could thus enable the foundation to act as an ideological leader in the development of higher education.

I am suggesting several things by designating corporate intellectuals as ideological leaders in the promotion of national higher education reform. The first is that corporate intellectuals consciously took the initiative in developing a theoretical critique of existing educational institutions. Second, this critique was formulated in terms of specific normative values (i.e., those associated with the commitment to social efficiency) that were developed historically by a rising class of corporate and finance capitalists. Furthermore, this initiative was undertaken to achieve clearly identifiable and specific objectives such as the reorganization of academic labor markets and an investment of educational capital that was more favorable to business interests.[43]

Moreover, as James MacGregor Burns has noted, an essential element in winning intellectual leadership of a movement is the ability of certain types of intellectuals to conceive their objectives and values in such a way that general ends, such as the corporate ideal of social efficiency, and specific means, such as administrative rationalization, are linked analytically in a coherent theoretical conception of social reform.[44] Cooke's study of academic and industrial efficiency was a powerful weapon in forging this link so as to bring the normative values of corporate capitalism to bear on a practical problem—namely, how to balance the demand for greater access to higher education (equality) with the rising costs of expanding access (efficiency). The specific implications of the corporate ideal for education reform were clarified in a way that could direct other leaders (corporate, educational, and governmental) toward the adoption of those policies implied by the corporate ideal. In other words, Cooke translated the ideals of corporate capitalism into a practical strategy for educational reform.

However, broader social conditions provided the opportunity for leadership by creating a predisposition, or "elective affinity," among other groups to accept these policies. On this level of analysis, references to the academic boom of the early twentieth century and its underlying culture of aspiration, play an explanatory role. The pressures on faculty time, plant utilization, and educational finance created by the academic boom supplied an opportunity, if not the proximate cause, for rationalizing corporate reformers to articulate their program of social efficiency to receptive audiences in educational administration, government, and the academic professions. Yet, equally important was the distribution and control over educational capital. By linking the availability of increased financial resources for higher education to the adoption of a corporate reform program, the foundations could use material pressures to reinforce the appeal of their proposed policies. They could, to quote Marx, represent their class interest "as the common interest of all the members of society," and thereby plausibly claim that their ideas were "the only rational, universally valid ones."[45] Hence, they could assert their program of educational reform as a socially hegemonic project.[46]

Indeed, in its second annual report (1907), CFAT articulated the relation between its administrative concerns and the interests of education as one in which greater academic efficiency would actually liberate teaching and research from the external constraints of a fiscal crisis. Academic efficiency would enhance the autonomy of the university by allowing its members to concentrate on teaching and research without external distractions. On the other hand, the report described the current condition, one familiar to all educators, as one in which "the sums of money now demanded for college support are so great that the mere question of raising money has come in many cases to overshadow the larger and deeper interests of many institutions."[47]

There can be little doubt that a growing and persistent fiscal crisis caused governing boards to focus on the problems associated with their fiduciary trust. The educational philosophy of academic efficiency gave business-dominated governing boards a ready-made solution which merely extended the application of concepts already familiar to them. It promised a further remedy to the fiscal crisis through an infusion of new capital from the foundations, but only if institutions adopted the foundations' standards.

THE MANAGERIAL REVOLUTION IN EDUCATIONAL ADMINISTRATION

Scientific management also drew a functional distinction between the roles of a governing body and an administrative body.[48] Consequently, foundation officials often cautioned governing boards against too much "direct administration." Boards were advised to institute a formal division of labor between themselves as policy-makers or governors and those who implemented policy, the administrators. The proprietary rights of ownership were distinct from the administrative expertise of the manager. The latter's specialized knowledge of organizational principles and the day-to-day details of industrial relations made him better suited for executing policies.

This was scientific management in theory. The problem in practice, however, was a shortage of specialized educational administrators with managerial expertise. Prominent college administrators initially met this demand through their own halting efforts. In 1900, Charles Thwing, president of Western Reserve University, wrote the first textbook on college administration. A few years later, Charles Eliot, the president of Harvard University, published another work on university administration in which he explicitly urged fellow presidents to adopt a new technique of executive recruitment. He advised presidents to select and groom younger faculty members for administrative positions on the basis of their proven business acumen, rather than on the basis of their talents for teaching or scholarship.[49]

In fact, Cooke found in his survey of major private universities in the Northeast that college administrators were already "expecting marked changes" in methods of administration to occur within a short time. He observed "that in most places these changes will be welcomed." Cooke found that everywhere he went "the question of functional efficiency" was "being raised among the responsible heads of institutions and the departments." Nevertheless, an article by Frank P. Graves, president of the University of Washington, probably best described the new anxiety of most university administrators. He complained that "the poor young college president, without a particle of specific preparation, is pushed out into the midst of things, and must stand or fall by the result." Graves was dismayed that no provision had as yet "been made for educating young men for executive work in our colleges."[50]

The "managerial revolution" associated with large-scale corporations actually made this problem common throughout the entire corporate economy beginning in the early 1900s. The corporate solution was to sponsor programs for "managerial development." Corporations increasingly financed conferences and institutes where administrators could share methods, techniques, problems, and successes. Their purpose was to "make managers—not just new managers out of nonmanagers, but also big managers out of small ones and good ones out of mediocre ones."[51]

The CFAT report *Academic and Industrial Efficiency* was a major contribution to this same movement transferred to educational administration. Cooke compiled extensive tables, charts, accounting forms, examples, and explanations of procedure designed to assist administrators in implementing the new policies. The effort was promoted further by the distribution of an additional CFAT publication in the same year, entitled *Standard Forms for Financial Reports*. All colleges and universities applying for admission to the CFAT pension system were required to use the standard forms and, by implication, to adopt the procedures which made these forms meaningful.

The General Education Board went a step further by providing on-site assistance to administrators undertaking the accounting and organizational reforms. For more than two decades GEB maintained a corps of expert "field representatives" who were sent to any campus requesting assistance with reorganization and managerial development. As early as 1913, however, the foundation reported that "the number of institutions desiring to reorganize their accounting system was so large that it proved impracticable to cooperate with them one by one." Thus, in 1915, GEB arranged for Trevor Arnett, chief auditor of the Chicago Great Western Railway, to write its own standardized handbook for college financial officers. This work, entitled *College and University Finance*, was intended to disseminate more widely the new accounting and administrative techniques. By 1924, 5,626 copies of the work had been distributed in the United States—roughly eight copies for every college and university in the country. In August of 1923, GEB also sponsored a national conference on university administration at the University of Chicago. According to GEB officials, the net result of all this activity was a "marked improvement" in college financial administration and accounting.[52]

The managerial revolution in educational administration did far more than simply separate administration from operations. It redefined the standards, strategies, and definition of a successful university president by institutionalizing corporate-derived bureaucratic norms of managerial behavior. As Robert Presthus notes, bureaucracies "are far more than mere devices for producing goods and services . . . they become sensitive and versatile agencies for the control of man's behavior, employing subtle sanctions that evoke desired responses and inculcate consistent patterns of action."[53]

The successful "managerial strategy" has always required outward intellectual and behavioral conformity "to the objectives and styles of those who hold power." For example, William Dewitt Hyde, a president of Bowdoin College, argued that "the expert financier is an indispensable member" of every board of trustees. Charles Eliot claimed in *University Administration* that the best trustee was a "business or profes-

sional man" who is "successful in his own calling," although prefera-
bly "highly educated" and "public spirited" as well.[54] The facts, of
course, were that no more than 30 to 40 percent of big business
executives had college degrees during the first three decades of this
century, while an informal survey of trustees in 1900 indicated that
most were politically conservative.[55]

Nevertheless, foundation publications advanced the expressive
imagery of this corporate ideal. The practice of appointing college and
university presidents as trustees of the major foundations assisted in
their socialization to the norms of the American corporation. The
foundations provided a forum in which leading educational administrators could pose and discuss common problems alongside the nation's leading businessmen. By reformulating educational issues within
the framework of business administration and scientific management,
corporate intellectuals offered practical business leadership in solving
educational problems. Foundations were thus instrumental in organizing the conquest of a key element among the traditional university
intellectuals and in integrating them under the hegemony of corporate
ideology.

Moreover, in relation to the corporate ideal administrative obedience
to recognized power became a necessary strategy for professional
advancement. It was not an "unknowing, involuntary submission,"
but as with all managers, a habit which "becomes so well practiced that
the manager can do it instinctively, responding not only to the overt
orders of his superior but even to inferred hints."[56] The previous
decade had clearly demonstrated to everyone that the only alternative
to this strategy was a curt dismissal notice from the governing board.
Presidents with populist political loyalties, or those who too strongly
defended the claims of faculty members against governing boards,
littered the decade of the 1890s.[57]

On the other hand, university presidents who adopted the ideology
of managerialism as their administrative model found themselves rewarded with prestige, higher incomes, foundation or corporate directorships, and offers for better university positions. Adoption of the
managerial role could easily be rationalized within the normative
framework of progressive democracy. Most presidents probably
wanted to adopt business means to achieve independent educational
ends.[58] As a result, most university presidents adopted the managerial strategy in good conscience and so "gradually took their mandate
to be assuring that the institution would be run in a businesslike
manner." Indeed, this role was so firmly entrenched by 1920 that John

Henry McCracken, the president of Lafayette College, complained "the college president today is expected to talk as glibly of overhead charges and per capita costs as the efficiency expert."[59]

The managerial strategy normatively redefined presidential loyalties to their institutions primarily in terms of economic and external prestige.[60] This first concern redirected administrators toward standard measurements of institutional achievement which placed a premium, as in all capitalist enterprises, on the accumulation of capital. An observant professor of psychology at the University of Wisconsin wrote that college presidents increasingly "like to be remembered by the buildings which were erected through their initiative [plant expansion], by the departments which have been added [new product lines], and the enrollment which has been increased [sales]. It is by urging these needs and presenting these successes that funds are secured [i.e. investment capital]."[61]

The accumulation of capital as a purely quantitative measure of academic efficiency was closely related to administrative anxieties about a school's prestige. Social efficiency—or the functional integration of institutional roles under the leadership of a managerial expert—was measured by the relative peacefulness of industrial relations within the university. A good administrator, therefore, "made determined efforts to keep the peace within his own institution, since if it appeared disunited it would lose prestige and influence" and, ultimately, the capacity to attract additional capital. Thus, the new texts on university administration generally advised "that quarrelsome debate, including that based upon conflicts among academic ideals, must be minimized or suppressed whenever it became threateningly serious."[62]

The redirection of administrative institutional loyalties also involved the adoption of a managerial style of leadership. University presidents gradually abandoned any "direct involvement in university life that chief administrators had formerly had" and shifted their attention to the accumulation of educational capital (e.g., benefactions, appropriations) and the elaboration of general rules and guidelines that could be enforced by subordinates with delegated authority.[63] Both activities widened the social and hierarchical distance between presidents and faculties.

The frequency with which presidents were now called upon to associate with wealthy businessmen in formal and informal settings required a change of mannerisms and characteristics that would enable them to "fit in" with polite society. The successful executive had to achieve and live up to a higher income and social status, while associating only with the "proper people" of an equal or higher status. This new position of authority and status had to be conveyed to subordinates by leaving old friends behind and assuming an air of poise and aloofness towards them. Managerial success in dealing with both higher authorities and subordinates always necessitated that it be done quickly.[64]

One professor at Adelphi College noted that faculty were aware of the new style. William Cranston Lawton observed that the president's "election to a position of absolute control over his associates usually changes his views with startling suddenness . . . he fondly believes himself elevated into a new and superior profession, — 'administration.' His new associates spend many times the incomes of his former colleagues; he cheerfully accepts the natural theory that he also 'must' have a social life, and therefore an establishment, totally different from that of a mere scholar and teacher."[65]

There was a widespread tendency among faculty to understand this new style as a radical break with recent historical traditions of the American university presidency. My own survey of eighty-nine university presidents at twenty-seven different institutions suggests that there was a great deal of empirical validity to their conceptualization of this development (see Table 3.3). Administrators were losing their institutional ties to college faculty and becoming a semi-autonomous managerial strata. In 1861, the majority of college presidents had been Protestant clergymen just prior to accepting their new administrative posts. By 1890, "a generation of college presidents who were preeminently scholars"[66] is indicated by the fact that 50 percent of university presidents had been professors before assuming their administrative position. In most cases, these administrative scholars rose to their positions only after developing close ties to the college community, usually as a member of the faculty for several years.

After the turn of the century, however, we see the emergence of college presidents who are professional administrators and lack a close relation to faculty as the result of a long ascent and socialization through the administrative machinery. In addition, their horizontal mobility from one institution to another increases as they continually assume new positions at more prestigious institutions by building national reputations as administrators. James McKeen Cattell, a professor of psychology at Columbia University, observed that this new type was likely to be selected by trustees exclusively for their "business qualifications."[67] President Graves of the University of Washington claimed that the corporate ideal of a university presidency was rapidly

Table 3.3. Occupational Origins of U.S. College Presidents, 1861–1929 (percentages)

Occupation	1861	1890	1915	1929
Minister	59	15	0	5
Professor	12	50	32	5
College dean	0	4	20	33
College vice-president or president	12	12	36	38
Public education official	0	4	8	10
Other	18	15	4	10
Total	101	100	100	101
Number	17	26	25	21

Source: Data compiled from general histories of the institutions and *Who Was Who in America*.

Note: Only new presidents elected during each time frame were included in each interval. The institutions were Princeton, NYU, Columbia, Rutgers, Drexel Institute, Amherst, Miami (Ohio), Vassar, Oberlin, Wellesley, Texas A&M, Howard University, CCNY, the Universities of Pennsylvania, Alabama, Mississippi, Arkansas, Massachusetts, Washington, Kansas, and North Dakota, and Indiana University, Kansas State, State College of Washington, North Carolina State, South Dakota State, and Iowa State.

becoming a fixed type: "A college president, according to this latest ideal, is an executive in the fullest sense of the word. Though in entire sympathy with education, he is a business man and a broad-minded man of affairs, with the gift of diplomacy and the alertness and poise of an entrepreneur. He may be a scholar—and very often is—or even a minister; but these qualities are merely incidental and have little to do with his success as an administrator.[68]

Faculty members lamented "the loss of the old-time president" and often reviled "the college president of our day" as a "disaster."[69] Some who wrote on the subject saw in these developments an opening through which business was invading the inner sanctum of the corporation of learning. Joseph Jastrow concluded that the new system of administration was due primarily to an irrelevant, pernicious, and "perverse application of glorified business procedure" to institutions that best flourish under conditions of a "wholly opposed character." He called this "externalism of government" the single most significant reason for the rise of the modern university presidency. Cattell described the new system as one in which a "small and compact group of men who represent a certain policy" elect an "absolute dictator, who in turn appoints minor dictators, and the result is an economical and powerful machine."[70]

THE IDEAL OF AN AMERICAN UNIVERSITY SYSTEM

The internal rationalization of university administration was only one component in a more comprehensive plan for the creation of a national university system. CFAT trustees were concerned that since "education was not touched by the Constitution," it had "no guidance from the central government looking toward unifying and coordinating the separate State systems." They similarly complained that "private initiative in the field of education has been both unguided and unrestrained by supervision on the part of State governments."[71] Consequently, by the turn of the century, there were hundreds of competing denominational colleges, secular liberal arts colleges, private universities, women's colleges, state universities, land-grant colleges, technical institutes, junior colleges, Negro colleges, and city universities. Every level of government, and competing religious, private, and political interests, were all involved in higher education.

As expressed by Frank Vanderlip of the Carnegie Foundation, these conditions went against the contemporary "keynote of economic life," which was "the tendency toward combination and away from useless competition." The corporate ideal of social efficiency persuaded CFAT officials that "underlying all other causes which tend to confusion in higher education is the fundamental one that American colleges have in the past been conducted as separate units, not as factors in a general educational system."[72] Rockefeller apparently shared this sentiment with Vanderlip, since he charged GEB with an explicit mandate in its charter "to promote a comprehensive system of higher education in the United States." Frederick T. Gates also explained that the Rockefeller endowment was: "not merely to encourage higher education in the United States, but . . . mainly to contribute, as far as may be, toward reducing our higher education to something like an orderly and comprehensive system."[73]

Daniel Coit Gilman, a GEB member and former president of Johns Hopkins, compared their task to eliminating "the paralleling of railroads."[74] His analogy was not without merit. The railroad engineers and accountants at the forefront of university rationalization had pioneered the intercompany standardization of corporate America. The uniformity of products (e.g., students), standardized specifications for performance and productivity (e.g., faculty), regularization of the process of production (e.g., time and plant-use requirements), and recognized standards of product quality (e.g., accreditation) all bore a striking resemblance to the same processes that had been necessary to the rise of national corporations a decade earlier.[75] For universities to be integrated into a single, coordinated system, the individual parts of this national machine had to be standardized so as to fit them together.

Likewise, scientific judgments about the efficient allocation and investment of educational capital could only be made once the data drawn from different institutions was comparable between units of production (e.g., departments) and between competing enterprises. For CFAT, the initial absence of standardization between institutions had presented an immediate investment dilemma. Its charter required the foundation to provide pensions to selected professors in all "private nondenominational colleges and universities" in the United States and Canada. The trustees required a working definition of these concepts, but discovered in their original surveys that no standard definition was self-evident in the current institutional use of those terms.

Their surveys revealed an absence of coordination in the diversity of mission statements and educational goals associated with institutions sharing similar designations as "colleges" or "universities." Some institutions nominally called colleges, or even universities, offered only two years of instruction. Some actually offered a level of instruction appropriate to high schools, preparatory schools, or academies. Others offered three or four years of instruction. In some places graduate education was merely a fifth year of undergraduate work. In others, graduate study required original research. There was a diversity of curricula, enrollment, staff size, finance and expenditure, quality and kinds of plant, libraries, accreditation, and admission requirements. Professorships were sometimes awarded only to faculty with a Ph.D., sometimes to those with an honorary Ph.D., and often to those with no advanced degree of any kind.

The CFAT solution to this problem was to rely, first, on a marginal utility calculation which yielded the optimum number of higher institutions that could be most efficiently financed and utilized in the United States and Canada. At the same time, the foundation was further constrained in its definition by the availability of pension funds. Its definitions had to be narrow enough to insure that applicants eligible for admission to the so-called Carnegie system did not exceed its financial capacity. Utilizing these twin criteria, the foundation established an empirical definition of the "college" and "university" which limited the number of institutions legitimately entitled to use these nomenclatures to a number CFAT officials concluded was most socially efficient.

The foundation then identified the minimum standards within these constraints for enrollment, student admission requirements, faculty certification, library volumes, plant, and laboratory equipment it considered appropriate for such institutions. The university was then distinguished from the college on the basis of graduate research and professional training leading to a post-baccalaureate degree. Universities were defined as primarily research institutions oriented toward graduate and professional education. Colleges were undergraduate teaching institutions that had two functions. Their primary role, as described by Nicholas Murray Butler, was to provide a "liberal" but "disciplined" education for the experts and future leaders of an emerging progressive democracy. He equated this task with "the training of American citizens who shall be educated gentlemen." The second role of colleges was to serve as a "vestibule to the university." Students who were broadly trained by "previous study of the liberal arts and sciences" would be fed into the "special fields of learning and research" offered by the major universities.[76]

It was this second function that created a further need for eliminating the current "chaos of standards and degrees."[77] As with any other national corporation, the routinization of intellectual labor processes required the standardization of parts and quality to insure that components being fed into the production process from widely dispersed suppliers met minimum specifications. Institutions excluded from the Carnegie group of colleges and universities were persistently encouraged to change their function to that of high schools, preparatory schools, academies, and junior colleges.

While there were already several other accrediting agencies in the country, CFAT was again unique in its ability to exert economic pressure on the universities and colleges. Access to the pension fund (a rarity at that time) made it possible for select institutions to offer an additional material incentive that could attract and keep prominent faculty members from around the country. Thus, it helped promote the development of a national labor market, while providing a competitive advantage to members of the Carnegie system.

As these universities succeeded in building nationally prominent faculties, their prestige increased relative to excluded institutions, and thus offered additional intangible professional status to those associated with these institutions. The widening stratification of institutional prestige resulted in a parallel stratification of the social authority inhering in the individual college or university to legitimize or delegitimize intellectual activity inside and outside the academic community. Association with one of these institutions carried with it a presumption of greater professional competence, individual prestige, and opportunities for professional advancement.

GEB engaged in similar activities that reinforced the actions of the Carnegie Foundation. In its own survey of the origins of American colleges and universities, GEB also concluded that "political, local, denominational, and purely personal factors have too often proved determinative." The board likewise decided that there were many "superfluous institutions" which "interfere seriously with the nutrition of those really needed." Furthermore, it asserted that rural geographical locations and population migration had left many institutions disadvantageously situated to compete in the educational market. GEB emphasized that these institutions "cannot be supported, cannot be manned, cannot procure qualified students," and yet continued to drain scarce educational capital out of the system.[78]

If there was excess capacity in the market, then inefficient competitors would have to be driven out of the market. The key to this foundation strategy involved placing GEB in a position to determine what universities survived and which ones did not; that is, to monopolize selectively access to educational capital. The number of colleges and universities actually continued to increase during this period because of rising consumer demand for access to higher education. Nevertheless, the foundation did manage to achieve its fundamental goal. Through a massive infusion of capital into selected universities, mainly for plant and equipment, GEB was able to elevate certain institutions into unparalleled giants (i.e., an oligopoly) on the higher education market, much as investment bankers had done with railroads, oil, steel, utilities, and other industries. From their strategic positions in this market, they could set trends and standards for the entire nation.

Abraham Flexner identifies Dr. Wallace Buttrick, GEB secretary and executive officer, as the originator of what board members called the "strategy of emulation" and "perpendicular development." Flexner admiringly recounts in his autobiography that Buttrick "had an eye for the strategical point, be it a state, a denomination, or an institution." The strategy was to show selected constituencies of business, alumni, university, or government officials what could be achieved through "financial cooperation" with the board. The board would build an institution's endowment, erect classrooms, purchase laboratory equipment, and reorganize its administrative structure, and then go to others and point to the results. Flexner notes that Buttrick "addressed himself to the pride" of those who were laboring under similar difficulties or aspiring towards similar goals.[79]

The perpendicular development of strategic institutions raised their visibility as "lighthouse" or "beacon" campuses which could point the way to others throughout the country. Flexner suggests that the entire board pursued a conscious strategy in which "the enormous increase in college and university endowments throughout the land" enabled them to set in motion a spirit of "emulation between states, emulation between denominations, emulation between different institutions" and to thus create a national system of higher education that was based in market structures. Once set in motion, emulation provided a stimulus to philanthropy from local businesses, alumni, and legislatures, who then saw the economic and political benefits of a strong college or university. The board found that "within a few years persons who had had no conception of the possibilities of the institution" became "deeply interested in it." Flexner claims that the growth of Harvard, Yale, Columbia, Princeton, and Chicago were not "essentially dissimilar" in this respect.[80]

In terms of sheer resources, no other single institution in the nation could exercise as much influence on higher education in the form of financial incentives and capital growth as could GEB. Since state activity was still relatively limited, and federal activity primarily restricted to the sixty-nine land-grant institutions, the field was essentially wide open to anyone who could exercise leadership. The incentives GEB offered for following its lead were enormous.

The influence of GEB expenditures in raising the national standards necessary to compete effectively in the educational market can be gleaned from a comparison of the GEB endowment to the total college and university endowments in the United States. In 1910, the total endowment held by colleges and universities in the country totalled just over $259 million. In 1909, GEB held an endowment of $53 million.[81] In other words, GEB possessed an endowment equivalent to 20 percent of all other college and university endowments accumulated in the entire history of the United States. In addition, it had the rare luxury of being able to deploy that entire amount toward a few institutions for strategic national goals. Endowments held by individual colleges and universities were scattered among hundreds of institutions. Similarly, CFAT's $15 million pension fund was equivalent to almost 6 percent of existing college and university endowments.

The implementation of a strategy of perpendicular development is clearly evident in the distribution of foundation expenditures. Between 1902 and 1934, the nine largest foundations (mostly those in the Carnegie-GEB group) appropriated $338,936,030 in grants to higher education. Seventy-three percent of this amount went to only 20 institutions. The five largest foundations gave approximately 86 percent of their disbursements to only thirty-six institutions from 1923 to 1929 among a total of over a thousand higher education institutions in the United States.[82] Thus, Hollis's 1938 study of philanthropy found "little doubt that foundations have been highly successful in applying their policies of concentration." The importance of concentrated grants in shaping American higher education led Frederick Rudolph to conclude subsequently that "philanthropic foundations became an apparent or hidden presence on every American campus."[83]

Once competitive market forces were set in motion by perpendicular development and emulation, the stratification of institutional prestige exerted further structural pressures toward systemization and a functional division of labor. The costs of funding competitive research, journals, professional associations, hospitals, laboratories, and libraries became so expensive that the vast majority of institutions simply could not compete in scholarship or graduate education with the new tier of nationally prominent research universities. As this gap widened, foundation officials were well aware that institutional survival would require most colleges to drop out of the competition and find their own local market niche within the new system.[84]

To the degree that foundations succeeded in constructing a national hierarchy of universities and colleges, the new structure of higher education bureaucratically restricted the number and location of places where prospective students or faculty members could aspire to the highest levels of intellectual authority, skill, and professional status. This simultaneously increased the professional influence of those intellectuals inhabiting these institutions by delegating to them a certain capacity to restrict or permit access to the best equipment and libraries, the most prestigious degrees, the journals and university presses being attached to these institutions, and the opportunity to penetrate their profession by training graduate students. In other words, there was an emerging stratification of access to the material means of mental production necessary to compete within the changing professional norms of the academic vocation.

This supported an introduction of external influences into the structure of professional development by providing administrative and governing personnel with a centralized capacity to regulate the intellectuals through their distribution of material and status incentives. Administrative and governing personnel acquired an increased ability to exert disciplinary authority within the academic fields by regulating the distribution of status (e.g., grants, journals, professional activities, promotions), and by supervising, carefully selecting, or dismissing key personnel at these institutions who themselves exercised disciplinary authority within their profession.

One of the most powerful techniques in the administrative regulation of the modern professions has been the introduction of an internal status hierarchy based in the bureaucratic delegation of professional authority, status, rank, and income.[85] Since administrators generally control these rewards at some point, by distributing them unequally they create "a situation in which organizational definitions of loyalty and competence are reinforced." "Status anxiety" and its related desire for an augmented share of organizational rewards may then provide "compelling reasons for individuals to accept authority."[86]

Thus, as Chester Barnard found, so long as a chief executive and his administrative allies can control and deliver these status inducements, they can create a "zone of indifference" within which most faculty will contentedly refuse to challenge authority, while simply going about their business.[87] Joseph Jastrow recorded early on that "the drift within the university is towards winning those marks of success upon which administrative dominance sets greatest store." He noted the emergence of a new "type of academician who pursues his career in a decidedly 'business' frame of mind," who was always "keen for the main chance, ready to advertise his wares and advance his trade, eager for new markets, a devotee to statistically measured success."[88]

CRITICISM OF AND OPPOSITION TO THE NEW EDUCATIONAL TRUST

Contemporary critics of foundation strategy were quick to recognize it as "the Standard Oil Company Plan of consolidation and concentration applied to educational institutions." GEB and CFAT were immediately characterized by many as an "educational trust" or a "collegiate monopoly" which aimed at "buying control of education."[89] But despite widespread criticism of the foundations, opposition to their policies was fragmented and sporadic.

Critics recognized that foundation grants enabled corporate leaders to decree "where new institutions should be located, what standards of efficiency they ought to conform to, what institutions are needless and should go out of existence, what institutions should be built up into large ones and which should remain small." As a result, one writer in the *New York Tribune* warned, with not much exaggeration, that "little colored pins" in the maps on Wall Street "will probably seal the fate of many a college."[90] Those with objections to this strategy generally fell into one of two groups: those who objected to foundation policies on procedural grounds and those with substantive ideological concerns.

Procedural objections largely centered on fears of "undue centralization." One prominent Harvard professor released "A Plea for Independence in Provincial Education" which berated foundation trustees as "professional standardizers."[91] Even some of those sympathetic to the aims of the foundations argued that national education reform was a task more appropriately carried out by a public institution such as the U.S. Bureau of Education. At least one professor was convinced that Henry Pritchett was already "in effect scarcely inferior . . . to the minister of education in the kingdom of Prussia."[92] Nevertheless, the only serious effort to organize opposition on this front was the passage of a 1914 NEA resolution that merely "viewed with alarm" current efforts by the foundations "to control the educational standards of the country."[93]

Other critics carried the procedural objections a step further with their recognition that foundations exercised a significant ability to decide the specific distribution of academic prestige in America by granting or withholding admittance to the pension system and by concentrating the material means of mental production. J. M. Cattell, one of the most vigorous foundation critics, feared that foundations' financial power would "tend to increase the autocracy of university administration and to limit not only the freedom of action but also the freedom of speech of the professor."[94] Many feared that administrators and trustees eager to enhance the reputation of their institutions were not likely to look favorably upon faculty members who offended the educational trusts by espousing doctrines inimical to big business and capitalism.[95]

Dr. Thomas E. Will, a former president of Kansas State College, who was fired for being a socialist and populist, suggested that in his experience "institutions may be expected to possess sufficient gratitude and business sense to refrain from biting the hand that feeds them." Similar incidents led another author to charge the educational trust with trying "to head off, if possible, the teaching of socialism" which was "on the increase . . . in a number of universities." Charles Eliot, a prominent trustee on both foundations, argued that as a matter of fact, while private benefactors did not have the right to dictate what was taught, they could "fairly claim that their benefactions entitle their opinions to be treated with consideration and respect, and not with contumely or scorn, in the institutions they have endowed, or by the professors whom their gifts support."[96]

Efforts to organize opposition on this second front were also still-born. Cattell played a leading role in creating a special committee on pensions as a founding member of the American Association of University Professors (AAUP) in 1913. The first task charged to his committee was the preparation of a report on the Carnegie pension system. The committee warned of a "menace to educational freedom" from "uniting in the Carnegie Foundation the function of critic and mentor of educational institutions with that of distributing financial benefits to such institutions."[97] Nevertheless, Cattell's experience convinced him that he dissented "from most of his colleagues in doubting the desirability of a uniform and centrally administered pension fund."[98]

POPULISM AND THE EDUCATIONAL TRUST

There was one source of opposition, however, which embarrassed, frustrated, and obstructed implementation of the foundations' strategies. In many of the western states, populist groups repeatedly opposed the collegiate monopoly. This confrontation was initiated in 1908 when the CFAT charter was amended to include public universities within the pension system. Pritchett was painfully aware that the construction of a genuinely national system in higher education necessitated their inclusion in that system. He was persuaded there could be no question that state universities were becoming "the seat of university education for the greater part of the whole country, including the Central, Western, and Southern States."[99]

In pursuing the integration of public universities into the national system, CFAT trustees viewed them as functionally no different than private ones. They adopted the same strategy of building on strength— which, in most states, meant the urban state universities. However, the trustees found that state universities also represented "a wide range of educational equipment and of educational standards," including some that were "still weak." Nevertheless, all such institutions at least "set before themselves the ideal of a strong institution crowning the state system of education."[100] A common functional aim directed these institutions toward the same role occupied in the East by major private universities. Consequently, those states which applied to the pension system were accepted only on the condition that the state university undertake internal administrative reforms. Frequently, CFAT made demands for administrative reform, institutional consolidation, and functional coordination of entire state systems.[101]

As part of these demands, CFAT launched an attack on the land-grant colleges. The imposition of higher requirements for student admission and the certification of full professors immediately excluded most of those land-grant colleges that did not already serve as the state university. Indeed, while debating the amendment of the CFAT charter, trustees concluded that "most of these institutions, and particularly those which have followed most closely the work of agricultural instruction, are not of academic grade."[102] The result was that independent land-grant colleges were criticized for wastefully diffusing scarce educational resources, promoting lower academic standards in the competitive market, and inefficiently duplicating curricula between schools. Furthermore, as designated schools of "agriculture and mechanic arts," A&Ms were acting contrary to a socially efficient division of labor in offering instruction in the liberal arts and humanities. CFAT was inclined to see them function only as agricultural trade schools.[103]

Finally, the A&Ms were blamed for continually introducing "politics" into higher education. Their efforts to claim a share of state appropriations or to maintain their autonomy against integration into a system stood in the way of constructing functionally coordinated and socially efficient public systems of higher education. CFAT trustees were perplexed by "the lack of a consistent ideal" among the land-grant colleges and by their reluctance "to articulate with the general system of education of their states." Ultimately, CFAT excluded most land-grant colleges from the pension system with an arrogant notice that "the Trustees of the Foundation are not in a position to deal with them as agencies of higher education."[104] GEB followed a similar policy.

In all of this there was certainly more than met the eye. According to the former president of Kansas State, the educational trust was aware that "the people's colleges and universities may at times pass into the control of the people's friends, and the tremendous enginery represented by these institutions be wrested from the grip of those who make of it a commercial asset and be employed in the interest of the people themselves."[105] In fact, since the 1890s, faculty and administrators at these institutions had been developing a rather coherent "philosophy of the land-grant college." This philosophy was derived from their assigned national mission to provide a "liberal education for the agricultural and industrial classes." The central component in this alternative philosophy was the democratization of truth. On the one hand, that meant that land-grant colleges identified their constituency not as "educated gentlemen," but as the farmers and workers of their state. This necessitated lower admission requirements, given the unequal availability of collegiate preparation between the classes.[106] Thus, raising admission standards relative to an abstract ideal not readily available to most members of these classes had unfavorable political implications.

Moreover, there is certainly evidence to indicate that land-grant colleges would upgrade their faculties when the opportunity arose by importing radical refugees banished from the private universities (see Chapters 7 and 8). Similarly, despite the constant assaults directed against them, A&Ms had already long since developed modern systems of administration and accounting in response to federal requirements and supervision. In the field of scientific research, the Department of Agriculture had already organized a clear division of labor between institutions constructed around a national research agenda.

Finally, the Morrill Act directed the institutions to provide a liberal education for the agricultural and industrial classes regardless of whatever division of labor the foundations may have thought best for the states. The land-grant conception of a liberal education was centered on the notion of "practice." A liberal education was a practical education, but in both an economic and political sense of the word. It did entail the acquisition of the arts and skills necessary to be farmers, mechanics, engineers, and schoolteachers. Yet, the social sciences were considered an equally practical "preparation for citizenship."[107] On assuming the presidency of Kansas State in 1897, Thomas Will had characterized the land-grant philosophy as that of teaching farmers "not only how to farm but also how to get their fair share of what they raised."[108]

Institutions like Kansas State, Missouri, Wisconsin, Nebraska, Montana, North Dakota, and Washington (all except the last two land-grant universities) were emerging as western islands where exiled radicals with Ph.D.'s could often find a safe mooring. It would be an exaggeration to say that Populists constructed "Socialist schools" in their wake, an accusation made by David Starr Jordan and Nicholas Murray Butler of CFAT. There is no doubt, however, that their social science faculties contained a disproportionate number of prominent advocates of bimetallism, public ownership of utilities, producers' and consumers' cooperatives, currency regulation, labor unions, nationalization of railroads and mines, and quite often even socialism. Agricultural scientists in these institutions were also turning their talents against mining companies, whose smelting fumes were damaging agricultural crops, and towards consumer issues of food additives, adulteration, and illegal weights and measures.[109]

It comes as no surprise, then, that the one major political showdown against Rockefeller and Carnegie took place in Nebraska. The first confrontation was initiated in April 1903, when John D. Rockefeller offered $66,666 to the University of Nebraska (a land-grant/state university) for the construction of a new building. The populist press immediately exploited the donation as a political issue. The *Nebraska World-Herald* expressed its hope "that the effort of this trust magnate to lay his foul hands upon the Nebraska state university will not succeed." The same paper later warned that "Mr. Rockefeller's willingness to send the Nebraska university $66,666 carries with it Mr. Rockefeller's purpose to dominate the faculty of Nebraska University." William Jennings Bryan also intervened to admonish Nebraskans that "Rockefeller's money smells too much of oil to allow him to put a building on our campus."[110]

The university was beset with financial difficulties, and the Regents accepted the donation. They justified their actions with the disclaimer that rejecting a donation on grounds that it was "ill-earned" would constitute a precedent in which "every subsequent donation to the University would be subjected to a similar test." The Nebraska legislature answered this embarrassment with a resolution declaring that the Regents' acceptance of the gift: "shall not serve before the people of the world as an indication that Nebraska has any sympathy whatever with the dishonest practices and the outrageous impositions for which John D. Rockefeller's great monopoly is responsible."[111]

Three years later, a similar issue was raised when the university Board of Regents sought permission to affiliate with the Carnegie pension system. This action required approval by the governor and the legislature. William Jennings Bryan was asked to address the legislature, whereupon he called the Carnegie pension "the most insidious poison that now threatens our nation" because it would "warp our teachers."[112] The Democratic party rallied to defeat the measure by only four votes.

It was a symbolic gesture at best, for by the end of the year, thirty-two legislatures had already given the necessary governmental approval to qualify their institutions for admission to the Carnegie system.[113] Hollis points out that "state officials were soon to learn that their acts were not merely perfunctory legal gestures."[114] Yet the Nebraska con-

frontation, and similar ones in California, Ohio, and Illinois, left foundation officials "always afraid, and rightly so," according to Flexner, that they might "through some misstep become mixed up in state
or local politics" in such a way as to permanently impair their influence.[115]

4

Building an Ideological State Apparatus, 1915–1928

THE PROGRESSIVE movement, which succeeded populism as the carrier of democratic demands, articulated the ideal of a democratic meritocracy in which leadership, status, and inequality of position were the results of individual achievement and talent. Progressive democracy assigned a crucial role to colleges and universities in legitimating its expressive order because they assumed responsibility for certifying talent strictly on the basis of individual merit and without reference to prior ascriptive distinctions. The "culture of aspiration" promoted by progressivism therefore could not authenticate its democratic claims except insofar as institutional avenues of social mobility—primarily colleges and universities—were in principle accessible to everyone.

The legitimation of progressivism as a democratic alternative to either populism or socialism thus partly hinged on the ability to expand access to higher education and the occupations to which it promised entry. From 1900 to 1930 the number of public higher institutions increased by 435 percent, or more than four times as rapidly as private institutions (which increased by 92 percent). During the same period, enrollments in public colleges grew by 1042 percent.[1] The proportion of persons aged 18–24 attending some form of higher institution rose from 2.89 percent in 1910 to 7.20 percent in 1930.[2]

Yet to eliminate the barriers of prior class distinction as an obstacle to individual achievement, public colleges were under legislative imperatives to offer the best possible education at the lowest possible cost. This meant state and local governments were expected to assume the increased costs of expanding educational opportunity. These financial requirements increased when many of the public institutions—California, Michigan, Wisconsin, Washington, Illinois, Iowa, and Minneso-

95

ta—began competing for recognition among the nation's top research universities. The real increase in public expenditures was further exaggerated by a prolonged period of price inflation. Inflation more than doubled the nominal cost of living from 1914 to 1919 and continued at a high rate until the Great Depression.[3] As a result, state and city spending on higher education more than doubled in every decade between 1890 and 1930.[4]

Despite the very real enrollment boom, however, most people still did not attend a higher institution, nor did they send any children to one. Most state universities identified their market with a local or regional middle class.[5] Consequently, political support for public higher education was often tenuous and ambivalent at best. Public college administrators and state legislators were subjected to conflicting demands for the expansion of public higher educational opportunities and a hostile popular reaction to its costs. For instance, Samuel Gompers in speaking for the AFL called for "universal higher education" and, at the same time, suggested that "the vast majority would profit far more by some other kind of education than that given in the traditional American college."[6]

Progressive campaigns for greater economy and accountability in state government did not exempt public higher education. Businessmen, private foundations, taxpayers' groups, and trade associations were quick to capitalize on this ambivalence as a means of mobilizing public support for administrative and financial reforms in higher education. In its biennial surveys of education, the USBE frequently discovered that such campaigns were crucial windows of opportunity through which the Carnegie plan could be introduced as a socially efficient solution to the fiscal crisis in state government.

An example of the degree to which public debate was captured by the "terms of American big business" is the comprehensive bibliography compiled by the USBE of works published by 1917 on the "money value" of education.[7] Most of these works justified expenditures on higher education by measuring the "value added" to graduates' lifetime incomes. Public higher education was thus increasingly redefined as a "social investment" in the economic growth of the state or local community. At the same time, however, this redefinition meant that continued growth of higher education had to be justified in terms of its rate of return to the public. That was usually measured in value added to the gross state or national product in the form of higher individual incomes. An indication of the speed with which this reconceptualization took place is that of 128 works listed in the USBE bibliography, only 2 were published before 1901. The remaining 126 were all published between 1902 and 1915.

Once the terms of public debate were altered, colleges and universities became susceptible to the same kinds of judgments about their "value" as any other economic institution. One USBE publication reported that the rise of a corporate ideal was eroding "the somewhat sacrosanct position which higher education had come to enjoy." The biennial survey found that by 1922 "people who had previously concerned themselves little about higher education" now "felt free to criticize and to make suggestions." The report notes the businessmen, in particular, became "free in their statements."[8]

The rise of the corporate ideal as a public image of the university was a significant ideological victory for business. It not only displaced traditional metaphors and myths with a new one, but structured debate under the leadership of business expertise. The progressive emphasis on the role of the expert meant that once educational questions were reformulated as problems of business organization and the investment of public capital, then presumably experienced businessmen—and not educators, farmers, workers, students, or the general public—could rightly claim to be the experts. This defined a scenario, as Veblen astutely observed, in which not only did appointing businessmen to boards of trustees or educational reform commissions seem legitimate, but in which doing the contrary would seem like mere "politics" instead of good public administration.[9]

Faced with the problem of expanding higher educational opportunities while controlling costs and accounting to the "public" for their expenditures, state legislators and educational administrators began to see the Carnegie and GEB methods as attractive solutions. Moreover, most boards of trustees were already sympathetically inclined to pursue business solutions for educational problems. The foundations were anxious to press their recommendations and even to provide administrative guidance through handbooks, conferences, and on-site agents. Yet, as previously noted, the foundations were always concerned that too direct an involvement in state or local politics would weaken their influence with charges of partisanship.

The problem was how to influence educational politics without appearing political. The larger aspect of this problem was how to exert that influence toward the goal of a nationally integrated, socially efficient higher educational system. A solution to the first part of the problem was the "educational survey." The solution to its second aspect was an ideological colonization of the U.S. Bureau of Education.

THE VERMONT SURVEY

The Carnegie Foundation and the General Education Board extended their strategy of emulation to the public sector while avoiding direct involvement in local politics by catalyzing a "survey movement" in higher education that carried the Carnegie plan into practically every state. The initial impetus for this movement emerged from Vermont, where an upsurge of public criticism was being directed at educational expenditures. The state legislature responded by approving a joint resolution on November 19, 1912, expressing its doubt about the "efficiency of our common school system" and "a similar doubt . . . among many friends of higher education regarding the adequacy of the return which the State is getting from its appropriation in aid thereof." The legislature then created a commission to "report upon the educational responsibilities of the State." The commission was broadly charged with conducting an inquiry "into the entire educational system and condition of this State. This commission shall report at the earliest possible date on the several rights, duties, and obligations of the University of Vermont and State Agricultural College, Middlebury College, and Norwich University, with such recommendations as will prevent unnecessary duplication and consequent financial waste."[10]

The governor of Vermont acted on this authority to appoint a commission whose members are listed in Table 4.1. Five of its ten members were businessmen, despite the fact that Vermont was a predominantly rural agricultural state. Its members included Theodore Vail, the president of AT&T; a railroad president; an insurance company vice-president; and Nicholas Murray Butler. Two of its members held positions within the Morgan–First National financial group, and one of these, Nicholas Murray Butler, was also a CFAT trustee. Nearly all of its members were prominent in the state or national Republican party. The group was a strong representation of northeastern financial capital, which was fairly homogeneous in its ideological and political perspective. Clearly, it was neither unbiased, nor even nonpartisan, in the simplest sense of the word.

Nevertheless, the members of this commission, when finally charged with the practical task of translating their vague demands for educational efficiency into public policy, were like most American businessmen, uncertain about how to proceed. Consequently, after only two meetings in January and February of 1913, the commissioners resolved that "in addition to the visitations, public hearings, and enquiries conducted by its own members," they would subcontract for

Table 4.1. Members of the Vermont Educational Survey Commission, 1913–1914

Member	Occupation	Party
Nicholas Murray Butler	Pres., Columbia Univ.; trustee, CFAT; director, Equitable Life Assurance	Rep.; U.S. V.P. candidate, 1912
James B. Estee	Investments lawyer; 2nd V.P., Nat'l Life Ins. Co. of Vt., 1902–11	Rep.; mayor of Montpelier
Theodore N. Vail	Pres., AT&T; owner/dir., of electrical companies in London and Argentina	Republican
Frank H. Brooks	Pres., E&T Fairbanks & Co., Merchants	Republican
Percival W. Clement	Pres., Bristol RR Co.	Republican; state legislator
John H. Watson	Judge, Vt. Supreme Court	Republican
Horace F. Graham	State auditor of accounts, Vt.	Republican
George L. Hunt	Lawyer	Unknown
Eli H. Porter	Former member, Vt. RR Commission	Unknown
Allison E. Tuttle	Pres., State Teachers' Association	Unknown

Sources: CFAT, *A Study of Education in Vermont* (Boston: Merrymount Press, 1914), pp. 3–4; *Who Was Who in America.*

an additional "expert study of the school system, including higher institutions of learning." On February 12, 1913, the commission invited the Carnegie Foundation to undertake this study.[11]

The purpose of the expert study was "to place in the hands of the Educational Commission the essential facts which will enable them to form conclusions, to make recommendations, and to propose legislation." CFAT eagerly accepted the invitation, since the Vermont survey represented "the first comprehensive effort on the part of a State to study its school system as a whole from the elementary school to the university."[12] Undertaking this survey would finally provide CFAT with a national showcase in which to demonstrate its methods, as well as the opportunity to influence the reorganization of an entire educational system.

CFAT approached the survey with a theoretical premise that "educational institutions in Vermont are not unrelated agencies, but form parts of one educational system."[13] This systems-analytic approach provided the general theoretical framework in which the concepts and techniques developed by Morris Cooke were then subsequently applied to individual institutions. What tasks the Vermont system should properly undertake were further defined relative to the ideal of a larger New England regional system of higher education.

On the basis of information and suggestions in the CFAT report, the Vermont Educational Commission recommended that the state almost wholly withdraw from higher education in the interests of regional efficiency. The commission recommended that Vermont restrict its work to the State Agricultural College, a land-grant institution, and that even this college should drop its offerings in engineering and the liberal arts to focus exclusively on agriculture and its supporting sciences. In the commission's opinion, this would "make a fruitful connection between the Agricultural College and the industries of farming, dairying, gardening, stock and poultry raising, and fruit culture."[14]

According to the CFAT report, liberal arts and engineering could more efficiently be left to other major universities in the New England region. Thus, it was also recommended that all state subsidies to the University of Vermont, Middlebury College, and Norwich University be terminated. The state was under no obligation to subsidize unnecessary duplication of curriculum at competing institutions within its own state, nor should it contribute to the inefficient fragmentation of educational resources in New England as a whole. The state's only obligation was to invest educational capital in those areas that would provide direct technical support and manpower training for the state's primary industry, agriculture. This policy would realize the highest yield on the state's investment and to that degree constituted the public interest in higher education.

Accompanying these reforms, the Educational Commission recommended a systemwide centralization of state control over education from the elementary school to the agricultural college. This administrative reorganization would supply unity of purpose in supervising the other changes, while providing further economies of scale. Likewise, the usual array of CFAT administrative and accounting reforms were recommended as standard procedures for all individual institutions within the state system.

When these recommendations were put to the next legislature, entrenched local and institutional interests among legislators obstructed full implementation of the Carnegie plan. The Vermont legislature did, nevertheless, adopt a compromise plan which the foundation considered an advance over previous policies. The administration of existing institutions was brought under the centralized direction of a single appointive body so that systematization was adopted as a principle. Individual institutions were also overhauled in order to introduce the new accounting, administrative, and managerial methods. The survey also attracted national attention among educators and government officials as a "scientific" method for resolving political disputes over the fiscal crisis in public higher education.[15]

A LEADERSHIP OF IDEAS

Indeed, the foundations were never interested in simply doing educational surveys. There was a broader political strategy of using opportunities like Vermont to set in motion a national survey movement. It is clear they hoped from the beginning that the reforms associated with the Carnegie plan would be adopted and carried forward by public authorities as long-term government policy. GEB conducted a half-dozen surveys, primarily in southern states, and then withdrew from the movement "on the theory that the proper authorities, local, state, or national would take over and develop any line of effort, the importance of which had been demonstrated on the basis of the Board's support."[16] Likewise, prior to the Vermont survey, Henry Pritchett, president of the Carnegie Foundation, had been lobbying the U.S. Bureau of Education to assume "the much larger function of scrutinizing and reporting upon educational methods and educational problems in the various states" toward the goal of developing and implementing a national policy on higher education.[17]

The foundations regarded education "as a national unifying and coordinating agency" that required "guidance from the central government looking toward unifying and coordinating the separate State systems."[18] The problem, of course, was that constitutional provisions did not authorize the federal government to exercise direct authority over education. The one federal educational agency was the U.S. Bureau of Education, which had been established in 1867 to supervise the land-grant colleges, and its only legislative mandate was the collection and distribution of statistics on education.

Nevertheless, as the result of an 1870 report by Robert Gallaudet, the bureau had early on established the institutional goal of becoming "a national clearinghouse for opinion" on educational questions.[19] As the sole institution in the country gathering current and historical national data on education, the bureau wanted to use its legislative mandate as a vehicle for becoming a dominant authority on the interpretation of national trends, problems, and policies in American education. The powers which the bureau lacked in direct constitutional or statutory authority it hoped to achieve through leadership. The authoritativeness of its recommendations would rest upon the ability to establish an overwhelming hegemony in national educational data.

The bureau was more or less succeeding at this enterprise by the early twentieth century. Government officials, educators, reformers, and private organizations turned to the bureau with ever increasing frequency to ask for statistical data, topical bibliographies, names of consultants, and policy recommendations. By the first decade of the twentieth century, the USBE was receiving an average of more than 1,200 letter requests per month and sending out more than 7,500 documents per month in response.[20] Its sheer capacity to focus volumes of information on almost any educational question put it in a strong position to direct current debates on the development of higher education.

This role positioned USBE as a perfect administrative instrument for executing foundation strategies in the public sector. It could exercise national leadership by defining statistical averages for judging the comparative performance of individual states or institutions. Yet, constitutional and statutory limitations would always prevent the bureau from ever assuming direct regulatory authority over national education. This was an appealing characteristic to business reformers, who saw federal leadership as necessary to educational change but were still wary of too much government control. A significant amount of evidence suggests that foundations were extremely successful in winning federal approval for their policies and, ultimately, in transferring leadership of the survey movement to the Bureau of Education, where ideologically sympathetic officials carried forward their strategies.

For instance, prior to becoming commissioner of education, E. E. Brown had actively lobbied government officials to grant the proposed General Education Board a federal charter of incorporation. While still a professor of education at the University of California, he wrote the secretary of the interior that he was "acquainted by personal inspection with the operations hitherto conducted by the persons named in the act of incorporation" and was convinced that "the course of action determined on by this body of men is wisely calculated."[21] Later, when the Carnegie Foundation was established in 1906, Commissioner Brown immediately wrote Henry Pritchett to inform him "I shall be very glad to see you at the Bureau of Education when you come to Washington and whenever you come to Washington, and if the Bureau can be of any service to you in your great work I trust you will call on me with the greatest freedom."[22]

Brown's successor was P. P. Claxton (1911–21), a professor of education from the University of Tennessee. Claxton had been a prominent member of the Southern Education Board, where he came in constant contact with the executives and trustees of the Rockefeller Foundation, the General Education Board, the Peabody Fund, and the Slater Fund. Claxton began his career in educational reform with a sense of southern noblesse oblige. Like many Progressives, he saw education as an avenue for uplifting the masses "into a life more or less like that of the professional and leisure classes" which, he thought, "was in some way very superior to the life of the farmer, the mechanic and the tradesman." By 1909, however, he concluded this view was a "mistake." He adopted in its place the standard foundation view that a liberal education was after all only for the "professional and leisure classes," and that education of the "masses" should be directed more toward the vocational promotion of industrialization, commercial development, and agricultural techniques.[23]

Bureau records indicate that during Brown's and Claxton's tenures in office, there was a regular exchange of information between the foundations and the government office similar to that which prevailed among the various foundations. GEB's annual reports were regularly forwarded to the commissioner of education.[24] CFAT and the bureau placed each other on their regular mailing lists so that each routinely received the other's publications, reports, circulars, bulletins, and monographs.[25] Similarly, the USBE compiled and maintained for its own use a complete set of the volumes of the proceedings of the Peabody Education Fund and the Slater Fund.[26]

Unfortunately, appointment books were either not kept or have been lost, so that a definitive empirical assessment of the levels of personal contact is not possible. Nevertheless, extant communications do reveal that GEB members frequently stopped at the commissioner's office to discuss policy when travelling south to SEB meetings. These documents indicate that commissioners of education routinely contacted CFAT or GEB members whenever they passed through New York City visiting colleges and universities. The commissioners would often meet with foundation executives at NEA meetings or the meetings of college and university associations.

However, an institutional analysis of the bureau suggests quite strongly that this otherwise free exchange of information and cooperation between public and private institutions was conducted with a very unequal flow of influence. The Bureau of Education became rapidly dependent on these well-funded private organizations to supplement its own routine statistical work with outside policy analyses. Despite the academic boom in the United States, the USBE's office budget only increased from $55,000 in 1890 to $72,000 in 1910. In the 1910 budget, almost 85 percent of bureau expenditures went for staff salaries and another 6 percent for office space rental. This left only about 9 percent, or $7,000, for maintaining and expanding a central reference library, bibliographic service, printing and distribution of documents, and data collection.[27]

The bureau was eventually so understaffed and underfunded that its clerical staff could barely catalogue the endless streams of information and empirical data, while its specialists were overwhelmed with answering routine letters and requests for information.[28] For example, the bureau was usually two to five years behind schedule in the compilation and publication of its own annual report. The workload associated with its basic legislative mandate proved so unmanageable that the yearly statistical compilations contained in the commissioner's *Annual Report* were finally replaced in 1916 with a *Biennial Survey*. This change only managed to keep the bureau from falling even further behind schedule. Consequently, when state officials and educators began turning to the bureau for policy recommendations, it was already reaching the limits of its organizational capacity. Conceptualizing and interpreting its reservoirs of information in relation to specific policy concerns would have stretched the bureau beyond its staff and time limitations.

In the last two years of his tenure, E. E. Brown addressed these problems by building and mobilizing a national education lobby. Its major success was a slight budget increase in which the additional revenues were earmarked for an expansion of publication activities and for hiring additional staff specialists in statistics, higher education, and land-grant colleges.[29] His goal was to deploy regular publications and staff expertise toward the conduct of "government by influence." He argued that strategy was primarily a problem of "the most effective collection and diffusion of the most useful knowledge."[30]

For the most part, however, Congress continually rebuffed the efforts of the bureau under Brown to assume "governmental functions belonging to the States."[31] The USBE finally circumvented restrictions on its personnel resources by turning to individuals employed full-time by foundations, universities, or other private agencies who could be paid for specific policy analyses as "outside experts" or "consultants" out of the new publications and documents budget. These experts and consultants undertook the task of writing the bulletins and circulars that interpreted the bureau's reservoirs of data for the purpose of converting it into policy recommendations.

Frequently, the bureau relied entirely on the foundations to conduct specialized studies which the bureau then publicized in lieu of its own works. In the commissioner's annual report for 1907–8, E. E. Brown made special reference to the fact that after only two years of operation "the recent publications of the Carnegie Foundation have proved of special interest and value."[32] The bureau's chief clerk later noted in a 1912 memo that "the publications of some of these foundations have rendered it unnecessary for this Bureau to issue publications on some phases of education and have thus enabled it to concentrate its efforts in other directions."[33] Bureau officials saw cooperation with the foundations and similar private agencies as a way to facilitate the over-burdened office's policy analysis activities. Policy recommendations accepted and publicized as official government positions on higher education were more often than not formulated with little or no modification by finance capitalists and other corporate intellectuals.

The influence of these publications within the bureau was best revealed in a 1912 study conducted by the New York-based Bureau of Municipal Research (BMR). As part of a study collecting information on "what has been done for public schools by citizens aside from voting, paying taxes, and serving on boards," the BMR asked the USBE to prepare a statement showing how far private agencies such as the major foundations "have been of value to the Bureau of Education."[34] P. P. Claxton issued instructions to the bureau staff asking them to comply with this request. The answers Claxton received were quite instructive, especially since he had already forwarded a reply to the BMR saying that "so far as I think there has been comparatively little cooperation."[35] Yet, these staff memos to Claxton soon revealed a very different picture, suggesting that the bureau had long been colonized by the foundations.

John Wolcott, chief of the Library Division, reported: "We find the publications of the Russell Sage Foundation, Carnegie Foundation, and of the National Municipal League of considerable assistance to us in our library reference work."[36] Such an acknowledgement was not insignificant, since one of the bureau's most important responsibilities was distributing information. As noted earlier, the bureau file of letters sent indicates the bureau was receiving dozens of requests every day for documents, circulars, special reports, references, bibliographies, and consultants. To the degree that foundations were able to "assist" in the collection and organization of this bibliographic material or focus this work on specific material, they were able to influence the bureau's activities in the direction of a specific educational philosophy.[37]

Along the same lines of endeavor, J. C. Boykin, chief of the Editorial Division, responded that his division had just republished a circular of the SEB at bureau expense in cooperation with Wickliffe Rose, the SEB president and an influential member of the General Education Board.[38] Similarly, another division replied: "While there has been no coopera- tion between this Div. of the Bureau and the Foundations, I have been able in many ways to multiply their usefulness by calling attention to the work they have done."[39]

A network of informal influence apparently permeated the entire bureau. Another note, probably from the Division of Statistics, re- ported a "large measure of cooperation between [the] B of E and [the] Carnegie Foundation and General Education Board."[40] Finally, one of the bureau's central clerks perhaps best summarized the situation by informing Claxton that

"while the most cordial relations have always existed between these great agencies and the U.S. Bureau of Education I have always felt that they are our debtors in the matter of exchange of favors. Their efforts are of great value as supplements to the work of the Bureau. By keeping track of what these agencies are doing we can avoid a duplication of work. They can do much that we cannot undertake for lack of facilities[,] and along certain lines they can make investi- gations which it would be unwise for a government office to attempt."[41]

Thus, the chief clerk's letter of response to the BMR was that

"some of the private foundations have been of considerable assistance in the work of this Bureau. We have found especially valuable in connection with the standardization of higher educational institutions data which have been col- lected by the Carnegie Foundation for the Advancement of Teaching and the General Education Board which members of our staff have been permitted to consult freely. In this way information has been placed in the hands of the Bureau that would have been practically impossible for us to obtain other- wise."[42]

Claxton was evidently surprised at the extent to which his staff was cooperating with the foundations. But if so, he was pleasantly sur- prised, because he had already decided to strengthen the bureau's cooperative relationship with the foundations. Before the replies from his staff ever made it to his desk, Claxton had already called a meeting of the secretaries of several of the foundations "for the purpose of discussing the possibility of closer cooperation and coordination of the work of the boards and the Bureau."[43]

At about the same time, Claxton was aggressively promoting the bureau's influence through a new policy of on-the-spot persuasion modelled after the foundations' use of "field agents." The idea was originally adopted by E. E. Brown as part of his strategy for "government by influence," but the policy came to fruition under Claxton. In one letter to the secretary of the interior, Claxton argued, "There is a great need at the present time in the Bureau of Education for the employment of additional specialists in several phases of education."[44] Claxton apparently envisioned a force of specialized field agents swarming across the country in an effort to bring federal policy directly to states and universities through face-to-face persuasion and consultation. In one report, bureau staff pointed to the SEB, Peabody Fund, and Sage Foundation as examples demonstrating that "placing able men actually in the field has been adopted by practically all agencies that have been successful in securing enlightened action." The same report also noted that "life insurance companies have all discovered that the publication of documents was not adequate in getting results. They have depended on the services of able men in the field."[45]

Claxton, like Brown, was unsuccessful in securing congressional appropriations for this purpose. He responded by shifting most of the office routine onto clerks and other staff members, while delegating his own purely administrative tasks to L. A. Kalbach, the chief clerk, who came to function as a de facto assistant commissioner. Meanwhile, he detailed himself and the two specialists in higher education on regular field visits throughout the country. In 1911, the total number of mandays spent in the field visiting educational institutions and attending educational conferences quadrupled (see Table 4.2). The number of states in which they visited institutions tripled. The following year, Claxton personally spent 254 days in the field, while Kendrick C. Babcock, the specialist in higher education, spent 154.

Claxton's failure to secure additional appropriations for a squadron of field agents simply drove the bureau closer to the foundations. GEB and the Phelps-Stokes Fund immediately stepped in and offered to supply appropriations to the bureau out of their own treasuries to help defray the costs of travel by bureau employees. Claxton wrote to the secretary of the interior on August 10, 1911, to ask if it was legally possible to accept "any funds from outside sources for the supplement-

Table 4.2. Visits by Representatives of the U.S. Bureau of Education to Educational
Institutions and Conferences: Total Days in the Field, 1906–1912

	1906	1907	1908	1909	1910	1911	1912
Commissioner of education	6	71	54	60	61	49	254
Specialist in higher education[a]					11	231	154
Specialist in land-grant college statistics[a]					26	130	61
Total man-days	6	71	54	60	98	410	469
Number of states visited	2	4	7	8	10	28	36

Source: Data compiled from information in the U.S Department of Interior, Letters from Commissioner of Education to the Secretary of the Interior, Secretary of the Interior's Central File, sec. 6, box nos. 1526 and 1538, RG 48, NA.

[a]Specialists' offices were not created until 1910.

ing of the statutory salaries" of any additional specialists he might hire. "It is possible," he wrote, "that outside assistance from private sources might be obtained to supplement the salaries of one or more positions provided by law."[46]

In forwarding a written response from the assistant attorney general for the department of the interior, Secretary Baker informed Claxton "that it is best to drop the idea you have in mind."[47] The assistant attorney general warned him that "the source of the contribution of such money might be a very material matter. . . . the source of the increased compensation might affect the integrity and efficiency of the payees. . . . I am therefore of opinion that such cooperation should not be accepted by the Bureau of Education unless authorized by Congress."[48]

Claxton countered this blow to his plans by proposing a wider and more systematic application of the outside experts scheme developed by E. E. Brown in relation to publications and documents. An arrangement was worked out with GEB and Phelps-Stokes whereby the foundations would pay the full salaries of certain specialists and field agents. The bureau would then pay these persons the nominal sum of one dollar per year for acting as "special collaborators."

The legal difference in this new arrangement was that the experts, instead of being government employees whose salaries were being supplemented by "outside agencies," would be employees of a private agency performing occasional service for the government for which they would be paid as consultants. Nevertheless, in their specific capacity as special collaborators, they would be entitled to act as official representatives and authorities of the USBE under the jurisdiction of the commissioner. The attorney general's office could offer "no legal objection" to this arrangement. The new opinion also informed the commissioner that the bureau could be reimbursed by outside agencies for specific work done by its employees if such work was undertaken as an official act of the USBE within its statutory mandate.[49] Under this arrangement, Claxton successfully built a national force of special collaborators in the field that included professors at colleges and universities throughout the country, foundation employees, and workers for various educational reform associations.[50]

Thereafter, the bureau worked hand in hand with GEB in the South. Elsewhere, the bureau encouraged other states and universities to follow the path blazed by Vermont. In his annual report and other publications, the commissioner continually called attention to examples of the emerging "Carnegie movement." Publication of the Vermont survey in 1914 was soon followed by a similar survey at CCNY conducted by the faculty in response to a resolution by the board of trustees requesting data on the costs of instruction per student hour. A report by the president of Smith College was praised by Commissioner Claxton as an illustration of the "growing tendency among progressive colleges and universities to survey themselves."[51]

One of the most significant examples to receive national exposure through USBE publicity was a 1914 efficiency survey of the Drexel Institute of Technology conducted by Dr. Hollis Godfrey. Godfrey was an engineer trained at Tufts University. Like Morris Cooke, he too was a well-known disciple of Frederick Taylor, as well as associate of Cooke's.[52] While Godfrey was in Philadelphia conducting a series of civil engineering surveys for the city, the Drexel board of trustees asked him to conduct a survey of the technical institute as well. Godfrey agreed and immediately turned to the techniques developed by Cooke in *Academic and Industrial Efficiency*. He adopted the "student-clock hour" as his basic measure of educational efficiency and productivity. This made him one of the first people in the country to independently adopt the concept.[53]

After Godfrey had completed the survey, the Drexel trustees appointed him as the institute's president and gave him a free hand to implement his recommendations. Godfrey boasted he would turn the institute into a "demonstration plant" of higher-education reform.[54] His first action was to drop or consolidate "inefficient" courses. In consolidating chairs, courses, and fields of study for administrative purposes, he simultaneously redefined the relationship between fields of study. Of particular significance in this respect was the administrative consolidation of natural sciences alongside technical fields of study in a single School of Engineering. This administratively linked the goals of natural science to the discovery of underlying laws of nature that would assist in solving immediate technical problems of capitalist development, product innovation, and plant efficiency. Other fields of study were reduced or eliminated in proportion to their academic efficiency and their ability to quantify a rate of return on educational investment.

Another link in the bureau's promotion of the Carnegie movement was the publicity Claxton conferred through his annual report on an otherwise obscure paper presented to the Ohio College Association in April 1914 by Raymond M. Hughes. Hughes was a striking example of the new managerial type of president. He started his career at Miami University as a professor of chemistry. He was eventually appointed university registrar, then dean, then acting president, and, finally, president of the university. Just before being made acting president, however, Hughes made an extended tour of England and the United States, visiting fifty-eight collegiate institutions along the way. He compiled two huge volumes of notes, commentaries, and ideas during the journey which he brought back with him as a working document.[55]

Once appointed president, Hughes conducted an institutional survey of Miami University using the Carnegie student-clock hour.[56] He recommended a reorganization of teaching schedules and curriculum that would both increase academic efficiency and link salaries to academic productivity instead of seniority. The Miami trustees received his recommendations favorably, although one visitor reports his "investigating proclivities" had "greatly annoyed" the faculty.[57]

THE SURVEY MOVEMENT, 1915–1928

In the midst of these developments, Henry Pritchett lobbied the bureau to take up the Carnegie survey as an instrument of national policy. As early as 1911, the year after Cooke's pathbreaking study, Pritchett was arguing with the secretary of the interior that whoever replaced E. E. Brown should be more active in using the bureau's new-found influence to direct higher education reform on a national scale. He knew that "it is, of course, impossible for the Government of the United States actually to control or regulate the systems of education set up in the various states, but," he argued, "there is no reason why the United

States Commissioner of Education, through his office, should not scrutinize and report upon these various state systems and state institutions with entire frankness and truthfulness."[58]

This vision was certainly in line with Claxton's new policy of an activist bureau. As far as personnel, the turning point in the bureau's ability and willingness to assume leadership of the emerging Carnegie movement was Claxton's appointment of Samuel P. Capen as the higher education specialist in 1914. Capen, a young professor of educational administration at Clark University, had become a leader of the educational reform movement in Worcester by advocating "administrative efficiency" in the public schools. He had also done some innovative work developing standardized methods for supervising and evaluating teaching. This work led to an invitation from Hollis Godfrey to join the Society for the Promotion of Engineering Education (SPEE) in 1912 as its first "educational engineer." It was in this capacity that Claxton selected Capen to replace Kendrick C. Babcock.[59]

Only two months after Capen arrived at his new post in Washington, the bureau received a request from North Carolina asking USBE to undertake a survey of that state's higher institutions. Claxton handed the project to Capen, who was ordered to do the fieldwork and then publish an official committee report with the cooperation of his predecessor, Babcock; the secretary of the Carnegie Foundation; and "the president of some southern college." Claxton informed him that the Carnegie Foundation had just completed a survey in Vermont that could be used as a model for the North Carolina survey.[60]

David Noble has demonstrated in another context that Capen "was thoroughly awed, even intimidated, by engineers." He was always impressed by their scientific rigor and was fearful that he might not "grade up" to their standards. Consequently, he was "anxious" to insure that whatever was done directly by his division "shall be as coldly scientific as I can make it." In this he considered himself a "humble associate" of the engineers.[61] Capen's anxiety was compounded, when upon arriving at the Bureau of Education, he realized that he "was not so strong on hard facts." He later wrote that "my flesh creeps" whenever he was referred to as an "expert" on higher education.[62] "The specialist in higher education," he wrote his wife, "is supposed evidently to be a specialist in almost everything known to the mind of man. It is too tall an order for one very young and inexperienced person to fill."[63]

Capen concluded within days of the assignment that he needed to be "Carnegieized." Claxton advised him "to go see Flexner," the GEB staff

member who was directing that foundation's Maryland survey, to "see
what he had to offer." Capen also apparently met with the full membership of the General Education Board.[64] A few days later, Capen
reports, his undergraduate college chum, none other than Hollis Godfrey, "blew into my office" and presented him with some "sound good
sense" derived from the reorganization of Drexel. He would later
characterize Godfrey's Drexel survey "as the best institutional study
yet made."[65] Two weeks after Godfrey's visit, Capen spent two days
with Raymond Hughes while on detail to the Midwest. He described it
as "one of the best visits I ever made anywhere or on anybody." Hughes
impressed him as "getting at a philosophy of college education which
is quite striking." Capen concluded that he was "far behind [Hughes]
in knowledge of college administration."[66]

The North Carolina survey turned out to be mainly a test run for the
bureau while Capen received his on-the-job training. GEB and SEB
ultimately assumed the leading political role in the North Carolina
reform movement. The small report authored by Capen (a mere twelve
pages) was circulated primarily among foundation members, North
Carolina educators, and state government officials.[67]

The critical events occurred early in 1915 when state legislatures
invited the bureau to survey the higher institutions of Washington and
Iowa, and the University of Oregon.[68] Claxton quickly accepted the
invitations. They were exactly the kind of leverage he needed to pursue
more aggressive federal intervention in shaping a national higher
education policy. Since he was acting at the invitation of the states, he
did not violate constitutional provisions which reserved education as a
power of the states. Similarly, federal participation in the surveys could
be justified under the bureau's existing statutory mandate to collect
statistical data. The legislatures agreed to assume the cost of the surveys from state appropriations, and the attorney general's 1911 opinion
had already authorized Claxton to accept nonfederal monies for specific work done by the bureau.

A survey team for Washington State was placed in the field in
February of 1915. Though it was chaired personally by P. P. Claxton,
most of the fieldwork and the authorship of the final report were
delegated to Capen and a support staff provided by the state. Claxton's
role was mainly political. He acted as the public relations advance man,
placating educators, building legislative enthusiasm, and smoothing
the entry of his survey team prior to its arrival at each campus. Claxton
seems to have been acutely aware that a national spotlight was focused
on Washington because of the political events that had finally led to the
survey invitation.

The state's population had almost tripled in the fifteen years prior to the survey. Most of this was concentrated in western Washington, particularly Seattle, where manufacturing output had more than doubled in the last decade. The state's secondary school system had expanded from 4 to 126 accredited institutions. The University of Washington's administration was continually articulating its "interest in meeting the practical problems of regional development."[69] However, it was exactly what constituted the "practical problems" of regional development that was at the center of a continuing political debate. Washington state politics had been a cauldron of turmoil for the last quarter century. During the 1890s, state government had temporarily fallen to the Populists, only to then be returned to conservatives in 1904. There were legislative divisions over the regulation of monopoly, real estate speculation, conservation, railroad regulation, and utilities. Even after the triumph of conservatism, the state remained a national stronghold for the Populist legacy, the Progressive party, the Socialist party, and the Industrial Workers of the World.

The Populist legacy to the University of Washington was an emerging reputation as one of the western islands of political discontent. The aggressive recruitment of refugee Populist scholars had brought it critical luminaries such as James Allen Smith and Vernon Louis Parrington.[70] Once conservatives regained control of the state in 1904, Governor Albert E. Mead made it known in his inaugural address that he was disturbed by professors' teaching "that our system of government is based upon fallacious principles and should, therefore, ultimately be overthrown!" He went on to promise that any instructor "engaged in the exploitation of such un-American ideas would be dismissed immediately."[71]

University of Washington President Thomas Franklin Kane had a different conception of university government. He was himself no political radical, but he was an extremely tolerant administrator who was willing to shield his faculty against external political forays by the governor, the legislature, and a governing board generally dominated by local industrialists, lumbermen, bankers, and real estate speculators. Kane believed that a university "should be as democratic as the State itself." Consequently, he promoted a free market of ideas within the academic community and relied heavily upon a committee form of university administration that decentralized decision-making in the faculty insofar as possible.

Kane's position became increasingly untenable as reactionaries gained the upper hand in the politics of Washington state. Another conservative governor was elected in 1912, and before the end of 1913, he had replaced every regent at the University of Washington. This time the new regents understood their marching orders and immediately set out to reorganize the university's administrative structure.

Kane was informed that a president "should not act as the leader of a constitutional republic but as the head of a large corporation." Kane rejected the regents' advice. He then refused the regents' request that the campus be closed to outside political speakers. He protested the regents' acceptance of a financial gift from a source he considered politically suspect. The last straw was his direct defiance of the regents' order not to hire a professor of political economy who was considered too radical. Kane was dismissed on June 14, 1914. His parting words were an attack on the regents for their "politically reactionary character" and "direct management" of the university.[72] The dismissal received national publicity because only two years earlier, Kane had been president of the National Association of State Universities.

Kane was replaced by Henry Suzzalo, a professor of education from Columbia University and a Carnegie protege of Nicholas Murray Butler.[73] Suzzalo had so impressed the Carnegie Foundation that he, rather than Claxton, had been Pritchett's preference as a replacement for E. E. Brown as commissioner of education in 1911. Pritchett had nominated him to the secretary of the interior as "a younger man of the best type with good training, courage, and good sense." Suzzalo shared Pritchett's enthusiasm for an active, interventionist bureau. Pritchett was convinced that Suzzalo "represented the type of man who could carry out such a conception." From Pritchett's perspective, Suzzalo was "one of the best men in education in the country."[74]

The Washington regents wanted Suzzalo to bring strong central leadership to the university as a prelude to more ambitious plans for its role in promoting regional economic development. Suzzalo argued after his arrival that the only way he could undertake this role "scientifically" would be on the basis of a detailed empirical survey of university operations and structure. He went on to insist that a single institutional survey would be insufficient, because even if strong central leadership was brought to the university, it was impossible to determine the university's proper role and pursue that goal vigorously unless the university's position was clearly defined relative to other institutions in the state. He claimed he could not make intelligent decisions about curriculum development, faculty recruitment, research funding, enrollments, or plant expenditures unless he had a state plan in which to frame his judgments.

In other words, the institutional reorganization he was being asked to orchestrate could be effectively accomplished only alongside a general restructuring of the state's entire higher educational system. Charles Gates observes that, consonant with CFAT dogma, Suzzalo naturally "assumed that the university should be the capstone of the State system of higher education . . . a key institution to which all others would be subordinated." He predicated this plan on the need to eliminate "overlap and duplication," a slogan that always won the attention of conservative state legislatures.

The chief obstacle to this plan was the land-grant college located in eastern Washington. Eastern Washington was primarily an agricultural center that had been a source of Populist strength in the state. Suzzalo drew the college and the entire region into a political confrontation by suggesting that his proposed reorganization required the transfer of all liberal arts, professional, and engineering curricula from the state college to the university. Efficiency could be realized only through a specialization and demarcation of functions between the two schools. This meant that the state college should be restricted exclusively to agricultural sciences and techniques.[75]

Suzzalo had one last demand to put before the state legislature. He knew that so-called local interests would obstruct any effort to achieve a socially efficient system of higher education. His last suggestion, therefore, was that any effort at reorganization should be accompanied by the consolidation of all higher institutions under a single board of regents with statewide powers to regulate curriculum and appropriations. This demand was always accompanied by the odd assertion that somehow a single centralized board would take higher education out of politics and professionalize its administration.

T. E. Will had diagnosed this phenomenon quite rudely by pointing out a decade earlier how strange it was that the educational trusts "insist that their representatives must permanently continue in control whatever may be the vicissitudes of State politics" because their views were "scientific." Any other policy was regarded as "gross spoilism" or "politics."[76] If centralized boards did take higher education out of politics, that was precisely the problem. It was already becoming evident to careful observers that wherever centralized boards appeared—Iowa (1909), Kansas (1913), Montana (1913)—there was a transfer of power over the institutions, always to a business coalition.[77] Thus, in Iowa, President Storm had been criticizing the centralized board as "tending to subject the State College . . . to a misunderstanding and unsympathetic control."[78]

Suzzalo's ambitious proposal was justifiably interpreted by Enoch

Albert Bryan, president of the state college, as a hostile attack upon the philosophy of the land-grant college. If higher education was to be scientifically administered by "experts," Bryan was curious to know in advance by what experts. He later reflected that in such contests "a curious notion prevails that business and political experience are the prime qualifications for membership on the board of an educational institution." Bryan was disturbed by this notion. He was convinced from his own experience that there was "no such thing as a separation between the 'business' and 'educational' functions of a college."[79] The state college board of regents followed Bryan's lead and notified Suzzalo and the governor that they would resist any attempts at statewide consolidation. The president of the state college board of regents rejected Suzzalo's proposed curriculum reform with an accurate rejoinder that the author of the Morrill Act "had never intended that the farmers' sons who attended these institutions should study only agriculture."[80]

In North Dakota, where the USBE would be called upon to conduct a survey the following year, the same battle was already being duplicated in the same terms between conservatives and the agrarian socialist Non-Partisan League. The North Dakota NPL was somewhat more poetic in its denunciation of the curriculum reforms, which it considered "an attempt to make our college into a trade school for peasants." Once a centralized board was in place in that state, the NPL would find it more and more difficult "to protect its sympathizers in college faculties and to ensure college administrations which were at least not hostile to its agrarian program."[81]

Bryan likewise argued that farmers and workers would learn to be more productive, while being denied the equally practical training in citizenship, political economy, government, history, and sociology. He believed, contrary to the corporate functionalists, that "all knowledge is based upon the primary sciences and their subdivisions and are so interwoven as to form a unity." Without this unity of science, one could easily acquire skills without obtaining knowledge. He suggested that "even to the novice who gives a little thought to the subject, 'duplication' will be seen to be a false cry."[82]

In spite of Bryan's effort to mobilize opposition to the survey, he later recounted that "a commission was created to hear and report, and provision was made for the conflict." Bryan did not expect an "impartial" survey by neutral experts. He knew that Claxton and Capen were "gentlemen with a hereditary bend [sic] toward aristocratic theory of education, with that lofty philanthropic view which looks upon the education of the industrial classes as a duty which we owe to our fellow men, but with the feeling that the education given must be adapted to their situation in life."[83] After reading an initial draft of the report, he wrote to Capen that "if it is merely a fight, we might as well have the fight without the preliminaries."[84] Nevertheless, the preliminaries were observed, and the Washington survey commission eventually brought its results before the state legislature in early March. Capen recounted that on the day his report was released, "I spent the evening in the [hotel] lobby . . . standing with lowered head before the attacks of Pres. Bryan."[85] His initial embarrassment was soon put to rest when other members of the bureau began calling the report a "masterpiece," a "monumental work," his "magnum opus," and "one of the best things the Bureau has published recently."[86]

The Iowa survey commission released its results at about the same time.[87] In that state, the USBE had been invited to conduct a survey with the explicit intention of "securing moral support for consolidation that would overcome local opposition" by conferring on "the investigation and consequent recommendations all possible authority and prestige."[88] Claxton appointed a survey team that carried exactly that kind of expert authority.

The Iowa commission was chaired by Capen, who kept other members informed of events in Washington. The other members were Raymond M. Hughes; Kendrick C. Babcock, the bureau's former specialist in higher education and now a dean at the University of Illinois; James R. Angell, a rising managerial type who was currently dean of faculties at the University of Chicago; Liberty Hyde Bailey, formerly a dean at Cornell's State College of Agriculture and a special collaborator for the bureau on agricultural education; and Henrietta Calvin, the bureau's specialist in home economics.[89] Capen wrote that in his opinion "there's only one crowd bigger and that one consists of [A. Lawrence] Lowell, and [Arthur T.] Hadley, and Pritchett."[90]

Claxton was delighted with both surveys, but he wrote to Godfrey that the Iowa survey was "the best thing of the kind that has been done in this country."[91] He was particularly pleased with that part of the report "showing the cost of a student-clock hour of instruction in each of the principal departments."[92] Both reports, in addition to their application of a standardized measure of efficiency to the higher institutions in the two states, made several recommendations which became routine in all subsequent surveys. Moreover, in both instances, the survey teams remained in the states to answer legislative inquiries, give testimony, lobby, assist in writing legislative bills, and even consult on the implementation of the legislation that eventually emerged from extended political contests.[93]

The proposals for internal administrative reform parroted the usual

CFAT recommendations: line-itemized budgets for stronger administrative governance of teaching, curriculum, and research; functionally differentiated hierarchical administrative structures with clear lines of authority; centralized business and accounting offices; pre- and post-audits of expenditures; centralized allocation of classroom space, plant, and equipment; and administration by full-time professional managers who would utilize sound business procedures.

The concept of a system was consciously applied to the problem of interinstitutional relations. There was to be one centralized board of regents responsible for all higher institutions in the state. This board would have authority to allocate curriculum between institutions according to that functional division of labor which was most cost-efficient.

The bureau did introduce a new concept which had the familiar ring of railroad administration. Political opposition to curriculum allocations from the land-grant colleges led the survey teams to modify their original position with the concept of "major and service lines" of instruction and research.[94] This modification required particular institutions to focus educational resources on a major line of instruction and research (e.g., engineering, liberal arts, agriculture). Major lines were to be allocated relative to local labor market segmentation (e.g., farming, professions, industry) and partly relative to an institution's proven ability to produce a major line more efficiently than other institutions in the state. Service lines of instruction and research would provide support personnel to the major line(s) (e.g., chemistry for agriculture, political science for law, or physics for engineering). Thus, all or most of the major disciplines would remain at each institution, but they would be redistributed, expanded, reduced, or altered in their substantive emphases with reference to their position as either a major or service line at each institution.[95]

The commissions recommended in this regard that all institutions keep detailed records of the occupational destinations of graduates to find out specifically what segments of the labor market actually constituted the demand for their product. This would allow colleges and universities to fine-tune curricula in relation to the relevant labor markets. The commissions concurrently recommended that all institutions establish placement centers with the function of maintaining a close watch on local or regional labor markets. These centers could help identify necessary adjustments in production (i.e., course offerings and research) and ease frictions in the labor market by facilitating movement out of the university into positions of employment.

These suggestions were a radical departure from the previous mission of American collegiate institutions. Colleges and universities were being charged for the first time with the responsibility to train people for jobs, rather than for character, citizenship, or leadership. There was an additional presumption that henceforth college and university degrees provided a meritocratic certification of competence (partly relative to the individual and partly relative to the prestige of the institution conferring the degree) that made one more qualified for a particular job or jobs, while disqualifying most others.

The Bureau of Education was subsequently invited to conduct a series of state-by-state surveys during the 1920s. By recommending decentralized adaptation to local and regional markets, the bureau shaped the construction of a national system which was still flexible enough to provide a maximum of direct service to states, cities, or private constituencies. This provided the greatest possible return to states and locales on their educational investment, while promoting a national interest in the socially efficient provision of an infrastructure for national economic and political development.

In the bureau's own estimation, the survey was "the most important of the advisory methods" at its disposal.[96] Capen concluded after less than a decade that the educational survey and its ability to promote a point of view persuasively was enabling the bureau to exercise an influence on American education "out of all proportion to [the bureau's] size and resources."[97] The vitality of that influence, he observed, lay in USBE's ability to provide "genuine intellectual leadership"— what he called "a leadership of ideas."[98]

The Washington and Iowa surveys started a survey movement which steadily acquired momentum. The following year, the USBE conducted surveys at the Universities of Nevada and Arizona. These were followed up with surveys of the state systems of North Dakota, South Dakota, and Alabama. In the fourteen years from 1915 through 1928, the USBE conducted or participated in a minimum of 114 higher educational surveys that embraced at least 240 separate institutions (see Table 4.3).[99] This means that at least one-third of all four-year higher institutions in the country were surveyed directly by the USBE. Most of these surveys were of public institutions. Figure 4.1 shows the geographic distribution of the surveys completed by the end of 1927. In fifteen states, the entire higher educational system (often including private colleges) was surveyed by the bureau. In nine additional states, the bureau surveyed only the state university. Similar surveys by CFAT and self-surveys by certain states are also included in the figure.

Table 4.3. U.S. Bureau of Education Surveys, 1910–1927

Type of survey	Number
National Study of Negro Education[a]	1
State systems of education[b]	11
State systems of higher education	10
Higher educational institutions	98
County systems of education	22
City systems of education	23
Building programs in city systems	15
Miscellaneous[c]	20
Total	200

Source: USBE, *Report of the Commissioner, 1927* (Washington, D.C.: GPO, 1928), p. 20.
[a]Includes higher institutions.
[b]Four of these include higher institutions.
[c]Includes national survey of land-grant colleges.

The bureau's activities as a standardizing and coordinating agency were extremely successful in carrying the Carnegie plan throughout the nation. Its recommendations followed a predictable pattern in every state. In a survey of its surveys published in 1928, the bureau reported:

"Whatever the main purpose of the survey, the same set of facts and conditions are studied and much the same means of dealing with specific problems are recommended. . . . All the surveys give considerable weight to problems of educational coordination, to methods of control, and the nature of support. . . . To settle disputes between two or more institutions regarding the proper fields of each, the Bureau of Education has consistently recommended the application of the principle of major and service lines. When lack of coordination between institutions exists, it has recommended a board to devise means of bringing about unity of purpose, or it has recommended the creation of a central board to govern the institutions. State surveys conducted by other agencies have followed the same general lines as have those of the Bureau of Education.[100]

A precise measurement of the survey movement is difficult because the bureau's own surveys do not fully measure the extent to which it swept through American colleges and universities. Unknown scores, perhaps hundreds, of small or little-known colleges conducted their own internal surveys in an attempt to identify niche markets for themselves in this burgeoning national apparatus. Many institutions surveyed themselves several times as a means of gauging the extent to which prior survey recommendations were being successfully implemented. The bureau did attempt to compile a comprehensive list of

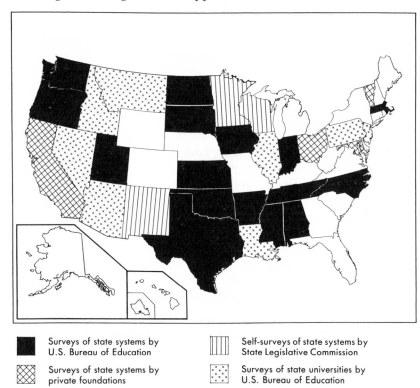

■ Surveys of state systems by U.S. Bureau of Education	▥ Self-surveys of state systems by State Legislative Commission
▨ Surveys of state systems by private foundations	⬚ Surveys of state universities by U.S. Bureau of Education

Fig. 4.1. The Survey Movement, 1914–1928

higher educational surveys at one point, but abandoned the project far short of its goal. The bureau's editorial staff concluded, "The list of such studies is increasing so rapidly and so many of them receive no circulation outside of the immediate campus vicinity that no adequate record or knowledge of this work exists anywhere."[101]

An exact assessment of the movement's impact is equally problematic. The bureau did not keep systematic records on which of its recommendations were actually adopted by institutions or state legislatures. Nevertheless, its one effort to collate the practical results of the survey movement in an internal 1928 document indicates that almost every survey was followed by some substantial change along the lines recommended.[102]

There is one study of indirect interest in this regard, undertaken by Jesse A. Bond in 1927. Bond's study was confined to an assessment of the impact of surveys at elementary and secondary schools. Yet, it does convey some general sense of the influence wielded by the survey movement, especially insofar as the administrative recommendations being made at this level were quite similar to those proposed at the university level. Bond sent a list of the major recommendations left by surveyors to each city where a school survey had been conducted. He found that 66 percent of the recommendations had already been adopted. Fourteen percent were "favored, but not yet completed." Another 7 percent were adopted with "major adjustments." Only 13 percent were actually thought "undesirable."[103]

Moreover, the bureau was able to report by 1928 that the merger of smaller private colleges with larger ones, and the formation of associated networks of public colleges, "had been effected in sufficiently scattered portions of the United States to indicate that a new method and form of organization" was "likely to be developed in higher education." It was noted that "higher education systems" were being constructed with one or two prestigious research universities at their core. One or more smaller colleges were then articulated around their periphery "to serve as feeders to advanced work."[104]

In this respect, the basic structure of a national ideological state apparatus was in place by 1929. It is probably best to conceptualize this apparatus as a decentralized network of federally coordinated, but formally independent institutions. At the polycentric core of this national apparatus, one finds several major research universities that were strategically located at key regional centers of economic activity and political power. The chief characteristic of these universities was that they were among the very few universities which awarded the Ph.D.[105]

In 1918, only forty-four universities, or about 8 percent of all four-year higher institutions, awarded Ph.D.'s in the United States. Sixty-one percent of these forty-four were private universities located mainly in the industrial Northeast and consisting precisely of those universities most closely and directly attached to the major northeastern financial groups. These private universities awarded 74 percent of all Ph.D.'s granted in the United States in 1918. Moreover, of the Ph.D.'s awarded by this group of private universities, two-thirds were granted by only five institutions: Harvard, Yale, Columbia, Cornell, and the University of Chicago.[106]

Similarly, one-half of all Ph.D.'s awarded by public universities were granted by only three institutions: the Universities of California, Illinois, and Wisconsin. Perhaps not coincidentally, California was reorganized as a consequence of a CFAT survey, while Illinois was the only institution surveyed by the USBE in that state. Wisconsin conducted its own survey because farmer-labor progressives were fearful of losing the state's higher educational autonomy. All three universities were among the only public institutions eventually admitted to the Carnegie pension system.

If these eight institutions are identified as the core of a national ideological state apparatus, then one finds that 1.5 percent of the four-year institutions in the United States awarded 63 percent of all Ph.D.'s granted in 1918.[107] A decade later, this pattern was essentially intact. The only difference was that more public universities had become prominent and had assumed positions at the core of the apparatus. Twelve universities, or about 1.7 percent of all four-year institutions in the United States, granted 65 percent of all Ph.D.'s awarded in 1928. The eight institutions listed for 1918 were all still present at the core of the apparatus. Johns Hopkins, as well the Universities of Iowa, Michigan, and Minnesota, took places at the core during this decade.[108]

Their presence at the center of the apparatus is linked not only to their participation in the survey movement, but also to their ability to tap directly into the reservoir of private national wealth. This capacity was also generally associated with local political ties to that class which exercised dominant control over wealth and income in an institution's regional social base. For instance, in 1918, the eight universities which dominated Ph.D. awards received more than 25 percent of all private benefactions given to higher education in that year.[109] In 1928, the twelve dominant institutions received 30 percent of all private benefactions to higher education.[110] The foundation strategy of perpendicular development, linked to the recommendations of the survey movement, constructed a core set of institutions that subsequently attracted disproportionate shares of private and public contributions to higher education. The peaks did get higher.

Thus, by the end of the 1920s, several tendencies had been set in motion that would shape the structure of American higher education in the coming decades. Individual institutions were developing into centralized corporate bureaucracies administered according to nationally standardized measurements of productivity and rates of return on investment. The entire educational enterprise was being restructured within these standards as a production process that was increasingly integrated into local or regional markets for labor, information, research, and professional expertise. This process was more and more a planned undertaking directed by the federal government. The construction of a national ideological state apparatus oriented toward solving the problems of capital infrastructure, capital accumulation, and political leadership within a capitalist democracy was well under way.

5

War and the Intellectuals: Building a Military-Academic Complex

IT HAS BEEN orthodox historiography for some time to regard World War I as a brief interruption in the development of the American university. Wartime precedents have been dismissed as fundamentally misleading events that played no significant role in the emergence of modern higher education.[1] More recent research is now suggesting, on the contrary, that World War I was actually a take-off point which accelerated existing tendencies, while institutionalizing these changes as permanent structures of the American university.[2] World War I was a unique window of opportunity, as Noble suggests, "to secure control over the entire higher education structure of the country, to coordinate it as never before, and to infuse it with the imperatives of corporate industry."[3]

The war generated an American ideology of national science that subsequently served as an ideological basis for reorienting the activities of intellectuals in two ways. The infusion of money, equipment, prestige, and political power which accompanied the intellectuals' participation in the war left them far more receptive to the principle of centrally administered, mission-oriented research. The principle of autonomy was therefore increasingly set aside for a concept of "public service."[4] Public service, however, was understood to mean the application of expert knowledge of "means" to achieving administrative goals—a national interest—that was defined by state executive elites. The national interest that emerged from World War I was a two-pronged attack on the problems of economic growth and national defense. Public service was institutionalized in research and manpower training programs that would promote capitalist economic development and in assigning intellectuals responsibility for defend-the American state against internal and external threats to its legitimacy.

HIGHER EDUCATION AND NATIONAL PREPAREDNESS

The American drift towards World War I was finally conceded by Woodrow Wilson and the Democratic Party when the demands of the national preparedness movement were met in 1916 by passage of a National Defense Act. The new law created a Council of National Defense (CND) with a civilian Advisory Commission to direct and coordinate the growing preparedness movement. By early 1917, however, the national preparedness movement was turning into a pro--allied war hysteria. Associations of bankers and businessmen, journalists, local politicians, military officers, the National Guard, farmers, and women voters (in that order) each successively demanded that America actively enter the war on the side of the Allies.[5] Finally, even the AFL national leadership, despite the union's official opposition to American participation in the war, declared that labor would support national preparedness and remain loyal in the event of war. In an atmosphere where all citizens were increasingly expected to declare their loyalty, the notable silence of leading educators and university intellectuals eventually led to cries that they prove their patriotism.

Nicholas Murray Butler was the first university president to respond to the challenge by thrusting Columbia University into the forefront of the national preparedness movement. On February 7, 1917, President Butler announced the appointment of a special university committee chaired by E. R. A. Seligman. Seligman was the notoriously conservative chair of Columbia's economics department.[6] The committee also included Frederick Keppell, university dean, and four Columbia scientists and engineers. It was charged with taking an inventory of the institution's human and physical resources. This inventory would then be used by the administration to develop proposals for a mobilization of the university in the event of a wartime emergency.[7]

The Columbia University board of trustees passed a resolution endorsing Butler's action a few days later and took the added step of offering the national government unrestricted use of the university laboratories and statistical department in case of war. On February 18, it was announced that in conjunction with the secretary of the navy, a comprehensive plan had already been formulated to nationalize temporarily "the entire resources" of Columbia University in a war emergency. Almost one hundred universities followed Columbia's lead over the next several weeks by offering their own plant and equipment to the national government.[8] The difficulty with these symbolic expressions of loyalty was that university administrators, with perhaps the single exception of Butler, had absolutely no idea of how to organize a college for warfare.

Federal agencies such as the War Department, the USBE, and the CND were flooded with requests from administrators and individual faculty members asking for national direction, guidelines, and policies. The USBE responded by distributing the "service form" developed by Columbia's inventory committee. That form provided a standardized procedure for colleges and universities to catalogue the national resources represented by their faculty, alumni, students, and physical plant. It was sent to every institution requesting advice on what actions would best contribute to national preparedness. Commissioner Claxton claimed that by the time the United States entered the war on April 6, 1917, the USBE had already "made a personnel index of the entire university body, perfected the internal organization of the universities, and established cooperative relations between the universities and the federal government."[9]

Official war planning policy, however, could come only from the Council of National Defense. Its civilian Advisory Commission eventually responded to requests for guidance on May 3, 1917, with the creation of a separate Committee on Engineering and Education (CEE). The committee's primary role was to develop policy guidelines and recommendations in engineering and education, while providing a central nexus of institutional coordination for college administrations and the national war planning agency (i.e., the CND). Hollis Godfrey of the Drexel Institute was appointed president of the committee. The committee itself was composed of eighteen prominent college and university presidents, two college deans (including Columbia's Frederick Keppel), and four government officials. Samuel P. Capen was appointed to the committee as a liaison between CEE and the USBE. A member of the Committee on Public Information (COPI), the government' s official war propaganda agency, was also appointed as a liaison member.[10]

Soon after America's declaration of war, Godfrey called an emergency conference of educational leaders in Washington, D.C., for May 5, 1917. Godfrey's goal was to establish "a medium of communication between the higher institutions and the departments of Government charged with the conduct of war." The conference was attended by about 150 representatives from the National Association of State

Universities, the Association of American Universities, the Association of American Agricultural Colleges, the Society for the Promotion of Engineering Education (SPEE), and a number of unaffiliated individual higher institutions.[11]

The first declaration of the emergency conference instructed all educators and institutional committees to direct any correspondence or other communication related to the war directly to CEE. Likewise, they were informed that henceforth all CND policy statements and answers to questions regarding the war effort would be channeled to them through CEE.[12] This declaration was followed by a five-point statement of principles that established the policy framework for government war policy in higher education for the duration of the conflict. These principles were that

1. Men below draft age (21) should continue in college.
2. Curricula and calendars should be modified to support the war.
3. Students in applied science should be allowed to complete training before being called into active service.
4. Military training should be given in all colleges with sufficient enrollment.
5. All communications from CEE should receive official government status and authority through issues of the USBE or USDA bulletins, circulars, etc.

In addition to these general principles, the emergency conference noted that the "sense of the meeting" was that "an educational responsibility rests on the institutions of higher learning to disseminate correct information concerning the issues involved in the war and to interpret its meaning." Additional meetings were therefore held on May 16 and May 26 "chiefly to discuss changes in curricula." The proposed changes were coordinated with the War Department's plans to broaden military training on campuses.[13]

The Bureau of Education publicized the results of these early meetings in a pamphlet entitled *Suggestions for the Conduct of Educational Institutions during the Continuance of the War.* In this pamphlet, Claxton informed colleges that specific measures were still being formulated within these policy guidelines but that in the meantime higher institutions should do two things: (1) keep students in college and (2) shift classroom instruction towards war issues, intensive engineering and technical professions, and chemistry, physics, biology, and "their practical application."[14] These recommendations received the official sanction of President Wilson on July 20, 1917, when Wilson wrote to the secretary of the interior that during the war "there will be a need for a larger number of persons expert in the various fields of applied science than ever before."[15]

This idea was ultimately the underlying thrust of war planning in higher education. Claxton emphasized in a letter to college faculty and administrators that "the war may yet resolve itself into a contest of engineering in the larger sense."[16] He explained that current surveys of colleges in foreign countries revealed that Germany was already more technically advanced than the Allies and still had an adequate supply of technical, scientific, and skilled workers. On the other hand, Allied countries had foolishly depleted their reserve of technicians and engineers by closing universities and sending all able-bodied men to the front as ordinary combat soldiers. Their technical workers were dying in trenches, and there were no students in the educational pipeline to replace them. As a result, "the supply of all the Allied Countries must come chiefly from the colleges, universities, and technical schools of the United States."[17] Claxton reiterated in a subsequent circular that "this is a war of engineers, of chemists, of physicists, of agriculturalists, of doctors, quite as much as of soldiers."[18]

Thus, the single most important contribution that higher institutions could make to the war effort was to keep students enrolled in classes and discourage them from enlisting in the military as ordinary combat soldiers. While specific measures were being formulated, the USBE devoted most of its energies during 1917 to a "stay in school" propaganda campaign. P. P. Claxton sent letters to all those even peripherally concerned with higher education to inform them that keeping the colleges fully enrolled was now a national war policy.[19] His letters were quickly followed up with similar communications from the secretary of the interior and the secretary of war. Copies of President Wilson's remarks were included in all of the letters.

This initial effort at war planning was actually quite successful. By the time the emergency conference reconvened on October 19–20, 1917, its statement of principles had been adopted as official government policy. Twenty percent of the institutions reporting had changed to a quarter system, as instructed, to accelerate training and graduation of students. ROTC had been expanded by the Army and Navy. Draft regulations were altered so that technical students could complete their collegiate training prior to active duty. Meanwhile, the Committee on Public Information (COPI) and the USBE had joined forces to create the National Historical Service Board (NHSB). The NHSB was assigned the task of rewriting social science and humanities curricula and of developing interdisciplinary "war issues" courses at colleges to help institutions meet their responsibility for interpreting the war correctly.

Once the general war mobilization was successfully under way, the proliferation of new institutions, functions, and policies led agency administrators to shift their attention temporarily to problems of internal administration and interoffice coordination. The USBE started to reorganize its internal procedures in early 1918. On January 31, 1918, Commissioner Claxton called a meeting of the bureau's specialists and division chiefs to serve as the agency "war council." The council's purpose was to develop a "comprehensive war plan" that would guide the bureau's internal operations within the context of broader policies originating with CEE and the CND. The first meeting resulted in a definition of the bureau's role in terms in terms of four projects: "1. the stay-in-school campaign (already underway), 2. propaganda and publicity (in conjunction with COPI)—*to receive priority*, 3. help others reach schools effectively, e.g., War Department, 4. redirecting all curriculum toward war issue."[20]

At a second meeting the following day, a smaller executive committee chaired by S. P. Capen was selected. At this meeting, the war council also asked Commissioner Claxton to issue "a very definite order as to [the] assignment of war work" following an internal bureau inventory of all "work on hand."[21] Documents in the bureau's files indicate that two inventories were actually conducted in compliance with this request. One was an inventory of "total work on hand by the bureau, that is, ongoing projects and routines. The other was a detailed breakdown of the distribution of this work among individual staff members and employees. Using this information, Claxton established priorities for all the projects in terms of their immediate relevance to the war effort. The memo he subsequently issued shows that by this time the war had become the one all-consuming activity of the bureau. All "non-war projects" were "postponed indefinitely" for the duration of the war.[22] After assigning priorities to the bureau's remaining projects, Claxton issued a twenty-seven-point "war plan" which itemized the specific tasks assigned to each member of the bureau staff.

Ten of these projects dealt with higher education. All but one of them was placed under the supervision of specialist Capen. The most important of these projects were centered on "the status of military training in the colleges," the use of college personnel and facilities "to teach the issues and purposes of the war," the war's effect on financial conditions in American higher education, and future problems in the postwar "readjustment" of colleges and universities.[23] Capen reported to CEE and the CND following this reorganization that he was now formally in charge of the bureau's war work in higher education and would report to them on the activities in progress.[24]

Shortly thereafter, Secretary of the Interior Franklin K. Lane called a meeting of government war planners from various agencies (at Claxton's request) to jointly formulate an administration-wide wartime education policy. Claxton's aim was to clarify the lines of authority between agencies, to coordinate related programs, and to insure continuing cooperation between agencies with overlapping jurisdictions. In early February 1918, several meetings were called that included representatives from the Departments of War, Navy, Agriculture, and Labor, and the U.S. Civil Service Commission. The result was a comprehensive wartime "education plan" that was approved and signed by the secretaries as a working document for these various departments. Although the plan mainly reiterated policies that were already in place, the document added that because of wartime resource shortages, "the schools should do everything possible to increase their efficiency."[25]

The administrative apparatus which finally emerged for the mobilization of higher educational resources during the war is illustrated in Figure 5.1. CEE acted as the central planning agency for higher education in its capacity as a specialized subcommittee of the CND's civilian Advisory Commission. Once CEE formulated its general goals for higher education, the locus of wartime activity shifted to the Bureau of Education, which possessed the information and inventories necessary for reformulating these goals into specific policies. These policies were then administered and implemented by several special committees, such as the National Historical Service Board and the Committee on Education and Special Training (CEST). The War Department exercised final authority in the administration of all technical and military programs, while the USBE and COPI oversaw propaganda and the restructuring of social science and humanities curricula in educational institutions.

Meanwhile, the war planning conferences called by Godfrey in May and October of 1917 had catalyzed a national organizing movement among the colleges and universities. The organizations and personnel represented at the earlier emergency conferences were joined in a January 1918 meeting by the NEA, the AAUP, the National Council on Education, the Association of Urban Universities, and the Catholic Education Association. At this conference, educational leaders decided that efficient wartime communication required more than the CEE nexus. It required a central institution capable of channelling these

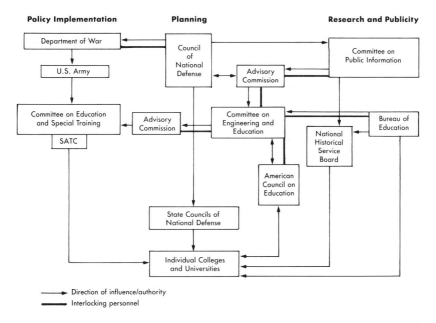

Fig. 5.1. Administrative Structure for Wartime Policy Coordination in U.S. Higher Education, 1917–1918

communications to the proper agencies. Thus, all of the major educational associations federated to establish the Emergency Council on Education (ECE) as their official liaison with national wartime administrative agencies.

The founding charter of the ECE declared its purpose "to place the educational resources of the country more completely at the service of the National Government and its departments."[26] A permanent headquarters was established in Washington, D.C., "where it could more easily serve as a mediating agency with the Federal Government in its effort to organize university resources for the war effort."[27] The ECE then called upon President Wilson "to take steps looking toward the immediate comprehensive mobilization of the educational forces of the nation for war purposes under centralized direction." Among the first resolutions passed by the new organization was a call for "increased scientific research for war purposes," a demand for "educational propaganda—lectures, pamphlets, etc.—to make clear the purposes of the war and maintain the morale of the people," and a request for instructions on a postwar "recasting of courses of study in light of the lessons of the war."[28]

By February 1918, the centralized command structure was in place.

The universities then demanded specific instructions. Government war planners finally initiated policies within this structure that clarified the role of universities and their expert personnel in terms of three support missions for corporations and the state. These were technical and professional manpower training for industry and the military, the conduct of mission-specific scientific research that was relevant to centrally designated problems of industrial or military innovation, and the development and promotion of an American ideology.

The first of these missions was implemented by the Student Army Training Corps (SATC) and the Committee on Education and Special Training. The organization of mission-oriented research was placed under the jurisdiction of the National Research Council (NRC). The formation and diffusion of an orthodox American ideology was carried out by the NHSB and USBE. All of these tasks were approached by war planners essentially as problems of human "engineering in the larger sense."

MILITARY-INDUSTRIAL MANPOWER TRAINING

The technical education of skilled and professional workers was a top priority for war planners because of its immediate relevance to wartime production and the deployment of troops. When the United States declared war on Germany, its regular army numbered fewer than 120,000 men. Yet, by the time of the signing of the armistice one and a half years later, the total number recruited was in excess of four million men.

The relationship between skilled manpower, industrial production, and modern warfare came to the attention of war planners with the first draft call in August 1917. The original Selective Service Law (passed May 18, 1917) had no provisions for exemptions. Consequently, when the first draft call for 687,000 men went into effect, the disruption of industry and agriculture was so severe that business and the military immediately moved to protect "essential industries" by modifying draft regulations.[29]

This task was first assigned to a Committee on Classification of Personnel (CCP) that was composed primarily of industrial psychologists, corporate personnel managers, and prominent business executives. The CCP identified military personnel needs by trade or profession, developed training specifications to be met by those filling these positions, and, in conjunction with the NRC Psychology Committee, proposed a method for rating individual personnel qualifications through widespread aptitude testing.[30] Eventually, some 9,586,000 registration cards were classified, so that it was possible to locate men with special skills and direct them to the appropriate units.[31]

In targeting these personnel needs, however, the CCP, discovered that estimates for trained technicians and skilled occupational personnel sent to them by various military units exceeded the supply available to the military by at least 200,000 men. It became quickly apparent "that the nation did not possess an adequate supply of technically skilled men to meet both the requirements of the military establishment and its essential supporting industries."[32] The War Department responded on February 10, 1918, with General Order 15, which created the Committee on Education and Special Training. CEST was directed "to study the needs of the various branches of the service for skilled men and technicians; to determine how such needs shall be met . . . to secure the cooperation of the educational institutions of the country and to represent the War Department in its relations with such institutions; to administer such plan of special training in colleges and schools as may be adopted."[33]

CEST was ready to implement a training program in only ten days. The secretary of war sent a letter to the presidents of educational institutions directing them to work through CEST on all problems related to technical training.[34] The CEST plan was to establish "vocational training detachments" at all technical schools with the requisite facilities. By early April, fifteen schools were under contract to begin training 6,000 men. Army officers were detailed to these institutions "to give the military training and maintain military discipline and routine" among the trainees.

The number of vocational detachments was increased every two weeks, until by July 1, 1918, there were 147 colleges and technical institutes training about 50,000 men. These institutions subsequently delivered about 25,000 trained technicians and workers to the Army each month. When the armistice was signed, more than 130,000 men had been trained, with 100,000 of these already delivered to the Army.[35]

A characteristically ambivalent cautionary note was sounded by the American Federation of Labor. The AFL National Executive Council's Committee on Education acknowledged "the urgent need for production, and the necessity of utilizing large numbers of so-called unskilled men" in skilled positions. The AFL grudgingly cooperated with CEST consonant with its promise of loyalty. However, the AFL Committee on Education warned its members, quite correctly, that CEST's "method of specialized training in a single operation, giving speed without adaptability or knowledge of the process as a whole, . . . is the general type of vocational training that many manufacturers attempted to introduce under peace conditions." The committee suggested—utimately without effect—that "organized labor should be on the alert to see that after the emergency is passed the system is not continued as an evil inheritance."[36]

CEST was soon called upon to assume similar functions in other areas of manpower training. Manpower shortages rapidly emerged in the higher technical professions such as engineering and in the available candidates for officer training camps. The Army Corps of Engineers estimated that "approximately six percent of the total force of a modern army had to be made up of engineer regiments." Similarly, the war industries that were now being "immediately stimulated" were the same industries "which chiefly demanded the services of engineers."[37]

The Corps concluded that by the spring of 1918, it would have to put 5,000 to 6,000 engineers into the field, along with additional technical support personnel, with the first 700,000 regular soldiers transported to Europe. Yet, the entire college class of 1917 included only 4,300 engineering graduates, and most of these were already, or soon would be, serving in the military. One-third of the engineers in the class of 1918 had already enlisted, while another 77 percent of engineering seniors and 40 percent of juniors; were classified "1a" (i.e., first draft call) for 1918.[38] Civilian industries had already encountered a shortage of engineers even before the war. Universities and businesses were thus also complaining that "it was becoming difficult to meet the industrial demand for engineers and chemists" because of the depletion of their already short supplies by military enlistments.[39]

There were similar shortages of professional officer candidates. The First Morrill Act had required land-grant colleges to offer military instruction because at the time of its passage in 1862, the Union Army had been suffering one defeat after another at the hands of Confederate troops. Many legislators attributed this to the military tradition prevalent in the southern academies and colleges, which made it possible for the South to mobilize rapidly a large cadre of professionally trained junior-grade field officers. Congressionally funded military training at the land-grant colleges was supposed to prevent a repeat of these early failures in any future wars. Congress had even authorized the Army to detail training officers to the campuses to direct instruction in military science and drill.[40]

By 1891, however, there were still no more than 7,400 students receiving military instruction of any kind. This number increased to

18,000 by 1900, but most of these students were still enrolled almost exclusively in the land-grant colleges, and the training and drills were generally considered silly by faculty and students. Few institutions, with the exception of Texas A&M, had ever taken the mandate for military training seriously. Many educators and students at the land-grant institutions considered military drill a threat to the democratic populist philosophy of the land-grant college. In fact, there had been occasional instances of student rioting in opposition to military drill at these institutions before World War I. The commissioner of education had reported in 1891 that "no department of instruction maintained by the [A&M] institutions . . . has been the subject of more criticism and adverse comment. . . . [There is a] widespread feeling of aversion . . . which while by no means confined to the farming element of their patronage, has certainly received its most frequent and open expression from that quarter."[41]

There is little doubt that military training on college campuses had been an unpopular and dismal failure.[42] The trend was reversed only in late 1915 and early 1916, when students at private eastern colleges and universities began circulating petitions demanding military instruction on their campuses. Bowdoin College launched the movement in Maine in the fall of 1915. As the national preparedness movement gained momentum in 1916, other campuses soon followed: Williams, Harvard, Princeton, Yale, Cornell, and Dartmouth (see Table 5.1).[43]

Congress answered the requests by expanding the Army's authority to offer military training on college campuses, creating the Reserve Officers Training Corps (ROTC) as part of the National Defense Act of 1916 (NDA). The War Department quickly called a conference in Washington, D.C., for October 17, 1916, to clarify details of the program with interested college administrators. Nineteen colleges and universities, including Harvard and Yale, were represented. In addition, the conference was attended by the secretary of war, General Leonard Woods (in charge of the Selective Service Office), the entire personnel of the Army War College, and other ranking officers.[44] The meeting resulted in formal recognition and substantive upgrading of the voluntary programs that most of the colleges in attendance had already established on their own initiative.

However, after the United States actually entered the war, it was discovered there would still be a shortage of 90,000 officers to command all the authorized units, despite the fact that in the intervening year the number of campuses offering ROTC had doubled.[45] Thus, while CEST was busy organizing vocational programs at the colleges, a

Table 5.1. Expansion of Military Training at American Universities, 1915–1917

Institution	Type of unit organized	Date	No. enrolled	Source of financing	Compulsory
Bowdoin College	Military Science/Drill	Fall 1915	—	College	No
University of Minnesota	Military Science/Drill	Fall 1915	—	College/War Dept.	Yes
Williams College	Infantry Battalion	Fall 1915	250	College	No
Yale University	Field Artillery	Fall 1916	—	College	No
Cornell University	Infantry Regiment	Fall 1916	2,000	War Dept.	Yes
University of Pittsburgh	Military Science/Drill	Fall 1916	—	War Dept.	Yes
Harvard University	Field Infantry	Spring 1916	1,200	College/War Dept.	No
Dartmouth College	Military Science	Spring 1916	—	College	No
Yale University	Infantry Regiment	Spring 1916	500	College/War Dept.	No
Yale University	Aerial Coast Patrol #1	Spring 1916	12	War Dept.	No
Harvard University	Aero Corps	Summer 1916	19	Aero Club of Am.	No
Princeton University	Military Science/Drill	Fall 1917	500	College	No
Columbia University	Aerial Coast Patrol	Spring 1917	125	War Dept.	No
Yale University	Aerial Coast Patrol #2	Spring 1917	20	War Dept.	No
University of Pa.	Aerial Coast Patrol	Spring 1917	—	War Dept.	No
CCNY	Military Science/Drill	Spring 1917	209	College	No
Lafayette College	Military Science/Drill	Spring 1917	—	War Dept.	No
New York University	Military Science/Drill	Spring 1917	—	War Dept.	Yes
Yale University	Aerial Coast Patrol #3	Spring 1917	8	Aero Club of Am.	No
CCNY	Aerial Coast Patrol	Spring 1917	—	War Dept.	No

Note: Chronological list by official date of organization.

special subcommittee of CEE mobilized the members of the ECE to lobby CEST for a program of military training which would keep not only engineers, but all other students on campus for higher technical or officer training.[46]

The CEST Advisory Board finally suggested the creation of a new cadet reserve corps in all collegiate-grade institutions. A proposal was submitted to the secretary of war recommending that military instruction be provided on all campuses, while students continued their regular studies. Cadets would then be drafted at age twenty-one when they graduated under the new quarter system. The secretary approved the program and soon issued a circular to the presidents of all higher institutions announcing that a new Student Army Training Corps (SATC) would begin operations in September 1918.[47]

Four officers from CEST were charged with administering the new program: Col. Robert I. Rees, General Staff Corps; Col. John H. Wigmore, Provost Marshall General's Office; Lt. Col. Grenville Clark, Adjutant General's Office; and Maj. William R. Orton, War Plans Division. The committee was assisted by a civilian advisory board which included James R. Angell, now president of the University of Chicago; Samuel P. Capen; James W. Dietz, electrical engineer and education director for Western Electric; Charles R. Mann, consulting engineer and consultant to CFAT on engineering education; Herman Schneider, a civil and railroad engineer and also dean of the College of Engineering at the University of Cincinnati; Hugh Frayne, president of the New York Federation of Labor and labor representative on the War Industries Board; and Raymond H. Pearson.

SATC was, in turn, placed under the direct regulatory authority of CEST, which created a special College Training Division to administer the program. R. C. MacClaurin, the president of MIT, was appointed director of the new division on July 17, 1918. MacClaurin immediately selected twelve "district directors" from among the more prominent college presidents. CEST and its College Training Division were ultimately subordinated to the Training and Instruction Branch, War Plans Division, of the General Staff, which all but placed the colleges within the direct command structure of the U.S. Army.[48]

CEST approved the actual details of the new program in May 1918. SATC was then formally authorized by the General Staff on June 28, 1918. The following day the adjutant general issued a circular to the presidents of all colleges and universities outlining the organization and regulations of the program.[49] Membership in SATC was voluntary for all male students eighteen through twenty years of age. However, individual university administrations had the authority to issue campus regulations making military training a compulsory part of the curriculum. The plan was to transfer SATC units out of the universities every three months as their members reached the age of twenty-one. Students studying medicine, chemistry, or engineering would remain on campus until their degrees were completed.[50] The U.S. government would pay each student's tuition and fees while he was enrolled in SATC and would provide him with lodging in the college barracks, board in the campus mess, uniforms, and thirty dollars per month in wages.[51] The War Department agreed to compensate the universities at a rate of one dollar per diem per student for subsistence and housing on campus.[52] The USBE ascertained through a follow-up survey that only 10 of 400 colleges responding to the call for SATC "raised the slightest objection to the plan, the objection in these cases being of secondary consideration."[53]

Voluntary enlistments in SATC were temporarily suspended when the Army announced its intentions to ask that Congress lower the draft age to eighteen. The Army had decided to mobilize two million men immediately. It was again brought to the Army's attention that a military force of this size would require 120,000 men in the Engineers Corps and at least 100,000 officers. Estimates were that no more than one-half this number could be secured through the regular draft. Consequently, the SATC authorization was amended on August 28, 1918, to place all SATC members on active duty rosters.[54] This meant students were now subject to direct military discipline independent of local college authorities. Colleges were now military camps under the command of the U.S. Army.

SATC units were organized at 525 collegiate and higher technical institutions (94% of all such institutions) by October 1, 1918.[55] Approximately 165,000 male students (74% of the total) enrolled in higher institutions were SATC recruits. Nearly 9,000 were actually transferred to central officer training camps before the armistice. Yet, after only two and a half months of operation, SATC was demobilized in December 1918 with the end of the war.[56]

MILITARY-INDUSTRIAL SCIENCE

A fairly clear division of scientific labor had already developed between universities, the national government, and industrial laboratories by the early twentieth century. University scientists were primarily interested in basic or pure research into the underlying laws and patterns governing natural and social processes. Industrial laboratories were primarily preoccupied with the development of new technologies and products. Most applied research took place in the various scientific bureaus of the federal government.[57] All of these investigations were conducted more or less independently and with very little interaction or coordination of purpose between them.

Prewar basic research was organized on an entrepreneurial model. It was conducted by university researchers in generally small scattered individual enterprises without external supervision. It centered on problems whose solution were mainly of interest only to other specialists in a particular research field.[58] On the other hand, industrial and technological development had usually been the result of "inspired inventors and talented tinkerers who were indifferent to science and the fundamental laws underlying their investigations."[59] For the most part, pure science and technological innovation were independent processes separated in location, intent, and social meaning.[60]

To the extent that applied research did occasionally supply a nexus between pure research and development prior to 1916, it came from the various federal bureaus operating under constitutional and statutory mandates to regulate standards and collect statistical data.[61] This research indirectly facilitated commerce, the standardization of products and processes, and occasionally the conversion of science into technology (but even then usually decades after the original research).

World War I resulted in a new set of institutional arrangements that more closely approximated the corporate ideal and that has aptly been described elsewhere as a national "state science."[62] The ideological and political leadership for this movement came from within the National Academy of Sciences (NAS) as part of the national preparedness movement in 1916. George Ellery Hale, director of the Carnegie Institution's Mount Wilson Observatory, and Robert A. Millikan, a professor of physics at the University of Chicago, had both been trying to revitalize the NAS and convert it from an honorary body into an institution that actively promoted scientific research within a national research agenda. They were also highly visible and staunchly pro-Allied, anti-German preparedness advocates.

Political sympathies were annexed to scientific and professional ambitions when Hale sponsored an NAS preparedness resolution that was passed in 1916. The resolution called on the NAS to form "a National Research Council, whose purpose shall be to bring into cooperation existing governmental, educational, industrial, and other research organizations" to facilitate national preparedness.[63] In a public letter dated July 25, 1916, Woodrow Wilson conferred quasi-governmental status on the NRC by agreeing to appoint representatives of various government bureaus as members.

The NRC held its first organizing meeting in September of 1916. Hale was elected chairman of the council and played a leading role in defining its basic principles with the support of other prominent figures and personal friends, such as Gano Dunn, president of the J. G. White Engineering Corporation; John J. Carty of AT&T; and Michael Pupin, a physicist. Collectively, they agreed upon three basic principles which guided the NRC's reorganization of scientific research.

The first principle constituted the foundations of an official NRC philosophy of science. It claimed that all research was similar in kind and differed only in the specific objects to be accomplished. Thus, there was a single and universal "scientific method" applicable to all research, whether it was pure, applied, or technological, and regardless of whether its object was natural or social. Any research not conforming to this method was by definition non-scientific.

Two additional principles defined an unofficial, but well-understood NRC methodology. The institutional aspect of this methodology emphasized "the value of cooperation" between all scientific researchers. The NRC accepted an institutional model of science patterned after the occasional cooperation between government bureaus and industrial laboratories. Its aim was to integrate basic university research into this organizational structure, routinize its relation to applied research, and thereby guarantee a regular stream of useful scientific discoveries that could be developed into products, technologies, and services.[64]

The final theoretical component of this new methodology was derived from industrial engineering. NRC elites promoted what was called a problem-solving approach. The NRC would establish a national hierarchy of research priorities or missions. These missions would be broken down into various projects which could be allocated to those teams of researchers best suited to carry out the projects successfully. The larger projects could then be broken down into a series of discreet problems to be solved by individual researchers at universities scattered throughout the country or working as part of a project research team.

The definition of the research missions rested with several appointive research committees in physical, mathematical, life, and behavioral sciences. Nevertheless, it was understood that funding for the NRC would be forthcoming only to the extent that it proposed missions to outside funding agencies that channelled research into useful lines of inquiry. Hale and his corporate colleagues on the NRC executive committee "clearly foresaw the coordination of science for industrial research as a postwar goal."[65] In fact, the NRC received its initial funding from the Engineering Foundation. This was followed by much larger grants from the Carnegie Corporation and Rockefeller Foundation.[66] The NRC could then redirect individual research through voluntary compliance by holding out opportunities for professional advancement, publication, and the prestige attached to research grants.

The NRC was provided with its first official research mission in February 1917, when the CND requested that it assume the task of organizing all "scientific investigation bearing on the national defense and on industries affected by the war."[67] The following year, Woodrow Wilson authorized the first federal grant of support, although more than half of its total funding continued to come from private sources. The NRC's leaders were extremely conscious that the war provided a unique opportunity to institutionalize their newly enhanced scientific status, as well as the opportunities it generated for funded research. They were equally conscious that any postwar continuation of these opportunities would depend on their present ability to be useful in the war effort. This would ultimately be measured "in the final analysis by its relations with the military," and this meant one thing: success "in the field of weapons research."[68]

There is no reason to believe that motivations to continue this attachment were merely cynical or purely self-interested. It is precisely the role of an ideology to conceal class interests behind a veil of public spiritedness and "national interest." The scientific, technological, and engineering successes of the war helped to consolidate the progressive claim that professional expertise in the service of democracy was essential to its survival in the modern world.[69] Amid national perceptions that America's new role was to make the world safe for democracy, scientists became its saviors insofar as they participated in the development of American military technology or the elimination of internally divisive social conflict. Indeed, the rush to public service was so great that Claxton recorded nearly one hundred colleges and universities which offered their plant and equipment to the government for military research during the first year of the war.

The NRC staff was quick to mobilize these campuses. After first conducting an inventory of scientific personnel and laboratory equipment, the NRC then determined which research projects would be allocated to individual universities or research teams. Under the NRC's general direction, major research universities and technical institutes were kept occupied with government work on military optics, ordnance, munitions, topography, food conservation, lethal gases, dyes, explosives, smoke screens, fuel substitutes, and submarine detection.[70] Virtually every field or discipline from physics to art (e.g., camouflage) could find some research task to perform in the interests of the war effort.

The military brain drain was so dramatic that the USBE reported "the withdrawal of the leading research scholars from the principal universities and colleges in order to carry on the research work of the Government." The withdrawal was so exhaustive that postgraduate and other research work was "practically eliminated" from most universities during the war. For instance, Harvard, Columbia, Chicago, and Michigan "lost nearly all of their leading professors of physics." The Universities of Pennsylvania and Cincinnati "suffered the loss of the greater part of their chemistry staffs."[71] The University of Wisconsin assured the USBE that "practically all scientific research has been directed into war channels." The University of Washington added an entirely new division "to furnish instruction in naval, military, and aeronautical science under the direction of government officers."[72]

THE AMERICAN IDEOLOGY

The militarization of science, its role in promoting corporate growth and efficiency, and its goal of socially efficient, functionally harmonious class relations became synonymous with public service. However, this imagery of the wartime scientist as a savior of democracy derived its plausibility from the idea that progressive democracy was threatened by foreign influences and subversion. Thus, an important part in the construction of an ideological state apparatus was the responsibility of humanists and social scientists in promoting a national consensus that could legitimate this symbolic imagery.

The major responsibility for this task during World War I was delegated to the National Historical Service Board. The NHSB was a group of historians from major universities and colleges called together on April 29, 1917, by the Carnegie Institute's director of the department of historical research. The group placed itself at the service of the national government and worked under the supervision of COPI and the USBE. In a span of one and a half years, the NHSB revolutionized American social science curriculum and made great strides toward standardizing its content as an American ideology.

NHSB wrote several pamphlets or "teachers' leaflets" which were printed and distributed by the USBE. These were utilized by professors, schoolteachers, newspapers, and innumerable private agencies promoting "education in patriotism."[73] Participants were again consciously aware that the undertaking was a radically new effort at engineering mass public consciousness toward a common end. The USBE was convinced that mobilizing public opinion was an integral component of modern warfare, equal in its importance to manpower training or technical innovation. Claxton suggested that the "success or failure of the Nation may turn very largely on the proportion of its citizens in whom the essential historic conception of their membership in a continuing community, more important than their own individual fortunes, has become a real motive force."[74]

Teachers at every level of education were informed by the Bureau of Education that they occupied a special role in the stabilization of public opinion. Educators were reminded in the first teachers' leaflet that history especially had a "power to help steady public opinion against superficial judgment."[75] This, it should be remembered, was in an environment where antiwar resistance, either on pacifist humanitarian grounds or because of ideological opposition to a squabble between imperialist powers, was resulting in mass demonstrations on the part of as many as a million people in New York City, including significant portions of the labor movement and most of the Socialist party.[76]

The first teachers' leaflet was careful to warn educators that using outright lies or false information was a "mistaken view of patriotic duty" that was likely to be counterproductive in the long run. Instead, it argued for the virtues of patriotic "interpretation" by emphasizing certain events as opposed to others, or by developing a moral theme, rather than a mere narrative presentation. The pamphlet observed that "history, properly studied or taught, is constantly reminding the individual of the larger life of the community. . . . This common life and the ideals which guide it have been built up through the sacrifice of individuals in the past, and it is only by such sacrifices in the present that this generation can do its part in the continuing life of the local community, the State, and the Nation."[77] The pamphlet went on to provide detailed suggestions on what to teach and how to teach history "properly" in the classroom. It urged teachers to stress the differences between Germany on the one hand, and France, Britain, and the United States on the other, as a conflict originating in the struggle between absolutism and democracy. This was a continuation of the same revolutionary struggle for liberty which America had initiated in 1776. If it had been America's manifest destiny to ignite the flames of democracy in the world and to carry democracy across a continent, it was now America's historical mission to come to the defense of democracy wherever it was threatened in the world. Moreover, the United States owed a particular historical debt to France for its own victory. This became the official state ideology for interpreting America's role in the world.

Teachers, professors, and journalists were charged with popularizing this viewpoint, although the leaflet was honest enough to acknowledge that some minor conflicts between the economic "interests and policies of the German Empire in the Western Hemisphere and in Asia" were "affecting those of the United States."[78] This was at least more subtle than the view of the Academy of Political Science, whose members adopted a resolution arguing that the World War should be used as a vehicle for "peaceful imperialistic expansion" into the Caribbean, Latin America, and Asia.[79]

The first teachers' leaflet left no aspect of the ideology to accident. It made recommendations on how to interpret and reinterpret events in ancient, medieval, and modern history—from Hammurabi (the origins of government by law) to Kaiser Wilhelm (its direct antithesis) to using the struggle between Sparta and Athens in the Peloponessian War as a historical metaphor for the present Great War. It even politely suggested that in teaching English history, the Teutonic elements of English civilization derived from the Saxon invasions should be deemphasized as relatively unimportant. This series of pamphlets subsequently provided official biographies of historical figures, course outlines, textbook recommendations, and other suggestions on how to interpret specific events in history.

The full-scale rewriting of history under state supervision not only facilitated a short-term justification of American participation in the war, but also helped to institutionalize a much broader and more permanent ideological conception of the United States in the social sciences and humanities. An entire network of propaganda agencies was set up to distribute this new consciousness through the universities, the government, the schools, and patriotic societies.[80] The NHSB maintained a steady correspondence with colleges and universities in an effort to "stimulate speaking and writing [by professors] of a kind calculated to educate public opinion."[81] COPI also "recruited the services of the best scholars in the fields of history, economics, and government," who, under the leadership of Dean Guy Stanard Ford of the University of Minnesota, prepared a "Red, White, and Blue Series" of popular monographs "on the background and issues of the war."[82]

Professors in economics, political science, philosophy, and history also worked with state and local branches of the CND to arrange public speaking engagements in order to "educate" the public about the official aims of the war and America's new role in the world. Speaking engagements were set up in public forums, guest visits to classrooms, evening adult education classes, extension courses, the meetings of private clubs or associations, labor unions, and wherever a public gathering could be found.

The SATC "war issues" course was another significant development in the formation of an American ideology. In April of 1918, CEST asked Dr. Frank Aydelotte to prepare a brief course on the "issues of the war." Aydelotte was a professor of English at MIT who also taught English to AT&T employees. He developed a course which was tested on a detachment of 250 men at Wentworth Institute in Boston during May 1918. According to a War Department report, "the work consisted of a series of discussions which endeavored to bring out the historical facts that led up to the declaration of war, the political and economic conditions that made the war necessary and differences in the social philosophies of the warring nations."[83] CEST found this experiment in propaganda so successful in raising war morale that arrangements were made in June to extend the war issues course to all detachments under CEST supervision. The new course was required for at least one hour per week of all men in CEST technical training and was extended to three hours for those enrolled in SATC. Individual schools and colleges assumed the burden of teaching the war issues course and, according to the War Department, "developed it with great success."

CEST did give the universities some general directions on how to conduct the course. Colleges were asked to report the name of the professor or professors who would be teaching the course for ongoing liaison. The course was to be designed as an interdisciplinary offering that included geography, government, history, economics, philosophy, and literature. It thus integrated the content of various liberal disciplines around a central theme—the American ideology. Materials for the course were distributed through COPI and similar sources, and CEST issued a brief bibliography containing the titles of works considered appropriate for the course.

CEST recommended that the course be collectively planned by a faculty committee representing the various disciplines under the direction of the college president. In a normal program the first three months were to be devoted to the historical and economic causes of the war. The next trimester would analyze the governments of the warring nations. The final trimester would analyze the "national characteristics and ideals" of the different countries. Each institution did this in its own way, but never as anything other than a variation on the official theme. A typical report, from the University of North Carolina, stated that its war issues course would clarify "American aims, purposes, ideals, etc." by emphasizing "the ideas of democracy." Dean Paul Boyd of the University of Kentucky was extremely pleased to report that even his arcane professors of German philosophy were contributing to the course by making "plain the roots of present day Teutonic madness" in the works of the great German philosophers.[84]

THE PERMANENT LEGACIES OF WARFARE

World War I did leave a permanent legacy, contrary to the assertions of some contemporary historians, by accelerating several movements in higher education that were already under way prior to 1917. The nationalization and standardization of university administration was one of the war's most obvious results. The necessity of conducting constant inventories of personnel and plant for national agencies hastened the diffusion of standardized measurements developed by the educational engineers. It promoted internal reorganization as an adaptation to national directives. One could recount innumerable examples of statements from engineers and foundation officials on the beneficial effects of the war on university administration. As a member of the CFAT executive committee, Nicholas Murray Butler was one of the first to recognize that "the war has distinctly helped us. . . . It has shortened by many years, perhaps by a generation, the path of progress to clearer, sounder, and more constructive thinking as to education, its processes, and its aims."[85] Similarly, George E. Vincent, president of the Rockefeller Foundation and a GEB member, noted in a speech before Yale alumni that the Great War had "opened the way" for continuing the curriculum and administrative reforms begun earlier.[86] He found that "sound business procedures" had made headway as a result of the war.

The war also deepened the fiscal crisis in American higher education and therefore set the stage for an explosion in the USBE survey movement during the 1920s. From 1916 to 1917, enrollments in American colleges and universities declined by almost 11 percent, as students left to enlist in the military, despite the stay-in-school campaign.[87] In many colleges, enrollment declines were as high as 20 to 50 percent of the student body. The result was a temporary decline in revenue ranging between 6 and 32 percent of projected budgets at individual institutions.[88] These problems were compounded when the Special Regulations of the SATC committed the War Department to pay only for those training costs incurred after October 1, 1918. This meant that most institutions had to absorb a substantial portion of the training costs incurred during World War I.

Many colleges and universities had incurred deficits and borrowed short-term money on the assurance of government SATC contracts which ultimately did not pay the full costs of the program. Furthermore, the War Department haggled over individual accounts for several months after the war, even while universities were still obligated to pay off loans. These problems were immediately made worse by a renewed postwar academic boom and postwar inflation that drove many institutions to the brink of bankruptcy. Pressed by financial exigencies, more and more institutions were receptive to business practices and corporate organization, so long as these moves promised efficiency and savings.

The war also drew higher institutions permanently closer to national politics. It accustomed many of them to the idea of looking to the national government for direction and policy initiatives. This corporatist arrangement was institutionalized when the Emergency Council on Education concluded at a meeting held in December 1918 that "there was continued need for such a central agency in order to unite the counsel of the several national education associations on numerous post-war problems." The American Council on Education was founded as a consequence and by 1920 had 16 constituent members (i.e., national education associations), 11 associate members (i.e., scientific or professional societies), and 120 individual institutional members.[89] ACE subsequently supplied an essential nexus for the integration of higher institutions into a genuinely national ideological state apparatus.

Samuel P. Capen, the USBE specialist in higher education, was elected ACE director in 1919. He was succeeded in 1925 by Charles R. Mann, the consulting engineer who had directed the CEST Education Section during World War I. Both directors played an important leading role by encouraging institutions to participate in the survey movement during the 1920s, to emphasize manpower training in curriculum reform, and to pursue designated industrial or state needs in scientific research.

The USBE assisted ACE and the NRC in these efforts by encouraging universities to convert their newly mobilized resources to the solution of peacetime social and economic problems. Thus, in addition to its

continuing survey work during the 1920s, the USBE led another movement to define a national agenda for public service by the universities.
Claxton's main priority for the bureau immediately following the war
was to continue the inventories, manpower planning, and labor needs
surveys during peacetime. The war had already led to an upsurge in
technical, engineering, and industrial-scientific work in the universities.[90] Claxton felt the bureau's main task was to facilitate the integration of this new work with the real needs of industry and government.[91]

Under the leadership of the USBE and ACE, a significant departure
was made in this direction when a special joint conference of industry
and higher institutions was held at the Drexel Institute on March 26–28,
1920. Representatives from over one hundred companies and colleges
attended, with the companies including AT&T, Eastman-Kodak, Standard Oil, United Gas Improvement, Du Pont, Goodyear, and many
other manufacturing, utility, mining, and paper milling companies
attached to the major financial groups. Claxton described the purpose
of the conference in a keynote address in simple and direct terms:
"Industry needs technically trained men. The higher institutions need
to know what kind of trained men are desired and in what numbers."[92]
The conference established a permanent "council of management education" composed exclusively of representatives from industry. The
industry council was designated as a "clearinghouse for all industrial
and educational matters in the country." Its main task was "to keep a
perpetual inventory of the educational needs of industry and the ability
of the colleges to meet these needs."[93] The council was ordered to
routinely cooperate with a newly created ACE committee on manpower.

ACE was charged with reviewing job specifications from the industry council and circulating them among colleges and universities. At
the first joint conference and at all subsequent ones held throughout
the 1920s, industry representatives submitted detailed requirements
for training business, executive, and technical personnel so that curriculum content and degree requirements could be adjusted to the needs
of a white-collar labor market. Industry and college administrators
worked together at these conferences to hammer out a clear national
division of labor in which individual universities would specialize in
"major lines" of curriculum relevant to the manpower needs of region-
ally or locally dominant industries.[94]

Government-oriented manpower training consisted primarily of a
reactivated ROTC program, with an expanded authorization to operate
at non-land-grant campuses. By January 1922, college ROTC units had

an enrollment of 57,419, approximately 14 percent of all male students. This was more than at any time in its previous history. ROTC remained compulsory at thirty-one state universities, twenty-seven land-grant colleges, and fourteen technical institutes. In 1925, 131 higher institutions were participating in the ROTC program, almost three times the prewar number.[95]

Similarly, as with so many of the war programs, a permanent pattern of cooperation between university scientists, industry, and the national government was also set in motion. Hale, Millikan, and others successfully lobbied Woodrow Wilson to declare the NRC a permanent auxiliary of the NAS with an Executive Order on May 11, 1918. Its wartime program of military and industrial research was replaced by an NRC Fellowship Program that was initiated by George E. Vincent. The Rockefeller Foundation, and later the Carnegie Corporation, funded fellowships that now provided university scholars with continuing opportunities for peacetime research, publication, and professional advancement.[96]

The institutional guarantee that research would be focused on appropriate or useful areas first involved the centralization of research funds and the allocation of research topics through the NRC. Individual scientists would be asked to submit proposals which were first judged on their scholarly merit by the peer review of a scientific elite selected on the basis of its prior accomplishments. This elite was generally already committed to the ideology of a national science. Private economic or state elites would play an "advisory" role in recommending areas of research and development which they thought were worthy of continued funding.

The first NRC advisory committee, established in 1918, included the presidents of AT&T, Phelps-Dodge, Eastman-Kodak, U.S. Steel, the Mellon Bank, Du Pont, GE, Warner-Swasey (founder of the Engineering Foundation), and Henry Pritchett of CFAT—all attached to major financial groups. Later, government appointees were vested with a veto over individual proposals. The net result was an institutional paradigm of national science structured under the hegemony of an "interlocking scientific directorate" in which the "same group of individuals encountered one another in slightly different combinations" on NRC committees, private foundations, and as trustees or faculty of recipient universities.[97] Henceforth, the national interest in science was understood to lay in discoveries that promoted economic development and technological innovation within the institutional, political, and social framework of advanced capitalist society.

Furthermore, as the progressive movement receded into prewar history, these institutional and social parameters were articulated by scientists such as Milikan at a high level of class consciousness. The elites of physical science especially began articulating a political component to the ideology of national science that was explicitly anti-socialist and anti-redistributive in its orientation to public policy. They successfully appealed to corporate and foundation elites for greater funding of basic and applied scientific research. Their appeals were frequently put forward on the grounds that a continual increase in the efficiency and technological level of production through scientific applications could raise the general standard of living for everyone, even within a highly unequal distribution of wealth.

NRC elites were convinced that a science-driven consumerism could ultimately undercut the source of class conflict and thus be a useful political ally to the corporation. A progressive science was offered as the corporate alternative to populism and socialism and took its place as a crucial element in the American ideology. This political vision of American science was developed throughout the 1920s with a high degree of formal precision at meetings of the NAS and other scientific societies. Indeed, by the coming of the Great Depression, most American scientists were vociferously anti–New Deal, and many were even advocating an engineering "Technocracy" of corporate and scientific elites as an alternative to liberal "democracy."[98]

As Noble points out, however, there was a well-understood "social problem" in containing these developments and their discontents within the implicit mandates of private property and the capitalist state. The natural scientists and engineers who dominated the NRC were equally convinced that proper empirical research combined with use of the scientific method would result in the discovery of social and cultural "laws." These laws could be employed to solve social and political problems in the same way that laws of physics could be employed, for instance, to discover methods of submarine detection.[99]

Beginning in June of 1919, the NRC made a concerted and conscious effort to address these problems by making a significant departure into the social sciences. The Engineering Foundation proposed to the NRC that it develop "a broad plan of investigation covering the whole question of personnel in industry." A new Committee on Industrial Personnel Research was set up under the direction of Samuel Capen, now the director of ACE, and Robert Yerkes, chairman of the NRC Anthropology and Psychology Division.

The new committee's definition of specific areas of study provides an excellent example of the precision with which national research agendas were being established by the various NRC committees in all fields. Among the items on its research agenda were

1. Finding the "causes of labor unrest and resultant excessive high turnover, low production, and high costs";
2. A study of the "physiological and pathological aspects of labor problems relative to health, efficiency, and productiveness in industry";
3. Continued "analysis, classification, and specification of industrial employments";
4. A determination of ways to overcome "misapprehensions and prejudices" of workers to capitalism;
5. Discovery of ways to counteract "similar industrial tendencies and fallacies" from becoming prevalent in the schools; and
6. A study of "the psychology and psychiatry of trouble-makers."[100]

This agenda was subsequently clarified and improved in meetings with major corporate leaders. It is of some interest that the committee and its corporate advisors apparently conspired to keep Samuel Gompers—a man who was always one step ahead of his union critics, but two steps behind his corporate opponents—out of the meetings until the agenda was a *fait accompli*. Individual research proposals, although submitted independently by scholars from around the country with a variety of individual motives (including mere scholarly interest), were ultimately judged and funded with reference to this national research agenda and their likelihood of producing results that might have practical applications in industry.

Individual scholars might have no interest in this agenda and might not share its motivation or values. Yet they could easily lend themselves to its purposes, while maintaining the subjective illusion of professional autonomy. Most scholars were probably not even aware that a national research agenda existed, except to the extent that professional interest led them to respond to indirect signals, such as what proposals were being funded, the kind of research being published, and the areas of inquiry that seemed to most interest professional scientific elites. A process of selection, professional advancement, and self-selection could therefore build, reinforce, and perpetuate the content of an ideological apparatus, even while scholars maintained their subjective delusions of autonomy. The ideological character of national science did not reside in the subjective intentions of any particular scholar, but in the institutional structure which directed that activity.

The next significant step toward converting the social sciences and humanities into forms of industrial, social, and political engineering was the creation of the Social Science Research Council (SSRC) as an adjunct of the NRC. The SSRC was a brainchild of Beardsley Ruml, director of the Laura Spelman Rockefeller Memorial. Ruml was a psychologist who specialized in mental testing and wanted an institutional vehicle to promote empirically oriented social science against the traditional historical and philosophical approaches which he thought were too polemical and explicitly "political."

Under Ruml's leadership, the SSRC was funded by the private foundations with a mandate to define and support a "behavioral research" agenda. Supported research was supposed to be empirical and statistical, particularly in the fields of sociology, economics, and political science. It was also expected that the results of any funded research would be able assist public or private authorities in the resolution of social problems and, hence, raise social science to the same level of technical and engineering success as the physical and mechanical sciences.

The University of Chicago was initially designated as the SSRC's showcase institution. Funds were later disbursed to other campuses for fellowships and training in the new empirical methods, for the development of courses in statistics and methodological techniques, and general department-building along the Chicago model.[101] The foundations worked in a similar manner to provide fellowships through the American Council on Education and the American Council of Learned Societies (founded in 1919).

Finally, the emergency atmosphere of war promoted one other change in the instrumental order of American pedagogy. The war's emphasis on "training" as opposed to "education," on the rapid acquisition of vocational skills, on problem-solving, on the mobilization of national consensus, and on the enforced regimen of sciences regarded as subdisciplines of engineering, all involved changes in the forms of pedagogy as well as its content and aims. The result was a militarized pedagogical order which emphasized the memorization of facts, preparation for aptitude tests, and acceptance of the results of these tests as indisputable, authoritative orders. While the university had pledged itself to make the world safe for democracy, it institutionalized the competing imagery of a militarized wartime production unit.

The war accelerated each of these tendencies by promoting a forced march through the university by students and by encouraging faculty to replace student oral presentations and discussion with large-scale dogmatic lectures that were periodically followed by standardized tests. P. P. Claxton observed in his annual report for 1918 that "a study of the new curricula" made it evident that "new and intensive methods of study and recitation will be adopted." He was pleased that "under the inspiring stimulus of war aims" students were acquiring "a spirit of concentration and scholarship seldom if ever equalled" in American higher education. On the other hand, Claxton concluded, there would henceforth "be little if any chance for genuine reflective or productive thinking" in American colleges.[102]

6

Is Anything to Be Done? The Intellectual as a Proletarianized Professional

THE ADOPTION of a corporate administrative ideal shifted managerial concerns onto items which hitherto had been regarded as peripheral conditions for the possibility of a university. The industrialization of American universities brought these conditions into focus as the standards for judging an institution's educational success. As Veblen observed, the industrialization of higher education had an "immediate and ubiquitous effect" on campuses. It led administrators to concentrate on "the tactful and effectual showing of efficiency reflected in an uninterrupted growth in size and other tangible quantitative features" of the campus.[1]

Among the most significant of these new measures were the following: (1) teacher productivity as measured by class size, student-teacher ratios, and numbers of publications; (2) educational capital gains such as buildings, grounds, and size of libraries and laboratories; and (3) educational output, in terms of the number of degrees conferred and the unit cost of awarding each degree. The industrialization of American universities consequently resulted in a concept of academic prestige that was measured through the productivity of an institution's labor force (i.e., faculty), its capital (i.e., plant), and its market share (i.e., enrollment).

THE PROLETARIANIZATION OF AMERICAN INTELLECTUALS

The practical result of this orientation was a two-pronged administrative emphasis on reducing labor costs and increasing the fixed or

154

Table 6.1. Average Dollar Value of Fixed Educational Capital per
        Student, 1890–1930

Year	Ave. dollar value[a]	Rate of increase
1890	$ 542	
1900	986	82%
1910	1,215	23
1920	1,239	2
1930	3,376	172

Sources: USBE, *Biennial Survey of Education, 1918–1920* (Washington, D.C.: GPO, 1923), p. 285; ibid., *1928–1930* (Washington,
D.C.: GPO, 1932), pp. 325, 337.
        [a]Includes buildings, grounds, libraries, and scientific apparatus.

constant capital of the educational enterprise. The university was thus
steadily transformed from a traditionally labor-intensive undertaking
into a capital-intensive industry that was subject, in this respect, to the
economic imperatives of corporate enterprise in advanced capitalist
society.[2] Table 6.1 illustrates the tendency towards capital intensity
from 1890 to 1930.

The levels of fixed capital necessary for educating students continually increased during this period. It rose in real terms during most
decades, including the highly inflationary 1920s. As capital expenditures became a fixed cost, necessary if colleges were to compete effectively in the educational market, the corporate imperative of measuring
efficiency in terms of marginal costs placed college administrators
under pressure from trustees and legislators to contain the costs of
"variable capital," primarily labor. Therefore, when the higher educational survey movement began in 1913–1914, the overriding emphasis
of the surveys was on the relative containment of faculty salaries
through higher rates of productivity.

Faculty salaries, at the time, were still the largest item in college and
university budgets. Consequently, relative reductions in labor costs
promised the greatest potential for improvements in educational efficiency. Unfortunately, the USBE did not collect comprehensive itemized figures on college expenditures until 1930. Nevertheless, it did
publicize the results of some of the first surveys which are at least
illustrative. The CCNY self-survey revealed that in its 1914 and 1915
budgets about 75 percent of all expenditures were for teaching, 14
percent for operations and maintenance, and 11 percent for administration. Ninety-five percent of all teaching expenditures or seventy-
two percent of the total budget were for instructional salaries.[3]

Raymond M. Hughes was the first nationally prominent administrator to address faculty productivity as an issue with his own survey of Miami University. In his pathbreaking study of costs at Miami, Hughes had made an important modification to Cooke's original calculus by completely excluding capital expenditures from his measurement of per capita instructional costs precisely on the methodological assumption that these costs were fixed and not subject to reductions.[4] Thus, he instead focused exclusively on faculty efficiency.

Hughes defined the variable per capita cost of instruction as a function of the number of student hours per instructor divided by salary costs. Hughes proposed that a faculty member could reasonably be expected to teach twenty-five students for a total of eleven hours per week. This made 275 student hours per week a "fair" workload. However, Hughes's survey found that the real average workload at his own university was only 214 student hours per week, or 22 percent below the optimum rate of teaching productivity. Evidence collected during his tour of other universities led him to conclude that such inefficiency was typical of higher institutions throughout the United States.

Similarly, Hughes calculated that the total cost of instruction per student year should be $91.77 if the optimum rate of work was enforced on faculty members. The actual cost, he discovered, was $140.00 or 53 percent higher than the optimum levels of teaching efficiency. The relationship between work loads, labor costs, and total budget expenditures was clear to Hughes. Thus, at a regional meeting of his colleagues in 1914, Hughes was already recommending the centralized formulation of teaching schedules, a reorganization of curriculum that emphasized the most efficient areas of instruction, and abandoning the seniority system in favor of salary schedules based on individual productivity.[5]

Hughes received strong support for his reform program from a board of trustees dominated by local Ohio businessmen. Trustees set the ideal class size at twenty students under Hughes's leadership. Hughes found that in 1915 only one-third of the total hours of instruction were actually given in classes with twenty or more students. The following year, Hughes increased that proportion to 62 percent. The proportion of instructional hours devoted to classes of fewer than ten students was reduced from 25 to 15 percent.[6]

As one would expect, total workloads increased substantially between the 1913–14 academic year and 1915–16 (see Table 6.2). Miami professors' average weekly workload increased by more than 17 percent in only two years. Nevertheless, Hollis Godfrey's 1914 survey of Drexel Institute argued that academic productivity could actually be

Table 6.2. Faculty Workloads at Miami University, Fall Terms 1913–1915

Year	Total student-clock hours	Weekly avg. student-clock hours per instructor
1913/14	5,364	214
1914/15	6,236	234
1915/16	7,323	251

Source: USBE, *Recent Movements in University Administration*, Bulletin, 1916, no. 46, (Washington, D.C.: GPO, 1917), p. 32.

increased further than Hughes had dared to suggest. Godfrey found that his faculty members were already reporting an average teaching load of 320 student-clock hours of instruction per week.[7]

The two surveys formed a base from which the USBE launched its national survey movement from 1914 to 1919 by surveying the public higher institutions of Washington, Oregon, Iowa, North Dakota, South Dakota, and Alabama. These initial reports, two of which were published and widely distributed,[8] were used to set a social average of efficiency as the national baseline from which to judge individual institutions throughout the country. The USBE surveys recommended that in lecture courses the only limit on class size should be "as many as may see and hear the professor."[9] Twenty to thirty students were recommended as the optimum number for recitation and discussion classes.

The USBE reports concluded that 300 student-clock hours was the statistically optimum weekly teaching load for professors at teaching colleges (i.e., twelve hours or four classes with twenty-five students each). The optimum workload for professors at research universities was set at 250 student-clock hours (i.e., ten hours or three regular classes plus labs of twenty-five students each). By the conclusion of the Alabama survey in 1919, the USBE was recommending that salary costs per student-clock hour should not exceed an institutional average of seventeen and one-half cents.[10]

The concept of major and service lines was also constructed with reference to the possibility that greater returns on social investment were possible when curriculum and research articulated with local industrial needs. Likewise, it promised economies of scale within the university. The results of the North Dakota survey made this possibility strikingly obvious (see Table 6.3). At the eight colleges surveyed in North Dakota, almost 72 percent of total instructional expenditures were on classes smaller than the USBE's recommended enrollment of twenty students. Similar findings elsewhere led the USBE to consis-

Table 6.3. Instructional Expenditures Relative to Class
Size at Eight Higher Institutions in North
Dakota, 1916

Class size (no. of students)	% of total instructional costs
1–9	42.1
10–19	29.5
20–29	18.3
30–39	5.8
40–49	2.9
≥ 50	1.2

Source: USBE, *Recent Movements in University Administration*, p. 29.

tently recommend the elimination of "small classes and the resultant excessive cost of instruction" incurred through them.[11]

All of these surveys emphasized that most colleges and universities were operating well below their optimum rates of productivity. However, the inefficiencies were not evenly distributed within the universities. The data shown in Table 6.4 revealed that teaching loads and class size could be substantially increased in nearly all fields relative to

Table 6.4. Percentage of Disciplines Operating at USBE Optimum Levels of Educational Productivity in Three Institutions, 1914–1915

	Depts. at or above 300 student-clock hours per instructor		Depts. at or above 250 student-clock hours per instructor	
	Fall Term	Spring Term	Fall Term	Spring Term
University of Iowa				
Liberal arts	27%	36%	55%	55%
Natural sciences	38	25	50	50
Iowa State A&M				
Liberal arts	14	43	29	43
Natural sciences	33	56	56	61
Engineering	75	75	75	75
University of Washington				
Liberal arts	29	21	64	57
Liberal professions	43	57	86	71
Natural sciences	78	67	100	100
Engineering	100	100	100	100

Sources: Figures compiled from data in USBE, *State Survey of Higher Educational Institutions of Iowa* (Washington, D.C.: GPO, 1916), Bulletin, 1916, no. 19, pp. 121–22; Samuel P. Capen, *A Survey of Educational Institutions in the State of Washington*, USBE Bulletin, 1916, no. 26 (Washington, D.C.: GPO, 1916), pp. 191–96.

Table 6.5. Average Instructional Cost per Student for Different Fields of
Study in Three Institutions, 1914–1915

	Fall term	Spring term
University of Iowa		
Liberal arts	$4.24	$4.44
Natural sciences	$3.45	$4.01
Iowa State A&M		
Liberal arts	$3.40	$3.51
Natural sciences	$2.54	$2.16
Engineering	$2.08	$2.11
University of Washington		
Liberal arts	$3.19	$3.36
Liberal professions	$2.76	$3.08
Natural science	$1.75	$2.12
Engineering	$2.62	$2.65

Sources: See Table 6.4.

the social averages established by the USBE. Yet, the liberal arts were
clearly the least efficient areas of investment, not only in terms of direct
economic returns on capital, but also in terms of educational productivity. The classics and the humanities were the least efficient of the liberal
arts (i.e., relative to the new social sciences).

A very quick way to realize increases in academic productivity was to
cut or phase out instruction in Greek, Latin, and classical literature
from all but a few select universities, where they could be concentrated
and taught efficiently through economies of scale. At the other end of
the spectrum, engineering classes emerged as a model of classroom
efficiency. The micro-economic viewpoint of a good business manager
made it inevitable that administrators would eventually draw certain
obvious conclusions. An efficient educational policy required them to
reallocate internal resources towards the most efficient areas of production (engineering), to restructure or consolidate some fields (social and
natural sciences), and to abandon unprofitable lines of production (see
Table 6.5).

Every academic field was thus subjected to additional structural
pressures (aside from those of the NRC) to become an ancillary of the
engineering discipline, by adopting not only its research methods but
also its teaching techniques and evaluative standards. The goal was to
produce equally quantifiable returns on social investment. The internal
administrative structure of the American university hence reinforced
the voluntary accommodation of natural science to industrial and military engineering, while increasing pressures on the social sciences and
the humanities to make similar adjustments.

A. Lawrence Lowell, the president of Harvard University and a prominent CFAT trustee, gave an instructive address to a joint national convention of the American Political Science Association and American Historical Association. Lowell was asked to explain why historians and political scientists were not consulted for advice as often as engineers or natural scientists. His answer was that they had failed to adopt any approximation of "the scientific method" and did not study the "real physiology of politics." Anyone willing to make the necessary adjustments, he suggested, would receive greater material rewards within the university, more money for research, greater opportunities for professional advancement, and enhanced prestige among nonacademic elites.[12]

The USBE was well aware of the disequilibrium between the various academic fields. It was even somewhat sympathetic to claims by social scientists and humanists that the new methods of administration distorted the measurement of educational success in these fields, where small nonlecture formats were often a more appropriate and effective instructional technique. A similar problem was that a costs-benefits analysis of educational investment could not really quantify the return on a good citizen or an intelligent leader in the way it could measure the return on a better laborer in terms of increased earnings or productivity.

Capen was apparently concerned enough to ask Leonard V. Koos, a professor at the University of Minnesota, to devise a method for adjusting administrative calculations of efficiency to account for the special needs, methods, and aims of different fields. Koos devised a method for adjusting teaching loads away from the social average by incorporating standardized differences for type of instruction, level of instruction, usual class size, and subject matter. The USBE published and distributed this revision of the CFAT methodology in 1919.[13]

Koos's adjustment calculations proved so difficult that his method was quickly dropped by everyone who tried to use it. A 1925 study of the Colorado State Teachers' College noted the method had been "too bulky" to prove useful.[14] Legislators, trustees, and university administrators under the immediate exigencies of a fiscal crisis used what methods and data were available and made the necessary financial adjustments. Consequently the generalized work speed-up being promoted by the survey movement fell with disproportionate weight on the humanities and social sciences, while the enhanced rewards of internal reallocation and corporate largess went to the natural and engineering sciences and to such social scientists as were willing to append themselves to the engineers.

The upward trend in faculty-student ratios and degrees awarded

Table 6.6. Student-Faculty Ratio in U.S. Higher Institutions, 1900–1930 (national average)

Year	No. of students	No. of faculty	Ratio
1900	197,163	18,220	11:1
1910	274,084	24,667	11:1
1920	521,754	42,882	12:1
1930	971,584	71,722	14:1

Sources: Tabulated from data in USBE, *Biennial Survey of Education, 1918–1920,* pp. 6–7; ibid., *1928–1930,* pp. 332, 334.

during the survey movement can also be used as rough indicators of the national trend toward higher rates of academic productivity. The figures suggest that a significant increase in productivity was achieved throughout the country. Table 6.6 indicates that the average faculty-student ratio increased by 27 percent in the two decades from 1910 to 1930. The work speed-up was most dramatic during and following World War I, when many faculty members assumed the burden of larger class loads to compensate for faculty on leaves of absence for special war activities and research. The postwar explosion in college enrollments, combined with the postwar fiscal crisis in education (especially the need for capital expansion), led most colleges to simply maintain the wartime workloads as an efficiency measure.

The number of degrees conferred (i.e., product output) per faculty member also indicates an intensification of the intellectual labor process during the same period. Faculty output of educated manpower increased by 72 percent between 1920 and 1930 (see Table 6.7). There is an empirical basis on which to suggest that labor costs, as a percentage of total higher educational expenditures, did decrease during this time as a result of increases in productivity. Since the USBE did not start

Table 6.7. Ratio of Faculty to Degrees Conferred in U.S. Higher Institutions, 1900–1930 (national average)

Year	Degrees conferred	Degrees conferred per faculty member	Rate of increase
1900	16,314	0.66:1	
1910	25,618	1.04:1	58%
1920	52,179	1.22:1	17%
1930	128,243	1.79:1	72%

Sources: USBE, *Biennial Survey of Education, 1918–1920,* pp. 6–8; ibid., *1928–1930,* pp. 332, 334.

Table 6.8. Percentage Distribution of Higher Education Expenditures, CCNY, 1915, and Nationwide, 1930

Item	CCNY, 1915	National, 1930	Change
Teaching	75.1	67.0	−8.1%
Plant/maintenance	13.9	20.4	+6.5%
Administration	11.0	12.6	+1.6%
Total	100.0	100.0	

Sources: USBE, *Biennial Survey of Education, 1928–1930*, p. 539; USBE, *Recent Movements in University Administration*, p. 32.

Note: For comparability the 1930 figures have been adjusted to include only those items also included in the 1915 CCNY budget. Thus, under "teaching," I have included both library and instructional costs. "Plant/maintenance" includes capital expenditures on new equipment.

Figures on the expenditures of three colleges in Iowa and two colleges in Washington are also available for 1915; however, the aggregate classifications used in these USBE surveys do not allow one to separate particular items and accurately compare them to the other figures available.

collecting national statistics on expenditures until the biennial survey of 1928–30, any definitive longitudinal comparison is currently impossible. However, if one compares the 1915 CCNY budget to the national figures for 1930, there is at least some reason to believe that relative instructional costs decreased during the survey movement (see Table 6.8). To the degree that such a comparison is meaningful, it is reasonable to conclude that educational resources were reallocated in real terms from labor to capital.

Consonant with this thesis is the relative as well as absolute decline in economic status experienced by intellectuals during the same period.[15] Even though higher educational expenditures rose at a rate far in excess of inflation between 1910 and 1930 (see Table 6.9), only a small proportion of these increases went toward salary and labor costs: total higher educational expenditures increased by 172 percent between 1910 and 1920, but professors received raises during this decade of no more than 10 percent. The following decade, when total higher educational expenditures rose by 163 percent, they received raises of 20 to 30 percent. Moreover, the enforced gains in productivity, whether measured by teaching loads or degrees conferred, proportionally exceeded pay increases, particularly during the 1920s.

There is substantial evidence to demonstrate that while capital expenditures outpaced inflation in real terms, salary expenditures lagged far behind inflation. The net result was an absolute decline in economic status for most college professors in the period under consideration.

Table 6.9. Total Receipts of U.S. Colleges and Universities, 1910–1930

Year	Total	Increase
1910	$ 88,369,734	
1920	$240,141,994	+172%
1930	$631,130,377	+173%

Sources: USBE, *Biennial Survey of Education, 1918–1920*, p. 285; ibid., *1928–1930*, p. 335.

For instance, an AAUP study found that during the period from 1910 to 1919, the cost of living in the United States increased between 40 and 70 percent "by the most moderate estimates." The average salary increment for professors during the same time was only ten percent.[16] A similar study published by *School and Society* in 1920 produced similar findings. It found that from 1912 to 1919 the salaries of full professors had increased by less than 7 percent, those of assistant professors by about 10 percent.[17] Indeed, a more recent analysis of the salaries at large state universities indicates that average pay for all professorial ranks reached its peak in 1908. Professors' real economic status declined by 33 to 37 percent between that year and 1919–20.[18]

Following World War I, a USBE survey found that faculty agitation over economic status was becoming so marked that 60 percent of American colleges and universities voted pay increases of 10 to 20 percent in 1918–19.[19] Nevertheless, faculty discontent continued to simmer. The AAUP voiced the collective dissatisfaction of American faculties with a declaration that the "generous" increases of 1919 did not offset "an increase in the price of necessaries of forty to seventy percent" during the previous decade. The organization well understood that the professor's "actual compensation—his real wage—has decreased."[20]

Another study published by the AAUP in 1929 claimed the same trend had continued during the following decade. Faculty pay increases were quite dramatic during the 1920s, but a Bureau of Labor Statistics cost of living index indicated a 70 percent inflation during the same period. Thus, the AAUP argued that professors, even at the most prestigious universities such as Yale, had suffered a further real decline of 12 percent in standards of living.[21] The evidence for this decade is the subject of continuing dispute among scholars, but even under the best possible scenario yet offered, real salaries only returned to 1908 levels by the end of the 1920s and then renewed their decline for the next quarter century.[22]

Yet, even if real salaries did return to earlier levels during the 1920s, this trend was set against even more dramatic relative shifts in social status within the university and relative to external occupations.[23] For instance, in the five years from 1922 through 1926 inclusive, the salaries of college presidents at land-grant colleges rose by an average of more than 33 percent. Deans' salaries rose on average by more than 13 percent during the same period. Faculty salaries registered an overall increase of only 9 percent.[24] The growing dichotomy between faculty and administration was compounded by a widening inequality of income and social status within the university. Administration was rewarded more than education, management more than labor.

The professors' condition deteriorated even more rapidly in comparison to the other "learned professions" by which university intellectuals had traditionally judged their own relative social status. According to an estimate by C. C. Bowman, the average faculty salary for all professorial ranks in 1893 was 75 percent higher than a minister's or clerk's salary, and quintuple that of elementary and secondary school teachers.[25] By 1920, the average salary paid to a male public school teacher was equivalent to that of an associate professor.[26] Elementary school teachers made real gains of 31 percent between 1904 and 1929, in comparison to the most optimistic scenario, which sees no real gains for professorial salaries across the same three decades.[27]

Under the best circumstances, there was a reduction of income differentials and in the distinctions of lifestyle which income made possible. In comparison to Bowman's figures, the study by Ruml and Tickton indicates that associate professors were making about 42 percent more in real terms than elementary school teachers in 1904 and 31 percent more by 1929. They were making 59 percent more than railroad clerks in 1904 and 53 percent more by 1929.

While the lower-middle class gained on American professors, professors simultaneously lost ground to the emerging business professions. A study by the American Association for the Advancement of Science found in 1929 that the average maximum salary a professor could ever hope to earn in the United States was no more than that paid to an "average salesman" or a factory shop foreman.[28] Railroad executive officials widened the existing salary gap between themselves and university intellectuals: their salaries went from 46 percent higher than an associate professor's salary in 1904 to 56 percent higher in 1929.[29] There is little doubt that professors' position on scales of American social stratification deteriorated, as represented by income, in relation to the new middle classes.

The absolute and relative decline in the intellectuals' status was

Table 6.10. Index of Union Wage Rates, 1913–1926

Year	Wage index
1913	100.0
1914	101.6
1915	102.3
1916	106.2
1917	112.4
1918	129.6
1919	147.8
1920	188.5
1921	193.3
1922	183.0
1923	198.6
1924	214.3
1925	222.3
1926	233.4

Source: U.S. Bureau of Labor Statistics, *Union Scale of Wages and Hours of Labor,* Bulletin no. 431, May 15, 1926.
Note: Table shows nominal wage increases from base year 1913.

perhaps exaggerated by the even more dramatic rise in the status of organized labor. The rapid economic, social, and political gains being made by the working class often prompted comparisons between the intellectuals and the industrial proletariat. As early as 1898, professors sporadically complained of being "on a par financially with conductors, machinists, foremen of works, and other occupations of like grade."[30] During the next three decades, these complaints continued to escalate in newspapers, scholarly journals, meetings of professional associations, and popular magazines. Progressive university presidents such as Jacob Gould Schurman of Cornell began warning trustees of an impending danger in "paying to their professors salaries smaller than the wages received by carpenters, mechanics, and trainmen."[31] By 1920, the commissioner of education was warning that "salaries of college professors and instructors have not only fallen far below those paid in many other professions, but they have been reduced to a level even below the average wage received by many mechanics and tradesmen."[32]

This perception was largely confirmed in 1926 when the U.S. Bureau of Labor Statistics (BLS) published a report on union wage scales in the United States.[33] The BLS report circulated widely among educators, businessmen, trustees, and legislators through a variety of published sources, including USBE bulletins and circulars. In fact, the USBE immediately used the BLS report as the basis for publishing a com-

Table 6.11. Index of Salaries in Higher Education Compared with Union Wage Rates,
          1922–1926

Year	Pres.	Dean	Prof.	Assoc. prof.	Asst. prof.	All trades
1922	100.0	100.0	100.0	100.0	100.0	100.0
1923	100.7	100.7	106.0	101.8	103.4	108.5
1924	106.6	104.2	106.0	105.5	103.4	117.1
1925	120.0	104.2	109.1	103.7	107.7	121.5
1926	133.3	113.4	109.1	105.5	107.7	127.5

Source: USBE, *Land-Grant Colleges, 1926*, Bulletin, 1927, no. 37, (Washington, D.C.:
GPO, 1927), p. 20.

parison of faculty salaries to union wages. It found that union wage
rates had increased by 133.4 percent between 1913 and 1926 (see Table
6.10). As Table 6.10 reveals, all but a small proportion of these gains
occurred in the eight years between 1918 and 1926. Thus, rather than
appearing as a gradual accretion, the proletariat's advance on the intelligentsia and within society as a whole must have seemed explosive at
the time—frightening to conservatives and a sign of its imminent rise to
more liberal intellectuals. In either case, it was impossible to ignore the
proletariat any longer or for university intellectuals to avoid comparing
themselves with this rising class. These comparisons indicated that
from 1922 through 1926 union wage rates had increased three times as
fast as those of associate professors. College presidents, on the other
hand, managed to move farther ahead of both faculty and unionized
workers (see Table 6.11) Figure 6.1 provides a graphic illustration of
these developments.

POPULISM VERSUS SOCIAL DEMOCRACY: THE CLASS
CONSCIOUSNESS OF THE INTELLECTUALS

The evidence seems conclusive that university intellectuals did under-
go declassment in the decades from 1890 to 1929. Their "proletarianization" was characterized by a de facto alteration in the customary
relations of production, a general decline in economic and social status
inside and outside the university community, industrialization, and
bureaucratization of the intellectual labor process. The alienation
which accompanied these events was in various ways expressed as a
hostility toward the so-called employee idea.

The employee idea first emerged during the 1890s and early twentieth century as an expression for the "employment at will" doctrine.
Several court decisions had firmly established employment at will as

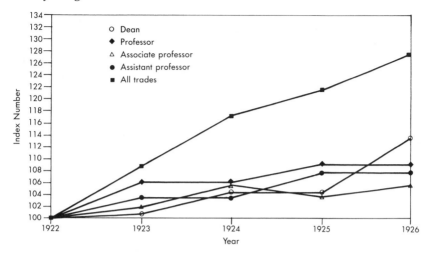

Fig. 6.1. Increase in College Salaries, 1922–1926

the legal doctrine governing relations between trustees and professors by the turn of the century.[34] In this manner, the basic laissez-faire conception of industrial relations prevalent throughout American industry was extended to the university. The doctrine meant simply that employment was at the will of the employer and could be terminated at any time without cause or explanation so long as there was no violation of any private contract between employer and employee.

It appears that trustees, conservative journalists, and sympathetic businessmen throughout the country first began articulating the employment at will doctrine as a coherent principle of academic-industrial relations during the controversies surrounding the dismissal of E. Benjamin Andrews from Brown University for his free-silver political economy. The principle is perhaps best articulated during this time by a writer for the *Philadelphia Ledger.* Employment at will meant quite simply that "if the issue should be raised between businessmen who support colleges and professors who live upon them, the latter will find their occupation gone." A series of interviews at the turn of the century with trustees from Northwestern, Cornell, Columbia, Yale, Princeton, Chicago, Johns Hopkins, and American University found that most trustees subscribed to this principle.[35]

The principle later received its clearest formulation during the Nearing Case (1915) at the University of Pennsylvania. After Scott Nearing was dismissed for his liberal economic views, the Pennsylvania governing board consciously invoked the Dartmouth case, which ensured that "the present equipment and endowment of the University are indeed the property of the trustees, to be administered . . . as they see fit." The faculty was informed rather bluntly that "the relation of a University professor to the trustees" is "the same as that of a day laborer to his employers." Any professor could therefore be removed "at the pleasure of the power by which they shall have been appointed."[36] A writer for the Pennsylvania *Alumni Register* thought it was "simple and elementary to believe that a man should do the things he is employed to do and for which he accepts remuneration."[37]

In articles that could be multiplied almost without end, professors increasingly complained that trustees had "come to regard themselves as the institution and the professors as merely their employees." Faculties resented being "mere employees to be hired as cheaply, worked as hard, as possible" and, hence, paid no more than a "skilled mechanic" or "hotel chef." The "stigma of servility" this attached to "the noblest of callings" was unacceptable.[38]

At the beginning of the century, college and university intellectuals had put forward a variety of counterproposals on institutional organization which Joseph Jastrow called the professors' "literature of protest."[39] An academic ideal emerged from this literature, and by 1920, it had become an official ideology of the intellectuals. The academic ideal was an amalgam of myth, real history, and wish fulfillment that constituted, as it were, a "noble lie" for the American intellectual.[40] The basic axiom of the ideology was its theoretical rejection of the employee idea in favor of efforts to reclaim intellectuals de facto position as a class with vested personal rights in the offices and property of the collegiate institution. Professors argued that the employee idea "cannot be admitted for an instant." The university was "not a student factory, nor an education works" regardless of what the courts or trustees might have to say about it.[41] Such statements can only be taken as socially meaningful utterances in relation to the historic ideal which these counterproposals were aimed at reclaiming.

The university was first and always defended as a preeminently cultural as opposed to a business institution. In most counterproposals, the faculty was thus proclaimed the rightfully sovereign authority in terms of this historic cultural ideal of the university. The exercise of sovereignty within the university was nearly always conceptualized as a direct democracy of autonomous actors in which decisions about educational policy were the result of collective deliberation by a faculty senate.[42] Educational policies were generally presumed to include all decisions concerning curriculum, course offerings, degree standards and professional certification, budget allocations, academic personnel decisions, and faculty promotion.

Most faculty members apparently saw no inherent conflict between this historic ideal and the corporate ideal of social efficiency. Faculties could also rightfully claim within the framework of either ideal (or so they thought) that they possessed the professional expertise on educational and cultural matters. Therefore, a socially efficient division of labor would also place them in control of university policies. In this respect, most university intellectuals considered the conflict between themselves and businessmen a simple misunderstanding by trustees of the correct division of labor, one that could be resolved through rational negotiation.[43]

Consequently, even while resisting the normative claims of the corporate ideal, college and university faculties were often calling for a clearer division of labor on the assumption that explicit lines of authority would somehow return the university to their control. A correct division of labor would always regard administration as a subordinate but necessary adjunct to an institution's primary cultural and educational mission. A proper division of labor would merely return administration to its historic ideal of executing or facilitating directives from a sovereign faculty. Administrators would be dispossessed of any authority over educational policies. Consequently, counterproposals frequently called for the election of major administrative officials such as deans and presidents.

Similarly, many faculties thought that a rational division of labor would confine trustees to their historical fiduciary tasks—primarily that of raising money and building endowments through investments or legislative connections. Some writers, such as James McKeen Cattell, were convinced that endowments would soon reach levels making it possible to altogether dispense with governing boards.[44] Others thought with equal naivete that progressive state legislatures would be willing to dole out millions to the universities without asking a question.

A final component of the academic ideal was the demand for a salary scale compatible with the self-imputed dignity of the academic calling. This was usually interpreted to mean a pay scale equivalent to that of attorneys and doctors, although less than that of high corporate executives. Most proposals were not adverse to merit pay for exceptional individual productivity. It could hardly be said that American faculties were possessed with the levelling spirit. However, they did generally demand some form of base scale, higher than the existing one, which would guarantee raises from year to year on the basis of seniority and the cost of living, as well as productivity. This would be accompanied by life-time tenure as an officer in the corporation of learning and a guaranteed pension upon retirement. It was assumed that the financial and individual autonomy of this structure would guarantee academic freedom and thus make that a peripheral issue once some approximation to this model was in place.

The first collective movement toward resolving the conflict between these competing ideals came as the result of a joint resolution passed by the American Economic Association (AEA), the American Sociological Society (ASS), and the American Political Science Association (APSA) in December 1913. The resolution authorized the appointment of a joint committee "to report on the present situation in American educational institutions as to liberty of thought, freedom of speech, and security of tenure for teachers." The joint committee was chaired by E.R.A. Seligman, the conservative political economist from Columbia who would later direct that institution's war preparedness committee; but the committee was otherwise a rather notable collection of progressive and liberal scholars. In addition to Seligman, the AEA representatives were Richard T. Ely, professor of political economy at the University of Wisconsin, and Frank A. Fetter, chairman of the Department of Economics and Social Institutions at Princeton. James Q. Dealey, professor of social and political science at Brown University; Herbert Croly, journalist and editor for the *New Republic*; and Frederick N. Judson, an attorney specializing in railroad regulation and labor relations were the APSA delegates. The ASS appointed Ulysses G. Weatherly, professor of economics and sociology at Indiana University; James P. Lichtenberger, professor of sociology at the University of Pennsylvania; and Roscoe Pound, professor of law at Harvard University.

The joint committee concluded that "the most fundamental point" of conflict between businessmen and intellectuals was their adherence to competing "ideals of employment." The report found that in most cases neither ideal wholly prevailed in practice, although it noted that "in some of the smaller colleges the private-employment concept is nearly realized," while "in some of the larger universities the public-employment concept is closely approached." Yet because most institutions fell somewhere in between, the result was that "almost everywhere there is great uncertainty of practice."[45]

The committee was convinced that difficulties between businessmen-trustees and university intellectuals were caused by mutual "misunderstandings" on both sides of "the fundamental theory of academic tenure," rather than by any inherent antagonism between the corporate and academic ideals of the university. Individual points of conflict were mainly problems of "departure from accepted standards; whether the departure is in the one direction or the other" was immaterial.[46]

Consequently, the joint committee recommended that the entire problem of university control and all its related issues be put on the table for negotiation. Its most significant departure from past practice was to reformulate each demand of the academic ideal as a series of open questions with negotiable answers. Academic freedom, tenure, salary, and faculty participation were reformulated from either/or propositions into questions of degree. In this context, the corporate ideal could be accepted as the historically real legal and political framework of negotiation. The academic ideal assumed the role of an existential ideology of the intellectuals—a political program—that oriented their negotiations with external social classes, political or administrative authorities. There was a belief that once the principles of tenure, salary, academic freedom, and faculty participation were reestablished, the logic of a functional division of labor would enable faculties to gradually strengthen these claims in practice. Intellectuals could at least carve out some relative autonomy within the general framework of corporate hegemony.

These principles were carried forward into the new AAUP by Seligman and other committee members the same year and an expanded version of the joint committee's original report was ratified by the AAUP in 1915.[47] This ideology of the intellectuals was later institutionalized as a framework of negotiation when the AAUP created a special Committee T in 1917 to investigate "the place and function of faculties in university government and administration." The committee, chaired by J. A. Leighton, conducted a three-year investigation. It finally released a report in 1920 which thereafter defined the AAUP's official position on the problem of university control.[48]

Committee T first surveyed the governing boards of twenty-five major universities. It confirmed earlier studies by Lightner Witmer (1915), Scott Nearing (1917), and the faculty of Colorado College (1917) that had demonstrated that university governing boards were, as suspected, controlled by businessmen and corporate attorneys.[49] Committee T pointed out to colleagues that these "busy men of affairs" had "no special competence to pass judgment on matters of educational policy."

Nevertheless, it conceded the legitimacy of their authority over the university precisely in terms of the rights attached to private property within the legal and political framework of American capitalism. Committee T offered as a fundamental axiom the idea that "trustees should be primarily the custodians of the financial interests of the university, *and as such* they should have the consenting voice in the final determination of its educational policies" as well as "final authority in the determination of the budget." Indeed, the committee went one step further in even recognizing the trustees' "right to take the initiative in matters of educational policy."[50] Educational policies were explicitly defined to include "standards for admission and for degrees; determination of the proper ratio between numbers of students, of courses and of instructors, respectively; numbers of teaching hours; the establishment of new chairs and departments of instruction, of new curricula and courses; the organization of new administrative units; the promotion of research; provision for publication; the abolition of any established form of educational or research activity; the distribution of income between material equipment and personnel."[51] The committee also conceded the principle that "the trustees' consent should be necessary . . . for the same reason, to all appointments, promotions, and dismissals of members of the teaching staff. " One may well wonder what space was left for negotiation after this litany of concessions? The AAUP asked only for what CFAT had been recommending to trustees since 1910.

It asked first that trustees limit their decision-making, for the most part, to approving or rejecting the policy initiatives of faculty and administrators. Committee T suggested that faculty members should act as "the legislative body" on educational matters through some forum of general representation such as a faculty senate. In those instances where trustees or administrators rightfully took the initiative, the AAUP merely requested that faculty representatives be "consulted" prior to a final decision. Committee T extended this recommendation to include giving faculty a "recognized voice in the preparation of the annual budget" through its representative body. It also asked to "participate, through appropriate committees, in the selection of full professors and executive officers of departments" and that "nominations to teaching positions of lower rank should emanate from committees consisting of the professors of the department."[52]

In all instances, it was recommended that faculties and trustees avoid direct contact or confrontation by recognizing the university president as the "chief administrative officer, both with regard to the functions of the trustees and those of the faculty." A strengthened university presidency was supposed to facilitate the incorporation of faculty demands into educational policy, since it was assumed that most university presidents were at least more sympathetic to faculty demands than business trustees. Moreover, strong presidents, acting as intermediaries between the separate proceedings of trustees and faculties could modify the exercise of university governance in a way that insulated individual faculty members from the eyes of potentially hostile or vindictive trustees. The success of this AAUP strategy was highly contingent on the good will and cooperation of benevolent university administrations—who themselves legally remained agents of the trustees.[53]

Committee T conducted a second survey of university government at 110 colleges and universities with respect to the particular items in this program. Its conclusions were that faculty "participated" in the control of educational policy to some degree by "constitutional or statutory authority" in 21 percent of the institutions. There was participation in another 37 percent by "custom." Nevertheless, that left 42 percent of American colleges and universities in which governance was characterized as "autocratic" even in terms of the relatively modest demands of the AAUP. The committee also found that general faculty exercised a formal "legislative function," as defined by Committee T in only 35 percent of the institutions. Faculty participated in the nomination or selection of academic personnel in only 16 percent of the institutions. Department heads were nominated by faculty in only 8 percent of the cases. There was some degree of participation in the formulation of university budgets in 30 percent of the surveyed institutions.[54]

Committee T concluded that despite what could have been deemed a dismal situation, there was "a growing tendency in the better class of institutions to accord the faculty official participation" within the restrictions the AAUP was willing to accept.[55] The committee was optimistic that competition among major universities for prominent or advancing faculty members would compel trustees and administrators to extend greater participation and higher salaries as a condition for attracting a prestigious faculty. Emerging market structures operated independently of everyone and therefore placed competitive pressures on administrations as well as on faculties.

The AAUP generally accepted these conclusions. It recommended that demands for salary and participation in university governance be put forward in local negotiations between individual faculties and administrations. Market structures would be relied upon to provide the pressure toward accommodating AAUP demands, rather than any national boycott, strike, or political tactics.

It is almost certain that the accommodationist strategy articulated by the AAUP accurately reflected the class consciousness of most intellectuals in the United States. It is important to recognize, in this respect, that the alienation of most American intellectuals was a "populistic" status-anxiety. It was an essentially defensive posture oriented toward the preservation of their status as independent guildmasters, freeholders, or entrepreneurs against their proletarianization, but not necessarily against the institutional structure of capitalism itself.[56] Intellectual's comparisons of themselves with industrial laborers were usually regarded as invidious distinctions.

Nevertheless, American intellectuals were still far from unanimous in their support or interpretation of AAUP policy. James McKeen Cattell could support strong presidencies as a founding member of the AAUP because he thought "their dictatorial power has been both harmless and useless." Likewise, he thought the "despotism" of corporate trustees was "only a passing phase in educational development," in the same way that capitalism itself was a passing phase in the history of societies. One could accept temporary accommodations with the educational trust because, in Cattell's view, it seemed likely "that in the end the people will control monopolies and the universities [be] supported by the profits of monopolies." Intellectuals would then no longer be dependent "on the generosity or caprice of millionaires."[57]

John Dewey, one of Cattell's departmental colleagues at Columbia and also a founding member of the AAUP, expanded on this often unstated social democratic ideal of the American university in a small paper delivered to the Pan-American Scientific Congress in 1915.[58] Like most academics, Dewey expressed his concern that the influence of business interests on the curriculum and internal organization of higher education was converting it into "an instrument for external ends." Yet, he argued, this should not force upon intellectuals the false dichotomy of a choice between competing philosophies of education that polarized these concerns in terms of traditional versus modern, cultural versus vocational, and scholastic versus technocratic conceptions of higher education. There was a modern democratic alternative to the corporate ideal which, he suggested, would ultimately triumph in conjunction with the victory of social democracy in America.

Dewey did not altogether reject the vocational aims of modern higher institutions because it was "industrial education" that would finally open the doors of American colleges and universities to the mass of workers who constituted the social base of a modern industrial democracy. There was also a certain inevitable sense in which higher education could not be anything other than a reflection of the dominant economic groups which controlled the scarce material resources of a particular society. However, Dewey claimed, the social meaning and political consequences of vocational education could be contested and rechannelled toward social democratic goals if it was brought under the direction of educators who made "the social and democratic factors supreme in industry, " instead of "pecuniary" concerns.

It was therefore important to negotiate as much relative autonomy as possible for the university so that higher education could avoid modelling "itself upon the automatic repetitiousness of machines" insofar as possible. This would enable it to act as a counterweight to the corporate ideal of industrial society by training students to participate as citizens of an industrial democracy in politics and in the workplace. It could formulate and guard an alternative expressive order through which to interpret the meaning of work and citizenship. Dewey emphasized to his colleagues that as educators possessing competing philosophies of education they were not merely engaged in scholastic or academic struggles. They were engaged in a conflict with the corporate class interests that had come to dominate the American university.

For the very same reason, Dewey concluded, any outcome of the conflict would be determined in the last analysis by "political factors" outside the university. The aims of social democratic educators in training participatory citizens for a modern democracy was simply one component in the wider contemporary struggle for industrial democracy by the working masses. Dewey knew that "to propose this is to invite the attack of those who most profit by [the] perpetuation of existing conditions." There was no doubt that "strong class interests stand in the way" of implementing this philosophy. For otherwise, he was certain that the "moral consensus" already accepted that education was a means of "bringing to more general recognition the evils and defects of present industrial aims and methods, and in making more widespread a knowledge of the means by which these evils are to be done away."

In this sense, Dewey took it for granted that populists and progressives had already succeeded in creating the "political machinery for securing control by the masses." Moreover, since a knowledge of modern social conditions "was an obvious concern of the masses" in their steady march toward social democracy, Dewey was optimistic that this same participatory spirit was "bound in the future to animate our educational system," in spite of its "seeming closer connection with existing economic forces."

Thorstein Veblen held a view that was similar in many respects. He too argued that providing people with the vocational skills necessary to survive efficiently in modern industrial society did not necessarily mean training them to be uncreative appendages of industrial machinery or the passive objects of bureaucratic management techniques. Education could be utilized to cultivate what he called "the instinct of workmanship," a notion he associated with the creative independence and artistic capabilities of the craftsman.[59] He apparently envisioned the future of higher education as a sort of guild socialism.

Veblen was somewhat pessimistic about the immediate prospects of this ideal. He thought that it would "avail little to speculate on remedial corrections" for the current "state of academic affairs so long as the institutional ground is the current system of private ownership." The legal and economic frameworks of private property were the "base-line in any inquiry into the policy that controls modern academic life and work."[60] The position of university intellectuals and their students could not dramatically change except with the abolition of capitalism.

This kind of observation led to more militant expressions of the social democratic ideal by the early 1920s. Upton Sinclair was one of the first American writers to move beyond the claim that American intellectuals were being treated like proletarians to the claim that they had actually become "intellectual proletarians" with "nothing but their brain power to sell." Sinclair pointed to their deteriorating economic status and their institutional dependence on a plutocratic capitalist class that now owned the means of mental production. He was convinced that American intellectuals were "proletarians, and the bulk of them will remain proletarians all their lives."[61]

Sinclair considered the structural transformation of the intellectuals as simply one aspect of a much broader polarization of classes that was developing within capitalist society as a whole. A general proletarianization of the working classes always characterized the structural development of industrial capitalism. This extended process is what compelled "the worker to organize in larger and larger units, and to take into solidarity a wider and wider proportion of the population." This same social force was now first "compelling the college professor to realize himself as a class, and second, to study the movements of other workers for freedom, to become more sympathetic toward them, and more identified with them in interest and action." Since labor was the only organized social force capable of overthrowing "the plutocratic empire," it followed "that the college professor's hopes are bound up with the movement of the workers for freedom."[62]

The implications of Sinclair's thesis were developed into an organizational program by J. E. Kirkpatrick in *The American College and its Rulers* (1926). Kirkpatrick who had been dismissed from Washburn College (Kansas) for organizing the faculty around a program of "academic democracy," concluded that American professors were actually "more like a mass of unorganized laborers than a self-respecting or responsible guild or profession."[63] He also proposed a form of guild socialism in which the university corporation was identified as the collective body of faculty, administrators, and students. Existing boards of trustees could be "entirely dispensed with" because equipment, plant, endowments, and other university property would become the cooperative property of the new corporation.[64] The university would be governed by a representative assembly elected from each of the constituent members of the corporation—faculty, students, and administrators.

Kirkpatrick suggested changes in curriculum such as a greater emphasis on democratic theory, citizenship training, and other social sciences. However, the important aspect of his recommendation was not that the content of these courses be of any particular ideological persuasion, but that the expressive order which gave meaning to intellectual life in the university would sustain and reinforce the broader values of an industrial democracy. This was not because faculty or administrators would necessarily share the same intellectual or ideological outlook, but because the institutional structure of education would require and encourage participation in and political debate about the institution's continuing mission, and would require defending the competing positions that would necessarily arise in the policy debates of the assembly. An educated person would emerge with vocational and citizenship skills, as well as a body of theoretical and cultural knowledge necessary to intelligent citizenship. The university could thus catalyze and support a social and political revolution without abandoning its own mission as an educational institution that promoted a free discussion of competing points of view.

INTELLECTUALS, SOCIALISM, AND THE WORKING CLASS

The most significant effort to forge an alliance between the movements for academic and industrial democracy was the Intercollegiate Socialist Society (ISS). The ISS was a rising organization on American campuses from 1905 to 1921, when it was superceded by the League for Industrial Democracy (LID). It was founded in New York City by Jack London and Upton Sinclair.

London and Sinclair were classic examples of the organic "working-class intellectual."[65] London was born to working-class parents in California, where, as a youth, he worked as a newspaper delivery boy, a helper on an ice wagon, and a pinstacker in a bowling alley. He later worked in a jute mill and as a furnace stoker while attending Berkeley in 1896. Sinclair had worked his way through CCNY and Columbia by writing dime novels for popular consumption. He continued to live on the extremely meager proceeds of similar publications long after his graduation. He joined the American Socialist Party in 1902.

The ISS was established as an organizational bridge between the labor movement, working-class intellectuals, and traditional intellectuals in the university, who, in Sinclair's words, were being compelled "to study the movements of other workers" as a result of their own proletarianization. It defined its mission as promoting the "intelligent discussion of socialism" as a possible solution to the problems of labor and democracy. The ISS was not officially attached to the Socialist party, although most of its members were apparently associated with the Party's social-democratic "right-wing" led by John Spargo, Victor Berger, and Max Hayes.

Jack London was elected as first president of the ISS at its founding meeting in 1905. In this capacity, he initially toured the Universities of California, and Chicago, Harvard, and Yale, where he delivered an address entitled "Revolution" to generate interest in the new society.[66] "Socialist Clubs" were subsequently established at each of these campuses to launch the ISS as an American collegiate association.

It has become popular wisdom among most contemporary American scholars to associate academic socialism with these campuses and to jokingly dismiss it as so much upper-middle-class ennui.[67] A caricature of the Mugwump parlor socialist has been etched in the tablets of American scholarship by a prior generation of scholars who were perhaps too much preoccupied with political self-justification in the aftermath of the Cold War. Yet, for all the ideological comfort that such a caricature seems to generate, it does not provide an accurate representation of socialism on the American campus.

The electoral strength of the American Socialist Party was located in the Midwest, West, and Southwest among miners, lumberjacks, dockworkers, railroad workers, various craft unions, and forgotten remnants of the more radical Populists (e.g., landless agricultural laborers and small debt-ridden farmers). Outside of New York City, its urban strength was in industrial cities such as Cleveland, Dayton, Akron, Chicago, Milwaukee, Duluth, and Seattle.[68] Farmer-labor and pro-

Table 6.12. Regional Distribution of Intercollegiate Socialist
Society Chapters, 1915

Region	No. of chapters	% of all chapters
New England	14	20
Mid-Atlantic	14	20
South	4	6
Middle West	32	46
Far West	6	9

Source: Data from Max Horn, *The Intercollegiate Socialist
Society: 1905–1921* (Boulder: Westview Press, 1979), p. 86.

gressive parties continued to find their most significant support in the
Midwest and Northwest during the 1920s.

Similarly, the majority of socialist university intellectuals appear to
have been located near these social bases, where they could receive at
least some degree of political protection in state legislatures. Upton
Sinclair argued that the University of Wisconsin had become "the most
liberal institution of higher education in the United States," primarily
because farmers' organizations kept jealous watch over the institution
to insure that it did not turn "into a place of academic snobbery."[69] A
regional breakdown of the ISS chapters active in 1915 shows that 46
percent of its chapters were actually located in the Midwest, with
another 9 percent in the Far West, including the mountain states (see
Table 6.12). Considering that most collegiate institutions and college
enrollments were then concentrated in New England and the Mid-
Atlantic states, it would seem that, relative to the distribution of institutions, faculty, and students, there was a disproportionate concentration of socialist intellectuals in those areas where a sympathetic or
protective social base was politically active.

The significance of this politically active social base and its ability to
mediate the general domination of colleges by business interests is
evident in the distribution of ISS chapters among different types of
institutions. Between 1910 and 1917, 104 colleges and universities
reported an official ISS national affiliate at some time or another. This
means that, on average, approximately 20 percent of all four-year
colleges and universities were the site of an ISS chapter during the prewar period. However, only 14 percent of all private colleges had sponsored chapters, while 35 percent of all public institutions had organized chapters of socialist intellectuals. Most of these were located in
the West and Midwest.[70]

Of the chapters located at private colleges 63 percent were on the campuses of small liberal arts or denominational colleges. This is not surprising, since most of these small colleges were usually engaged in the production of small town provincial elites from the middle and lower-middle class. This constituency was suffering its own status decline relative to urban professional elites, industrial and financial magnates. Many of the small denominational colleges had long traditions of messianic and evangelical social reform movements, including utopian and Christian variants of socialism. Hofstadter suggests that clergymen "were probably the most conspicuous losers from the status revolution." They were "at times antagonized by the attitudes of some of the rich men in their congregations" and simultaneously saw "the churches losing the support of the working class on a large and ominous scale." The institutional interests of the church, as well as the class interests of the clerical intelligentsia, often pointed towards a radical courtship with the working class.[71]

Less than 12 percent of the ISS chapters ever formed were located on the campuses of major private universities. Quite the contrary: the everyday reality of academic socialism was one of ex-populists involved in the farmers' movement, Christian socialists engaged in various reform movements, and intellectuals directly attached to the labor movement and left-wing parties. Once these political and ideological alliances were consciously articulated, further attempts were made to integrate the radical intellectuals directly into the working class through union activity. The radical conceptualization of the intellectuals as "proletarians" and "brain workers" did find some institutionalized support throughout the country, particularly after the World War I work speed-up.

The first breakthroughs in union organization occurred in January 1919 at the University of Illinois and Milwaukee Normal College. Union locals affiliated with the new American Federation of Teachers (AFT) were organized on both campuses.[72] The University of Missouri, an old populist stronghold, then quietly organized its own "professors' union" in November of 1919. The union boasted forty-seven members (20 percent of the entire faculty) within one month of its first recruitment drive. Although the unions at Illinois and Milwaukee had encountered difficulty recruiting any members beyond the ranks of instructor and assistant professor, more than one-half of the first members at Missouri were full professors.

One month later an even more dramatic union drive was mobilized at the University of Montana at Missoula.[73] Ninety percent of the Missoula faculty joined the new union within days. The Missoula union immediately drew national attention because it had a notorious reputation (at least among corporate and conservative leaders) as a result of its faculty's close political ties to the Montana Non-Partisan League and the Missoula Federation of Labor. The other side of Anaconda Copper's grip on state government was an agrarian socialist farmers' movement and an AFL local in Missoula that was one of the most solid and militant proponents of the Socialist party anywhere in the United States. The Industrial Workers of the World found a large following among the state's miners as well.

The Missoula union raised the consternation of conservatives by instantly filing a grievance on behalf of Professor Louis Levine. Levine had been dismissed for publishing a costs-benefits analysis of mine taxation in Montana. Levine had argued that mining companies were being taxed at less than the benefits they derived from state and local government. He had therefore recommended increasing taxes on the Montana mining industry. The Missoula union used the issue to challenge the university governing board directly by calling for the introduction of "democratic principles" into university administration and governance.

Shortly after the formation of the Montana union, the University of North Dakota faculty followed suit by organizing its own branch of the AFT.[74] The publicity meted out to these western islands of dissent by the New York City press apparently backfired by encouraging a wave of similar activity in that city. AFT locals soon appeared on major campuses in New York City: Columbia, NYU, CCNY, Hunter College, Adelphi College, Union Theological Seminary, Pratt Institute, and many other campuses.[75] John Dewey added the weight of his considerable prestige as a philosopher of education by joining the Columbia local.[76]

Likewise, individual professors from all over the country began joining the AFT even where locals had not been established. The union movement received additional momentum when the New York locals began establishing contact with these scattered professors to help build and direct a national network of unionized intellectuals. Other unions were subsequently organized at Illinois State Normal, Howard University, Washburn College, and Yale.

At about the same time, Samuel Gompers actually invited "the intelligentsia" to join the AFL. Gompers reiterated the relative decline in salaries and the industrialization of labor processes among the intelligentsia as indications of their proletarianization. He agreed that these developments were bringing the interests of the intelligentsia increasingly into harmony with those of the working class. He went so far as to accept the idea that intellectual workers "have the power to create wealth." It was "immaterial whether this service [i.e., labor] is the mechanical work of the elevator conductors, the technical work of the engineers, or the teaching work of the teachers or professors." Gompers asked college men to carry the trade union viewpoint into the colleges and called for a coalition of labor and educators united to win democratic control of university governing boards and local boards of education.[77]

Gompers was in fact communicating what soon became an official AFL position. At its 1920 national convention, the AFL unanimously endorsed an amendment to its educational platform which claimed that "the most effective guarantee of democracy and progress in the schools is the affiliation of the teachers with the great democratic force of organized labor." The 1920 amended educational platform called for "vigorous and effective support for progressive educational measures," an upward revision "of the salary schedule of teachers in public schools, normal schools, and universities to meet the increased cost of living," and a "democratic voice" for teachers in the conduct of schools and universities. The AFL Executive Council, as well as all state and city central labor unions, were encouraged by the convention "to give every assistance to the American Federation of Teachers."[78]

The more moderate leadership of the AAUP intervened at this point to discourage any further movement towards unionization. Arthur Lovejoy, a professor of philosophy at Johns Hopkins University, was at that time president of the AAUP. He observed in his 1919 presidential address that many members of the association had "written the officers asking their opinions as to the propriety of university teachers joining" the AFT.[79] Others were calling on the AAUP to affiliate directly with the American Federation of Labor. Lovejoy attributed this "agitation" to the "deplorable economic situation" of the "the younger teachers." Although Lovejoy was a liberal who supported trade unionism among manual workers, he cautioned the AAUP's membership against professorial unionism and offered "three decisive reasons" for his position.

Lovejoy first insisted that as a practical matter "the great majority" of American professors would simply not join a "teachers' union affiliated with the American Federation of Labor." Consequently, he claimed, "the utterances of a dissident faction" were not likely to carry any weight "with governing boards of institutions." An organization of university professors had to rely on rational persuasion, and it would therefore only "possess influence precisely in proportion as it is representative" of the entire profession. Therefore, Lovejoy argued, university professors would wield more influence "organized in an independent professional body, rather than as part of a national federation of labor unions." A professional association was the organizational form "in which the largest possible number of members of the profession can be united."

In terms of their economic condition Lovejoy conceded that university professors were really "employees, and that their economic position is, therefore, in certain respects the same as that of a wage-earner." On the other hand, professors were not as a rule "employees of establishments conducted for the private profit of individuals." As a result, "their relation to their employment" was essentially different "from that of the wage-earner bargaining with the private capitalist over the division of the profits of industry." Though intellectuals now occupied a position contingently like that of the proletariat, they could not in essence be technically designated proletarians, because intellectuals did not create surplus value for anyone. Thus, Lovejoy also rejected the theoretical analysis which supported calls for faculty unionization.

Finally, there was the problem of autonomy and objectivity. Lovejoy insisted that "the professional investigator" should in principle "refrain from identifying himself with powerful bodies representing organized special interests, whether of capital or labor." Union affiliation would naturally create the presumption "both by members of other trade-unions and by non-unionists" that social scientists especially "were committed in advance to a general support of the policies and activities of the American Federation of Labor." Such a commitment could be justified only in terms of the intellectuals' historical mission "if it could be safely assumed a priori that in the future all the demands of organized labor" would be those of "the community at large." Since Lovejoy concluded this was a patently unjustified assumption, there was exactly the same kind of reason against adhesion to the AFL as to "any similar organization of employers."

The Missouri unionists utilized Lovejoy's polemic as an opportunity for initiating further debate on the question of unionization in the AAUP's *Bulletin*. In a collective response to Lovejoy and the official position he represented, the Missouri group attempted to clarify their own relation to the AAUP by pointing out that the interests of the two organizations were "sufficiently different to permit both to flourish side by side." The political problem of choosing between conflicting types of organization had in their opinion been falsely formulated by Lovejoy.[80]

The Missouri group was particularly interested in debunking the claim that a commitment to labor organization would necessarily "prejudice the freedom of teaching in the social sciences." They argued this was a necessary conclusion only if one assumed a priori that the AFL was "committed in advance to some cut-and-dried formula for interpreting social phenomena." On the contrary, the group pointed out, the AFL was "composed of organizations and individuals having the most diverse opinions about political, social, and even economic questions." Furthermore, the confederated structure of the AFL guaranteed the autonomy of individual unions. Consequently, there was no reason to believe that affiliation with the AFL would subordinate the intellectuals to any single set of directives.

The Missouri group contended for this reason that the whole problem of academic freedom had to be formulated "as a question of institutions, rather than of individuals." It was observed that "no teacher was ever persecuted for exhibiting the perfections of the existing order." Regardless of the individual professor's subjective intentions, certain teachings were implicitly protected by the hegemony of business interests within the current institutional structure of capitalist society. Consequently, it was far more likely that the universities would be "freer as institutions" to the degree that labor exhibited an interest in higher education and "a readiness to check any tendency toward the censoring of economic teaching." The AFT was a necessary complement to the AAUP's own work on academic freedom, since the participation of college professors in the AFT/AFL was "at present the most practicable means of awakening and guiding the interest of organized labor in the schools."

Despite the Missouri group's rejoinder, or perhaps because of it, the leadership of the AAUP decided that the unionists were an "intransigent minority." Lovejoy advised local officers of the AAUP that it was "unnecessary and inadvisable to prolong the discussion of this subject."[81] The issue never reappeared in its official bulletins. It was not until recently ever raised again in an official forum of the AAUP.

The AAUP position was again probably indicative of most professors' attitudes. The AFT succeeded in organizing only twenty faculty locals on college and university campuses during the 1920s. These attracted only slightly more than 600 members. Thus, even where locals existed, they were relatively powerless and generally did not represent a majority of the faculty. They certainly did not represent the bulk of associate and full professors.[82]

Union organizers found that administrators had already successfully constructed wide zones of indifference among faculties with various bureaucratic incentives. These grew wider as one moved up through the professorial ranks. A Wisconsin organizer reported that professors were a self-centered lot. He reported that "if they are satisfied as far as they are concerned, it is impossible to get them to move."[83] An Illinois organizer complained that professors "regard theirselves [*sic*] on a plane above labor, believe in Carnegie pensions, and dream of good pay positions in the future under the present system."[84]

This indifference, combined with antiunion administrative pressures, led to the failure of most locals. Faculty members were pressured to withdraw from union membership at Howard and at Illinois State Normal. Farmers in the Missouri legislature were afraid higher taxes would accompany higher faculty salaries. Moreover, they found it inconceivable that learned men with an easy job would need the protections of a union.[85] Yellow-dog contracts were adopted at the University of Illinois. At Washburn College the entire membership of the local, including J. E. Kirkpatrick, was fired. By 1929, there were only three locals left on collegiate campuses.[86]

7

Discipline and Punish: Defining the Institutional Limits of Academic Freedom, 1894–1916

THE PROBLEM of academic freedom is a peculiarly modern one in terms of our contemporary definition of the concept. It not only presupposes an open conflict of ideologies, but an institutional commitment to the principle that any restraint on the free trade in ideas is an inherently illegitimate combination that distorts the intellectual marketplace.[1] The problem of academic freedom has emerged mainly as a result of efforts to regulate this market within the functional requirements of a corporate ideal of social efficiency. Consequently, as a historical phenomenon, the problem of academic freedom has appeared almost exclusively as an element of the fundamental class conflicts associated with the development of advanced industrial society.[2]

The historical origins of the problem can be assigned a fairly precise date in the United States. The problem begins in 1894, and as Veysey has observed, the date was not coincidental.[3] The first confrontations were played out on a stage which had seen the rise of a new American Federation of Labor, the financial Panic of 1893; the formation and first victories of the Populist party, the Pullman strike, and the organization of Eugene Debs's American Railway Union. The Pullman strike and the Populist campaigns of 1894 sharpened class conflict and, for the first time, led American capitalists to seriously fear the possibility of an apocalyptic challenge to the existing social and economic order.

Many leading intellectuals from major colleges and universities attempted to forge an alliance between social theory and political action by legitimating the new demands of farmers and laborers as sound

186

social science. The contours of the initial class struggle between intellectuals and business is generally defined in terms of several prominent cases during this time which set procedural and symbolic precedents for future confrontations. These cases involved Richard T. Ely, Edward Beemis, E. Benjamin Andrews, Edward A. Ross, and John R. Commons.

HISTORICAL ORIGINS OF THE PROBLEM OF ACADEMIC FREEDOM

The incident that is usually considered to have been the first to raise modern issues of academic freedom was the case of Richard T. Ely at the University of Wisconsin in 1894. Ely—a nationally prominent political economist, chairman of the Wisconsin political economy department, and secretary-founder of the American Economic Association—had published several important works in political economy establishing him as one of the pioneer socialist academicians in the United States.

His treatises *French and German Socialism* and *Socialism and Reform* had suggested a mild form of democratic socialism, what today would be called a "mixed economy," as the best solution for reconciling competing claims among Americans for individual liberty and class equality. Ely had also published a major work, *The Distribution of Wealth*, in which he examined the effect of political and legal institutions on the existing distribution of wealth and therefore upon the reproduction of classes and class conflict. Ely's publications ware in large part responsible for the founding of a school of "institutional economics" which emphasized the significance of historical economic and political institutions in determining the production and distribution of wealth in American society.[4] He avidly defended the demands of the Populist party as scientifically legitimate economics. He dismissed "political economy, as it has been hitherto taught" as a "cloak" and "balm" for suppressing "the voice of outraged conscience."[5]

An incident involving his economic theories began when Oliver E. Wells, the Wisconsin state superintendent of schools, charged him in a national publication with being "the college anarchist." Wells went on to accuse Ely with "believing in strikes and boycotts, of justifying the one while employing the other, and in teaching, both in his books and classroom, pernicious socialist and anarchist doctrines."[6] The immediate provocation for this charge was actually a protest by Madison businessmen that Ely was aiding a local printers' strike by boycotting a firm that employed non-union labor as scabs and strikebreakers.

A committee of the university's regents was convened to investigate Wells's charges. However, the regents' main concern was apparently confined to investigating whether or not Ely was an anarchist. Believing in strikes, boycotts, and even socialism was not likely to carry much weight in the Wisconsin of 1894, but "anarchism" was a word still charged with memories of the Haymarket bombing. Yet, in precisely this respect, the issue of academic freedom made a false start with the Ely case, primarily because Ely easily and deliberately circumvented the charges.[7]

Wells failed to appear at the hearing, but sent a lengthy written statement indicating that his charges were based largely on a reading of Ely's major publications.[8] Ely answered by explaining to the regents' committee that his position was clearly not that of an anarchist. He then went on to suggest that while he did consider strikes a "necessary evil," his politics had become more conservative since his writing of *Socialism and Reform*.[9] The committee absolved Ely of the accusation, and various journals throughout the country optimistically applauded his successful ability to "explode" the charges against him. A belief that the "German principles" of academic freedom had been transported to America was reinforced when the Wisconsin regents censured Wells and released a policy statement that "in all lines of academic investigation it is of the utmost importance that the investigator should be absolutely free to follow the indications of truth wherever they may lead."[10]

Wisconsin did develop into a genuine oasis for academic dissent, but this was largely related to its fairly idiosyncratic capacity to sustain populist, farmer-labor, socialist, and progressive movements well into the twentieth century.[11] The conclusion that academic freedom was a *fait accompli* was a misreading of general political conditions in the nation, although one that is easily understood, in retrospect, as the populist and labor movements gained momentum during the 1890s. Moreover, those who celebrated Ely's acquittal failed to recognize that the regents' substantive decision was based not so much on the principle of academic freedom as on the fact that Ely was not an anarchist. The result was that most scholars misunderstood the real political outcome of the Ely case.

In one sense, it was still too early to judge the long-term effects of Ely's encounter but recent scholarship indicates that Ely thereafter retreated from his enthusiastic socialism into an opportunistic strategy of individual career advancement. He later began advising his own graduate students to adopt similar tactics. "Backing off" one's socialism quickly emerged as a conscious strategy of adaptation and survival that is now called the "Ely model."[12] The other side of this model was that a *threat* of dismissal was evidently a sufficient regulatory tool against even a prominent national scholar. However, the implicit contours of this model were not readily understood by American scholars, who now assumed that "academic freedom" would be guaranteed as a fundamental right in American universities. This illusion did not last long. The political grounds for academic freedom shifted onto more unfavorable terrain in following years.

A "Beemis confrontation model" emerged in three subsequent cases, those of Edward W. Beemis, E. Benjamin Andrews, and Edward A. Ross. The Beemis case took place in 1895 at the University of Chicago, which at the time was being changed from a small Baptist college into a modern university almost entirely with Rockefeller funds. Its governing board was composed exclusively of Chicago investment bankers, railroad men, steel manufacturers, and corporate attorneys attached to the Chicago financial group. Edward W. Beemis was a professor of economics at Chicago and was a moderate academic adherent of the Populist movement. In scholarly papers and roundtables of the AEA, Beemis was advocating an international bimetallic agreement, cooperative agricultural banks, public ownership of utilities, trade unionism, and the introduction of a progressive income tax "to reach the rich of our cities and secure a fund for the great improvement of the roads and schools of the rural districts."[13] He also maintained regular ties with the Chicago labor movement. An incident was again initiated when local businessmen complained to the trustees of the University of Chicago that Beemis had met with Eugene Debs during the Pullman strike.[14]

President William Rainey Harper warned Beemis to stop his controversial activities off campus, but without result. Unlike Ely, Beemis not only failed to heed the warnings: he took them as an opportunity to confront the administration publicly by invoking the principle of academic freedom and his rights as a citizen to assemble off-campus with labor officials or anyone else. He was finally dismissed after several confrontations with Harper that were publicized on campus and in the local press. Beemis's friends at the university complained that his dismissal was politically motivated by his prolabor populist ideology. There were many hints (probably incorrect) that John D. Rockefeller lay behind the dismissal.

A group of professors from other institutions attempted to investigate the case but were rebuffed by Harper and the trustees who regarded their presence as an "unwarranted interference."[15] Harper eventually denied that the case had political implications and suggested that Beemis was dismissed because of poor teaching. Beemis fell strangely silent after the dismissal and apparently took Harper's warnings one confrontation too late. It was not until twenty-seven years later that he revealed to Upton Sinclair that President Harper had told him face to face that he was dismissed because of "his attitude on public utility and labor questions."[16] He had gone silent after Harper threatened to blacklist him at other universities.

In fact, the aftermath of his confrontation was that Beemis did become an academic pariah. He was later recommended by colleagues for positions at Iowa College, Oberlin, Amherst, Smith, Northwestern, Illinois, Nebraska, and Colorado. The trustees or president vetoed the appointment in every instance. Beemis only managed to secure a temporary appointment from Thomas E. Will at Kansas State during the Populists' brief control of that college. He lost that appointment with the Populists' and Will's departure in 1899.[17]

The Rockefeller shadow fell across another campus in 1896, when E. Benjamin Andrews was forced to resign the presidency of Brown University. Andrews was an ordained Baptist minister, and like Francis Wayland, his predecessor at Brown, he continued a long institutional tradition in "moral and political economy." Andrews assumed the presidency in 1889 and during his tenure rose to international prominence as a Populist political economist. He served as U.S. commissioner to the International Monetary Conference held at Brussels in 1892. He was particularly well known as a vehement opponent of "trusts" and as an equally committed advocate of bimetallism. Indeed, two of his most popular works were *Wealth and Moral Law* (1894) and *An Honest Dollar* (1894). The latter was a popular tract on free silver which Andrews specifically wrote for the Peoples' party. The tract was so widely read that by the end of 1894 Andrews was considered "a leading academic defender of monetary reform."[18]

Andrews's troubles with his board of trustees began when he invited William Jennings Bryan to address the Brown University commencement in 1896. The following year, the trustees asked him "to cease promulgating his opinions." They attributed a decline in endowments and personal bequests to the fact that wealthy friends of the college were put off by his activities. Brown University was another of Rockefeller's favorite objects of philanthropy. His name was again circulated as a shadowy figure in the background of the trustees' growing concern. The suspicion was magnified because Rockefeller, Jr. (later of the GEB), was currently attending the university as an undergraduate.[19]

Andrews eventually resigned in protest. This time, however, there was a national outcry from prestigious scholars throughout the country. The trustees asked him to reconsider, and he withdrew his resignation. He continued to publicize Populist theories, despite continuing pressure from the trustees, and was subsequently forced to resign a second time. Republican editors defended the dismissal as "the unquestionable right" of trustees, who were justified in their expectation that "a servant shape his teachings in economics to meet their views."[20] The Populist press "pictured him as a martyr to the cause of truth and honesty betrayed by the plutocrats who controlled the eastern universities."[21] After a short stint as superintendent of public schools in Chicago, Andrews became president of the Populist-controlled University of Nebraska. He served at that institution until the Fusionists lost control of the Nebraska Board of Regents in 1908.

The last major case of the Populist decade was that of Edward A. Ross at Stanford University.[22] The Ross case was one of the most infamous among Populists for the simple reason that, in this instance, a wealthy trust magnate came out of the shadows into the forefront of the confrontation. It was the kind of western showdown that made good muckraking in the Populist press. There had only been vague suspicions of Rockefeller at Chicago. The Brown University trustees had referred only to dissatisfaction among anonymous wealthy benefactors. On the other hand, Mrs. Leland Stanford, the widow of the Stanford University's founder, was quite outspoken in directing that Ross be dismissed even over the objections of Dr. David Starr Jordan, the university's president.

Ross had been invited to teach sociology and political economy at Stanford beginning in 1893. He had achieved some standing among the founding generation of American political economists primarily on account of two positions. One of these was opposition to the immigration of orientals into the United States. He argued that immigrant labor was undercutting organized labor by putting downward competitive pressure on American wages. This was the same position on immigration currently articulated by the AFL. The position was controversial, but particularly repugnant to the widow of a man who had built the Union and Southern Pacific railroads with the sweat of coolie labor and thereby accumulated a personal fortune.

Second, Ross believed that available evidence had already demon-

strated the superiority of public ownership in certain fields of industrial activity, including utilities and railroads. Public ownership, in his
view, was not only more responsive to the public interest, but also
more efficient from a purely economic standpoint. When the Populists
seemed to offer a political program in line with his own academic work,
Ross agreed to travel the Pacific coast as an advocate of bimetallism.
Ross also carried his advocacy into the 1895 convention of the AEA,
where he found allies among Ely, Andrews, and John R. Commons.
Like Andrews, Ross was asked to publish a bimetallist tract, *Honest
Dollars* (1896) which similarly enjoyed a wide popular circulation.
Ross's western campaign proved so successful that the *California Bank-
ers' Magazine* was forced to counter his views with a public rejoinder.

Mrs. Leland Stanford began criticizing Ross in public. She openly
pressured trustees to remove him from the university. The trustees
were perfectly willing to comply, but President Jordan pleaded for her
indulgence. Meanwhile, he tried to rescue Ross from the brink with
requests that he stop his controversial campaigns. Ross refused, and
the confrontations continued to escalate back and forth, with Jordan in
the middle, until Ross finally resigned on November 14, 1900. Ross was
fortunate in that E. Benjamin Andrews was now strategically placed as
president of the University of Nebraska. Andrews immediately invited
Ross to join that institution. Ross later left Nebraska, in 1906, when the
political situation destabilized after the Fusionist defeat. He then
headed north to the University of Wisconsin at the invitation of Richard
T. Ely.

There is one additional case which deserves more attention than it
has received from scholars, mainly because it probably represents the
way in which most conflicts over academic freedom were actually
resolved. This is the case of John R. Commons. Commons was a young
political economist who had helped found the national Christian
Socialist movement along with Ely, W.D.P. Bliss, and George D. Herron
of Iowa College. He had published an important book, *The Distribution
of Wealth* (1893), while holding an assistant professorship at Indiana
University. Commons was an outspoken defender of Populist economics at national conventions of the AEA alongside Ely and Ross. He also
favored proportional representation in Congress with seats distributed
to represent economic and industrial groups, rather than geographic
districts. His positions soon created a silent tension among Indiana's
board of trustees, who in 1894, began pressuring Joseph Swain the
university president to do something about Commons.

Unlike Ely, Andrews, Beemis, or Ross, Commons was not yet a

prominent scholar. The likelihood is that no one would have ever known, or cared about what happened to Commons except for the fact that he emerged as a major American labor historian some two decades later. As a matter of fact, Swain was clearly intent on avoiding the kind of national publicity that other cases had generated, so when Syracuse University offered Commons a new position in 1895, Indiana's president assisted him and actually tricked him into accepting it. Commons had intended to use the offer as leverage for securing a promotion and pay increase at Indiana. Swain led him to believe that he would be successful in this goal, but not until he had nominally accepted the Syracuse offer so as to make the threat more real to Indiana's trustees. Once he accepted the offer from Syracuse, however, Swain refused to renew his contract, thus managing to get rid of Commons in a way that avoided an imminent confrontation, but without a public humiliation for Commons. Indeed, to outward appearances, it looked as if Commons was moving up to a better position.

The pattern defines a "Commons model." The key is that Commons silently accepted his fate and left for Syracuse. Indeed, he repeated the same pattern a few years later. In 1899, shortly after he made some public speeches that praised Henry George and Karl Marx, the chancellor of Syracuse advised him that his sociology chair was being abolished for financial reasons. The financial reasons for his termination, the chancellor said, stemmed from refusals by several important donors to contribute to the university so long as Commons remained on the faculty. Commons' version of the story was that the chancellor also warned him of an agreement reached at a recent meeting of university presidents not to hire any "radicals." A blacklist was being circulated. Commons' name would be kept off the list if he voluntarily resigned and kept silent. He struck the bargain and retired in silence. Richard T. Ely later hired him at Wisconsin. Once at Wisconsin, Commons became an Ely protege and adopted a more and more conservative, scholastic, and careerist strategy of survival.[23]

There are far more historical examples of the Commons model than of the Beemis model, although the latter received most of the contemporary publicity and is still the object of most subsequent historical analysis. Yet, examples of the Commons model continue to be discovered in what were usually fairly obscure places. For instance, I. A. Hourwich left the University of Chicago in 1894 with very little disruption. James Allen Smith, a young Populist political economist, was dismissed from Marietta College along with four other Bryan supporters in the spring of 1897.[24] Beemis and Frank Parsons, a socialist political economist, both left Kansas State in silence when the Populists lost control of that institution in 1899. George D. Herron was forced out of his chair of Applied Christianity at Iowa College without too much turmoil for his Christian Socialism. Vernon Parrington quietly left the University of Oklahoma in 1908 when the Populist movement was finally unseated in that state.[25]

It is probably impossible to arrive at even a reasonable approximation of the real extent of ideological repression occurring at the time. Most of the cases never received more than local attention. Most involved unknown scholars or teachers at small colleges and universities whose institutional histories may never be written. Commons, Smith, Parrington, and others are known only because they found refuge on the western islands and survived to become major figures in the history of American social science. Among the hundreds of small American campuses, however, it is perhaps not too much to surmise that if trustees did not hesitate to remove scholars with national reputations, they were certainly no less inclined to pressure faculty members with far less standing in the academic community. It is equally no less plausible to suspect that others, like Commons, learned a lesson from Beemis by concluding that their own survival depended on emulating Ely or in seeking silent refuge at another campus.

THE MANAGERIAL CONCEPT OF ACADEMIC FREEDOM

The passing of the Populist storm was accompanied by a temporary and dramatic decline in the incidence of ideological repression on American campuses. However, its legacy was a continuing and wide-ranging discussion among university faculties and administrators about the meaning of academic freedom. Those scholars who were even interested in the topic usually defended an absolutist position imported from Germany: an unconditional right to academic freedom on campus and the equivalent rights of free speech, petition, and peaceable assembly enjoyed by all citizens off-campus. University governing boards claimed that professors were employable-at-will "servants" and therefore obligated to teach and publish within the range of expectations of their employers.

College and university presidents, even when sympathetic to professorial claims (and they often were sympathetic), were on more ambiguous terrain. They could side with the faculty, but by 1900, it was obvious that the price of doing so was nearly always immediate dismissal. Other administrators believed that trustees were correct and willingly served as the paid hatchetmen for business interests. Yet, it was equally difficult to govern a campus without some base of support among the faculty. Thus, from about 1900 to 1915, leading college and university presidents were actively drawn into the ongoing debate. A managerial concept of academic freedom emerged from these discussions. It is probable that this concept was adopted by most college and university presidents by the end of the 1920s.

A precise comprehension of the managerial concept is crucial to an understanding of how college and university administrators could so often stand before their own faculties after 1900 and declare in good faith that no threat to academic freedom existed anywhere in the United States. The basic premise of the managerial concept was its distinction between academic freedom and academic license. Nicholas Murray Butler of Columbia University argued that "the *proper* freedom of speech of university professors" presupposed what he called "habits of self-control, self-direction, and self-ordering."[26] This was not merely an abstract personal characteristic but involved a "reasonable presumption," according to Butler, that what already exists must carry greater moral and intellectual authority in the academic profession than "untested and untried" theories. Academic freedom was therefore always disciplined by the moral and political values of the status quo.

Moreover, insofar as the academic profession was concerned with examining untested theories of society, practitioners were further restricted by the emerging disciplinary boundaries which defined professional expertise. For instance, an economist had no right to talk about *political* institutions. An expert on the rural family could not speak professionally about income taxation. In this respect, the genuinely *professional* expert, as opposed to a pseudoscientist, was always confined to the teaching and publication of empirical "facts" that were generally accepted by other experts in the field. Academic freedom became academic license when professors went beyond these facts to theoretical speculations about untested alternative political, moral, or social arrangements.[27]

Butler was more precise than most administrators in specifying exactly what he meant by untested theories. Academic freedom crossed over into academic license at any one of five different points. The first was "irreverence" for the "religious faith or the political convictions of others." This certainly excluded any positions that might be construed as atheistic or overtly partisan. A second boundary was crossed in the advocacy of "all forms of artificial equality." Academic license was also at work any time a professor took classroom time to express personal opinions on any subject. Similarly, a professor engaged in academic license whenever he or she used the authority of professional expertise to "pronounce publicly on issues of current public controversy." In this respect, Butler argued, "the serious, scholarly, and responsible investigator" was not a "demagogue" or "propagandist." He defined a propagandist as anyone who supported "the agitation in favor of woman suffrage," prohibition, "trial marriage," and "what is called socialism."[28] The concept of academic freedom was not a refuge for any type of "radicalism." Butler concluded, from this standpoint, that no more than two "genuine cases" could be found since 1870 in which academic freedom had actually been violated in the United States.

It is significant that Butler considered these self-disciplines the foundation of a liberal university. He considered liberalism the ground that stood between "the philosophy of anarchy" (including not only anarchism, but the "industrial autocracy" of unrestrained laissez-faire capitalism) and an "unprogressive civilization." Since the colleges and universities were entrusted with training leaders for a progressive democracy, Butler felt there was every reason why students should be protected from the "outside influences" of "agitators and propagandists." Liberalism, in his view, could not include anything that was "queer, odd, unconventional, otherwise minded, " or "in perpetual opposition." It excluded "freaks, oddities, revolutionaries."[29] The development of a progressive industrial democracy required leaders with a liberal education, but this had to be balanced by self-restraint and discipline if liberalism was to avoid degenerating into a competition between demagogues or into reckless social experimentation. Academic freedom was always balanced by the principle of "academic responsibility."

There is no doubt that Butler's position represented a conservative extreme among university presidents. But while other administrators might draw the line between academic freedom and license in a different place, increasingly they all did draw that line. However, the broad range in which administrators could draw the distinction in practice made the theoretical concepts of radicalism and license equally ambiguous. For the Columbia University administration radicalism encompassed virtually everything except the platform of the Republican party. At the University of Wisconsin it included virtually nothing but anarchism.

Most university presidents probably occupied positions somewhere between Butler at Columbia and Charles Van Hise at Wisconsin. Yet, there was a tendency to move toward Butler, since individual university presidents often resolved this ambiguity by general reference to the corporate ideal of the university. Presidents who adopted a managerial strategy identified their role with the interests of the institution as a whole, rather than with the interests of any particular faculty member. Thus, an irresponsible professor was in practice generally one who in some way seemed to threaten the interests of the larger institution.

It is probably for this reason that faculties often failed to understand the managerial concept of academic freedom. Faculties identified the university exclusively with themselves as a collective body. Consequently, their concept of academic responsibility and institutional loyalty precluded a priori any notion that a faculty member could ever act against the interests of the university. They *were* the university, as well as the historical agents of the academic ideal to pursue truth for its own sake. The idea that academic responsibility or professional loyalty could impose external restraints on research or teaching was inconceivable.

Presidents, on the other hand, understood the college and university as a far more extensive and complex institutional matrix that encompassed several groups in addition to the faculty. President William Dewitt Hyde of Bowdoin College identified the university as a compound composed of six elements: founders, donors, trustees, president, faculty, and public constituents. The president's managerial role was to insure that all groups cooperated in a socially efficient manner toward the institution's common mission. Academic freedom was thus circumscribed in principle by the functional imperative of social efficiency and the specialized division of labor which defined the "rights" of an institution's various groups. Hyde even defined academic freedom as "the harmonious working of the six constituent elements of the university." He indicated that any person who could not cooperate harmoniously with individuals within the other "elements" had "no place on a college faculty."[30]

Hyde's formulation of this vision was that the initial academic mission of an institution was imposed by founders and trustees. Founders had the right to designate an institution's goals (whether public or private), while trustees were the contemporary guardians of that mission. Hyde, like most presidents, agreed with faculty that even private higher institutions were a public trust with a public constituency. Yet, for exactly that reason, as Butler argued, the principle of academic responsibility imposed a requirement that professors not offend "common morality, common sense, common loyalty, and decent respect for the opinions of mankind."[31]

The "public" constituency had a specific meaning for most administrators, but it was a meaning that faculties were slow to understand
because professors often regarded the public as some abstract general
will. Hyde, however, defined its "most important element" as the
"institution's own alumni." These were followed by "donors and benefactors" who had an "obvious right" to satisfy themselves as to "the
wisdom of the policy of the institution to which they give their
money."[32] This was the real public that made an institution possible
through contributions and benefactions. Thus, the precise point at
which a president's managerial judgment led him to deem a particular
professor's actions as academic license often came down to the point at
which his presence threatened the institution's capacity to generate
revenues from alumni, legislators, or wealthy benefactors. A professor
who engaged in public political activities, strikes, and boycotts; wrote
popular pamphlets and newspaper editorials; or caused public confrontations on the campus was obviously more likely to produce this
effect.

In this respect, President Hadley of Yale concluded that conflicts with
faculty would be unavoidable precisely because "teaching costs
money." Hadley recognized that a university was "more likely to obtain
this money if it gives the property owners reason to believe that vested
rights will not be interfered with." He was perfectly willing to concede
"academic freedom in theory." However, he warned faculty that in
practice "the outcome of the conflict is generally in favor of the corporation, be it public or private, and against the individual teacher or group
of teachers. This is partly due to the corporation's material advantage in
holding the base of supplies."[33]

Faculty could press the issue if they wanted, but like Socrates, they
would drink hemlock. Prudence entailed an acceptance of the practical
limitations imposed by the necessities of financing a university.
Hadley's presentation of this argument deviated from the most liberal
president's only in its self-consciously aggrandizing cynicism. Its conclusion was a necessary consequence of the managerial presidency and
its underlying corporate ideal.

Presidents frequently conceptualized this managerial practice as a
theoretical distinction between politics and ideas. Academic freedom
meant *academic* freedom to most administrators. As a result, most of the
early cases followed a similar pattern with reference to this distinction.
The complaints were all initiated by local businessmen or trustees
whose attention was first drawn to a faculty member as a result of
participation in off-campus "politics." This was followed by what presi-

dents considered a fair warning from the administration to withdraw from political activities.

The outcomes associated with the Beemis confrontation model, as opposed to the Ely or Commons models, are that Beemis ignored the warnings, while Ely and Commons understood their implicit meaning. Ely distanced himself from the printers' strike. Commons, Parrington, Smith, and others silently withdrew and struck out for safer territories in the West without drawing more than local attention to themselves. In each case, a professor was dismissed or finally asked to resign only after declining donations and benefactions could be traced directly to dissatisfaction with a particular faculty member.

As Furner notes, for instance, there were philosophically far more radical men than Beemis at Chicago. Charles Zeublin and Thorstein Veblen went about their business unmolested, but "their work was theoretical and did not bring them into conflict with corporations" as readily or as directly as the writing of popular pamphlets.[34] No one beyond a few colleagues had the faintest idea what a Veblen or a Zeublin were up to with their time. Beemis, Andrews, and Ross were political activists and popular heroes.

Individual professors could maintain a certain degree of autonomy within this framework, but it was always an inherently insecure position. One could never be entirely certain at what point various ideas would be considered politically controversial. Administrators could apply such a distinction between politics and ideas equally to all faculty and hence regard the rule as constituting fair warning and due process for everyone. Yet, the simple fact of life in a capitalist society was that advocating the platform of the Republican party at a local meeting of the Chamber of Commerce would never be regarded as controversial by the public constituency which administrators considered most relevant to managerial decisions; populism, progressivism, trade unionism, or socialism might be controversial under various circumstances.[35]

These circumstances were highly contingent on the character of local politics, on what movements were perceived as a real threat by local capitalists, or on the mere attentiveness and aggressiveness of individual university trustees. Controversy could be sparked by an ill-considered statement quoted in a local newspaper or an off-the-cuff remark overheard at a church picnic. Thus, once one moved outside a relatively narrow range of safe opinions, what academic freedom really meant at any particular institution was often an accident of local circumstance subject to wide fluctuations. A change in the university presidency, a new party majority in the state legislature, local labor unrest, or a new member on the board of trustees could quietly widen or narrow the range of academic freedom. Its meaning often shifted without warning at particular institutions and could easily catch by surprise anyone bold enough to be standing on its boundaries.

In this respect, the Ely and Commons models represented strategies of survival for the radical intellectual. The survivors were people who could navigate the shadows cast by the ambiguity of the managerial concept of academic freedom. The widening zones of indifference could also work in their favor, but only if they did not threaten the financial well-being of the institution and, hence, the perks and prestige of their colleagues. This required an occasional political hibernation during winters of reaction or a periodic migration to other campuses. When the latter became necessary, it always required a radical to accept fate with the dignity of a professional. This was quietly demonstrated in the ability to be a personable colleague devoted to the larger interests of the university.[36]

An institution like Wisconsin was idiosyncratic in the larger national arena. Elsewhere, it was often not clear when a professor's politics became "politics" from a managerial standpoint, but the general rule was when unfavorable publicity threatened the financial strength of the institution. At that point, university presidents expected institutional loyalty to take precedence over off-campus activities. Most presidents were willing to negotiate ideas. None of them—not even the most liberal—was willing to negotiate personal politics. Some interesting illustrations of the process can be found in three subsequent cases: those of John M. Gillette, and Joseph Lewinsohn, and another incident involving Edward A. Ross.

John M. Gillette was a Kansas minister whose scholarly publications at the turn of the century established him as the American founder of rural sociology. Gillette was a fervent Progressive and a religious agnostic and had often expressed his affinity for many of the socialist policies articulated by Eugene Debs. These views were well known to President Merrifield of the University of North Dakota when Gillette was asked to interview at the campus for an academic appointment in 1907. In a letter sent prior to the interview, Merrifield advised Gillette "to strike a conservative tone" with the trustees. Gillette complied and was offered the position.[37]

Once Gillette was on campus, Merrifield reiterated his advice as a permanent warning not to be interpreted as merely a temporary tactic for securing the appointment. He wrote to Gillette in a subsequent letter:

I judge from what I learn that your views are those of a collectivist. . . . The utmost freedom of individual belief is conceded to everyone on our faculty. At the same time, I would be unwilling to have members of our faculty express in public or in their classes views which would be so distasteful to the North Dakota community in general that their expression would alienate from the University the cordial sympathy and confidence of the average citizen of the State."[38]

Merrifield went on to explain that the university had already been attacked as a "hotbed of anarchy." He did not want these accusations rekindled by irresponsible faculty members. On the other hand, Gillette would be safe so long as he confined his activities to scholarship.

The seriousness of these warnings was demonstrated five years later when Joseph Lewinsohn was dismissed from North Dakota.[39] Lewinsohn accepted an appointment as professor of law at the University of North Dakota after serving on the national platform committee of the Progressive party. He continued to make public speeches during the 1912 Presidential campaign on behalf of Theodore Roosevelt. Frank McVey, the new president of North Dakota, was a well-known advocate of academic freedom. Yet, like most of the new managerial presidents, he wished to avoid unnecessary confrontations with his board of regents. McVey initially asked Lewinsohn to restrict his off-campus political activities to municipal politics. He apparently reasoned that local politics was identified with a more progressive constituency that was less likely to find Lewinsohn's views controversial. Lewinsohn would therefore be less likely to capture the attention of statewide political officials. Lewinsohn rejected the advice.

The very conservative Louis B. Hanna was elected governor of North Dakota in 1912. He immediately filled two vacancies on the university's sharply divided board of regents with political allies. An unstable ideological stalemate on the board was resolved to the conservatives' advantage. Moreover, Lewinsohn's progressive politics had not escaped Hanna or his appointees during the election. McVey was pressured by the new majority to dismiss Lewinsohn. McVey subsequently ordered him "to get out of politics or leave the university." Lewinsohn chose the latter and resigned his position. Professor Charles E. Carpenter was then dismissed by the board for criticizing its political bias in the Lewinsohn action. The dean of the Law School attempted to defend Lewinsohn and gain a hearing for Carpenter. He failed on both accounts and finally resigned in protest.

Edward A. Ross encountered similar limits even at the University of Wisconsin. Shortly after his arrival on campus at the invitation of Richard T. Ely, President Charles Van Hise issued a suspiciously timed statement asking "controversial members of the faculty to exercise circumspection." Van Hise was himself a political economist sympathetic to Wisconsin's farmer-labor progressivism. He was known to be an ardent defender of academic freedom, but even this most liberal of the university presidents warned that discretion was "necessary at times of public clamor about the 'radicalism' of the University unless its financial support be curtailed."[40]

Ross went about his usual business and, predictably, soon embarrassed the administration by announcing in his classroom the time and place of an off-campus lecture by Emma Goldman. The administration was scandalized when Wisconsin papers later reported that Goldman had appeared in Ross's office and been given a grand tour of the campus by him. The administration censured Ross for the Goldman incident, but he had apparently not yet crossed the informal line that prohibited anarchism. Ross was then censured a second time when he allowed a Progressive educator to address his class without receiving prior permission from a new campus lecture committee. He was allowed to slip by on his alleged ignorance of the new procedures.

Ross submitted to the new procedures when in 1917 he tried to schedule an on-campus lecture on socialism by Max Eastman. The committee exercised prior restraint by denying Eastman access to the campus. Ross and other sponsors complained to the administration that they were being treated unfairly. The administration responded that everyone was receiving equal treatment and pointed out that suffragettes had also been denied access to the campus. Ross pushed his case to even Wisconsin's institutional limits of toleration, but in the last instance accepted the administration's ruling and, one suspects, avoided what might have been the third termination of his career. Ross was twice punished and now finally disciplined. This time he understood the meaning of administrative fair warning and backed off at the appropriate time.

Leading administrators informally adopted the managerial concept as a practical way to resolve the conflict between faculty and business trustees. Lecture committees like the one at Wisconsin emerged on campuses throughout the country as one mechanism for exercising the prior restraint necessary to deflect faculty participation from campus activities that might draw the attention of trustees, conservative legislators, or local businessmen. As a practical policy, however, it depended upon an unstable triangular balance of three factors.

First it required the disciplined cooperation of a faculty willing to abide by and understand the practice of fair warning. It required, on the other side, a relatively non-intrusive or inattentive board of trustees that was equally willing to accept the division of labor between governance and administration. This was the essential basis of a managerial authority that was both strong and relatively autonomous. Finally, this informal regulatory structure ultimately hinged on the occupation of managerial positions by individuals who were personally both strong and tolerant. The strong managerial presidency, when occupied by a weak or intolerant individual, turned its holder into either a servile political hack or a petty tyrant.

The structure worked only with a president who was tolerant enough to win the cooperation of his political faculty and confident enough to fend off restless trustees at precisely those moments when they were most likely to push for ideological repression. Van Hise at Wisconsin, Alexander Meiklejohn at Amherst, and perhaps Lowell at Harvard were such men, but they were the exception more than the rule. Consequently, the informal regulatory structure in place by the Progressive era was a highly unstable balance that collapsed if any of its three pillars was weakened or if any of its participants failed to understand and observe the managerial rules of the game. As the Progressive era would demonstrate, the contradictions of the regulatory structure were most likely to break down and generate confrontations during periods of political turmoil.

INTELLECTUALS AS A CLASS-CONSCIOUS SOCIAL MOVEMENT

The Progressive era gave birth to a second wave of ideological repression that began about 1909 and steadily escalated until the end of the Red Scare in the early 1920s. This second phase of the contest for academic freedom was not confined to "a few inferior universities"— despite the claims of certain contemporary historians—but struck at the research and teaching centers of the emerging ideological state apparatus.[41] Conservative trustees became ever more aggressive in their efforts to deepen the administrative structure of prior restraint by rooting out radicals or prohibiting their entry into the university. Moreover, what began as scattered acts of repression on the part of individual boards of trustees became increasingly systematic and centrally directed by government during this second phase.

The Columbia University board of trustees, under the leadership of Nicholas Murray Butler, was one of the most self-conscious and systematic in its actions to overturn the institution's reputation as an eastern haven for academic radicals. Charles Beard reports a case in 1909 that seemed spurious to the Columbia faculty at the time but in retrospect was seen as the opening shot in a new round of contests between faculty and trustees. Following the retirement of John W. Burgess, a professor of constitutional law, the Columbia Faculty of Political Science unanimously recommended a replacement whom Beard would refer to only as "Professor X." Professor X was critical of current Supreme Court rulings on child labor, unionization, and other labor issues. He had published a book "in which he justified criticism of the Supreme Court as a means of bringing our constitutional law into harmony with our changing social and economic life." Unlike Gillette at North Dakota, Professor X was not successful in "striking a conservative tone" with the trustees. His appointment was vetoed by the trustees. The position was instead awarded to W. D. Guthrie, a successful corporate attorney who was a business partner of one of the trustees. Beard claimed that "the whole affair was settled by backstairs negotiations, and it was understood by all of us who had any part in the business that no person with progressive or liberal views would be accepted."[42]

Columbia's trustees targeted James McKeen Cattell shortly after the Professor X incident.[43] Cattell was a pioneer in experimental psychology who directed Columbia's renowned psychology laboratory. He was at the time organizing a national campaign to oppose the Carnegie pension plan and had just published a collection of critical articles on that topic. The Columbia trustees subsequently discussed a resolution that recommended his dismissal specifically because of the criticisms directed at CFAT. The initial resolution on his termination was defeated by a majority of the trustees, who considered dismissal too harsh a punishment. However, President Butler convinced them to assume administrative control of the psychology laboratory and dismiss Cattell as its director. Butler apparently hoped that a public humiliation of so prominent a scholar would provoke an angry resignation.

It had the opposite effect. Instead, Cattell published a second critical work, *University Control* (1913), in which he attacked the role of businessmen in university administration and proposed a form of faculty democracy in its place. The trustees soon informed Cattell they intended to ask him for an early retirement at their next meeting. That action was forestalled only after a series of formal protests from all of the graduate faculties. The trustees retreated and bided their time, rather than risk a full-scale confrontation with the entire faculty.

The election of 1912 was soon followed elsewhere in the country by a wave of reprisals in which trustees were again growing attentive to the activities and utterances of individual faculty members. One professor was dismissed from the University of Iowa in 1913 for no apparent reason. The case became public when President Bowman threatened to resign over the trustees' failure to consult him prior to the dismissal.[44] The same year, Professor Willard C. Fisher was asked to resign from Wesleyan University after reports to trustees of an incidental utterance at a men's literary club in which he "disparaged church going and Sunday Observance."[45] In another prominent incident, Professor A. E. Morse resigned his chair in political science at Marietta College in early 1914, claiming that he was "practically forced to resign for political reasons." The college administration released an official bulletin in response to public protests by Morse informing the curious that "it is the sacred duty of the trustees to administer the affairs of the institution according to their own judgment and the dictates of their own conscience."[46] Two department chairs who had defended Morse were then given the choice between resignation or involuntary dismissal.

A long list of similar cases had accumulated by the end of 1914. Some received national publicity. Most were local confrontations with trustees. Yet enough incidents were becoming known in complaints to *Popular Science Monthly* that it noted, "Scarcely a month passes without the occurrence of one or more events disquieting to those who would make our universities the homes of scientific scholarship and social progress."[47] Moreover, a pattern was becoming evident in this second wave of political dismissals and forced resignations. In 1914 Howard C. Warren of Princeton University published an extensive list of recent cases in which he found that "interference with freedom of inquiry and instruction in recent years has been largely confined to the departments of philosophy, psychology, and economics, particularly the last."[48]

It was obvious to everyone that businessmen had a direct interest in regulating economic thought in the universities. However, their intrusions into other fields such as philosophy, psychology, anthropology, and political science now indicated a much deeper comprehension of their long-term class interests in the regulation of ideology and curriculum. The long-term stabilization of collective orientations required the imposition of a uniform set of presuppositions across fields and disciplines. For instance, psychology, anthropology, and philosophy had to be regulated because they dealt with the "innate" tenets of human nature, rational man, and self-interest. As new social science concepts like "ideology" and the "collective unconscious" were imported from

Europe, scholars were developing theoretical frameworks which fundamentally challenged the basic assumptions of classical economics and conservative political thought. As one college trustee suggested, it was feared that "psychologists might venture to attack certain innate and fundamental truths, such as moral judgment and rational intention."[49]

The problem of academic freedom quickly grew to such proportions that it finally received extensive attention in Commissioner of Education P. P. Claxton's 1915 annual report. Claxton observed that "within the past two or three years . . . there have been so many recurrences of disciplinary action directed by trustees and presidents of prominent institutions against professors reputed to hold unorthodox political, economic, or religious views that the question of academic freedom has become temporarily one of the foremost issues in university administration." Claxton also found that "instructors in the field of economics and political science are at the present time especially in danger."[50] He thought no one would deny "that there is always pressure exerted in academic communities, as elsewhere, to keep radical propagandists quiet and to discourage destructive criticism of the existing order." The problem emerged, for Claxton, when this pressure became so intense that it discouraged the constructive and loyal criticism necessary to a progressive democracy. Claxton thought that such a point was now being reached "in large universities which are supposedly free," although such pressure "as a rule" was "exerted subtly" and "often unconsciously" by those in authority.[51]

The pressure was so intense that one by one those fields which were under attack finally mobilized the existing professional associations as a base of resistance. The first organized response came in 1913 when Dr. John M. Mecklin, a professor of philosophy and psychology, tendered a forced resignation from Lafayette College. Lafayette was formally under the jurisdiction of the Presbyterian church, although like most denominational colleges by this time, its board of trustees consisted of local manufacturers, railroad men, and coal operators. The trustees' alleged reason for requesting the resignation was that Mecklin had violated a "common understanding" that "teachings in such departments are generally to be in harmony with the doctrines of philosophy usually taught and held in the Presbyterian Church."[52]

Dr. Mecklin was at this time a member of the American Philosophical Association and the American Psychological Association. Both organizations concluded they were not satisfied with the official explanation provided for Mecklin's dismissal. A joint committee was appointed to investigate the incident. The committee legitimized its authority to conduct the investigation by asserting that its purpose was to discover whether or not the dismissal might "have the effect of injuring the professional standing and opportunities" of any member of the two associations. Furthermore, it wanted to ascertain for the benefit of its members what "doctrinal limitations" were currently "imposed in teaching philosophy and psychology" at Lafayette College.[53]

The college administration "courteously declined" to provide any information. The committee could therefore only note that the corporation's official charter expressly prohibited the imposition of any doctrinal limitations at the college. It also established that Mecklin was a Presbyterian minister in good standing with the church whose orthodoxy had never been questioned by ecclesiastical authorities.[54] The findings added to suspicions that the trustees' official explanation was merely a smoke screen.

There was little the committee could do in this particular case except try to focus public attention on inconsistencies in the official explanation. However, the Mecklin case was used as a vehicle for making the first formal statement on academic freedom by a professional association. A general statement of principles began by distinguishing between two different classes of American higher institutions: "those in which freedom of inquiry, or belief, and of teaching is, if not absolutely unrestricted, . . . at least subject to limitations so few and so remote as to give practically no occasion for difference of opinion; and those which are frankly instruments of denominational or political propaganda."[55]

The committee immediately distanced itself from any claim to an absolute right of academic freedom. It agreed there could be no assertion of a right to academic freedom in the latter institutions so long as the pertinent restrictions were explicitly stated as a condition for employment in individual contracts or college charters. There was a presumption of academic freedom only where doctrinal restrictions were not specified in advance. The joint committee then asserted that professional associations had the right to investigate colleges only for three specific reasons:

1. to ascertain which institutions do, and which do not officially profess the principle of freedom of teaching,
2. to ascertain with a fair degree of definiteness, in the case of those institutions which do not, what the doctrinal limitations imposed upon their teachers are and,
3. to call public attention to all instances, in institutions of the former sort, in

which freedom of teaching has been violated, or in which . . . restrictions other than those laid down, appear to have been imposed ex post facto.[56]

The committee finally claimed that whenever academic freedom or doctrinal restrictions were at issue, all professors had a right to have the charges against them stated and presented to them in writing. It was recommended that these charges, along with any supporting evidence, should then be brought before the full faculty and board of trustees for a fair hearing according to an assumed rule of due process.

University administrations were outraged by this assertion of academic rights, despite the fact that in retrospect, the committee report seems a model of deference and moderation. The report was a full-scale retreat from the more radical claims to unconditional rights of academic freedom, political participation, and university democracy. The report did not even put forward a claim to academic freedom except in those instances where it was specified in university charters or implied by past administrative practices. The committee only requested that limitations be made explicit, but it never challenged the right of university administrations to impose such restrictions. On the contrary, it narrowed the issue to one of technical due process and, hence, sidestepped any serious confrontation with the political and ideological conflicts which underlay the current problem.

Three other professional associations took similar actions shortly after the Mecklin case. The American Political Science Association (APSA), American Sociological Society (ASS), and American Economic Association (AEA) each independently established general committees to investigate the state of academic freedom in their respective disciplines. The AEA committee consisted of three department chairs from major universities: E.R.A. Seligman (Columbia), Richard T. Ely (Wisconsin), and Frank A. Fetter (Princeton). The APSA committee was composed of Frederick N. Judson, an attorney specializing in railroad regulation and labor arbitration; James Q. Dealey, professor of social and political science at Brown University; and Herbert Croly, journalist and editor for the *New Republic*. The sociology committee included Ulysses G. Weatherly, professor of economics and sociology at Indiana University; James P. Lichtenberger, professor of sociology, University of Pennsylvania; and Roscoe Pound, professor of jurisprudence, Harvard University.

The three committees were soon merged into a single joint committee with E.R.A. Seligman as its chair for the purpose of investigating the Fisher case at Wesleyan University. The new joint committee accepted the theoretical framework laid down by its predecessor in the philosophical and psychology associations as the basis of its investigation. It concluded, from this perspective, that Fisher did not have a legitimate complaint, since Wesleyan University was expressly a denominational college. While many suspected that the real reason for Fisher's dismissal was "the objection felt by the president and some of the trustees of the college to his political and social views,"[57] the trustees had officially based their dismissal on unorthodox public religious utterances.

The joint committee continued its original work following the Fisher case and finally released a preliminary general report on academic freedom in December 1914. The committee once again reiterated the principle that a right to academic freedom could not exist in any institution expressly "designed to spread specific doctrines of any kind." It concluded that elsewhere, a problem was prevalent in American higher institutions. The committee was convinced that, on the one hand, faculty misunderstood "the nature and limits of academic freedom," while on the other, trustees had failed to understand "the fundamental theory of academic tenure." In that respect, the current problem resolved "itself into one of departure from accepted standards" on both sides. Faculty and trustees had both failed "to observe the duties no less than the rights of their position."[58] The solution to that problem, therefore, lay in a clarification and specification of the limits on academic freedom and the contractual terms of academic tenure.

The committee refused to offer any specific guidelines of its own, but instead attempted to clarify the relevant questions that individual faculties and administrations needed to negotiate at each individual campus. These included defining the status of a tenured professor (i.e., was it absolute, as in Europe, or something less permanent?), the rights associated with various professorial ranks (e.g., probationary status), the ownership of pension funds, and the definition of mutually acceptable rules of due process in dismissals.

The questions presumed that the problem of academic freedom would automatically be resolved once these ambiguities in the terms of tenure were eliminated at individual campuses. It is probable, as Veysey suggests, that the joint committee report again accurately reflected the current class consciousness of university intellectuals. Academic freedom was a lofty ideal around which to rally, but the real concerns of most professors were far more mundane. They were more concerned with "matters of security, status, salary, and power."[59] The concept of academic freedom was not so much a principle for most professors as a political symbol which appeared to be inextricably linked with their general loss of status and university control. It was possible to mobilize a broad base of professional support for academic freedom precisely because academic freedom and tenure initially seemed to be the same issue.

Several well-known scholars had already set about the task of mobilizing this professional support in conjunction with the joint committees of the existing professional associations in the spring of 1913. A number of senior professors from Columbia and Johns Hopkins University broached the idea of creating a national organization of university professors to be specifically concerned with problems of academic freedom, tenure, salary, status, and university government. The faculties of ten leading universities were canvassed on the question. The results proved encouraging, so that a call was issued for a November meeting to be held in Baltimore.

Representatives attended from Columbia, Cornell, Johns Hopkins, Harvard, Yale, Princeton, Clark, and the University of Wisconsin. This initial delegation decided the new organization would be national in scope and open to all professors regardless of rank or institution. The convention elected a twenty-five-member organizing committee with at least one representative from each major disciplinary field to write a constitution. John Dewey of Columbia was elected committee chair. James McKeen Cattell and Richard T. Ely were other important members.[60]

The new American Association of University Professors issued its first public statement in early 1914. The AAUP explained that while the various learned societies did an admirable job of caring for "the scientific and specialized interests" of American university faculties, no organization currently represented "the common interests of the teaching staffs" by dealing with "the general problems of university policy."[61] The AAUP proposed to organize faculty across disciplinary lines to pursue their common occupational interests as a social category. Its major goal was to promote and defend "the interests of the profession as a whole."[62] The AAUP claimed 867 dues-paying members at sixty institutions by the end of 1915.[63]

The first issue on the AAUP agenda was the problem of academic freedom and academic tenure. It immediately appointed a new committee of thirteen members which included six of the original members of the earlier AEA-APSA-ASS joint committee, and in addition, Charles E. Bennett, professor of Latin, Cornell; Franklin H. Giddings, professor of sociology, Columbia; Frederick W. Padelford of the University of Washington; Howard C. Warren, professor of experimental psychology, Princeton; Henry W. Farnam, professor of economics, Yale; Charles A. Kofoid from the University of California; and Arthur O. Lovejoy. Seligman was again selected as committee chair.

The committee soon turned its deliberations to a Utah case that erupted shortly after its formation. The case succeeded in establishing the AAUP as a credible and legitimate professional association among faculty whose task was to mediate disputes between faculty and trustees through investigations of faculty complaints. The Utah incident could not help but draw national attention for the simple reason that it was an academic holocaust.

On March 17, 1915, the University of Utah Board of Regents dismissed four members of the faculty and demoted one other professor without warning or prior notice. Seventeen faculty members resigned in protest over the next five weeks. None of those dismissed had any history of radicalism. The most prominent of the four, A. A. Knowlton, was a physicist. In this instance, the managerial concept of "politics" had been extended to embrace internal relations between faculty and administration. The official charges against the four were "speaking in a very uncomplimentary way about the administration, speaking very disrespectfully of the chairman of the board of regents, speaking in a depreciatory way about the university before classes, and working against the administration."[64]

The incident was particularly significant as a vehicle for widening the AAUP's base of national support. The case pitted faculty against administration in a peculiar situation where academic tenure and freedom of speech were spliced together by the employment-at-will doctrine. The board of regents declared that it alone was responsible for the management of the university and would not "be influenced by protests coming from others."[65] Thus, the case cut across disciplinary and ideological cleavages to mobilize faculty as a cohesive social category in opposition to the businessmen-trustees. The case was perfectly suited to a mass mobilization of the professoriate because it incorporated the question of academic freedom into broader concerns with tenure, status, and university control.

Academic appointments at the University of Utah, as elsewhere in the country, were for a *de jure* period of one year. In asserting the employment-at-will doctrine, the members of the administration were well within their legal rights as trustees of the corporation's property. This was precisely the problem. There was a traditional presumption among American faculties that contracts were automatically renewed each year, as a matter of routine, unless teachers were notified well in advance. The University of Utah had been founded in 1850, and so far as can be determined, that tradition had never been violated until 1915.

It was becoming evident that long-accepted standards of university tradition were no longer secure. Trustees had decisively asserted the employee idea. The university president had indicated that unacceptable politics now included challenges to the internal functional division of labor between administrators and faculty. It served notice that no one was in principle exempt from dismissal for a range of political reasons that even included disagreements over internal policies.

The AAUP investigating committee sharpened the conflict by challenging the employment-at-will doctrine with an alternative theory of public trusteeship. State universities were unquestionably public institutions that were owned by the citizens of the states. Consequently, they were under a special obligation to tolerate a diversity of viewpoints and conflicting opinions on all matters. The board of regents was, as a consequence, a public trust whose role should be to guarantee this diversity. University administrators were public officials and, hence, had to accept criticism of their policies and persons like any other public officer in a democracy. Moreover, this right could not be arbitrarily denied to university professors, who as citizens, enjoyed the same rights to criticize government officials and policies. The AAUP committee found the Utah board's action "unjustified in general," but "peculiarly unsuitable in officials of a State University."[66]

The board answered the statement with a rejoinder that it had "no doubts as to the correctness of its past action and the rectitude of its own motives and those of the president." None of the professors were reinstated in their former positions. The AAUP' s only gain, other than a boost in membership, was the winning of a new rule at Utah that required consultation between regents and faculty prior to any future terminations. The AAUP credited even this modest achievement "to the professors who by their resignations made effective protest."[67] This kind of confrontational boycott was a tactic few professors were willing to support in practice.

Following the Utah incident the AAUP was severely attacked as a "professors' union" by university administrators, conservative politicians, and businessmen. Yet, the issues involved in the Utah case were those which attracted a more conservative membership of the kind that would not support unionization or union tactics. The paradox was that any influence the AAUP might hope to exert depended solely on its capacity to cooperate with university administrations and wield some degree of professional persuasion with trustees. As a result, the organization was now under pressure to prove to administrators that it was not a union which would instinctively come to the defense of any professor who filed a grievance.

It was able to make some movement in that direction the same year with the investigation of a case at the University of Colorado. The case involved James H. Brewster, a professor of law, who was hired for the 1914–15 academic year. During his tenure at Colorado, Brewster delivered highly publicized testimony to the U.S. Commission on Industrial Relations (December 7–8, 1914) that was extremely critical of industrial practices in the state following the infamous Ludlow massacre. He also appeared as counsel for the United Mine Workers before a U.S. Congressional committee in February and March of 1915. The chairman of the Commission on Industrial Relations then asked him to testify for the commission a second time.

Brewster was not rehired for the following year. He attributed the unannounced termination to his political and legal activities in opposition to Colorado mining interests. In fact, the AAUP investigating committee discovered that the governor had intervened and pressured the university president to dismiss Brewster earlier. Nevertheless, the AAUP exonerated the university on grounds that the administration had been planning a "reconstruction of the law faculty" before Brewster was hired and that his appointment was never intended to extend beyond the time when financial conditions made this reconstruction possible. Unfortunately for Brewster, that time had come after only one year.[68] The Colorado case provided an inroad toward administrative cooperation with the AAUP by demonstrating that a full disclosure of evidence could actually work to an administration's advantage.

Critics of the AAUP cited the Colorado case as an example of how focusing on technical issues of due process, tenure, and contract would submerge the substantive ideological aspects of academic freedom.[69] Why was Brewster not rehired instead of someone else? It was perfectly possible within well-defined rules of tenure and employment to selectively hire and dismiss individual professors. Administrative adherence to the technical details of procedural rules would not prevent politically or ideologically motivated retaliation. It would only require the actions to follow a specified procedure. Upton Sinclair saw the case merely as evidence that university presidents were learning how to structure dismissals within a bureaucratic framework of rules that concealed the problem of academic freedom.

THE SCOTT NEARING CASE

The professional tendency toward submerging substantive questions of academic freedom beneath the procedural concerns of academic tenure was temporarily arrested when the Scott Nearing case erupted at the University of Pennsylvania in 1915. The Nearing case, according to Commissioner of Education P. P. Claxton, aroused "even greater public interest than the Utah situation."[70] No other single case brought the class conflict between intellectuals and business trustees into such relief by intertwining the tenure issues raised in Utah with the problems of ideology and academic freedom.

Dr. Scott Nearing was an assistant professor of economics at the Wharton School of the University of Pennsylvania.[71] He was known in Pennsylvania as an advocate of child labor laws. He had written extensively on the topic and served on the Pennsylvania Child Labor Commission from 1905 to 1907. Nearing continued to publish books and articles on wages and child labor that were highly critical of current labor practices after accepting an appointment at the Wharton School in 1907. The child labor issue was so hotly contested by Socialists and progressives in the Pennsylvania state legislature that mere publications were enough to constitute "politics" in this particular instance.

Nearing was frequently criticized by name in the *Philadelphia Ledger*, a newspaper owned by investment financier Anthony J. Drexel, and was also criticized by conservative alumni, other faculty, and students in various forums. In many respects, Nearing had the unfortunate honor of being a lightning rod for much deeper and generalized dissatisfaction with the university that was simmering among trustees and alumni. Nearing's eventual dismissal was merely the denouement to a long series of complaints, threats, and harassment of faculty over several years at Pennsylvania. These were directed against what trustees and alumni claimed were "settled points of orthodox economic theory and accepted social standards" concerning child labor, public ownership, and religion.[72] The criticism was most vehement when faculty members challenged so-called generally accepted ideas outside the classroom. Frustrated by their inability to control liberals and radicals on the college faculty, Philadelphia's bankers, railroad men, coal operators, and steel manufacturers decided to make the young and rather naive Nearing an example that would serve as a standing warning to the remaining faculty.

The trustees had first voiced their discontent by censuring the dean of the Law School for having advocated the recall of judicial decisions by popular vote. Another professor was denied permission to publish an address entitled "The Agitator in History" in the official university journal. Many professors had had promotions denied or postponed because of unfavorable reports from conservative students or because of critical articles and editorials about them in the *Ledger*. One assistant professor was threatened with termination because of a report from one student about "a remark he had made in the classroom." In this case, the issue was dropped only when the professor's department chair threatened to resign over the dispute. Following vigorous faculty condemnation of such actions, the trustees responded by releasing a statement "favoring" academic freedom in 1914. The statement was accompanied by a warning that "dismissal might follow from any unauthorized teaching."[73]

The trustees' actions were closely related to the growing discontent among leaders of the General Alumni Society. Ten of twenty-four trustees were nominees of the society. The alumni association had been complaining for years about the admission of women to the university. It condemned larger enrollments for opening the university to Philadelphia's "urban masses." Alumni opposed a growing dependence on state appropriations on the grounds that it would subject the university to "public control" and the vagaries of "mass education."[74] In addition, alumni continually pressured trustees to assert control over the faculty. A 1914 article in the Pennsylvania *Alumni Register* perhaps best summarizes the frustration of alumni, who were apparently giving antecedent support to any dismissals. The article complained that a "mania for making laws to reform the universe has been unbridled without regard to the economic fallacies involved in the proposed statutes. Laws to regulate wages and the hours of labor have disregarded the law of supply and demand . . . it is a courageous thing for the trustees of a university to stand firm for sound thought and a guarded education in these crises, as against the whim of popular fancy."[75]

Nearing received a promotion from instructor to assistant professor in June of 1914. A year later, on June 14, 1915, Nearing was informed that he would not be reappointed, despite a unanimous recommendation from the Wharton faculty and the dean. The case was a national sensation by the end of the year.

The board of trustees refused to issue any official explanation for its action. On the other hand, individual trustees were making private statements which confirmed pervasive suspicions that Nearing's dismissal was political. For instance, Harrison S. Morris, a trustee for the Joseph Wharton estate, which endowed the school, made an inquiry to

see if terms of the endowment protecting academic freedom had been
violated by the action. He was informed by George Wharton Pepper, a
university trustee, that

if by free speech is meant the unrestricted right of the teacher to adopt any
method he pleases for the propagation of any view he happens to hold, then I
could not bring myself to advocate such license . . . a man might feel himself
justified in advocating a disregard for moral principles regarded by the rest of
us as fundamental. If, on the other hand, free speech means the right to
proclaim views not discordant with the ethical sense of the community and so
proclaimed as to evidence due consideration for the sensibilities of those
holding different views, I shall be happy to enlist in a campaign for free speech
at the university.[76]

What is interesting in the ensuing debates is the degree to which the
relevant community for making such judgments was identified almost
exclusively with alumni, trustees, and wealthy benefactors. The
"moral principles" which constituted its "ethical sense" were always
defined in terms of private property, axioms of laissez-faire economics
and government, and the religious practices of conservative orthodox
Protestant denominations (e.g., Episcopalianism and Presbyterian-
ism). The concepts of laissez-faire economics and public morality were
so intertwined in the minds of Philadelphia businessmen that what
began as a dispute over Nearing's "economic fallacies" in advocating
the abolition of child labor ended with trustees accusing him of religious heresy and immorality.

The Alumni Society aggressively defended the university governing
board against the public outcry. It released one statement that approved
the board's action. The occasion was also used as an opportunity "to
express [the society's] condemnation of the 'fallacious conclusions' of
certain members of the teaching staff which when stated publicly were
'likely to arouse class prejudice.' "[77] Similar statements crystallized the
problem of academic freedom for many throughout the country. Lightner Witmer, a professor of psychology at the university, concluded "that
certain representatives of the privileged classes have determined upon a
campaign for the control of research and teaching."[78] From as far away as
Scotland, T. H. Huxley declared that "the attacks upon Nearing are made
. . . because he attacks the aggressions of associated capital; attacks
made because associated capital knows that its aggression upon the
economic rights of the people is nefarious and cannot stand against
adequate presentation of the demands of the people."[79]

The international controversy surrounding the case finally roused the AAUP into action, but its investigating committee met with a decidedly hostile reception when it arrived on campus. J. Levering Jones, a trustee engaged in finance and real estate, made the governing board's position clear in the *Philadelphia Ledger* (June 19, 1915), noting that the University of Pennsylvania was not a public institution and that the trustees were therefore "answerable only to our sense of duty and responsibility. No one has the right to question us."[80] The AAUP was conciliatory, but not even a moderate investigating committee could fail to draw the obvious conclusion. AAUP investigators were reluctantly "compelled to conclude that at least a contributing cause of Dr. Nearing's removal was the opposition of certain persons outside the university to the views . . . expressed by him in his extra-mural addresses."[81]

Nearing was not reinstated, nor did the trustees alter their understanding of academic freedom, but the Nearing case did convince the University of Pennsylvania trustees to unanimously adopt a new set of statues concerning appointments and tenure.[82] These new statutes clarified the meaning of professorial ranks, the length and terms of appointment for each rank, and procedures for advancement and promotion. The assistant professorship was explicitly designated as a "probationary" rank. The new statutes institutionalized "consultation" with a faculty committee prior to the removal or nonrenewal of any faculty member. The board was required to give written notice of nonrenewal well before the end of the academic year. Professors who were denied tenure automatically received a one-year grace period prior to permanent termination.

The statutes essentially clarified the procedural meaning of due process at the university and were equally important for stabilizing capitalist relations of production within the university. Formal recognition of the governing board's authority *not to accept* faculty recommendations was the price of due process. The new statutes, approved by the faculty, conceded that "the provost and board of trustees shall proceed to make such reappointments as their judgment approves."[83]

The USBE publicized the new statutes as an event of "very great significance in the evolution of a just and efficient method of university government in the United States" and recommended that other university trustees and administrators consider similar statutes.[84] Likewise, the AAUP praised the statutes as a breakthrough in the cause of academic freedom. Effigham B. Morris, chairman of the Pennsylvania trustees, had been pushing for the adoption of similar rules well before the Nearing incident. The Philadelphia corporate executive had understood the logic of bureaucratic authority better than his colleagues. The Nearing incident enabled him to convince other trustees that if they had received the prior approval of a faculty committee acting in a representative capacity or had given Nearing fair warning within a set of accepted procedures, the outcry against the trustees would not have been possible.[85]

The second annual meeting of the AAUP convened in the midst of the Nearing dispute. It was at this meeting that the association adopted its first report on academic freedom and academic tenure. The declaration of principles was framed and adopted with an eye to the Nearing case. It was therefore something of an ideological coup for the association's left-wing which was being led by Richard T. Ely, J. M. Cattell, and John Dewey.

The document was divided into two parts that seem to reflect the different concerns of the association's liberal and conservative wings. The document could thus serve as the manifesto of either wing, depending upon which part was placed in the forefront of the problem of academic freedom. Part I was a "general declaration of principles designed to clarify and specify the precise issues which constitute the dispute over academic freedom." Academic freedom was defined to include "freedom of research, freedom of teaching within the institution, and freedom of extra mural utterance and action." In relation to this principle, "the nature of the trust reposed in the governing boards" was "emphatically declared to be public." Governing boards were considered "trustees for the public." Consequently, it was asserted "they cannot be permitted to assume the proprietary attitude and privilege . . . they have no moral right to bind the reason or the conscience of any professor."[86] The AAUP militantly reasserted the academic ideal by claiming that faculty were "appointees, but not in any sense the employees" of the governing board. Their status was essentially that of freeholders with permanent tenure in a public office: "University teachers should be understood to be, with regard to the conclusions reached and expressed by them, no more subject to the control of the trustees than are judges subject to the control of the President with respect to their decisions."[87]

The report was particularly bold in situating these claims against the backdrop of current historical developments. It pointed out that in the earliest days of American higher education, the church had been the major threat to academic freedom. Physical sciences had been the major object of repression in that era. In the modern era, the locus of institutional power had shifted toward businessmen, who were now the "enemy" of academic freedom. This had shifted the academic "danger zone." Academic repression was now explicitly aimed against: "the expression of opinions which point toward extensive social innovations, or call in question the moral legitimacy or social expediency of economic conditions or commercial practices in which large vested interests are involved."[88]

The ideological statement concerning the principles of academic freedom was intended as a theoretical framework for interpreting the meaning of Part II of the report. Part II essentially outlined the procedural details for avoiding and resolving disputes over academic freedom and tenure. They were substantively little different from those eventually adopted by the University of Pennsylvania board of trustees.

The only statement of tactics in the 1915 declaration was a naively optimistic and typically progressive appeal to the pressures of "an overwhelming and concentrated public opinion."[89] The following year, the AAUP officially repudiated the notion that the association was an occupational union that would attempt to achieve its aims by any form of coercion. The influence of publicity was to be its only means of negotiating with trustees. Despite its failure to rectify a single case of academic repression, the AAUP continued to cling to the notion "that such abuses will cease when they are made known and when their full significance is understood."[90]

The commissioner of education attempted to facilitate this process by circulating 3,000 copies of the new declaration to college presidents and trustees and by reprinting it in his 1916 annual report, where he advised college administrators that the AAUP report "would bespeak the careful consideration of university boards and executives."[91] The adoption of statutes regulating academic freedom and academic tenure also became a regular recommendation of future USBE survey teams. The AAUP further publicized the declaration in newspapers and libraries throughout the country.[92]

For the time being, however, the AAUP really made very little headway in convincing other universities to emulate the Pennsylvania example. In the years following the Nearing case, violations of academic freedom continued to multiply. Committee A, on Academic Freedom and Academic Tenure continually received complaints from every part of the country. However, a shortage of personnel and travel funds meant that delegations from Committee A could investigate only a small proportion of the complaints—probably never more than 10 percent. Nevertheless, of the seven cases the AAUP had investigated by the end of 1917, it found violations of academic freedom or tenure in six of them.

Moreover, the complaints received by the AAUP did not include cases falling under the Commons model, in which faculty silently accepted their situation. When investigations were conducted, they revealed that cases receiving publicity were often only the last incident in a long pattern of administrative tyranny which had finally driven a faculty to its collective breaking point. The Nearing investigation unearthed evidence of at least four or five other incidents of harassment. An investigation at the Colorado School of Mines revealed that Dr. Charles D. Fest and Professor John C. Bailar were dismissed for refusing to raise the grades of students with influential relatives after direct requests from the board of trustees. This investigation uncovered four other unpublicized incidents of arbitrary termination.[93]

In the midst of these findings, tactics remained a point of contention between liberals and leftists in the association, with leftists continuing to prefer unionization, strikes, and boycotts over professional persuasion and censure. There was also tension between those who wanted to firmly establish a German principle of academic freedom that was explicitly political in its protections (e.g., Ely) as against those conservatives, like E.R.A. Seligman who preferred focusing on procedural issues of tenure and university government. Seligman moved strategically to drive this wedge deeper through his position as chairman of Committee A once the aftershocks of the Nearing case subsided, by orchestrating a major shift away from Part I of the 1915 declaration. The crucial moves were made during the war years of 1917 and 1918.

8

Twilight of the Idols, 1917–1928

SELIGMAN and his allies moved to drive a wedge between liberals and the left in the AAUP once the concerns of the Nearing case subsided and were finally lost in the war hysteria of 1917 to 1918. Conservatives successfully neutralized the organization's left wing during World World I, as liberals rushed to defend democracy and the American state against German autocracy. Anything perceived as German—whether Marx, Nietzsche, Freud, university traditions of academic freedom, historicism, institutional political economy, or social scientific method—was immediately suspect as treasonous or as the propaganda of a foreign agent. Any attempt to speak out against the war left one open to attacks as an unpatriotic and disloyal opponent of democracy.

WORLD WAR I AND THE POLITICS OF ACADEMIC FREEDOM

It was a strange prescience on the part of President Van Hise to be the first administrator to respond to signs of an approaching storm on American campuses. He encircled Wisconsin with a blanket policy of prior restraint as early as 1914. The faculty was advised to "refrain from using the university platform, either in classroom or otherwise, for discussing any of the questions relating to the War."[1] The campus and its faculty would remain officially neutral. The Wisconsin campus, with all its populist, progressive, and socialist radicals, would provide a striking picture of internal peace over the next few years.

Wisconsin stood in sharp contrast to Columbia University where Nicholas Murray Butler and E.R.A. Seligman would jointly establish the campus model for systematic ideological repression. Columbia University became the major staging ground for the first concerted assault against "disloyal" leftist radicals during the war. The war finally gave Butler and the Columbia trustees an opportunity to eliminate several leftist faculty they had long considered troublesome. Seligman was more than willing to organize faculty consent and even carried these policies back into the AAUP.

Most universities, including Columbia, imposed no prior restrictions, so that as the debates over national preparedness escalated in late 1915 and early 1916, university professors were also increasingly vocal in their positions on the war. Debates on whether the United States ought to abandon its official neutrality were being held in public schools and universities throughout the country. Columbia and CCNY became vital centers of war resistance. Strong campaigns were organized at Columbia and CCNY to resist military training on campus, to collect petitions against the war, and to hold antidraft demonstrations. Both student leaders and faculty members were active in the movement, although most administrators blamed the turmoil on the influence of irresponsible professors. Annoyance turned to alarm as Butler and his trustees watched the activity on their campus spread from Columbia into a formal regional network of organized campus resistance that eventually linked up with off-campus political groups.

A board of trustees' committee on education made the first move to discourage the antiwar activities in early 1916. Professor of history Benjamin Kendrick and Dr. Leon Fraser, an instructor in politics, were summoned to appear before the committee on education. They were censured for delivering speeches at a student meeting in which they criticized military discipline as an influence that violated the educational mission to train leaders committed to democratic institutions in the country. Both professors singled out the controversial military camp at Plattsburgh as a danger to the democratic values of New York's students.[2]

Despite the censures, Columbia faculty members continued participating in student and off-campus debates on the neutrality issue. A nationally publicized incident associated with one such debate roused Butler and the trustees back into action in early 1916. A speaker at one debate asked the audience "to defend the flag." Someone in the audience retorted, "To Hell with the Flag!" The statement was subsequently plastered across the front page of newspapers across the country as evidence that "pacifism" was motivated by "unpatriotic impulses."[3] The incident temporarily turned national debate away from whether or not America should enter the war to the question of whether or not public schools and universities should be allowed to sponsor debates on the war. Proponents of national preparedness argued that prolonging the debate would weaken civic morale by exposing the public to poor citizenship and foreign propaganda.

On April 21, 1916, Charles A. Beard, a professor of history and political science at Columbia University, entered the debate with a speech to the National Conference of Community Centers. Beard expressed the opinion that public schools were legitimate forums for public debate on any issue. After all, he casually suggested, the world's strongest republic could certainly withstand the inconsequential effects of a single "To Hell with the Flag" uttered by an anonymous man in a crowded New York City schoolhouse.

Most newspapers accurately reported Beard's off-hand remark. However, one newspaper hysterically declared that the already controversial Professor Beard was now in sympathy with the statement "To Hell with the Flag!"[4] Beard was already in the midst of an academic civil war that was spilling over beyond the boundaries of professional discussion with the publication of his *Economic Interpretation of the Constitution*. The respected Edward S. Corwin had already berated Beard for trying to demonstrate "the truth of the socialistic theory of economic determinism and class struggle." The noble Henry Cabot Lodge, a man not unknown to the 1912 Republican vice-presidential candidate, Nicholas Butler, also intimated that such works were motivated by "Socialist proclivities."[5] Neither charge was without merit.[6] At the same time, however, Beard was an advocate of American entry into the war, if only as a historically necessary assault on the remnants of feudal absolutism in Europe.[7]

The newspaper report was used as a pretext to summon Beard before a closed meeting of the Columbia trustees' committee on education. Beard said nothing at the time, but later reported he had "speedily disposed of the flag incident" as an obvious mistake on the part of a single newspaper. The trustees apparently accepted his version of the event. However, he notes:

The flag incident being at an end I prepared to leave the room when I was utterly astonished to have Mr. Bangs and Mr. Coudert [two trustees] launch into an inquisition of my views and teachings. For half an hour I was "grilled" by these gentlemen. Dr. Butler and certain colleagues from the Faculty of Political Science (who were present at the inquisition) made no attempt to stop the proceedings. Mr. Coudert denounced my teachings in vigorous language, in which he was strongly seconded by Mr. Bangs. . . . When the inquisitors satisfied themselves, the chairman of the committee ordered me to warn all other men in my department against teachings "likely to inculcate disrespect for American institutions."[8]

Professors Kendrick and Beard became silent for the time being, but Leon Fraser continued working for the Association of International Conciliation. Fraser had been organizing courses for the association on the principles of pacifism and international conciliation at campuses throughout the country. Thus, in the spring of 1917, President Butler warned the Faculty of Political Science not to renominate Fraser for a continuation of his academic appointment. Butler informed the faculty that Fraser was not acceptable to Mr. Bangs. The faculty defiantly renominated Fraser. Butler then dropped Fraser from the payroll for "financial reasons" associated with the declining enrollments during wartime. According to Beard, he then "informed the College authorities that in case the attendance in the college in the autumn warranted the appointment of additional instructors, under no circumstances should Dr. Fraser be renominated."[9]

The trustees adopted a more systematic approach to rooting out radicals following Fraser's release from the faculty. On March 6, 1917, the same day that the trustees expressed their "full support" for Butler's national preparedness activities (see Chapter 5), they adopted a second resolution which created a special investigative committee. The committee's preparedness role was "to inquire and ascertain whether doctrines which are subversive of, or tend to the violation or disregard of the Constitution or laws of the United States or of the State of New York, or the principles upon which it is founded, or which tend to encourage a spirit of disloyalty are taught or disseminated by officers of the university."[10]

The trustees appointed to the new committee were Nicholas Murray Butler; George L. Ingraham, an attorney and former Justice of the New York Supreme Court; John B. Pine, an attorney; William Parsons, a consulting civil engineer; Stephen Baker, president of the Bank of Manhattan and a director for the Bowery Savings Bank and the New York Clearinghouse Building Company; and Francis Bangs, an attorney.

The appointment of an official inquisition won immediate response from around the nation and was held up as an example for all loyal universities to emulate. The *New York Times*, for instance, carried an editorial that not only praised the trustees' action, but simultaneously encouraged the committee to rebuff any assertions of a right to academic freedom. The editorial expressed its concern that a "noisy brood of boy disloyalists, anarchists, and pacifists" were being spawned in American schools and colleges and it concluded that "if anywhere patriotism is being poisoned in the young, if anywhere our children and youth are exposed to the inculcation of fatal doctrines by their teachers, the fact cannot be faced too soon. There will be the customary patter about 'academic freedom.' That freedom cannot protect teachers, if such they be, who are undermining the patriotism of the next generation."[11]

Three weeks later the trustees responded to faculty protests by appointing nine senior faculty members to the committee. E.R.A. Seligman was appointed chairman of the faculty subcommittee. John Dewey was the only member who had any affinity with the left. Dewey had favored neutrality. Once hostilities began, however, he argued that social democrats should participate in the war effort to influence its goals and consequences.[12]

Seven months later, on October 1, 1917, the joint trustee-faculty committee recommended action against two professors. The trustees finally succeeded in dismissing James McKeen Cattell, on charges that he "had disseminated doctrines tending to encourage a spirit of disloyalty to the Government of the United States."[13] The committee based its charge on several personal letters Cattell had written to congressmen urging them to vote against sending troops to Europe. One can only speculate on how the committee got these letters, but it certainly required the collaboration of congressmen or someone in their offices.

Henry Wordsworth Longfellow Dana was dismissed at the same time. Dana was an undistinguished assistant professor of English whose main claim to prominence was his indirect descent from the more famous literary Longfellow. The committee did not specify any reason for Dana's termination, but he was currently teaching "the social interpretation of literature" at the Socialist Party's Rand School of Social Science. He later became an early though unimportant supporter of the Russian Revolution and a fellow traveller of the Workers' (Communist) party. He personally attributed his dismissal to participation in the antiwar activities of the People's Council, an umbrella resistance organization led largely by the left wing of the Socialist party.[14]

Yet, the internal dynamics of this committee remain obscure. John Dewey resigned from it without explanation after Cattell's termination but refused to speak about its proceedings. The intrigue at Columbia then reached new levels the following week when Charles Beard resigned from the faculty in what at first appeared to be a sympathetic protest against the committee's actions regarding Dana and Cattell. Beard himself said that he felt compelled to leave because "the institution had fallen under the control of a small and active group of trustees" who were "without standing in the world of education . . . reactionary and visionless in politics," and "narrow and medieval in religion." Beard was again a front page item in the *New York Times* when it revealed that he had already been investigated a second time for stating that free speech should continue during the war.[15]

Beard's resignation proved to be the catalyst that finally brought the simmering confrontation to a violent conclusion. The day after his resignation a hundred students met spontaneously to request that he withdraw it from the administration. Will Durant stepped forward to harangue the students and protest the expulsions. Beard refused to withdraw his resignation. Five hundred students gathered the next day to put forward the same request. This time it was accompanied by a series of provocative speeches denouncing "the autocracy of the Trustees."[16] Seven hundred students met for a third time on October 12. This time a formal resolution was passed demanding the trustees alter their position on academic freedom and allow Beard to return. Similar demonstrations continued for several days until, by the end of the week, sporadic fist fights and minor brawls were occurring between supporters and opponents of Beard. Finally, a quasi-organized guerrilla "war" erupted between roving gangs of "radical" and "patriotic" students and culminated in full-scale riots on the campus.[17]

The flame was then fanned by one of Beard's close personal friends on the faculty. Dr. Raymond H. Mussey, an assistant professor of economics at Barnard College, resigned on December 3, 1917, in a show of sympathy after having spent seventeen years at the institution.[18] However, most of Beard's liberal sympathizers criticized him for having resigned in what they interpreted as "a fit of anger." Trustees played off this criticism to trivialize the incident.

Beard answered his critics in "A Statement," published in the December issue of the *New Republic*. Beard outlined a long and well-considered program by the trustees to reshape the ideological complexion of the Columbia faculty going back to the Professor X incident in 1909. Cattell's dismissal was, in his presentation, only the latest in a long line of similar incidents at Columbia. In his view, "It was the evident purpose of a small group of the trustees (unhindered, if not aided, by Mr. Butler) to take advantage of the state of war to drive out or humiliate or terrorize every man who held progressive, liberal, or unconventional views on political matters in no way connected with the war. The institution was to be reduced below the level of a department store or factory and I therefore tendered my resignation." Beard also claimed that in early October he had been "positively and clearly informed by two responsible officers of the University [whom he did not name] that another doctrinal inquisition was definitely scheduled for an early date."[19] Beard had it on good authority that he was the committee's next target. He chose to resign rather than submit to further harassment by the trustees.

President Butler indirectly confirmed these claims in his own 1917 annual report on Columbia University. He observed in the report that "Bolsheviki of the intellect" had become too prevalent in the United States. He went on to suggest that "economic determinism . . . has in recent years obtained much influence among those who for lack of a more accurate term call themselves intellectuals. . . . The time has not yet come, however, when rational persons can contemplate with satisfaction the rule of the literary and academic Bolsheviki or permit them to seize responsibility for the intellectual life of the nation."[20]

Columbia's special investigations committee was formally disbanded on October 6, 1917, but pressure was apparently still being exerted on faculty members who failed to heed its warning. Dr. Ellery C. Stowell, a renowned professor of international law, resigned on March 1, 1918. Stowell had been a vocal critic of the special investigations committee, attacking it in local newspapers as "Prussianistic." Stowell complained in his own resignation that he was heavily pressured by university administrators and other faculty members to stop criticizing the university's wartime policies. However, he explained, his departure was primarily motivated by administrative "interference with my liberty of action, especially in regard to the expression of my views on international affairs through the medium of newspapers."[21]

The repercussions of the Columbia massacre were national in scope, as other institutions emulated Columbia's strategy. James Wechsler, a journalist, later observed that newspapers across the country lauded President Butler's example "as the epitome of conduct to which college presidents should aspire" during the war. Columbia was now the beacon illuminating the path which other campuses would follow. Presidents and trustees understood the signal and acted appropriately against "disloyalists" on their own campuses. Joseph Freeman, a Columbia undergraduate at the time, credited the Columbia dismissals with initiating a "reign of terror in the intellectual world."[22]

The incidents were widespread. For instance, all but one member of the University of Minnesota faculty was accused of being in open rebellion against the country. The charges were pure nonsense. Nevertheless, the regents conducted a full-scale hearing before the charges were put to rest. Professor William Schaper, chairman of the political science department, was the only faculty member dismissed because of the hearings. Schaper was vigorously supporting the war effort but was terminated because he thought it would be unwise for the Allies to completely destroy the German government and leave the nation in anarchy after the war.[23]

There were scattered incidents elsewhere in the country. A Professor Patten was dismissed from the University of Pennsylvania for antiwar activities. Allan Eaton, an instructor at the University of Oregon, was summarily terminated for attending a meeting of the Peoples' Council. Three professors were driven from the University of Nebraska, not because they opposed the war, but because they, respectively, lacked aggressive Americanism, supported the principle of internationalism, and disbelieved atrocity stories about the Germans. Seven other professors were driven from the University of Michigan for alleged "pro-German leanings." In a similar incident, Professor William E. Walz was banished from the University of Maine after eighteen years of service for creating "the impression that in this war his sympathies, as well as his convictions, are with Germany." The University of Illinois warned its faculty that anyone "deriding Liberty Bond salesmen" would be punished.[24]

Finally, the Communist issue was introduced during the war. Dr. Lyford Edwards, a sociologist, was run out of Rice Institute for possessing "certain views in respect to Russia so contrary to the fundamental principles of our government as to utterly destroy his further usefulness."[25] These are but a sampling of the known cases. There are probably many more still hidden in unindexed local newspapers or buried in university archives that are waiting to be told in the hundreds of as yet unwritten institutional histories.

The AAUP was not only unwilling to offer its limited assistance to those being driven off the campuses, but took decisive steps to lend its support to this round of academic repression. Social-democratic leaders like John Dewey were paralyzed and obviously confused by a failed policy of pragmatic complicity with the war. Others were neutralized in silence, if not by prior restraint, like Ely and Jastrow at Wisconsin, then by individual strategies of discreet, quiet survival. This left a reactionary like Seligman or an opportunist such as Lovejoy free to rampage unchallenged through the AAUP.

The direction of things was clear within a month of the Columbia massacre. Frank Thilly, a Cornell professor of philosophy who succeeded Dewey as president of the AAUP, issued the first official proclamation on the war in his annual address. He cast an approving eye on the events at Columbia with a declaration that the members of our profession stand loyally behind the President in this war. . . . They have no sympathy with the disloyal and even with the indifferent, and they do not believe that this is a time for ill-considered sppech and action. . . . They believe in the vigorous prosecution of the war upon which our country is engaged. . . . They do not look with favor upon those who, in times like these, insist upon an inalienable right to say whatever they please on every and all occasions."[26]

Thilly's position received wider sanction from the AAUP membership through a special Committee on Academic Freedom in Wartime, chaired by Arthur O. Lovejoy. It released a report in early 1918, ratified by the national convention, which recommended that "members of college or university faculties should . . . be required by their institutions to refrain from propaganda designed, or unmistakably tending, to cause others to resist or evade the compulsory service law or the regulations of the military authorities; and those who refuse to conform to this requirement may be and should be, dismissed, even before any action has been taken against them by the law-officers of the state."[27]

The wartime policy was cleverly institutionalized by Seligman at the same annual convention which ratified the Lovejoy report. Through his position as chairman of Committee A, Seligman engineered a decisive move while the left was still neutralized in silence. The committee reported that during 1916–17 it had received more than thirty complaints reporting violations of academic freedom or academic tenure. The committee concluded that less than a third of these cases involved real issues of academic freedom. The rest were procedural disputes over academic tenure. The committee observed that "experience has shown pretty clearly that we can rarely expect to obtain the actual redress of an individual grievance." However, the committee felt it had been fairly successful in negotiating changes in general procedure and in the definition of tenure. Consequently, the committee recommended that as far as having any practical effect, the AAUP should shift its emphasis away "from the problem of academic freedom to the more general problem of the security of academic tenure."[28]

Part I of the 1915 statement was effectively nullified in practice. It was not because the problem of academic freedom had been resolved by the AAUP. Quite the reverse: it was the committee's conclusion that it could not resolve the problem which led the AAUP to abandon any pretense to a political principle of academic freedom. Moreover, the committee stated its intention to henceforth conduct on-site investigations only in cases that offered some possibility for negotiating changes in tenure and university governance.

The academic left was further isolated by the war issue in another way which altered its complexion after the war. In April 1917 the American Socialist party had split wide open at its St. Louis convention over whether to support American participation in the war. The party's new left-wing majority denounced the war as a conflict between rival imperialist powers. It went on to form a nucleus for the People's Council and the American Peace Federation that served as national umbrella organizations for mobilizing antiwar and draft resistance. The left wing's participation in the council, and in related movements, made it easier for college administrations to dismiss militant and revolutionary socialist academics on the loyalty issue.

On the other hand, J. G. Phelps-Stokes, president of the Intercollegiate Socialist Society (ISS), had denounced the Socialist party's position in a declaration stating: "We believe the cause of socialism, of industrial democracy, of the progress of the world's workers toward a better and nobler life, is indissolubly bound up with the cause of the United States and its allied democracies."[29] The ISS cited Marx's support for the Union in the American Civil War as a precedent justifying the aggressive overthrow of a backward social structure which denied workers basic liberties and freedoms. The net result was that most university socialists, who already occupied its far right, broke with the Socialist party, severed their ties with the more militant sections of the labor movement, and joined the rush to defend American democracy. What remained of the academic left had itself moved right.

Consequently, the ISS "suffered comparatively little harassment from the federal authorities" in contrast to the Socialist party. On the other hand, Max Horn, who has written the only study of the ISS, found it "difficult to document the extent of interference with chapter activities by the college authorities during the war." Administrative interference differed from one institution to another "depending on local traditions, the ingenuity of chapters, and the degree of external pressure on the institutions." Nevertheless, it is certain that "the activities of almost all chapters were curtailed and that an unknown number of chapters were suppressed."[30]

The ISS was confident enough in its security that it launched a campaign to reorganize left-wing intellectuals even before the armistice. But, it encountered the legacy of war as an unspoken strategy of self-restraint and silence. Former members distanced themselves from the socialist label, its policies, and its politics.

One survey at the University of Minnesota is indicative of the new problem. The student newspaper there claimed in early 1919 that academic freedom had been suppressed on campus since the Schaper case. The local chapter of the AAUP asked the university president to call a general meeting of the faculty to investigate the allegation and explore the general problem of academic freedom. The faculty meeting appointed a committee "to investigate, hear testimony, gather and sift the evidence and sense the feeling of individual faculty members."[31]

The committee found that although no specific incidents of further repression could be uncovered, the effects of the Schaper case still lingered on campus as an aura of fear and inhibition. A broad structure of academic terror had been set in place over several years and then consolidated during the war. The Minnesota committee found that the problem of academic freedom was "psychological" and "was often a matter of tacit understanding, recorded . . . much more clearly in a feeling of what might . . . impend rather than by what had already happened." The committee found enough of this elusive feeling to conclude "that the university has here a real and serious problem."[32]

The problems encountered by the ISS suggest this psychological undercurrent was so pervasive that it now penetrated almost every campus. There were very few people who drew fine distinctions between the philosophy of the ISS, the Socialist Party, the IWW, and the new Communist movement. Socialism, anarchism, syndicalism, pacifism, and communism were all easily lumped together as criminal "radicalism" and "espionage." The strategy of survival dictated that leftists keep their distance from any group that could fall under this label, especially as the war hysteria was simply replaced by a "red scare."

The ISS was unable to attract most of its former constituency in this atmosphere. Consequently, its national officers conducted their own survey of college and university campuses in the fall of 1919 in order to determine whether interference with freedom of speech was still continuing on campuses in a way that prohibited the reorganization of local chapters. They received replies from faculty at more than sixty campuses. Their conclusions were identical to those reached at Minnesota six months earlier: "Although there existed little or no formal machinery to stifle free discussion, one could discern a more subtle and pervasive climate of repression."[33]

THE RED SCARE AS STATE TERROR

This climate ceased to be subtle or unspoken by the end of 1919. The Russian Revolution set off a worldwide panic among capitalists and conservative political leaders. The threat to democracy and national security shifted from Germany to Russia. Radicals suddenly changed from being viewed as German spies to being construed as Russian agents.

A. Mitchell Palmer, the current U.S. attorney general, launched an American red scare by convincing the U.S. Senate to initiate a federal investigation of "Bolshevik propaganda" in the United States. A resolution instructing the Senate Subcommittee on the Judiciary to conduct such an investigation was passed on February 4, 1919.

The bulk of the investigation focused on developments in Russia, and on such major Socialist Party activists as Morris Hillquit, Eugene Debs, Victor Berger, Max Eastman, and John Reed. In addition, however, several prominent university intellectuals—including Scott Nearing, H.W.L. Dana, and Ellery C. Stowell—were investigated. The committee was particularly disturbed by Stowell's reluctant revelation that between 25 to 50 percent of the Columbia University Faculty of Political Science had been for "peace at any price." They found a disturbing presence of "the intelligentsia" and of "intellectuals" in American radical movements.[34]

The War Department Intelligence Division also submitted to the committee its own list of sixty-two prominent people "whose activities had not been helpful to the country during the war."[35] There were again several university professors on the list, as well as Henry Laidler, secretary of the ISS. Many others were listed as members, endorsers, or sympathizers of the ISS.

The lists of names, coupled to nationally publicized investigations, hearings, testimony, and newspaper reports, were crucial to a successful strategy of terror without violence. Public attention was brought to bear on specific individuals who by implication were deemed traitors, foreign agents, and un-American enemies of democracy. It did not matter whether or not the charges were true. What was important was that state harassment, arrest, subpoenas, slander, accusations, innuendo, and legal prosecution generated an atmosphere in which others pursuing a strategy of individual survival were less likely to associate with these persons or affiliate with blacklisted organizations.

Furthermore, the federal investigations created a political atmosphere that sanctioned and lent direction to other investigations which could penetrate more deeply into the structure of various social institutions. State, local, or educational officers could pursue similar policies within this framework to target local officers and reach even further into a suspect organization's local membership. The most impressive example in this second tier of investigations was that of the New York

Joint Legislative Committee Investigating Seditious Activities. The report of New York's so-called Lusk Committee was a monumental effort of over four thousand pages and one million words published in four large volumes.[36] This report, *Revolutionary Radicalism,* went beyond the identification of persons and organizations to propose a series of practical steps required to stamp out socialism in the United States.

The Lusk report recorded and analyzed the historical rise of revolutionary socialism in every major European country, both as a theoretical doctrine and in terms of its relationship to the labor movements of those countries. The report then traced socialism's alleged importation to America through the immigration of certain ethnic groups, labor leaders, and criminal revolutionaries. The Lusk committee staff marshalled impressive and detailed historical documentation to support the official state ideology that all leftist radicalism was an "un-American" doctrine related to the economic immigration of a European underclass and to the education of American scholars in countries whose traditions of class structure were different from those of America. The committee concluded that intellectuals and the underclass jointly endorsed a doctrine of class hatred that was developed under conditions inapplicable to the United States. Moreover, it claimed that enemies of American democratic capitalism (e.g., Germany and Russia) were able to utilize this immigration as a screen for the infiltration of foreign agents who could play on the naivete of intellectuals and the ignorance of immigrants to stir up trouble and discontent.

The report provided a lengthy examination of how socialist ideology was supposedly diffused throughout the immigrant population. The indoctrination of immigrants had occurred, it claimed, through a sophisticated institutional network of left-wing political parties, churches involved with Christian socialism and settlement house work, civic organizations such as the YMCA, charitable organizations, mutual aid societies, left-wing publishing houses (e.g., Charles H. Kerr), public schools, and labor colleges. In the process of revealing this network, the committee collected and published extensive lists of the officers and members of suspect organizations which included party officials, trade union officers, schoolteachers, and college professors. The report was so exhaustive that it republished excerpts from professors' public addresses, attacked specific courses taught by individual professors, and censured innumerable scholarly books.

The Lusk committee concluded from its analysis that the menace of socialism could best be met with a two pronged attack on labor radicalism and the intellectuals. The preservation of capitalism first required that its defenders deflect the American labor movement into a non-European path of development. On another level, public education had to be utilized as a mechanism for shaping the way Americans were taught to think about their society, economy, and government. The Lusk report stands out as a remarkably calm and well-conceived plan of action amid the hysteria that is usually associated with the red scare.

In its effort to influence the ideological character of the American labor movement, the Lusk committee targeted nine "revolutionary industrial unions," including the ILGWU and IWW. The committee warned that these unions "presented the real spectre of revolution on the American horizon." Their leaders had to be prevented from gaining any further ascendancy within the labor movement.[37]

However, the Lusk committee advised public officials against using overt forms of repression (such as strikebreaking or police), because these had actually steeled radical labor in the past and in other countries. Instead, it suggested three alternatives. (1) immigration control, (2) cooperation with Samuel Gompers, and (3) public education.

The chief political objective of immigration control was to stem the tide of foreign workers from which the revolutionary industrial unions recruited most of their membership. Immigration control had to include the deportation of radical aliens like Emma Goldman, Alexander Berkman, and the leaders of revolutionary industrial unions. Deportation was to be accompanied by a more subtle use of the legal system. Political and labor radicals could be prosecuted, imprisoned, or deported for violating the antisedition laws, the federal Espionage Act, and labor injunctions. This would enable government officials to portray radicals as mere criminals, foreign agents, or threats to democratic law and order.

The report noted that the machinery for these tactics was already in place. Attorney General Palmer was deporting scores of radicals each month. Congress was already tightening immigration laws in an appropriate way. The federal Espionage Act had been extended to peacetime. Furthermore, during and just after World War I, thirty-five states passed their own criminal syndicalism laws which made it illegal to advocate in writing or speech various beliefs that encompassed pacifism, socialism, communism, syndicalism, anarchism, or any revolutionary overthrow of the government.[38] Even the AAUP observed in regard to these laws that "never before in American history has such a wholesale effort been made to regulate public opinion."[39]

The final policy proposed by the committee encouraged support for Samuel Gompers. The Lusk committee went to great lengths to demonstrate that Gompers' wing of the AFL did not challenge capitalism or the existing social structure. It did not challenge the existing two party system with an independent labor or socialist party. On the contrary, Gompers had always opposed a labor party and spent his life actively combatting socialists in the AFL. Therefore, the committee argued, capitalists and government officials should quit placing obstacles in his way, leave Gompers alone, and let him do the necessary dirty work in the unions.[40]

The other side of the conservative reaction focused on education. The committee argued that the spread of socialism in America was primarily the consequence of "persistent propaganda by Socialist, communist, and anarchist groups . . . stimulating in thousands of workers who are ignorant of our institutions and laws a contempt for our form of government."[41] Schools and colleges had to intensify citizenship and Americanization programs to counter this propaganda with an understanding of Americanism. The committee surveyed public schools throughout the country and again concluded that progress in this direction was already under way. The war had led to a more extensive introduction of civics and citizenship courses in the elementary and secondary schools. Adult education programs were offering citizenship training through English and Americanization courses for immigrants. Various coalitions of educators and businessmen were successfully promoting required college courses in American government and history based on the National Historical Service Board's war issues model.

Yet, the Lusk committee did uncover the disturbing outlines of what it considered a well-organized network of socialist professors, especially in the fields of economics, sociology, psychology, and political science.[42] It identified this network through subpoenaed personal letters which indicated the existence of personal contacts between socialists on a national scale. The report also found that socialist professors were disproportionately located in Western and Midwestern states outside its jurisdiction. The committee nevertheless expressed dismay that college administrators in these regions often knowingly hired socialists and were occasionally sympathetic with their beliefs. It was also able to focus more attention on the ISS. In New York, the Lusk committee threw its spotlight on several individual professors at major universities such as Columbia, CCNY, and Union Theological Seminary.

Contemporary liberals are fond of portraying men like Lusk, his staff, and his committee associates as merely paranoid extremists who represented bizarre deviations in American history. Yet, these portrayals minimize the fact that despite hysteria, exaggerations, and oversimplifications in the committee's analyses, Lusk was closer to the truth than those who would deny his allegations. He did name names and correctly. He and others like him did identify left-wing organizations, institutional coalitions, leading theorists, journalistic associations, and trade union leaders.

The other side of minimizing these episodes, however, is to obscure just how important state terror was to the building of a liberal consensus among labor leaders and intellectuals. It was an important factor, though by no means the only one, in undercutting the left-wing alternatives to liberalism and in confining challenges to capitalism within the institutional framework of progressive democracy. It is interesting just how few liberals or progressives at the time ever raised an objection to state terror until after the damage was done. It would not be the last time they stood silently on the sidelines until the proceedings ran the risk of engulfing them.

SOCIALISTS AS THE LIBERAL LEFT

The red scare dissipated by the end of 1921. It was perhaps officially over when the New York State Assembly repealed its own antisedition "Lusk Laws" on April 24, 1923. A new postwar generation of ISS leaders decided to reestablish the society during these years. Reflecting, however, one legacy of the red scare—that socialism had become a prohibited word even among socialists—the former ISS changed its name to the League for Industrial Democracy (LID). The LID was a "loose alliance of socialists, trade unionists, and assorted liberals and progressives."[43] Norman Thomas and Henry Laidler were named executive directors; Charles Beard, John Dewey, Reinhold Niebuhr, and A. A. Berle were other well-known members.

While the name change was partly an attempt to circumvent the lingering fear associated with joining a socialist society, it was also an indication of a different political orientation among the new leadership. The ISS had been devoted to the "intelligent discussion of socialism." The LID boldly announced that its new goal would be "education for a new social order based on production for public use and not for private profit."[44] The league shifted its focus away from campus activities and towards a section of the trade union movement and practical politics that eventually coalesced around LaFollette's 1924 Progressive party.

In part, the LID represented the new awareness among leftist intellectuals that the problem of academic democracy was inseparable from the general conditions of industrial labor. The labor problem and the problem of academic freedom were both problems of private property and its unequal distribution within capitalist relations of production. The LID was most successful in developing a relationship with the remaining socialist labor leaders in the AFL such as James Maurer, president of the Pennsylvania Federation of Labor, and John Brophy, president of District 2 (Pennsylvania) of the United Mine Workers.

The relationship was already showing results by the end of 1922. The UMW established a three-member "Nationalization Research Committee," chaired by Brophy, which reported a plan on December 29, 1922, the calling for the nationalization of all anthracite coal mines. The mere suggestion of nationalization from a major industrial union sent shock waves through the corporate community. The *New York Times* carried the report as its lead story the next day.[45]

The plan was not that surprising in terms of its call for nationalization. The UMW was known to have a strong socialist presence among its local and district leaders. The report was a new departure because it marked a new level of sophistication in the development of a practical plan for democratic nationalization. This was not a vague call for socialism.

The committee based its proposal on specific economic evaluations and assessments of the total book value of the American coal industry and its capital assets. The plan suggested precise methods for financing the acquisitions over a period of years, along with technical details for legal procedure and changes of management. The plan had worked out rules for turning over administration of the industry to the workers through a self-management program of industrial democracy. Corporate executives and the press suspected there was more to this than met the eye.

Their suspicions were confirmed when further details for the proposed nationalization were released by the UMW committee at an LID meeting in New York city one month later. Mine owners and political conservatives immediately denounced the plan as "having been prepared for the committee by some well-known New York radicals who have no connection whatever with the coal industry."[46]

Corporate hostility to the LID spilled over into another industry when railroad employees made a similar proposal. The March 1923 *Railway Review* carried an article critical of this proposal. Entitled "Miseducation of Railway Employees and Industrial Workers," the article was deemed important enough to warrant a full reprint in the *New York Times*. The article warned corporate and government officials that "labor leaders representing the major sections of organized labor in the United States have entered into an alliance with the leaders of radical thought in American colleges and a group of ex-college professors who have achieved prominence in the Socialist movement." It described this alliance between labor and intellectuals as "the most extensive program of revolutionary propaganda ever attempted in the United States" by "labor leaders, ex-college professors, college Bolsheviki." It pointed out that "the college radicals . . . by adding their strength to the radical group in the unions have virtually become the real leaders of organized labor. Under the invisible leadership of the radical alumni who direct the Socialist movement in America, the labor unions are turning more and more toward revolutionary objectives."[47] The old ISS and now the LID were identified as two of the groups perpetrating this "revolutionary conspiracy."

Mining and railroad executives were convinced that this alliance posed an immediate threat to the entire social and economic order. In this respect, business executives considered the prospects for social revolution to be far more favorable than did LID, the declining Socialist Party, or socialist union leaders. Miners' and the railroad employees' proposals were certainly not revolutionary in their political tactics. They adhered to the principle of full compensation and constitutional due process in the nationalization of all corporate assets. The reaction of corporate executives, however, does reveal the degree to which any hint of a leftist alliance between intellectuals and labor, no matter how moderate or constitutional, was immediately interpreted as the signal and cause of an impending socialist revolution.

This post–red scare panic was exacerbated by the eruption of student discontent on American campuses. The roaring twenties was not only speakeasies and campus flappers. The vacuum left by the dismantling of the old ISS was slowly filled by a new generation of Liberal Clubs and Social Science Clubs. Perhaps twenty of the clubs had arisen from the ruins of former ISS chapters by the end of 1919.[48] Forty-five clubs could be identified by early 1920.[49]

These spontaneous local groups finally merged at a convention which met at Harvard University on April 2–3, 1921. There, 250 representatives from twenty-seven colleges and universities founded the new Intercollegiate Liberal League. Its acronym—ILL—was an appropriate description of the American left by that time. Its constitution was similar to that of the ISS, but its mission statement was indicative of a growing movement on the intellectual left to withdraw from any firm ideological statement of a socialist political alternative. The ILL vaguely defined its purpose as "a fair and open-minded consideration of social, industrial, political, and international questions by groups of college students."[50]

Several speakers addressed the founding convention with a view to infusing the new movement with its old sense of mission. Walter Lippman, a former ISS member, warned students there was to be "a heresy hunt in the American colleges" which it was their obligation to "fight when it comes." Henry Laidler of the LID asked them to resist all encroachments against academic freedom and to resist "the present state of hysteria." John Hayne Holmes, a Christian socialist minister, told students that the best "way to amount to something is to identify yourselves to the limit with the labor world."[51]

The usual round of conservative denunciations soon followed the ILL founding convention. Two days after the convention the *New York Times* was already proclaiming that so-called Liberal Clubs were really a cover for "eager young Socialists and radicals, overturners and over-throwers" who "bleat the revolutionary notions they have borrowed from liberal weeklies." Archibald E. Stevenson, counsel for the Lusk Committee, decried the ILL as "a phoenix sprung from the ashes of the Intercollegiate Socialist Society" and expressed his regret that colleges were already again "granting increased hospitality to radical ideas."[52]

J. Mayhew Wainright, the assistant secretary of war, delivered a speech in which he offered the Harding administration's position that the new student radicals were "organized enemies, often led and financed by aliens." He claimed that "these sinister forces aim to wipe out the army and navy and turn America into a weakling nation." Wainright tied this foreign subversion to the present struggle between labor and capital. He suggested that "where there should be mutual confidence, respect, and reciprocity, there is continual fomentation of distrust, which is like a smouldering fire springing up when least expected into flames."[53]

The political response was not limited to verbal denunciations. For even in the absence of direct government repression, speeches of this character were still signals to private associations that sanctioned vig-ilante actions as part of "the new virility" in America.[54] Patriotic so-cieties like the American Legion and the National Security League (a coalition of businessmen, conservative politicians, and military offi-cers) were not averse to hiring thugs to break up meetings with the full knowledge they would never be prosecuted.

One week after the ILL founding convention, the National Security
League had plans under way to counteract the ILL initiative. The NSL
was already leading the movement to introduce required citizenship
training into the college curriculum. It was successful in setting up a
model course at Columbia University with the cooperation of Nicholas
Murray Butler. The NSL announced that it would now "attempt to
offset the influence of Socialist societies among college students and
make a particular effort to counteract the influence of the ILL." Asserting that, "the traditional role of our colleges and universities" had been
their service as "the cradle of Americanism and Nationalism," and that
socialists were now using the ILL to "strike at the foundation of Americanism," the NSL announced that it would establish campus branches
of the NSL "in every college and university in the country in which the
ISS or the new ILL is working." NSL leaders claimed with satisfaction
that "this plan was applied by us with great success during the war."

The claim had some basis in fact. The NSL war clubs had a notorious
reputation as being composed of rowdy hordes of college athletes and
fraternity members, usually paid and financed by local businessmen,
armed with clubs to intimidate and beat student antiwar protestors.
The techniques that businessmen used to break strikes in coal fields or
steel mills had proved just as effective in breaking student strikes. The
NSL leaders had no doubt that "the poison can best be counteracted by
militant patriotic organizations of the loyal students not yet affected."[55]

Boards of trustees were equally concerned with the new student
revolt. Butler's position that university administrators had an obligation to protect students from academic licentiousness was frequently
echoed in public addresses by trustees throughout the country. Frank
Hiscock—a Syracuse attorney, bank director, and former Republican
U.S. senator from New York—made such an address as chairman of the
Cornell University Board of Trustees, noting in a 1923 address that a
university "owes it to the commonwealth which has been so generous
in its support, to the fathers and mothers who are trusting their sons
and daughters to our care, to see to it that these are not swept away by
false and delusive doctrines . . . no greater purposes will engage the
earnest mind . . . than that of maintaining in and around the University that atmosphere of fidelity to American ideals and institutions."[56]

In the opinion of those responsible for regulating student conduct
there was little doubt about who to blame for the problem of student
rebellion. Left-wing professors always lay at the root of the problem.
Henry MacCracken, the president of Vassar College, concluded in an
article on the student movement that "professors with strong pro-

clivities toward social sympathy with the downtrodden have, by close association, fostered the development of [student] strike leaders." Professors had "produced the student movement of our time" simply by applying "their own knowledge to current problems" in the classroom. MacCracken noted: "This is recognized by the supporters of the unchanged order of things, who in denouncing the youth movement very seldom denounce the student leaders of it, but bitterly attack the professors for saying what they believe."[57]

Clear cases of academic repression continued to proliferate in this political environment. Several important cases which not even the AAUP could avoid were investigated and publicized during the first half of the 1920s. Louis Levine, a professor of political economy, was expelled from the University of Montana for publishing a costs-benefits analysis of state mine taxation. Herriot C. Palmer, a professor of American history and political science, was dismissed from Franklin College in Indiana. Dr. James E. Kirkpatrick was run out of Washburn College after organizing the faculty around his program of academic democracy. W. H. Lawrence, Jr., a professor of history, and James G. Stevens, professor of economics, were both terminated at Middlebury College for clearly ideological reasons. Arthur Fisher, a professor of law, was also released from the University of Montana. The Phelps-Dodge Corporation struck a blow at the University of Arizona by forcing the termination of a professor of agricultural chemistry for daring to argue before the state legislature that copper smelting fumes were damaging local crops.[58] There were more than a dozen terminations at major Southern universities (e.g., the University of Tennessee) because of the evolution controversy.

The AAUP would not reverse its position. The 1918 report of Committee A was reaffirmed during Arthur O. Lovejoy's tenure as president from 1919 to 1920. The first postwar national convention of the AAUP reiterated in its platform that its basic goal was to mediate between local faculties and administrations in the development of "a set of principles that will insure against the arbitrary exercise of administrative authority."[59] Committee A continued following the Seligman line from case to case. It released another major report in 1924 which noted that "reports of this committee in previous years have mentioned that complaints with which it has to deal are based more frequently upon principles of infringement of tenure than upon those of freedom in teaching or expression. This continues to be the experience of the Committee."[60] The committee conceded that "real questions of freedom may lie below the surface" of many dismissals; unfortunately, however, administrators were becoming more sophisticated in their termination strategies. They were now more careful about pursuing them within procedures and guidelines that had been formulated by the AAUP. Consequently, the AAUP was locked inside its own legalistic approach, which defined academic freedom as a merely incidental item in the wider problem of academic tenure. Committee A could offer no solution to this problem within the current programmatic guidelines of the association.

This was part of the truth. The other part, as pointed out by Arthur Livingston, a professor of Italian at Columbia University, was that "ninety percent of American professors" were "uninterested in the advancement of learning." Academic freedom was not a problem which touched their daily lives, nor one which most of them were ever likely to encounter. Most professors were "content with the chance to live in relative peace, teaching in the traditional manner of the secondary schools, but with fewer hours' work and more concessions to their vanity." That was the real purpose of the AAUP. However, in that mundane goal it still represented a "decay of academic courage." The AAUP could not even offer "effective trade unionism" but was content to "draw up long-winded pseudo-judicial opinions, which the newspapers rarely print and which people never read." These "amalgams of dignity and righteousness" seemed only to satisfy the professoriate's craving for self-importance.[61]

The AAUP was so moribund less than a decade after its founding that it could not find a violation of academic freedom at the University of Tennessee when everyone involved, including the administration, admitted that professors were dismissed for teaching evolution. Because the dismissals were properly structured within existing personnel regulations, the association could find no grounds on which to intervene. The *New Republic* accurately surmised that the AAUP had "become so rigidly committed to the scrutiny only of technical legal points of tenure and prerogative that it is now, apparently, automatically limited to infractions of the professional code."[62]

INTELLECTUALS, CAPITALISM, AND THE AMERICAN STATE: THE HISTORIC ACCORD

The AAUP's steady drift towards proceduralism established the early groundwork for a historic accord between intellectuals and American business later in the 1920s. University trustees made a decisive breakthrough from the other direction during the publicity and debates which accompanied the Alexander Meiklejohn case at Amherst College in 1923. Meiklejohn was a former professor of philosophy at Brown University who had been one of E. Benjamin Andrews' last appointments prior to his resignation from that institution. Meiklejohn was appointed president at Amherst in 1912 for the express purpose of shaking the college out of a conservative rut. He apparently accomplished that task a little too well over the next decade. Wealthy alumni began voicing objections to Meiklejohn about 1921. The criticism escalated when a faculty report dominated by aging traditionalists rebuked the president for the importance he attached to economics, philosophy, and political economy in his personnel and administrative policies. Meiklejohn had been slowly restructuring the faculty with new appointments in these fields which alumni and senior faculty considered too radical.[63]

George Bosworth Churchill, a professor of English literature and local Republican party activist, followed up the report by publicly reproving Meiklejohn for believing "the goal of the liberal college is freedom."[64] Churchill argued that Meiklejohn's administrative policies were responsible for the looseness of conduct and disrespect for authority among students at Amherst. He complained that many students now felt there were no standards, moral or intellectual, to which they were bound to conform at the college.

The faculty submitted its report to the trustees amidst Churchill's accusations. The trustees then formed their own investigative committee. The committee was abolished the next year (1922) for reasons that are not clear. However, it was immediately reorganized with an explicit mandate to investigate "the educational policies and personal affairs" of Dr. Meiklejohn. The committee was ordered to report back by June of 1923. It consisted of an impressive group of bankers, corporate attorneys, and Republican activists: Dwight W. Morrow, banker and member of J. P. Morgan and Company; Edward T. Esty, lawyer-banker and trustee for Worcester County Institution for Savings; George A. Plimpton, financial analyst for the Federal Reserve Board; Arthur L. Gillette, Congregationalist clergyman and Republican Party activist; Stanley King, corporate attorney, manager, and director for International Shoe Company (Boston).

While the committee was conducting its investigation, wealthy Amherst alumni, usually businessmen from New York City or Boston, stepped up their own attacks on Meiklejohn. He was accused of engaging in "propaganda activities," "pacifism, " and "radical tendencies." Yet, amid the flurry of accusations, Harry E. Taylor, president of the alumni association, enunciated a significant distinction that business-men had often previously failed to articulate. Taylor claimed that Meiklejohn had taken liberties with his mandate to liberalize the col-lege by radicalizing it. Taylor insisted: "There is no issue as to whether Amherst is a liberal college or not. I know of very few alumni who would have it otherwise, provided the liberty of liberalism is not inter-preted as the license of radicalism."[65]

For the first time, representatives of corporate business consciously extracted liberalism from the broad swath of radical ideas. This did not make the institutional limits of academic freedom any less nebulous from a theoretical perspective, but as a practical policy it did signifi-cantly widen the boundaries of acceptable teaching and narrow the range of unacceptable politics. The principle of a liberal college was no longer at stake, only the details of its regulatory structure. The new boundaries were clarified for trustees in highly publicized debates over the charges levelled against Meiklejohn. Liberalism degenerated into radicalism whenever a university professor came to the support of any anarchist, socialist, or communist movement. Moderate democratic socialists could, of course, negotiate some tenuous leeway on the fringes of this definition by claiming to be merely left-leaning liberals or ultra-liberals. In addition, liberalism crossed into radicalism when-ever professors failed to defend the American state during periods of international crisis such as warfare. Liberalism therefore excluded paci-fism. An equally important administrative principle was established for trustees during the Meiklejohn debates. It was that presidents, not trustees were responsible for regulating the boundaries between liberal freedom and radical license. Presidents who failed to defend these frontiers would be held accountable. This again was an important departure from previous debates involving college presidents. Meikle-john was not threatened for his own ideological commitments or politi-cal activities, nor for defying trustees' authority by refusing to dismiss radical faculty. Rather, he was under assault for having failed to prevent radicalism in the first place. This constituted irresponsible and careless administration.

In this regard, the Meiklejohn debate finally settled on two specific incidents that were used to substantiate his administrative failures. He was accurately quoted as having affirmed on one occasion that he "would hire a Bolshevik if he was a good teacher."[66] Meiklejohn had also refused to allow some pro-preparedness speakers to use the campus as a public forum several years earlier unless anti-preparedness speak-ers were allowed to share the same platform. Meiklejohn had therefore indicated his willingness to violate the limits of acceptable academic freedom as an administrator by tolerating communism and pacifism. The Amherst board of trustees expressed similar observations when it met to call for Meiklejohn's resignation on June 16, 1923. The board concluded that Meiklejohn had failed as an administrator. He was, from the standpoint of the liberal university, not a good manager.

Amherst students immediately reacted with protests and a petition drive demanding that trustees withdraw their request for Meiklejohn's resignation. Students pointed out that the trustees' in their discussions of Meiklejohn, had frequently used terms like "class consciousness." The student rebels argued that good administration was being equated with intellectual supervision in the Meiklejohn case. Managerial concepts were simply being used to obscure the underlying ideological concerns. Trustees and alumni answered the protests in a very straightforward manner. Many of them pointed out that while they had been students at Amherst, they too had enjoyed such freedom, but after maturing in the real world of business, they had come to see that too much freedom was not good for the reputation of the college or the moral character of its graduates.[67]

Meiklejohn finally agreed to resign on June 19, 1923. That evening students broke into the college chapel and tolled the bell in symbolic mourning for "the death of liberalism" at Amherst. The trustees replaced Meiklejohn with an eighty-year-old professor of mathematics who had taught at Amherst since 1891.[68]

Meiklejohn was allowed the courtesy of delivering one final commencement address to the class of 1923. In a highly publicized address, Meiklejohn called for the abolition of all boards of trustees at American colleges and universities as a first step toward academic self-management and intellectual freedom. This call was related to the broader theme of democracy in America. Meiklejohn optimistically observed that "America is trying to be a democracy." His optimism was tempered with doubts about whether American higher institutions would be allowed to fulfill their historical mission in that process. It was still a fact that, despite its best efforts, "America doesn't know how to be a democracy. America cannot think in democratic terms. America still thinks in terms of privilege and possession and social clique. America must learn to think in other terms than those, and it has a long task."[69]

Many of Meiklejohn's appointees made the sympathetic gesture of resigning after his last commencement address. This merely accelerated the housecleaning. Six professors resigned by June 25: John M. Gaus, associate professor of political science; Walter W. Stewart, professor of economics; Walton Hamilton Hale, professor of economics; Albert Park Fitch, professor of the history of religion; Howard E. Hinners, instructor in music; and Walter R. Agard, instructor in Greek. Thomas Reed Powell, a professor of political science at Columbia, and Henry A. Ladd, a professor of English at Oxford, both refused to assume positions they had previously accepted from Meiklejohn. Four more professors subsequently resigned over the next three weeks.[70] The resignations all expressed outrage over Meiklejohn's dismissal and a belief that academic freedom no longer existed on the campus.

Nevertheless, the Meiklejohn case marked a new departure for trustees. The trustees were more concerned with administrative structure than with the particular president or individual faculty members. They moved closer to the managerial presidency and away from direct administration by incorporating a regulatory principle of license into their own concept of responsible presidential administration. The Meiklejohn case was a forum for articulating this modification to the employee idea.

Meiklejohn's removal put college and university administrators on notice that they were managerial employees responsible for preventing academic radicalism and license by regulating its frontiers. The key was regulatory prevention, not *ex post facto* repression. An administrator had already failed by the time his trustees found it necessary to intervene in the matter. This principle was subsequently institutionalized in the managerial concept of the college presidency. It was so well understood that Frank L. McVey and Raymond M. Hughes would later write in their classic textbook, *College and University Administration:* "Boards are made up chiefly of conservative men and women. They are sensitive to criticism regarding radical statements or actions by the faculty . . . the able president will see that such persons are not appointed to the faculty."[71]

The Meiklejohn case does seem to have led to a wider repositioning and a rethinking of their role by trustees throughout the country. Governing boards gradually withdrew from direct administration during the rest of the decade. The pattern of escalating academic repression that began in 1909 apparently peaked in 1924.[72]

In the five years from 1920 through 1924, inclusive, the AAUP investigated twenty-one cases where violations of academic freedom and tenure were alleged by faculty. The AAUP agreed that violations had occurred in thirteen (62%) of the cases by its own conservative standards. Only six incidents were investigated from 1925 through 1929, but violations were confirmed in all of them. Insofar as these figures

permit any kind of measurement, they suggest that levels of overt
academic repression fell to less than one-half their previous levels in
the second half of the postwar decade.

The most obvious explanation for this decline is that by the end of the
decade university governing boards had been more or less successful
in eliminating the far left wing of American faculties. Those remaining
on its ambiguous frontier had been silenced, repositioned, driven
underground, or at least removed from off-campus politics and trade
unionism. The tendency toward political and social isolation by the
academic left was reinforced by movements within and outside of the
university.

The ISS and LID had broken with the far left wing of the American
labor movement during World War I. Consequently, as socialists and
progressives were pressed into full-scale retreat within the AFL, the
academic left were beached on shore like stranded whales. The only
alternatives were either to make a leftward reversal toward the revolutionary industrial unions or to follow the AFL further right toward the
emerging liberal consensus. Anyone who chose the first alternative
was well outside the acceptable boundaries that distinguished liberals
from radicals. When LaFollette's Progressive campaign was defeated in
1924, socialist intellectuals saw their last political vehicle disappear.

At the same time, the events and aftermath of the Meiklejohn case
provided a new climate in which liberals could negotiate an historical
accommodation with businessmen. Once business trustees were willing to remove liberalism and progressivism from the index of prohibited ideologies, the problem of academic freedom became negotiable on
both sides. The AAUP had already taken the single most important step
toward an accommodation with its 1920 report on university governance. Its acknowledgment that trustees wielded final authority on all
educational policies by virtue of their control or ownership of academic
property had removed the most radically nonnegotiable issue of class
conflict from the table. The rights of private property were conceded in
exchange for the consultative senates.

The AAUP made further concessions in a 1925 Committee A report
when it even backed off the salary issue. The association "frankly
acknowledged that the financial rewards of successful academic effort,
even under very favorable circumstances, will not equal those of an
equally successful business career." The AAUP offered to exchange "a
comparative security of tenure" in return for accepting its subprofes-
sional compensation. The threatening character of the potential autonomy offered by tenure was mitigated by accepting the idea of a proba-

tionary period during which the young professor would be "on trial." If he or she failed to meet the approval of colleagues, administrators, or trustees, the probationary assistant professor could be terminated at will by a veto from any one of these groups.[73]

Finally, by establishing a concept of managerial responsibility, the Meiklejohn case helped initiate a wider movement toward the separation of governance and administration which the Carnegie Foundation and AAUP had been requesting in their publications for a decade. This altered the pattern of interaction between administrations and faculties. It meant that faculty members could bargain with trustees through administrators, and vice versa. As the AAUP had hoped, university presidents tended to be somewhat more conciliatory in their negotiations with faculty members, so long as they accepted the proprietary limitations imposed upon the administration by boards of trustees.

With all the chips on the table, the Association of American Colleges took the next step toward a comprehensive resolution of the conflict in 1924. The AAC adopted a formal "declaration of principles of tenure" explicitly modelled on the one developed by the AAUP.[74] The following year, the American Council on Education (ACE) called a Conference on Academic Freedom in Washington, D.C., for January 2, 1925, to "coordinate action on questions of academic freedom, tenure, and promotion."[75] ACE agreed to mediate the conference through Samuel P. Capen, its current president, and Charles R. Mann, a consulting engineer and ACE president-elect. The AAUP sent a delegation of three persons led by Arthur O. Lovejoy. Trustees were represented by a delegation from the Association of Governing Boards. Administrators sent delegates from the Association of American Colleges, the Association of American Universities, the Association of Urban Universities, the National Association of State Universities, the Association of Land-Grant Colleges, and the American Association of University Women.[76]

The AAC presented its own declaration as a framework for negotiation at the conference. After a day of discussion, the conference elected Arthur Lovejoy, Samuel Capen, and John R. Effinger (president of the AAC) as a working committee to revise the AAC statement. The working committee reported back at a subsequent meeting of the full conference. The new ACE declaration on academic freedom, tenure, and promotions was endorsed by the delegates from every major higher educational association in the United States.[77] It was then adopted over the next three years by every association that had sent delegates to the convention. These in turn recommended that member institutions adopt the ACE principles or some variation on them.

Committee A could report by 1929 that "considerable progress has been made in the formulation and general recognition of principles governing academic freedom and tenure." The AAUP was pleased that "the general conditions of Academic Freedom and Academic Tenure throughout the country are undoubtedly more satisfactory than they were a generation ago."[78] The intellectuals had finally reached a procedural accommodation satisfactory to themselves and to the ruling powers, even if neither completely trusted or understood the other.

9

Hegemony and Autonomy:
The Political Economy of
American Intellectuals

CONTEMPORARY social theorists continue to conceptualize the role of intellectuals in terms of the two competing ideal types developed during the class struggles that accompanied university modernization.[1] The now dominant ideology has been constructed around the assertion that intellectuals compose an autonomous and relatively classless stratum pursuing knowledge for its own sake.[2] Those who dissent from this view continue to argue that intellectuals are structurally part of a class or classes and therefore have no sociological status independent of the competing classes which constitute capitalist society.[3] Nevertheless, there is a consensus on both sides that contemporary intellectuals have been historically shaped by the social forces of university professionalization.[4]

Professional associations are now usually identified with the definition and rise of expert disciplines. It is the university, however, which unites these diverse disciplinary practitioners into a relatively cohesive social force capable of articulating collective interests independent of, and even in opposition to, those of other groups in society.[5] Thus, an important measure of political and ideological autonomy is the degree to which professional institutions, particularly the universities, establish an autonomous or heteronomous relationship between social classes and organized communities of scholars. The competing ideal types of the intellectual diverge primarily in the analysis of this relationship.

Adherents of the autonomy thesis have emphasized formal guarantees of academic freedom, the role of professional peer review in assessing the quality and importance of scholarship, and the importance of faculty self-governance in defining standards of academic certification, professional achievement, promotion, and tenure. Adherents of the heteronomy thesis emphasize three phenomena: the social composition of boards of trustees, the influence of corporations and private foundations, and the importance of federal coordination in directing research towards specific political, economic, and military agendas. What does a historical analysis indicate in regard to the validity of one or the other of these viewpoints? The most superficial measure of university modernization has been the transfer of formal control from religious to secular authorities in the half century between 1880 and 1930. More revealing, however, are the large number of empirical surveys which consistently indicate that secularization of university control and ownership has been synonymous with the transfer of power to American businessmen. The patterns of business control identified by Scott Nearing as early as 1917 have only become more pronounced in the seven decades since. An obvious conclusion is that contemporary concepts of modernization and rationalization are ideological euphemisms concealing the class conflicts which shaped and still structure American universities. Yet, for exactly that reason, it is important to not be content with such facile demystification. It is a conclusion that few would any longer dispute.

In Chapter 3, I suggested at least one important theoretical modification to the ideology critique. The local and regional nature of most American universities has been reflected in the composition of their governing boards, which appear to be extremely sensitive to local and regional variations in social structure. It is true, in this sense, that governing boards reflect locally dominant class and political interests, but that dominance itself must be understood as a concrete and shifting balance of power between classes. Ideological power is not a fixed institutional or social structure in capitalist society so much as an organized pattern of social relations *between* intellectuals and competing classes. These relations are at least partly constituted by conscious actors within the university itself and are not automatic adaptations to capitalist economic imperatives or purely the result of the scholarly intentions of free-floating intellectuals.[6]

The state plays a decisive role in regulating this balance of power by intervening in the academic class struggle through national leadership, centralized resource allocation, and strategic coercion. The ability of state elites to formulate a coherent national interest in higher education can be used to legitimate specific policies that actually grant preferen-

tial treatment to particular class interests. Immediate political concerns
with promoting economic development and national defense have
tended toward a natural alliance between state and capital. Moreover,
this alliance is a pivotal component of capitalist class hegemony. It
allows the interests promoted by this alliance to mobilize national
resources, institutional support, and public constituencies against political oppositions that are typically dispersed and fragmented because
of the decentralized structure of American higher education. The state
is thus a national leadership center that facilitates coordinated political
action among those who can successfully colonize its executive agencies.

The state can further consolidate a particular balance of power by
offering material incentives that strongly encourage intellectuals' collaboration with hegemonic educational and scientific projects.[7] Research grants, stipends, and consultantships in turn play a significant
role in the opportunities for publication, promotion, and tenure that
influence individual positions within the university. The success of this
strategy would seem to require either blind naivete or a certain degree
of bad faith by the intellectuals, but of a kind that makes them opportunistic servants of power, rather than members of any particular
class.[8]

The academic class compromise that now prevails cannot absolutely
prevent other kinds of research, teaching, or publication. It may discourage it through an unequal system of rewards and incentives.
However, the negotiated range of theoretical free space between absolute autonomy and totalitarian control is real and substantial. As a
balance of social power, hegemony does not consist in totalitarian
control or domination. It is, as Miliband suggests, a structure of ideological competition that is "so unequal as to give a crushing advantage
to one side against the other."[9] In this respect, ideological hegemony
consists of a structured institutional capacity to regulate intellectuals
through market forces, rather than control them as individuals or as an
oppressed group.[10] The growing predominance of state-funded scholarly and scientific research enables administrative officials to skew
research significantly toward specific methodological frameworks and
policy agendas. The centralized institutional structures established for
awarding these incentives also enable strategically placed political and
administrative appointees to secretly veto unacceptable projects.[11]

Finally, the state can intervene in a coercive manner to maintain or
reassert the balance of power when academic class struggles threaten
the disintegration of the existing compromise. The state can either
sponsor coercive activities of its own or indirectly sanction private

control during periods of political crisis. In fact, the American state has consistently intervened in a coercive capacity to sustain regulatory structures that are destabilized under the pressures of political conflict. The fact that it must apparently do so with almost generational regularity suggests that intellectuals and businessmen are, in some sense, antipathetic social forces whose uneasy truce must periodically be reestablished in capitalist society with coercive sanctions.[12]

There is no doubt that a major component of this regulatory structure today is the imperfect institutionalization of a corporate ideal within the university. It has promoted the introduction of corporate managerial techniques into higher education that have a real impact on the kinds of activities and scholarship that are rewarded. It has facilitated organizational strategies which promote (through financial incentives) closer ties between capital, state, and university.

These administrative developments have been accompanied by the appearance of an ideology of higher education which explicitly defines the university as merely another business organization. University expenditures are defined as a social or educational investment that must efficiently yield some tangible return in the form of usable knowledge, technical innovation, and marketable skills for white-collar and professional labor. Return on educational investment is now one of the chief measures for judging whether a university has successfully performed its public service mission or offered a quality product to its consumers (students and taxpayers). The ideology clearly originated with a corporate elite that has successfully forged a long-term educational coalition with other political, bureaucratic, and administrative officials, who remain its chief proponents. It thus organizes a concept of university governance and public service which grants priority to the articulated interests of an economic and political ruling class.

The other side of hegemony, however, is conflict. The democratic political ideals of public education, as well as the professional claims of intellectuals themselves, cannot be denied completely. If the modern university is to achieve political legitimacy in a democratic society, or even within the university community, business has found that it too must continually accommodate the demands of independent scholarship and the concerns of a wider public. It is certainly an unequal exchange at present. Corporate capital in the United States has probably been more successful than elsewhere in pursuing its educational program. Nevertheless, a preexisting pattern of institutional checks and balances has never been completely eliminated by proponents of the corporate ideal. These include tenure, peer review, consultative faculty senates, and the nomination of new faculty. The subordinate role of such checks rarely makes useful for offensive strategies within the university, but they do set up defensive barriers which protect a certain free space and prevent it from being eliminated altogether.

THE IDEOLOGICAL STATE APPARATUS: A BALANCE OF POWER

The ideological state apparatus is thus best conceptualized as a state-centered regulatory structure for managing the intellectuals and, thereby, the production and distribution of knowledge (i.e., research and teaching). It must successfully manage the conflict between intellectuals and business within the university, as well as the wider contradictions between capitalism and democracy, to avoid an educational crisis. It must successfully manage the contradiction between the reality of class exclusion from the university and the culture of aspiration that legitimates the institution as a democratic meritocracy. There is no guarantee that these contradictions can be successfully managed on a permanent basis.

As a result, the key to maintaining this balance of power has been the tripartite accommodation between business, administration, and faculty that structures the ideological state apparatus. This accommodation requires a very reluctant concession from businessmen that they leave the details of university life to administrators and faculty. Yet, their proprietary relationship to the institution creates a continual temptation to exert direct control at precisely those moments when the potential for confrontation is greatest. Thus, a crucial pillar in the existing balance of power has been the managerial ability of educational administrators to restrict autonomy without eliminating it. The modern system of administrative management achieves this task primarily through the elaboration of endless regulations that constitute fair warnings and rules of the academic game. These discipline behavior before the fact and, hence, legitimate the punishment of those who violate the rules of the game. Team players are rewarded with an array of quite desirable material and social incentives. The occasional renegade is still punished in a symbolic public spectacle.[13]

However, the weakness of the strategy is exactly that it does rely on the renegade's appearing to be a renegade and on the uninterrupted ability to deliver material incentives. Administrators have found time and time again that regulation is an easy task in times of relative social peace and political consensus, but that once competing forces challenge dominant elites, intellectuals are pulled *en masse* into outside social movements which cause the fragile balance to collapse. Meanwhile, the fiscal crisis of the state periodically undermines the ability of university and government administrators to offer widespread incentives. It is seemingly impossible to know in advance at what point these restrictions cease to foster even greater competition or elitism, and at what point they breed generalized discontent among the intellectuals. However, the widespread unionization of faculty during the 1970s, the growing attacks on the neutrality of peer review, and complaints about the unequal distribution of government research funds suggest the line may have been crossed sometime during the last two decades.

Yet, American intellectuals have historically been divided in their response to these problems. A majority were originally represented by the newly formed AAUP, which favored a negotiated class compromise with trustees, administrators, and state elites by conceding major elements of the corporate ideal in exchange for the individual procedural guarantees that constitute the relative autonomy of American colleges and universities. It was a defensive strategy which aimed to negotiate as much political distance as possible between intellectuals, businessmen, and government officials while accepting the bureaucratic-capitalist mission that successfully conquered the university. This settlement was achieved in the 1928 agreement between administrative, governing, and faculty associations that was mediated by the American Council on Education.

A second group of intellectuals was represented by the American Federation of Teachers and the Intercollegiate Socialist Society. These two organizations were attempts to ally university professors economically and politically with the American labor movement. Their aim was to challenge capitalist hegemony directly by embracing a new group identity. This identity defined intellectuals as workers instead of as autonomous professionals and, hence, equated their long-term political interests with an oppositional activism that would realign the balance of economic and political power throughout American society. It was to be an alliance of industrial and academic democracy.

It is actually from this continuing dispute among intellectuals that the competing ideal types have appeared as components of larger ideologies that define specific historical missions for intellectuals.[14] Neither position is actually an adequate theoretical framework for the sociology of knowledge because neither of them presents an accurate empirical description of American university intellectuals. In fact, the current and historical ideal types are at best existential ideologies of the intellectuals. They orient the individual and collective actions of intellectuals when confronted by the necessity of justifying their political position in relation to broader social conflicts. It is therefore my contention that any adequate theoretical conceptualization of American intellectuals must place this continuing historical conflict at the center of its explanatory account.

My aim has been to illustrate this point with an institutionally based concept of ideological hegemony which is necessarily related to an empirical concept of relative autonomy. The two concepts are not mutually exclusive; properly understood they are necessarily related components of the contradictory position occupied by intellectuals in capitalist society. In advancing this argument, I have attempted to straddle two fundamentally antagonistic ideal types of the contemporary intellectual. This is not only because each of them has a partial existential validity in orienting intellectuals, but also because that validity is itself derived from the real ambiguity of their position in capitalist society.

In the current work, I have emphasized those factors which historically circumscribe the autonomy of the intellectual and which therefore demonstrate that autonomy is necessarily relative and not absolute. I would suggest that any theorist who wants to argue consistently the autonomy of intellectuals must be able to answer two simple questions: autonomous from whom and relative to what? The concept of autonomy is meaningful only *in relation to* a specifiable context of institutional and ideological hegemony.[15] It is not a defense against contemporary notions of an ideological state apparatus, particularly when the empirical contours of that apparatus are explicitly delineated as a framework for the measurement of autonomy. Instead, it is the relation to class conflict that defines the ground on which we understand and measure the extent of autonomy.

At the same time, it is the relative autonomy instituted by the university that mediates the formation of the intellectual as a social type.[16] This delineates the concept of the intellectual as an empirical referent that is meaningful only in relation to social class, but which necessarily requires avoiding the identification of that concept with social classes that are defined by their direct economic relations to production. Intellectuals exist and are constituted on their own sociological terrain, albeit one that is continually beset with all the pressures and contradictions of class conflict.

It is clear from a historical analysis that intellectuals do at times identify and organize themselves as a distinct stratum with distinct interests. It would seem to make more sense to look at the relation between intellectuals and social classes as a consequence of the intellectuals' institutional mobilization into coalitions and social movements.[17] These long-term coalitional mobililizations are the referent for our idea of an ideological apparatus.

This means that explanatory concepts of hegemony and relative autonomy are defined effectively when they are specified in terms of concrete historical and institutional social relations. These parameters (as regulatory boundaries) expand and contract from place to place and across historical time, contingent upon levels of class conflict and the consequent balance of social power. It is precisely this historical and local variability which the concepts of hegemony and relative autonomy can conceptualize, if they are understood in terms of the concrete institutional conditions and social-political conflicts which determine intellectuals' level of relative autonomy in relation to that balance of power.

Hegemony and the relative autonomy of intellectuals is therefore at any given time the result of a historical balance of power between intellectuals, administrators, and economic and political elites. The precise boundaries of that autonomy are always the outcome of real conflicts that are subject to temporary fluctuations as well as long-term critical realignment. Consequently, the free space which defines a relative degree of autonomy expands or contracts depending upon a variety of historically contingent factors, such as the willingness of elites to use various forms of repression, coercion, or incentives on intellectuals; the posture taken by administrators in promoting academic freedom or vice versa; the ability of intellectuals to organize themselves cohesively for bargaining with external groups; and intellectuals' ability to mobilize supporting alliances with other social groups challenging the society's dominant elites.

CONTEMPORARY POSTSCRIPT

The range of fluctuation between absolute autonomy and totalitarian control seems to establish the contours of a recurring cyclical crisis in the liberal university. The construction of a national ideological state apparatus in the United States has been a continuing process that appears to closely parallel the development of economic and legitimation crises. The same cycle of events that took place from 1894 to 1928 was essentially repeated from 1929 to 1962. The Great Depression and the events leading up to World War II resulted in another left-wing academic rebellion. The Veblen genre of academic criticism was carried forward by writers such as Robert S. Lynd, E. C. Lindeman, James Wechsler, and Hubert Park Beck.

The same patterns of compromise and coercion were then repeated once again over the next two decades. Left-wing organizations formed a united front with the New Deal heirs of progressivism to save democracy in a second world war. Science and engineering was permanently integrated into the military-industrial complex which now structures the permanent war economy of American capitalism.[18] A second red scare erupted on the Lusk model of state terror, once the national unity of world war collapsed amidst a new wave of violent industrial unrest and international tensions.

The AAUP responded to the crisis by adopting a new 1940 Statement on Academic Freedom and Tenure that was even more concessionist than its original 1915 document. It went so far as to warn university professors against even introducing "controversial material" into the classroom. This second cycle was consolidated in another survey movement and in the National Defense Education Act. Other measures of national policy expanded opportunities for research and prestige for those intellectuals willing to collaborate with state and corporate elites.

We now seem to be in the midst of a new wave which, if past history is any guide, will probably not end until sometime well into the next decade. American campuses passed through a third cycle of academic unrest that began in 1963. The cycle has been followed, as usual, by a new round of state and national education survey commissions beginning with the 1972 Carnegie Commission report designed to more closely integrate curriculum, institutional missions, and research with the needs of capital accumulation and national defense. The radical demands for a curriculum relevant to life in a democratic society have been reshaped over the last decade to mean a further vocationalization of curriculum. Demands for academic self-management have been countered with proposals for reprofessionalizing the intelligentsia through increased incentives and meritocratic rewards.

In one respect, each of these cycles has resulted in deeper penetration and stronger regulation of the university by corporate capital and the capitalist state. Yet, that hegemony has also accelerated the countervailing tendencies which historically have always been present in the contradictory structures of the ideological state apparatus. Thus, an internal polarization of universities is as much the organizational consequence of corporate hegemony as the growing domination of universities by corporations and the state. This unequal polarization is identifiable in at least two phenomena: faculty unionization and the growth of the left academy.

The continuing advance of academic and state bureaucracy has finally been met with a renewed wave of faculty unionization. There is no doubt that most of these unions are fairly non-militant professional associations whose primary concerns are still status, income, tenure, and personal security. Thus, it is likely, that if the state can successfully manage its current fiscal crisis, a new intellectual class compromise will be served up at a feast on the carcasses of American workers.

Nevertheless, the growth of faculty unionization does set in motion a historic alteration of the intellectuals' class consciousness. It would seem to indicate that American intellectuals are reaching a critical juncture at which they are willing to abandon an essentially medieval conception of the academic vocation. Notions of professional autonomy are being silently replaced with a concept of academic and industrial democracy. In this respect, unionization still offers the possibility for an alteration in the balance of power in any future confrontations. It opens up a whole new field of organizational tactics and off-campus alliances with the labor movement that have been lacking in previous confrontations.

Moreover, the rebellion of the 1960s has not been followed by the expected round of reprisals and state terror to the same extent as in previous cycles. There were and continue to be isolated instances, but nothing approaching the two red scares. It may be a premature prognosis, but the ideological legacy of the New Left is far more powerful on campus at this late date in the cycle than in previous periods.[19] Any future outbreak would thus begin from an advanced position.

It may be, as Jacoby has recently claimed, that the increased tolerance on campus is the other side of an opportunistic strategy of survival from which the left has emerged so academic that it does not currently pose any serious threat to American capitalism or the capitalist state.[20] We may have become a generation of Elys, Veblens, and Zeublins whose political scholarship has become so opportunistic or so esoteric that it is irrelevant. It is equally possible that the left academy is a real victory in the academic class struggle which marks the widened boundaries of an uneasy and deceptive truce. That stalemate will hold only so long as the conditions which make truces necessary and possible remain unaltered. A more liberal drift in the electorate, a rise in student activism, a major economic crisis, or another imperial skirmish will reassert all the same pressures which have led to conflict in the past.

Notes

Sources Consulted

Index

Notes

Introduction

1 Bob Jessop, *The Capitalist State* (New York: New York University Press, 1982); Martin Carnoy, *The State and Political Theory* (Princeton: Princeton University Press, 1984); Samuel Bowles and Herbert Gintis, *Democracy and Capitalism* (New York: Basic Books, 1986); and cf. Robert Dahl, *A Preface to Economic Democracy* (Berkeley and Los Angeles: University of California Press, 1985).

2 Charles Lindblom, *Politics and Markets* (New York: Basic Books, 1977); Stephen L. Elkin, *City and Regime in the American Republic* (Chicago: University of Chicago Press, 1987).

3 Fred L. Block, "The Ruling-Class Does Not Rule: Notes on the Marxist Theory of the State," *Socialist Revolution* 7, no. 3 (1977): 6–28.

4 James O'Connor, *The Fiscal Crisis of the State* (New York: St. Martin's, 1973); Jurgen Habermas, *Legitimation Crisis* (Boston: Beacon, 1975); Claus Offe, *Contradictions of the Welfare State* (Cambridge: MIT Press, 1984).

5 Charles Tilly, *The Formation of National States in Western Europe* (Princeton: Princeton University Press, 1975).

6 Steven Lukes, *Power: A Radical View* (London: Macmillan, 1974); Ralph Miliband, *The State in Capitalist Society* (New York: Basic Books, 1969), pp. 49–55.

7 Ekhart Zimmermann, "The 1930s World Economic Crisis in Six European Countries: A First Report on Causes of Political Instability and Reactions to Crisis," in Paul M. Johnson and William R. Thompson, eds., *Rhythms in Politics and Economics* (New York: Praeger, 1985); Richard Scase, ed., *The State in Western Europe* (London: St. Martin's, 1980); Alan Wolfe, *The Limits of Legitimacy: Political Contradictions of Contemporary Capitalism* (New York: Free Press, 1978). Cf. Harry Cleaver, *Reading Capital Politically* (Austin: University of Texas Press, 1979); Harry Cleaver and Peter Bell, "Marx's Crisis Theory as a Theory of Class Relations," *Research in Political Economy*, no. 5 (1982); Joachim Hirsch, "The State Apparatus and Social Reproduction: Elements of a Theory of the Bourgeois State," in John Holloway and Sol Picciotto, eds., *State and Capital* (Austin: University of Texas Press, 1978), pp. 57–107.

8 Heide Gerstenberger, "Class Conflict, Competition, and State Functions," in Holloway and Piccioto, *State and Capital*, pp. 148–159.

9 Alvin W. Gouldner, *The Future Of Intellectuals and the Rise of the New Class* (New York: Continuum, 1979), p. 31, notes correctly, in my opinion, that "for the most part, classes themselves do not enter into active political struggle; the

263

active participants in political struggle are usually organizations, parties, associations, vanguards. Classes are cache areas in which these organizations mobilize, recruit, and conscript support and in whose name they legitimate their struggle. Classes as such are never united in struggle against others." Thus, following Karl Mannheim, *Ideology and Utopia* (New York: Harcourt, Brace, Jovanovich, 1936), p. 276, I argue that of all the social groupings possible in a capitalist society, class stratification remains "the most significant, since in the final analysis all the other social groups arise from and are transformed as parts of the more basic conditions of production and domination."

10 Karl Marx and Friedrich Engels, *The German Ideology* (New York: International Publishers, 1970), pp. 46–48: "Empirical observation must in each separate instance bring out empirically, and without any mystification and speculation, the connection of the social and political structure with production." The method of historical materialism starts out from an investigation of social relations in "their actual, empirically perceptible process of development under definite conditions."

11 James O'Connor, *The Meaning of Crisis* (London: Basil Blackwell, 1987); Philip Abrams, *Historical Sociology* (Ithaca: Cornell University Press, 1982); Anthony Oberschall, *Social Conflict and Social Movements* (Englewood Cliffs: Prentice-Hall, 1973); Charles Tilly, *From Mobilization to Revolution* (New York: Random House, 1978). Cf. Edward P. Thompson, *The Making of the English Working Class* (London: Gallancz, 1963), and Mike Davis, *Prisoners of the American Dream: Politics and Economy in the History of the U.S. Working Class* (London: Verso Books, 1986).

12 For example, Wolfe, *Limits of Legitimacy*, Theda Skocpol, "Political Response to Capitalist Crisis: Neo-Marxist Theories of the State and the Case of the New Deal," *Politics and Society* 10 (1980): 155–201.

13 William Appleman Williams, "A Profile of the Corporate Elite," in Ronald Radosh and Murray N. Rothbard, eds., *A New History of Leviathan* (New York: E. P. Dutton, 1972), pp. 1–6; G. William Domhoff, *The Higher Circles: The Governing Class in America* (New York: Random House, 1970).

14 Skocpol, "Political Response to Capitalist Crisis," p. 200.

15 Ibid., p. 199. See also Carnoy, *State and Political Theory*, pp. 246–261; Jessop, *Capitalist State*, pp. 211–259; and cf. Theda Skocpol, *States and Revolution* (Cambridge: Cambridge University Press, 1979).

16 Jean L. Cohen, "Between Crisis Management and Social Movements: The Place of Institutional Reform," *Telos* 52 (Summer 1982): 21–40; O'Connor, *Meaning of Crisis*, p. 139.

17 Louis Althusser, "Ideology and Ideological State Apparatuses," in *Lenin and Philosophy and Other Essays* (New York: Monthly Review Press, 1971); Miliband, *State in Capitalist Society*, pp. 49–55; Nicos Poulantzas, *State, Power, Socialism* New York: New Left Books, 1980), pp. 28–34, 54–62; Martin Carnoy, "Education, Economy, and the State," in Michael W. Apple, ed., *Cultural and Economic Reproduction in Education* (London: Routledge and Kegan Paul, 1982), pp. 79–126.

18 Joel H. Spring, *Education and the Rise of the Corporate State* (Boston: Beacon Press, 1972); Stephen Skowronek, *Building a New American State* (Cambridge: Cambridge University Press, 1982); James Weinstein, *The Corporate Ideal in the*

Liberal State, 1900–1918 (Boston: Beacon, 1968); Robert H. Wiebe, *Businessmen and Reform: A Study of the Progressive Movement* (Cambridge: Harvard University Press, 1962); Robert H. Wiebe, *The Search for Order,* 1877–1920 (New York: Hill and Wang, 1967); Samuel P. Hays, *Municipal Reform in the Progressive Era: Whose Class Interest?* (Boston: New England Free Press, 1960).

19 Richard Hofstadter, *The Age of Reform* (New York: Vintage Books, 1955).

20 Wolfe, *Limits of Legitimacy,* pp. 13–79.

21 Arthur M. Okun, *Equality and Efficiency: The Big Trade-Off* (Washington, D.C.: Brookings Institution, 1975). Cf. Samuel Haber, *Efficiency and Uplift: Scientific Management in the Progressive Era,* 1890–1920 (Chicago: University of Chicago Press, 1964); Samuel P. Hays, *The Response to Industrialism,* 1885–1914 (Chicago: University of Chicago Press, 1957); Samuel P. Hays, *Conservation and the Gospel of Efficiency* (Cambridge: Harvard University Press, 1959).

22 Ronald C. Tobey, *The American Ideology of National Science, 1919–1930* (Pittsburgh: University of Pittsburgh Press, 1971). See also Frank J. Goodnow, *Politics and Administration* (New York: Macmillan, 1900); Herbert Croly, *The Promise of American Life* (New York: Macmillan, 1909); Charles McCarthy, *The Wisconsin Idea* (New York: Macmillan, 1912).

23 Mary O. Furner, *Advocacy and Objectivity: A Crisis in the Professionalization of American Social Science, 1865–1905* (Lexington: University Press of Kentucky, 1975); Burton J. Bledstein, *The Culture of Professionalism* (New York: W. W. Norton, 1976); Thomas L. Haskell, *The Emergence of Professional Social Science* (Urbana: University of Illinois Press, 1977); Magali Sarfatti Larson, *The Rise of Professionalism* (Berkeley and Los Angeles: University of California Press, 1977).

24 Jerome Karabel, ed., *Power and Ideology in Education* (Oxford: Oxford University Press, 1977); Martin Carnoy, ed., *Schooling in a Corporate Society* (New York: McKay, 1977).

25 Basil Bernstein, *Toward a Theory of Educational Transmissions,* vol. 3 of *Class, Codes, and Control,* (London: Routledge and Kegan Paul, 1975), p. 38, identifies the intellectuals' "instrumental order" with those activities related to the teaching and acquisition of specific skills. Cf. Samuel Bowles and Herbert Gintis, *Schooling in Capitalist America* (New York: Basic Books, 1976), pp. 201–44, and Alain Touraine, *The Academic System in American Society* (New York: McGraw-Hill, 1974).

26 Bernstein, *Class, Codes, and Control,* 3:38; David O. Levine, *The American College and the Culture of Aspiration, 1915–1940* (Ithaca: Cornell University Press, 1986). Bernstein identifies the "expressive order" of education with the conduct, character, and manners of education which transmit an image of the social and educational order.

27 Michael W. Apple, *Education and Power* (London: Routledge and Kegan Paul, 1982), pp. 14–28.

28 Ibid., pp. 54–55; idem, *Ideology and Curriculum* (London: Routledge and Kegan Paul, 1979); idem, *Ideology and Practice in Schooling* (Philadelphia: Temple University Press, 1983).

29 Jerome Karabel, *Trends in the Racial, Sexual, and Class Inequalities in Access to American Higher Education* (Cambridge: Huron Institute, 1981); Samuel Bowles, "Unequal Education and the Reproduction of the Social Division of Labor," in Carnoy, *Schooling in a Corporate Society.*

30 Laurence R. Veysey, *The Emergence of the American University* (Chicago: University of Chicago Press, 1965); Roger L. Geiger, *To Advance Knowledge: The Growth of American Research Universities, 1900–1940* (New York: Oxford University Press, 1986).

31 Roger Dale, "Education and the Capitalist State: Contributions and Contradictions," in Apple, *Cultural and Economic Reproduction*, pp. 127–161; David N. Smith, *Who Rules the Universities?* (New York: Monthly Review Press, 1974).

32 Geoffrey Price, "Universities Today: Between the Corporate State and the Market," *Culture, Education, and Society* 39 (Winter 1984/85): 43–58; Theodore Draper, "Intellectuals in American Politics: Past and Present," in Nissan Oren, ed., *Intellectuals in Politics* (Jerusalem: Magnes Press, 1984); Irving Howe, "Intellectuals, Dissent, and Bureaucrats," *Dissent* 31 (Summer 1984): 303–8; Edward Shils, *The Constitution of Society* (Chicago: University of Chicago Press, 1972), p. 191; Paul J. Piccard, ed., *Science and Policy Issues* (Itasca, Ill., F. E. Peacock Publishers, 1969); Chester E. Finn, *Scholars, Dollars, and Bureaucrats* (Washington, D.C.: Brookings Institution, 1978).

33 Clyde W. Barrow, "Intellectuals in Contemporary Social Theory: A Radical Critique," *Sociological Inquiry* 57 (Fall 1987): 415–30.

34 For instance, Russell Jacoby, *The Last Intellectuals: American Culture in the Age of Academe* (New York: Basic Books, 1987); Allan Bloom, *The Closing of the American Mind* (New York: Simon and Schuster, 1987); E. D. Hirsch, *Cultural Literacy* (Boston: Houghton-Mifflin, 1987).

35 Ira Shor, *Critical Teaching and Everyday Life* (Boston: South End Press, 1980); idem, *A Pedagogy for Liberation* (South Hadley, Mass.; Bergin and Garvey, 1987); Theodore N. Norton and Bertell Ollman, *Studies in Socialist Pedagogy* (New York: Monthly Review Press, 1978); Joel H. Spring, *Educating the Worker-Citizen* (New York: Longman, 1980).

36 Noam Chomsky, *Problems of Knowledge and Freedom* (New York: Pantheon Books, 1971); Conor Cruise O'Brien and William Dean Vanech, eds., *Power and Consciousness* (New York: New York University Press, 1969); Jean-Paul Sartre, *Between Existentialism and Marxism* (New York: Pantheon Books, 1974), pp. 230–87.

Chapter 1. Economic Origins of the Corporate Ideal

1 Thorstein Veblen, *The Higher Learning in America* (New York: Augustus M. Kelley, 1965), pp. 59, 18. Adam Smith, *An Inquiry into the Nature and Causes of the Wealth of Nations* (New York: Modern Library, 1965), pp. 120–25, traces the concept of the university to the corporate structure of medieval guilds. He notes that all incorporations—whether of scholars, bakers, smiths, or tailors—"were anciently called universities, which indeed is the proper Latin name for any incorporation whatever."

2 Robert Paul Wolff, *The Ideal of the University* (Boston: Beacon Press, 1969), pp. 3–8; Max Weber, "Science as a Vocation," in Hans H. Gerth and C. Wright Mills, eds., *From Max Weber: Essays in Sociology* (New York: Oxford University Press, 1946), pp. 129–56.

3 Veblen, *Higher Learning*, p. 59. See also Mannheim, *Ideology and Utopia*, pp. 154 –156; Talcott Parsons, "The Intellectual: A Social Role Category," in Philip Rieff, ed., *On Intellectuals* (Garden City: Doubleday, 1970), pp. 15–16;

Talcott Parsons, "Considerations on the American Academic System," in Walter P. Metzger, ed., *Reader on the Sociology of the Academic Profession* (New York: Arno Press, 1977), p. 503; Everett Carl Ladd and Seymour Martin Lipset, *The Divided Academy: Professors and Politics* (New York: W. W. Norton, 1975), pp. 174–76; Richard Hofstadter, *Anti-Intellectualism in American Life* (New York: Vintage Books, 1963), pp. 408–9; Gouldner, *Future of Intellectuals*, pp. 3, 18–19; Charles Kadushin, *The American Intellectual Elite* (Boston: Little, Brown, 1974), pp. 337–38; Robert K. Merton, *Social Theory and Social Structure* (New York: Free Press, 1968), p. 266; Lewis Coser, *Men of Ideas: A Sociologist's View* (New York: Free Press, 1965), pp. 267–80.

4 Max Weber, *The Methodology of the Social Sciences* (New York: Free Press, 1949), p. 65.

5 Geiger, *To Advance Knowledge*, pp. vi, 67; J. McKeen Cattel, "Concerning the American University," *Popular Science Monthly* 61 (June 1902): 179; An American Professor, "The Status of the American Professor," *Educational Review* (December 1898), p. 420.

6 Marx and Engels, *The German Ideology*, p. 64; Geiger, *To Advance Knowledge*, p. 67.

7 Merton, *Social Theory and Social Structure*, p. 264; Edward Shils, *The Intellectuals and the Powers* (Chicago: University of Chicago Press, 1972), p. 15. We would not accept it as legitimate if a licensed plumber practiced medicine or law on the authority of a plumber's credentials. We would also be less likely to believe that a licensed physician practicing medicine in the rear of a hardware store was a competent practitioner. Not only the certification, but the *social location* of a particular occupational practice will be interpreted as evidence of competence, skill, and even the right to claim a particular occupational label. Universities occupy a social location in contemporary societies which confers an expressive image of expertise upon contemporary intellectuals.

8 There were two attempts at vesting the proprietary rights of a "tenured freehold" in the professorial office that included the physical plant of university corporations: *The Reverend John Bracken* v. *The Visitors of William and Mary College,* argued by the agrarian radical John Taylor of Caroline and decided by the Virginia Court of Appeals in 1790, and the Dartmouth College Case, argued by Daniel Webster and decided by the U.S. Supreme Court in 1819. In the former, John Marshall represented the Visitors of the College of William and Mary. In the latter, he was Chief Justice of the U.S. Supreme Court. In both precedents, the claim to a freehold tenure was denied by the court. The university was imputed to be a "corporation" no different than any other in principle. Proprietary rights were vested in the "governing board." See Richard Hofstadter and Walter P. Metzger, *The Development of Academic Freedom in the United States* (New York: Columbia University Press, 1955), pp. 460–64.

9 European law has a concept of the "foundation" as a property that exists without an owner, whereas in American legal tradition all property must have an owner. Thus, the European foundation may exist independent of the persons who administer it and even of the state which supports it. No Such concept exists in American law. See Arthur Livingston, "Academic Freedom," *New Republic,* November 17, 1917, pp. 69–71; Samuel P. Capen, *The Management of Universities* (Buffalo: Foster and Stewart, 1953), pp. 4–6.

10 Louis Althusser and Etienne Balibar, *Reading Capital* (London: New Left Books, 1970), pp. 212–13, 226–33.

11 Marx and Engels, *German Ideology*, p. 64.

12 Lukes, *Power: A Radical View*, p. 41. My analysis suggests a radical application of the concept of power. Lukes observes that an "attribution of the exercise of power involves, among other things, the double claim that A acts (or fails to act) in a certain way and that B does what he would not otherwise do." Influence as a form of power exists where A's mere "reputation for power" results in B's anticipating A's reaction in what B does without any overt or covert threat of coercion in any particular case. Lukes is explicit about using the term "do" to include "think, want, feel, etc."

13 Cf. Gabriel Kolko, *The Triumph of Conservatism* (New York: Free Press, 1977); Louis Hacker, *The Triumph of American Capitalism* (New York: Columbia University Press, 1940).

14 Ernest Mandel, *Long Waves of Capitalist Development: The Marxist Interpretation* (Cambridge: Cambridge University Press, 1980).

15 Paul A. Baran and Paul M. Sweezy, *Monopoly Capital* (New York: Monthly Review Press, 1966), pp. 219–26.

16 David Noble, *America by Design: Science, Technology, and the Rise of Corporate Capitalism* (New York: Alfred A. Knopf, 1977), pp. xvii–xxvi.

17 David M. Kotz, "Finance Capital and Corporate Control," in Richard C. Edwards, ed., *The Capitalist System*, 2nd ed. (Englewood Cliffs, N.J.: Prentice-Hall, 1978), p. 150.

18 Baran and Sweezy, *Monopoly Capital*, pp. 220–21.

19 Percentages tabulated from figures in U.S. Bureau of the Census, *Historical Statistics of the United States: From Colonial Times to 1970* (Washington, D.C.: GPO, 1972), p. 239.

20 Ibid., p. 232.

21 Ibid., pp. 11–12, 22, 457. An "urban" center is technically designated by the U.S. Census Bureau as an incorporated unit of 5,000 or more inhabitants.

22 Alfred D. Chandler, *Strategy and Structure* (Cambridge: MIT Press, 1962).

23 Gardiner Means, "Business Concentration in the American Economy," in Richard C. Edwards, ed., *The Capitalist System* (Englewood Cliffs: Prentice-Hall, 1972), p. 148; U.S. Bureau of the Census, *Historical Statistics of the United States* (Washington, D.C.: GPO, 1960), p. 413.

24 Chandler, *Strategy and Structure*, pp. 21–38, 40–41.

25 Eric Hobsbawn, "The Crisis of Capitalism in Historical Perspective," *Socialist Revolution* 6 (October–December 1976): 77–96, finds that long-wave global crises of capitalist accumulation occurred from 1873 to 1896 and from 1917 to 1948.

26 See Karl Polanyi, *The Great Transformation* (Boston: Beacon, 1944), ch. 7, for a similar analysis of British industrialization. As soon as British Whigs successfully created free markets, British businessmen clamored for an end to them.

27 Douglas Dowd, *The Twisted Dream: Capitalist Development in the United States since 1776* (Cambridge: Winthrop Publishers, 1974), ch. 3.

28 Foregoing argument from Kotz, "Finance Capital," pp. 150–51.

29 John Lintner, "The Financing of Corporations," in Edward Mason, ed., *The Corporation in Modern Society* (New York: Atheneum, 1969), p. 180; Daniel Creamer, Sergei P. Dobrovolski, and Israel Borenstein, *Capital in Manufacturing and Mining* (Princeton: Princeton University Press, 1960), pp. 192–93. Cf.

Franz Hilferding, *Finance Capital: A Study of the Latest Phase of Capitalist Development* (Boston: Routledge and Kegan Paul, 1981).

30 Lewis Corey, *House of Morgan: A Social Biography of the Masters of Money* (New York: G. H. Wyatt, 1930), p. 172. Ben Fine, *Marx's Capital* (London: Macmillan, 1975), p. 51, attributes a general overdevelopment of productive forces to the anarchy of production that prevails in laissez-faire capitalism.

31 Kotz, "Finance Capital," p. 150.

32 Ibid., p. 151.

33 Dowd, *Twisted Dream*, ch. 3; Temporary National Economic Committee (TNEC), *Investigation of Concentration of Economic Power: Final Report* (Washington, D.C.: GPO, 1941), p. 7; Gardiner C. Means, *The Structure of the American Economy* (Washington, D.C.: GPO, 1939), pp. 100–108, 239, 277; idem, "Business Concentration," p. 147.

34 U.S. Congress, House Banking and Currency Committee, *Report of the Committee Appointed Pursuant to H.R. 429 and 574 to Investigate the Concentration of Money and Credit*, 62nd Cong., 2nd sess., 1913; TNEC, *Investigation*, ch. 10; Means, *Structure of the American Economy*, ch. 9.

35 Means, *Structure of the American Economy*, p. 161: "Interlocking directorates alone are not sufficient evidence of a close relationship between corporations. Neither is the possession of a minority stock interest alone evidence of close association. Nor is a single instance of the underwriting of a corporation's securities by a particular investment house evidence of a close association between the two. But when a corporation was initially promoted by a particular investment firm, when all its new securities issues are handled by that firm, when the two have directors in common, and when other evidence of a less precise nature points to a close association between companies, it seems appropriate to treat them as part of a single interest group."

36 Financial groups are structured as long-term financial relationships. Those identified by the U.S. House Banking and Currency Committee in 1912 were all essentially intact with little change, in Means' 1935 investigation. Most of them have persisted to the present day with even higher levels of integration; see Ralph L. Andreano, ed., *Superconcentration/Supercorporation* (Andover, Mass.: Warner Modular Publications, 1973).

37 For an excellent empirical description of the geographic core and periphery of American industrialization, see Elizabeth Sanders, "Industrial Concentration, Sectional Competition, and Antitrust Politics in America, 1880–1980," *Studies in American Political Development* 1 (1987): 142–214.

38 Means, *Structure of the American Economy*, pp. 161–62.

39 Hofstadter, *Age of Reform*, p. 135.

40 Ibid., pp. 135–36; estimate found in Sidney Ratner, *American Taxation: Its History as a Social Force in Democracy* (New York: W. W. Norton, 1942), p. 136.

41 Quoted in Hofstadter, *Age of Reform*, p. 136. See also C. L. Merwin, "American Studies of the Distribution of Wealth and Income by Size," in *Studies in Income and Wealth* (New York: Columbia University Press, 1942), pp. 3–84, for studies of the distribution of wealth in the United States during this time.

42 TNEC, *Investigation*, ch. 8, esp. pp. 171–74.

43 Sanders, "Industrial Concentration," pp. 146–84; Richard Franklin Bensel, *Sectionalism and American Political Development* (Madison: University of Wisconsin Press, 1984).

44 Among the 200–300 individual histories of American colleges and univer-

sities, there are only a handful which devote any serious attention to the political aspects of university development. In most of these works, there appears to be a strained effort to ignore or gloss over political conflict in order not to offend the trustees or alumni for whom such books are usually written.

45 Charles A. Beard and Mary R. Beard, *The Rise of American Civilization*, 2 vols. (New York: Macmillan, 1930), is the general philosophy of American history which informs the present work.

46 For more detailed analyses of class structure in the postbellum South, see TNEC, *Investigation*, pp. 199–203, and Robert W. Shugg, *Origins of Class Struggle in Louisiana* (Baton Rouge: Louisiana State University Press, 1939), ch. 8.

47 Antonio Gramsci, "Americanism and Fordism," in Quintin Hoare and Geoffrey Nowell Smith, eds., *Selections from the Prison Notebooks* (New York: International Publishers, 1971), pp. 277–318; Claude Lefort, "What Is Bureaucracy?" in *The Political Forms of Modern Society* (Cambridge: MIT Press, 1986), pp. 89–121.

Chapter 2. Who Owns the Universities?

1 Geiger, *To Advance Knowledge*, pp. 1–2. Also, Veysey, *Emergence of the American University*; Frederick Rudolph, *The American College and University* (New York: Alfred A. Knopf, 1962); John S. Brubacher and Willis Rudy, *Higher Education in Transition* (New York: Harper and Row, 1976); Elbert Vaughn Will, *The Growth of American Higher Education* (Philadelphia: Dorrance and Co., 1936).

2 Bledstein, *Culture of Professionalism*, p. xii; Levine, *American College*. Also, Haber, *Efficiency and Uplift*, pp. xi–xii.

3 Geiger, *To Advance Knowledge*, pp. 1–11.

4 Veysey, *Emergence of the American University*, pp. 315–16; see also Hofstadter and Metzger, *Development of Academic Freedom*, pp. 453–54.

5 Veblen, *Higher Learning*, p. 45.

6 Ibid., p. 46. Also see Thomas C. Cochran, *Business in American Life* (New York: McGraw-Hill, 1972), p. 180.

7 Earl J. McGrath, "The Control of Higher Education in America," *Educational Record* 17 (April 1936): 259–72.

8 Lightner Witmer, *The Nearing Case* (New York: B. W. Huebsch, 1915), pp. 103–6; Scott Nearing, "Who's Who among College Trustees?" *School and Society* 6 (September 8, 1917): 297–99; Faculty of Colorado College, *Report on College and University Administration*, General Series no. 94 (Colorado Springs: Colorado College Publications, 1917); J. A. Leighton, "Report of Committee T on Place and Function of Faculties in University Government and Administration," *Bulletin of the AAUP* 6 (March 1920): 17–47; Hubert Park Beck, *Men Who Control Our Universities* (New York: King's Crown Press, 1947); Bettina Aptheker, *Big Business and the Universities* (New York: Institute for Marxist Studies, 1966); *Who Rules Columbia?* (New York: North American Congress on Latin America, 1968); Morton A. Raugh, *The Trusteeship of Colleges and Universities* (New York: McGraw-Hill, 1969); James Benet, "California's Regents: Window on the Ruling Class," *Change*, February 1972; Troy Duster, *The Aims of Higher Learning and the Control of the Universities* (Berkeley, n.d.).

9 The difference is clearly attributable to McGrath's institutional sample. It underrepresented land-grant colleges. Land-grant colleges accounted for about one-half of all public institutions in the United States at the time (i.e., excluding normal schools and junior colleges).

10 Henry Adams, *The Education Of Henry Adams* (New York: Modern Library, 1931), p. 32. See also, Ronald Story, *The Forging of an Aristocracy: Harvard and the Boston Upper Class, 1800–1870* (Middletown: Wesleyan University Press, 1980).

11 "Every social group, coming into existence on the original terrain of an essential function in the world of economic production, creates together with itself, organically, one or more strata of intellectuals which give it homogeneity and an awareness of its own function not only in the economic but also in the social and political fields." Antonio Gramsci, "The Intellectuals," in Quintin Hoare and Geoffrey Nowell Smith, eds., *Selections from the Prison Notebooks of Antonio Gramsci* (New York: International Publishers, 1971), p. 5.

12 Beck found, further, that 40 percent of those trustees holding business positions held three or more such positions and that those holding more than three "averaged slightly over eight such positions in as many different business firms." See *Men Who Control Our Universities*, ch. 9.

13 This conclusion is drawn from the raw data on individual institutions that is summarized in Tables 2.3 and 2.4.

14 Upton Sinclair, *The Goose-Step: A Study of American Education*, rev. ed. (Pasadena: privately printed, 1923), found similar patterns at major public and private institutions throughout the United States.

15 Veblen, *Higher Learning*, p. 48.

16 Tabulated from figures in U.S. Bureau of Education, *Report of the Commissioner of Education, 1872* (Washington, D.C.: GPO, 1874).

17 U.S. Bureau of Education, *Report of the Commissioner of Education, 1905* (Washington, D.C.: GPO, 1907).

18 Veblen, *Higher Learning*, p. 47.

19 Cochran, *Business in American Life*, p. 183; Charles Coleman Sellers, *Dickinson College: A History* (Middletown, Conn.: Wesleyan University Press, 1973), p. 480.

20 Cochran, *Business in American Life*, p. 181. See also Veysey, *Emergence of the American University*, p. 303.

21 Jay M. Gould, *The Technical Elite* (New York: Augustus M. Kelley, 1966), pp. 33–58, 124–25.

22 Charles R. Mann, *A Study of Engineering Education*, Carnegie Foundation for the Advancement of Teaching, Bulletin no. 11 (New York, 1918), a survey of executives in 120 manufacturing establishments. See also Noble, *America by Design*, pp. xxiii–xxv.

23 W.H.G. Armytage, *The Rise of the Technocrats: A Social History* (London: Routledge and Kegan Paul, 1965), pp. 245–46; A. Hunter Dupree, *Science in the Federal Government: A History of Policies and Activities to 1940* (Cambridge: Harvard University Press, 1957), pp. 288–97.

24 Mann, *Study of Engineering Education*, pp. 6, 19.

25 Gould, *Technical Elite*, pp. 162–63.

26 R. T. Crane, *The Utility of All Kinds of Higher Learning* (Chicago, 1909), chs. 4–6.

27 Veblen, *Higher Learning*, p. 53; Hofstadter, *Anti-Intellectualism*, p. 237 (quote).

28   Hofstadter and Metzger, *Development of Academic Freedom*, pp. 451–67; Merton, *Social Theory and Social Structure*, pp. 268–72.
29   Stanley M. Herman, *The People Specialists* (New York: Alfred A. Knopf, 1968), pp. 14–18.
30   George E. Peterson, *The New England College in the Age of the University* (Amherst: Amherst University Press, 1964), pp. 78–79.
31   Hofstadter, *Age of Reform*, ch. 4; John Barnard, *From Evangelicalism to Progressivism at Oberlin College, 1866–1917* (Columbus: Ohio State University Press, 1969), for an excellent example.
32   Weinstein, *Corporate Ideal*, ch. 4; Haber, *Efficiency and Uplift*, p. xi; Tobey, *American Ideology of National Science*, pp. 3–19.
33   Peterson, *New England College*, pp. 196–206.
34   There were only brief and isolated interruptions in this pattern of control during Reconstruction. Some institutions, such as the University of South Carolina, were governed temporarily by coalitions of Radical Republican carpetbaggers and southern white scalawags. A few southern blacks were even appointed to these governing coalitions. This short-lived challenge dissipated before the end of the 1870s.
35   Abraham Flexner, *I Remember* (New York: Simon and Schuster, 1940), pp. 203–18.
36   U.S. Bureau of Education, *Survey of Negro Colleges and Universities*, Bulletin 1928, no. 7 (Washington, D.C.: GPO, 1928), p. 5.
37   In "The Point of View," *Scribner's Magazine* 42 (1907): 122–24, an anonymous professor impressionistically observes that in rural state universities and colleges "the regent may be a country lawyer or editor or even a farmer."
38   Nearing, "Who's Who among College Trustees?"; Leighton, "Report of Committee T," p. 20.
39   Beck, *Men Who Control Our Universities*, p. 59.
40   G. William Domhoff, *Who Rules America?* (Englewood Cliffs, N.J.: Prentice-Hall, 1967), p. 77.
41   Miliband, *State in Capitalist Society*, p. 252.

Chapter 3. Corporate Power and Social Efficiency

1   Miliband, *State in Capitalist Society*, p. 68.
2   For general historical background see Jesse B. Sears, *Philanthropy in American Education*, USBE Bulletin 1922, no. 26 (Washington, D.C.: GPO, 1922); E. C. Lindeman, *Wealth and Culture* (New York: Harcourt, Brace, and World, 1936); Ernest Victor Hollis, *Philanthropic Foundations and Higher Education* (New York: Columbia University Press, 1938); Raymond B. Fosdick, *Adventure in Giving* (New York: Harper and Row, 1962); Merle Curti and Roderick Nash, *Philanthropy in the Shaping of American Higher Education* (New Brunswick: Rutgers University Press, 1965); Smith, *Who Rules the Universities?* chs. 3–5.
3   Lukes, *Power*, pp. 41–42.
4   Smith, *Who Rules the Universities?* p. 95
5   Ibid., p. 98.
6   Flexner, *I Remember*, p. 205.
7   Ibid., p. 208.
8   Ibid., p. 209. In his autobiography, Flexner, who was later a prominent GEB executive provides an interesting insight into the small-group dynamics that

structured influence within the foundation. It illustrates what Lukes, *Power,* pp. 42–43, refers to as an issue agenda, structured through a "power reputation operating on anticipated reactions." As executive officer, Dr. Buttrick was responsible for formulating "the tentative docket." In this task, he "always felt that we were on safe ground if we could meet any possible challenge from Mr. Gates or Mr. Rockefeller," though of course "criticism and suggestions were gladly entertained from any member."

9 USBE, *Report of the Commissioner of Education, 1902–1903* (Washington, D.C.: GPO, 1905), p. 379.

10 Flexner, *I Remember,* pp. 213–15. Flexner also claims that Wallace Buttrick personally selected Wickliffe Rose (a long-time GEB member) "to be his successor as head of the Peabody Fund" (p. 228). Buttrick also encouraged the selection of James H. Dillard to head the Anna T. Jeannes Fund.

11 CFAT, *Annual Report,* 1906 (New York, 1906).

12 CFAT, *Thirtieth Annual Report* (New York, 1935), p. 31.

13 Hollis, *Philanthropic Foundations,* p. 28.

14 Henry S. Pritchett, "Shall the University Become a Business Corporation?" *Atlantic Monthly* 96 (September 1905): 289–99. On how CFAT policies were to promote this corporate model, see Henry S. Pritchett, "Policy of the Carnegie Foundation," *Educational Review* 32 (June 1906): 83–93; Henry S. Pritchett, "Organization of Higher Education," *Atlantic Monthly* 102 (December 1908): 783–89; Henry S. Pritchett, "Scope and Practical Workings of the Carnegie Foundation for the Advancement of Teaching," *Journal of Education,* December 17, 1908, pp. 656–57.

15 Pritchett, "Shall the University Become a Corporation?" p. 294. It is not surprising that an educational administrator who was also a railroad director would make this connection: see Stephen Hymer, "The Evolution of the Corporation," in Edwards, *Capitalist System,* p. 123; Alfred D. Chandler and Fritz Redlich, "Recent Developments in American Business Administration and Their Conceptualization," *Business History Review* (Spring 1961): 103–28; Chandler, *Strategy and Structure,* pp. 21–41.

16 Pritchett, "Shall the University Become a Corporation?" pp. 293–94.

17 Ibid., pp. 293–97.

18 For example, Frank A. Vanderlip, *Business and Education* (New York: Duffield and Co., 1907), pp. 3–5, was convinced that academic specialists suffered from a "tendency toward narrowness" on questions of education in contrast to the "wisdom" displayed by businessmen. He claimed that "keen foresight, a shrewd knowledge of humanity, a wise and well-seasoned judgment of the practical value of things, ordinarily go to make up the mental equipment of the man who has made a million dollars." An educational policy under the direction of businessmen was therefore more likely "in all respects to follow the best lines." Similarly, he recounts that Nicholas Murray Butler, after researching the history of Columbia University, informed the committee "that every great progressive step which the university had taken in one hundred and fifty years had been against the protest and the opposition of the faculty." The advance of higher education had been possible, in his opinion, only where trustees assumed "responsibility upon themselves."

19 Kenneth E. Trombley, *The Life and Times of a Happy Liberal: A Biography of Morris Llewellyn Cooke* (New York: Harper, 1954), pp. 6–11.

20 Noble, *America by Design,* pp. xiv–xxv, 62, 207; Daniel Nelson, *Frederick Taylor*

and the Rise of Scientific Management (Madison: University of Wisconsin Press, 1980); Haber, *Efficiency and Uplift*; Weinstein, *Corporate Ideal in the Liberal State.*

21 Henry S. Pritchett, Introduction to Morris L. Cooke, *Academic and Industrial Efficiency,* CFAT Bulletin no. 5 (Boston: Merrymount Press, 1910), p. iii.

22 Cooke, *Academic and Industrial Efficiency,* p. 3.

23 Ibid., p. 8.

24 Samuel P. Capen, "The Supervision of College Teaching," *Pedagogical Seminary* 18 (December 1911): 544–46; William Cranston Lawton, "The Decay of Academic Courage," *Educational Review* 32 (1906): 395; Charles W. Eliot, "Academic Freedom" (1907), in Walter P. Metzger, ed., *The American Concept of Academic Freedom in Formation* (New York: Arno Press, 1977), p. 2; John J. Stevenson, "The Status of American College Professors," *Popular Science Monthly* 66 (December 1904): 122–23; James E. Kirkpatrick, *The American College and Its Rulers* (New York: New Republic Press, 1926).

25 Cooke, *Academic and Industrial Efficiency,* p. 7; Frederick Taylor, *The Principles of Scientific Management* (New York: Harper and Bros., 1911); Frank Gilbreth, *A Primer of Scientific Management* (New York: D. Van Nostrand, 1912).

26 Cooke, *Academic and Industrial Efficiency,* p. 8.

27 Ibid., p. 19.

28 Ibid., p. 26.

29 Pritchett, Introduction to Cooke, *Academic and Industrial Efficiency,* p. iv.

30 Frederick Taylor, quoted in Herman, *People Specialists,* p. 41.

31 Cooke, *Academic and Industrial Efficiency,* p. 21.

32 CFAT, *Annual Report,* 1919, p. 31.

33 Geiger, *To Advance Knowledge,* p. 224, finds that even as late as 1930, between 33 and 75 percent of faculty members at major research universities had received all or part of their graduate education from the institution in which they were currently teaching. In most of the institutions he examines over 50 percent of faculty were inbred.

34 Cooke, *Academic and Industrial Efficiency,* p. 23. See also Capen, "The Supervision of College Teaching," 547–48.

35 Cooke, *Academic and Industrial Efficiency,* p. 24.

36 Ibid., pp. 24–25.

37 Ibid., pp. 86–88, 95.

38 Ibid., pp. 35–36.

39 Ibid., pp. 36 and 103 (Table 8).

40 Ibid., p. 59.

41 Ibid., pp. 32–34, 57.

42 CFAT, *Standard Forms for Financial Reports of Colleges, Universities, and Technical Schools,* Bulletin no. 3 (New York, 1910), pp. 2–3.

43 My concept of ideological leadership is a technical modification of Burns's notion of intellectual leadership; see James MacGregor Burns, *Leadership,* (New York: Harper and Row, 1978), pp. 142–63.

44 Ibid.

45 Marx, *German Ideology,* pp. 65–66.

46 Jessop, *Capitalist State,* p. 243, defines a hegemonic project as "the mobilization of support behind a concrete, national-popular programme of action which asserts a general interest in the pursuit of objectives that explicitly or implicitly advance the long-term interests of the hegemonic class (fraction)

and which privileges particular 'economic-corporate' interests compatible with this programme whilst derogating the pursuit of other particular interests that are inconsistent with it."

47 CFAT, *Annual Report, 1907*, p. 101.
48 CFAT, *Annual Report, 1919*, p. 31.
49 Charles Thwing, *College Administration* (New York: 1900); Charles W. Eliot, *University Administration* (Boston: Houghton-Mifflin, 1908).
50 Cooke, *Academic and Industrial Efficiency*, pp. 5, 56; Frank P. Graves, "The Need of Training for the College Presidency," *Forum* 32 (1902): 680–85.
51 Herman, *People Specialists*, p. 156.
52 GEB, *Report of the Secretary, 1924–1925*, p. 12; GEB, *Report of the Secretary, 1914–1915*, pp. 44–45; GEB, *Report of the Secretary, 1923–1924*, pp. 9–10.
53 Robert Presthus, *The Organizational Society* (New York: Alfred A. Knopf, 1962), pp. 15–16.
54 Herman, *People Specialists*, pp. 164–65; William D. Hyde, "Academic Freedom in America," in Metzger, *American Concept of Academic Freedom*, p. 7; Eliot, *University Administration*, p. 2.
55 Gould, *Technical Elite*, pp. 162–63; G. H. Shibley, "The University and Social Questions," *Arena* 23 (1900): 294–296.
56 Herman, *People Specialists*, p. 165.
57 For example, George M. Steele of Lawrence University, H. E. Stockbridge of North Dakota Agricultural College, E. Benjamin Andrews of Brown University, George A. Gates of Iowa College, Henry Wade Rogers of Northwestern University, and Thomas E. Will of Kansas State College.
58 Veysey, *Emergence of the American University*, p. 354.
59 Geiger, *To Advance Knowledge*, p. 16; John Henry McCracken, *College and Commonwealth* (New York: Century Co., 1920), p. 241.
60 Veysey, *Emergence of the American University*, p. 309.
61 Quoted in Joseph Jastrow, "The Academic Career as Affected by Administration," *Science* 23 (1906): 561–74. See also Lawton, "Decay of Academic Courage," p. 398.
62 Veysey, *Emergence of the American University*, p. 308.
63 Geiger, *To Advance Knowledge*, p. 16.
64 Herman, *People Specialists*, p. 158.
65 Lawton, "Decay of Academic Courage," p. 398.
66 Cattell, "Concerning the American University," p. 180.
67 Ibid.
68 Graves, "The Need of Training," p. 683.
69 Stevenson, "Status of American College Professors," p. 125.
70 Jastrow, "The Academic Career," pp. 568–69; Cattell, "Concerning the American University," p. 180.
71 CFAT, *Annual Report, 1911*, p. 14.
72 Vanderlip, *Business and Education*, p. 6; CFAT, *Annual Report, 1908*, p. 152.
73 Quoted in Fosdick, *Adventure in Giving*, pp. 127, 129.
74 Daniel Coit Gilman, *University Problems in the United States* (New York: Century Co., 1898), p. 292.
75 Noble, *America by Design*, pp. 69–82.
76 Nicholas Murray Butler, *Scholarship and Service* (New York: Charles Scribner's Sons, 1921), pp. 62, 107. Also see Gilman, *University Problems*, pp. 290–98.
77 Butler, *Scholarship and Service*, p. 102.

78   GEB, *The General Education Board: An Account of Its Activities, 1902–1914* (New York, 1915), pp. 105, 109.

79   Flexner, *I Remember,* pp. 210–11.

80   Ibid., p. 236. Also see Wickliffe Rose quoted in Fosdick, *Adventure in Giving,* p. 230. Vanderlip, *Business and Education,* p. 8, indicates that CFAT also consciously pursued the same strategy.

81   USBE, *Biennial Survey of Education, 1918–1920* (Washington, D.C.: 1920), p. 285 (1910 statistics in decennial table); GEB, *General Education Board,* p. 221.

82   Hollis, *Philanthropic Foundations,* pp. 274–75; Curti and Nash, *Philanthropy,* p. 221.

83   Hollis, *Philanthropic Foundations,* p. 275; Rudolph, *American College and University,* p. 431. Hollis's chapter 13 is a detailed empirical account of concentration in foundation grants.

84   GEB, *Annual Report of the General Education Board, 1928–1929* (New York, 1929), p. 7.

85   Larson, *Rise of Professionalism,* pp. 136–77.

86   James G. Anderson, *Bureaucracy in Education* (Baltimore: Johns Hopkins Press, 1968), p. 114.

87   Chester Barnard, *The Functions of the Executive* (Cambridge: Harvard University Press, 1954).

88   Jastrow, "The Academic Career," pp. 566–67.

89   "Mr. Rockefeller's Educational Trust," *Current Literature* 42 (March 1907): 253; Thomas W. Churchill, "Carnegie Foundation," *Journal of Education,* September 3, 1914, pp. 174–75.

90   Quoted in "Mr. Rockefeller's Educational Trust," in *Current Literature* (March 1907), pp. 253–54. I say "with not much exaggeration" because eight years later just such a map was included in GEB, *The General Education Board,* p. 110.

91   CFAT, *Annual Report, 1909,* p. 161; CFAT, *Annual Report, 1914,* p. 54.

92   Charles C. Heyl, "The Carnegie Foundation and Some American Educational Problems," *Journal of Education,* May 26, 1910, p. 565.

93   "The Carnegie Pension," ibid., April 28, 1910, p. 459.

94   James McKeen Cattell, "The Carnegie Foundation for the Advancement of Teaching," *Science* 29 (April 2, 1909): 533.

95   "A Serious Situation," *Journal of Education,* February 25, 1915, p. 208.

96   Thomas Elmer Will, "A Menace to Freedom: The College Trust," *Arena* 26 (September 1901): 248; "Mr. Rockefeller's Educational Trust," p. 254; Eliot, "Academic Freedom," p. 4.

97   Quoted in James McKeen Cattell, ed., *Carnegie Pensions* (New York: Science Press, 1919), pp. 228–29.

98   Cattell, "The Carnegie Foundation," p. 533.

99   Pritchett, "Shall the University Become a Corporation?" p. 292.

100 CFAT, *Annual Report, 1909,* p. 84.

101 Ibid., p. 83; Hollis, *Philanthropic Foundations,* pp. 56–57.

102 CFAT, *Admission of State Institutions to the System of Retiring Allowances of the Carnegie Foundation* (New York, 1907), pp. 33–35.

103 CFAT, *Annual Report, 1909,* pp. 85–88.

104 Ibid., pp. 84, 97, 102.

105 Will, "A Menace to Freedom," p. 248.

106 Edward Danforth Eddy, Jr., *Colleges for Our Land and Time: The Land-Grant Idea in American Education* (Westport, Conn.: Greenwood Press, 1956), pp. 83–85.

107 Ibid., p. 118.

108 Quoted in James C. Carey, *Kansas State University: The Quest for Identity* (Lawrence: Regents Press of Kansas, 1977), pp. 73–74. On assuming the presidency, Will increased the number of Ph.D.'s on the faculty from one to four. He also instituted a required course on political economy for all students that was taught by a socialist and increased social-science requirements from fifteen to forty-two hours.

109 Cf. Carey, *Kansas State University,* pp. 70–77; Robert N. Manley, *Centennial History of the University of Nebraska* 2 vols. (Lincoln: University of Nebraska Press, 1967), 1:150; Sinclair, *Goose-Step,* pp. 199–202.

110 Quotes in Manley, *Centennial History of the University of Nebraska,* pp. 152–53.

111 Ibid., p. 154.

112 Quoted in ibid., p. 209.

113 CFAT, *Annual Report, 1909,* p. 83.

114 Hollis, *Philanthropic Foundations,* p. 57.

115 Flexner, *I Remember,* p. 242.

Chapter 4. Building an Ideological State Apparatus

1 Tabulated from data in USBE, *Report of the Commissioner of Education,* 1900 and 1910; USBE, *Biennial Survey of Education,* 1920 and 1930. Public institutions increased from 46 in 1900 to 246 in 1930; private institutions increased from 434 in 1900 to 832 in 1930. Enrollments in public institutions went from 34,177 in 1900 to 390,397 in 1930.

2 U.S. Department of Health, Education, and Welfare, National Center for Education Statistics, *Digest of Education Statistics* (Washington, D.C.: GPO, 1979), table 85.

3 USBE, *The National Crisis in Education: An Appeal to the People,* Bulletin, 1920, no. 29 (Washington, D.C.: GPO, 1920), p. 13.

4 USBE, *Biennial Survey of Education, 1918–1920,* p. 285; USBE, *Biennial Survey of Education, 1928–1930,* p. 335. Spending by states and cities in nominal dollars was $4,464,405 in 1900 and reached $133,179,356 by 1930.

5 Levine, *American College,* pp. 113–35. A survey of the University of Illinois found that in 1915 only 12 percent of the enrolled students came from urban working-class backgrounds, while 32 percent were from families engaged in farming or agriculture. The rest reported parents pursuing business or the professions. See the *New York Times,* February 21, 1915, part 4, p. 4. Likewise, a 1926 survey of higher education in Indiana found that at Purdue (a land-grant college) only 3.6 percent of students were from working-class back-grounds. At Indiana University the figure was 2.8 percent. About one-quarter were from farming or agricultural families. The rest were pursuing business or the professions. Indiana Survey Commission, *Report of a Survey of the State Institutions of Higher Learning* (Indianapolis: William Burford, 1926), p. 43.

6 Samuel Gompers, "For Higher Universal Education," *American Federationist,* November 1922, 843–44. A similar view is expressed by the AFL Executive Council, Committee on Education, *Report of the Proceedings of the Thirty-Eighth Annual Convention of the American Federation of Labor, Held at St. Paul, Minnesota, June 10th to 20th, 1918,* p. 320.

7 USBE, *Biennial Survey of Education, 1922–1924,* p. 2; A. Coswell Ellis, *The*

Money Value of Education, Bulletin, 1917, no. 22 (Washington, D.C.: GPO, 1917); Geiger, *To Advance Knowledge,* pp. 41–42.

8   USBE, *Biennial Survey of Education, 1922–1924,* p. 2.

9   Veblen, *Higher Learning,* pp. 46–47.

10 Quoted in CFAT, *A Study of Education in Vermont,* Bulletin no. 3 (Boston: Merrymount Press, 1914), p. 3.

11 Ibid., p. 4.

12 Ibid., pp. 5, 7.

13 Ibid., p. 5.

14 Ibid., p. 200.

15 "A Survey of the Vermont Survey," *Journal of Education* 79 (March 26, 1914): 350–51; Ide G. Sargeant, "Vermont and the Carnegie Survey," *Journal of Education* 81 (May 13, 1915): 508–11.

16 GEB, *Report of the Secretary, 1914–1915* (New York, 1915), p. 41; Flexner, *I Remember,* p. 249; Dewey W. Grantham, *Southern Progressivism* (Knoxville: University of Tennessee Press, 1983), pp. 246–74.

17 USBE, Henry S. Pritchett to Hon. Walter L. Fisher, Secretary of the Interior, May 29, 1911, p. 2. Historical File no. 100; NA.

18 CFAT, *Annual Report, 1911,* p. 14.

19 Durrell Hevenor Smith, *The Bureau of Education: Its History, Activities, and Organization* (Baltimore: Johns Hopkins Press, 1923), pp. 66–67. For the Gallaudet report see USBE, *Report of the Commissioner of Education, 1871* (Washington, D.C.: GPO, 1876).

20 Figures tabulated from USBE microfilm copies of letters in the National Archives.

21 USBE, Commissioner of Education to the Secretary of the Interior, January 8, 1903, in Press Copies of Letters Sent, 1870–1908, Microfilm Roll no. 67, p. 170, NA.

22 USBE, Elmer E. Brown to Henry S. Pritchett, August 13, 1906, ibid., Microfilm Roll no. 54, p. 501, NA.

23 Quoted in Grantham, *Southern Progressivism,* p. 263.

24 USBE, letters in Historical File no. 106, NA; U.S. Secretary of the Interior, GEB Annual Reports, Secretary's Central File, RG 48, NA.

25 USBE, Lovich Pierce, Acting Commissioner of Education, to A. LeF. Derby, Assistant Secretary of the Carnegie Foundation for the Advancement of Teaching, October 3, 1906, in Press Copies of Letters Sent, 1870–1908, Microfilm Roll no. 54, p. 233, NA. Letters received from CFAT and GEB indicate a regular correspondence with the bureau from the time the foundations were incorporated; see USBE, *Indexes to Letters Received,* vols. 9–11, NA.

26 USBE, Elmer E. Brown, Commissioner of Education, to Dr. Samuel A. Green, Massachusetts Historical Society, April 18, 1907, in Press Copies of Letters Sent: 1870–1908, Microfilm Roll no. 55, p. 243, NA; USBE, Chief Clerk of the Bureau of Education to Mr. Basil M. Manly, January 20, 1915, in Historical File no. 106, NA.

27 USBE, Report prepared by L. A. Kalbach, Acting Commissioner of Education, and Submitted to Secretary of Interior Bollinger for Use by Senator Bourne, Jr., Chairman, Committee on Public Expenditures, August 20, 1909, p. 2, in Historical File no. 100, NA.

28 Samuel P. Capen to Mrs. Samuel P. Capen, February 1914, Capen Papers, Box

7, SUNY—Buffalo University Archives. Samuel P. Capen was the bureau's specialist in higher education from 1914 to 1919. Soon after assuming the position, he wrote to his wife that "this business of answering inquiries is the principle routine of my office." His letters constantly refer to problems of understaffing, overtime, and discontent among clerks, assistants, and statisticians.

29 See the following from USBE, Historical File no. 100, NA: L. Gulick, "What the Bureau of Education Should Be and Do to Further Education in America," October 1909; Memorandum of Conference at Luncheon at the Hotel Willard, Washington, D.C., Saturday, March 26, 1910; Memorandum of Meeting Held at the Ebbitt House, Washington, D.C., March 27, 1910 at 12:30 A.M.; Elmer Elsworth Brown, Memorandum; Report on the Campaign in Behalf of the United States Bureau of Education.

30 Elmer Elsworth Brown, Memorandum, ibid., p. 1; Elmer E. Brown, *Government by Influence and Other Essays* (London: Longman, Green, 1909).

31 USBE, James A. Tawney, Chairman, Committee on Appropriations, House of Representatives to Hon. Elmer E. Brown, Commissioner of Education, June 10, 1908, Historical File no. 100, NA.

32 USBE, *Report of the Commissioner of Education, 1907–1908*, p. 16.

33 USBE, Chief Clerk of the Bureau of Education to Miss Elsa Denison, March 2, 1912, Historical File no. 106, NA.

34 USBE, Miss Elsa Denison, Bureau of Municipal Research, to P. P. Claxton, Commissioner of Education, January 31, 1912, Historical File no. 106, NA.

35 USBE, P. P. Claxton to Miss Elsa Denison, February 3, 1912, ibid. Capen praised Claxton as a "hustler" who was "making the Bureau felt in every corner of the educational world." He notes, however, that "the universal verdict" among bureau employees "seems to be" that Claxton is "off his head," or rather, has his head "up in the air." Claxton was preoccupied with meetings, lobbying, and travelling to universities in an effort to build the USBE's national influence. For this reason, "he was not much of a man for minor details" or "internal details" of office routine. Capen quotes the specialist in foreign education, a Miss Smith, as saying, "You can make your own plans . . . and get all the credit for it. Ten chances to one Claxton will not know anything about it." Employees informed Capen that E. E. Brown had been exactly the opposite: an excellent organization builder with no vision of how to use its emerging influence. See Letters from Samuel P. Capen to Mrs. Capen, February 4, 19, and 20, 1914, and April 8, 1914, Capen Papers, Boxes 7, 8, SUNY—Buffalo University Archives.

36 USBE, undated loose handwritten note, signed JDW, Historical File no. 106, NA.

37 Robert A. Dahl, *Polyarchy* (New Haven: Yale University Press, 1971), p. 82, finds that knowledge and information are key political resources "with which an actor can influence the behavior of other actors in at least some circumstances."

38 USBE, undated loose handwritten note, signed J.C.B., Historical File no. 106, NA.

39 USBE, undated loose handwritten note, signed, F.B.D., ibid.

40 USBE, undated loose handwritten note, signed Kle.B, ibid.

41 USBE, undated loose handwritten note, signed A.S., ibid.

42 USBE, Chief Clerk to Miss Elsa Denison, March 2, 1912, ibid.

43 USBE, P. P. Claxton to Miss Elsa Denison, February 3, 1912, ibid. The foundations' influence within the bureau was such that Secretary of the Interior Walter L. Fisher wrote to Henry S. Pritchett for his advice on who should be nominated to replace E. E. Brown in 1911. See Henry S. Pritchett to Hon. Walter L. Fisher, May 29, 1911, Historical File no. 100, NA.

44 USBE, P. P. Claxton to the Secretary of the Interior, August 10, 1911, ibid.

45 L. Gulick, "A Brief for the Extension Plans of the United States Bureau of Education," p. 3, ibid.

46 USBE, P. P. Claxton to the Secretary of the Interior, August 10, 1911, ibid.

47 USBE, Acting Secretary of the Interior to P. P. Claxton, August 28, 1911, ibid.

48 USBE, Assistant Attorney General for the Department of the Interior to the Secretary of the Interior, August 20, 1911, pp. 3, 7, ibid.

49 USBE, Assistant Attorney General for the Department of the Interior to the Secretary of the Interior, November 9, 1911, ibid.

50 For a list see USBE, P. P. Claxton to Hon. Franklin K. Lane, Secretary of the Interior, January 13, 1917, ibid.

51 USBE, *Report of the Commissioner of Education, 1915–1916*, pp. 129–30.

52 Noble, *America by Design*, pp. 62, 209.

53 Edward D. MacDonald and Edward M. Hinton, *Drexel Institute of Technology, 1891–1941* (Philadelphia: Drexel Institute of Technology), p. 55.

54 Noble, *America by Design*, p. 209.

55 An account of Hughes's travels and his octavo volumes is in Samuel P. Capen to Mrs. Capen, March 30, 1914, Capen Papers, Box 8, SUNY—Buffalo University Archives. I have been unable to find a copy of Hughes's paper.

56 USBE, *Report of the Commissioner of Education, 1913–1914*, pp. 128–29.

57 Capen to Mrs. Capen, March 30, 1914, Capen Papers, Box 8.

58 USBE, Henry S. Pritchett to Hon. Walter L. Fisher, Secretary of the Interior, May 29, 1911, Historical File no. 100, NA.

59 Noble, *America by Design*, pp. 212–19.

60 Capen to Mrs. Capen, February 22, 1914, Capen Papers, Box 7.

61 Noble, *America by Design*, pp. 212–13.

62 Capen to Mrs. Capen, April 10, 1914, and March 11, 1915, Capen Papers, Boxes 8, 9.

63 Capen to Mrs. Capen, May 1, 1914, Capen Papers, Box 8.

64 Capen to Mrs. Capen, March 8, 1914, and February 22, 1914, Capen Papers, Box 8.

65 USBE, S. P. Capen to P. P. Claxton, May 17, 1916, Historical File no. 501, Box 104, NA.

66 Capen to Mrs. Capen, March 30, 1914, Capen Papers, Box 8.

67 Samuel P. Capen, *A Report on the Colleges of North Carolina* (Raleigh: Office of the State Superintendent of Public Instruction, 1916).

68 P. P. Claxton had delivered an address to the convention of the National Association of State Universities, held in Washington, D.C., on November 9–10, 1914. He offered the bureau's "extended experience" and "broad outlook" to any state or institution "which might desire a survey of its work or organization." See S. P. Capen, *Report of a Survey of the University of Oregon*, University of Oregon Bulletin, N.S., Vol. 13, no. 4 (Salem: State Printing Department, 1915), p. 2.

69 Charles Marvin Gates, *The First Century at the University of Washington, 1861–1961* (Seattle: University of Washington Press, 1961), pp. 117–18.

70 Eric F. Goldman, "J. Allen Smith: The Reformer and His Dilemma," *Pacific Northwest Quarterly,* July 1944, pp. 195–214; James L. Colwell, "The Populist Image of Vernon Louis Parrington," *Mississippi Valley Historical Review* 49 (June 1962): 52–66.

71 Quoted in Gates, *University of Washington,* p. 133.

72 Ibid, pp. 137–39.

73 Nicholas Murray Butler delivered the keynote address at Suzzalo's inauguration; see Samuel P. Capen to Mrs. Capen, March 19, 1916, Capen Papers, Box 10.

74 USBE, Henry S. Pritchett to the Secretary of the Interior, May 29, 1911, Historical File no. 100, NA.

75 Gates, *University of Washington,* pp. 146–48.

76 Will, "A Menace to Freedom," pp. 248–49.

77 CFAT, *Annual Report, 1913,* p. 82; USBE, *Report of the Commissioner of Education, 1913–1914,* pp. 162–63; USBE, *Report of the Commissioner of Education, 1914–1915,* p. 140.

78 Ross, *Iowa State College,* p. 263.

79 Bryan, *State College of Washington,* pp. 380–82.

80 Quoted in Gates, *University of Washington,* p. 146.

81 Louis M. Geiger, *University of the Northern Plains: A History of the University of North Dakota, 1883–1958* (Grand Forks: University of North Dakota Press, 1958), pp. 283–84; "Political Revolt in the Northwest, III: Making the Schools an Issue," *New Republic,* November 17, 1917, pp. 71–73.

82 Bryan, *State College of Washington,* pp. 380–81.

83 Ibid., pp. 381, 383.

84 USBE, E. A. Bryan to S. P. Capen, March 8, 1915, Historical File no. 501, Box 106, NA. Capen wrote that Bryan's letter was "the most indignant and threatening letter I have ever received." It worried him because Bryan "is the strong man of the state educationally and to a certain extent politically, a czar in his own domain." Samuel P. Capen to Mrs. Capen, March 10, 1915, Capen Papers, Box 9.

85 Capen to Mrs. Capen, March 6, 1915, Capen Papers, Box 9.

86 Samuel P. Capen, *A Survey of Educational Institutions in the State of Washington,* USBE Bulletin, 1916, no. 26 (Washington, D.C.: GPO, 1916); Capen to Mrs. Capen, June 26 and 29, 1915, Capen Papers, Box 9.

87 USBE, *State Higher Educational Institutions of Iowa,* Bulletin 1916, no. 19 (Washington, D.C.: GPO, 1916).

88 Ross, *History of Iowa State College,* p. 297.

89 Capen reported that Hughes's knack for "collecting and marshalling figures" enabled him to take "the center of the stage" in the meetings of the Iowa commission "almost before we knew." Capen to Mrs. Capen, November 10, 1915, Capen Papers, Box 10.

90 Capen to Mrs. Capen, November 15, 1915, Capen Papers, Box 10. Hadley was a former professor of political economy and lecturer in railroad administration who was by this time president of Yale and a member of the CFAT executive committee. Lowell, a former professor of political science, was president of Harvard and also a CFAT trustee.

91   USBE, P. P. Claxton to Hollis Godfrey, February 23, 1916, Historical File no.
     501, Box 105, NA.

92   USBE, *Report of the Commissioner of Education, 1915–1916*, p. 125.

93   Capen to Mrs. Capen, March 7 and 11 and June 29, 1915; February 15, 16, and
     17, 1916; all in Capen Papers, Boxes 9 and 10.

94   Chandler, *Strategy and Structure*, pp. 22, 38. Railroad administrators had
     originally pioneered the division of railroad operations into "major" and
     "ancillary" units. The major units consisted of those activities directly associ-
     ated with transportation, i.e., carrying passengers and freight. Ancillary
     units provided "services" for the major operation, e.g., ticket sales or loco-
     motive repair.

95   Samuel P. Capen, "The Status of the Land-Grant College as Outlined in
     Reports of Surveys Recently Made by the United States Bureau of Education,"
     April 7, 1919, Capen Speeches, SUNY—Buffalo University Archives.

96   Smith, *Bureau of Education*, p. 70.

97   Quoted in *Bulletin of the AAUP*, March 1922, p. 10.

98   Samuel P. Capen, "The Colleges in a Nationalized Educational Scheme,"
     School and Society 9 (May 24, 1919): 613–18.

99   This figure was derived from USBE, "Information about Surveys Compiled
     for Use by Appropriations Committee," January 2, 1922, and "Higher Educa-
     tional Surveys since 1921," January 5, 1926, in Historical File no. 501, NA. A
     published but far less complete listing of these surveys can be found in USBE,
     Report of the Commissioner of Education, for the years 1922 through 1928 and in
     USBE, *Educational Surveys*, Bulletin, 1928, no. 11 (Washington, D.C.: GPO,
     1928).

100 USBE, *Educational Surveys*, pp. 1, 4.

101 USBE, *Biennial Survey of Education, 1926*, p. 24.

102 USBE, "Results of Educational Surveys Conducted by the U.S. Bureau of
     Education," September 1928, Historical File no. 501, NA. The one exception I
     can find was Mississippi.

103 USBE, Jesse A. Bond to P. P. Claxton, January 19, 1927, Historical File no. 501,
     NA; Jesse A. Bond, "Results of School Surveys" (M.A. thesis, Education
     Department, University of Southern California, 1927).

104 USBE, *Report of the Commissioner of Education, 1927–1928*, p. 4.

105 One cannot discount the role of conscious planning in the emergence of
     several of the major research universities as a consequence of foundation
     grants. GEB, *General Education Board*, p. 133, notes as part of its strategy that
     "our college planning, in so far as it endeavors to develop institutions that
     have not yet attained full power, must give weight to the consideration that the
     modern university thrives and is most useful in close association with
     population, industry, and wealth."

106 Percentages tabulated from figures in USBE, *Biennial Survey of Education,
     1916–1918*, esp. p. 698.

107 Ibid.

108 Percentages tabulated from figures in USBE, *Biennial Survey of Education,
     1926–1928*, esp. p. 699.

109 Tabulated from figures in USBE, *Biennial Survey of Education, 1916–1918*, pp.
     710–12.

110   Tabulated from figures in USBE, *Biennial Survey of Education, 1926–1928*, pp. 700–701.

Chapter 5. War and the Intellectuals

1   Geiger, *To Advance Knowledge*, pp. 105–7.
2   Levine, *American College*, pp. 38, 23–24.
3   Noble, *America by Design*, p. 206.
4   Tobey, *American Ideology of National Science*, p. xi.
5   See the *New York Times*, January 5, 1917, p. 8; January 23, 1917, p. 8; February 8, 1917, p. 22; February 9, 1917, p. 6; February 18, 1917, p. 5; March 8, 1917, p. 2; March 19, 1917, p. 9; March 26, 1917, p. 6; April 24, 1917, p. 6; May 7, 1917, p. 2; September 6, 1917, p. 4, for a representative sampling of statements, resolutions, and opinion polls of the major associations of various social groups.
6   Joseph Freeman, a Columbia undergraduate who later achieved prominence as a Communist journalist, notes that "socialists had for years attacked" Seligman "from soapbox and platform as the chief economic apologist of capitalism." *An American Testament* (New York: Octagon Books, 1973), p. 110.
7   *New York Times*, February 8, 1917, p. 22.
8   Ibid., February 13, 1917, p. 8; February 18, 1917, p. 7; USBE, *Report of the Commissioner of Education, 1918*, p. 15. Ninety-five percent of Harvard's administration and faculty signed a petition calling on President Wilson "to lead the people to defend at all costs the integrity of the nation." *New York Times*, March 9, 1917, p. 6. The presidents and faculties of eight women's colleges pledged their collective loyalty to Wilson in the event of war. Ibid., March 31, 1917, p. 2. CCNY was a bastion of antiwar resistance, but finally capitulated and pledged its "full cooperation" during the war. Ibid., April 6, 1917, p. 15.
9   USBE, *Report of the Commissioner of Education, 1917*, p. 2.
10   USBE, *The Work of American Colleges and Universities during the War: A Report of the Work of the Education Section of the Committee on Engineering and Education of the Advisory Commission of the Council of National Defense*, Higher Education Circular no. 2, June 8, 1917, pp. 1–2. (These circulars are cited by circular number after the first reference.)
11   USBE, *Report Of the Commissioner of Education, 1917*, p. 2; Charles F. Thwing, *The American Colleges and Universities in the Great War, 1914–1919* (New York: Macmillan, 1920), pp. 26–27.
12   USBE, Higher Education Circular no. 2, pp. 1–2.
13   USBE, *The Work of American Colleges . . . during the War: A Report of the Work of the Education Section of the Committee on Engineering and Education of the Advisory Commission of the Council of National Defense*, Higher Education Circular no. 5, December 15, 1917.
14   USBE, *Report of the Commissioner of Education, 1917*, p. 3.
15   USBE, Woodrow Wilson to Franklin K. Lane, July 20, 1917, Commissioner's File no. 107, NA.
16   USBE, Commissioner P. P. Claxton to College Officers and Teachers, August 16, 1917, ibid.

17 Ibid.; USBE, *Report of the Commissioner of Education, 1918*, p. 14.

18 USBE, *The Work Of American Colleges . . . during the War: Contribution of Higher Institutions to the War and to Reconstruction*, Higher Education Circular no. 4, August 30, 1917, p. 1.

19 These included state governors and superintendents of public instruction; the presidents and faculties of all colleges and universities; the editors of all farm, business, trade-association, church, and scholarly journals; popular magazines; the secretaries of local chambers of commerce, boards of trade, and central trade unions; religious leaders; and women's clubs. See USBE, undated memo and copies of August 16, 1917, Claxton letter, Commissioner's File no. 107, NA.

20 USBE, Minutes of 3:30–5:15 Conference, Thursday, January 31, 1918, ibid.

21 USBE, Minutes of Conference, Friday, February 1, 1918, ibid.

22 USBE, "P. P. Claxton, Activities in Connection with War Work," ibid.

23 USBE, "Bureau of Education: Suggestions for War Service," ibid.

24 S. P. Capen, "Report of the Division of Higher Education to the Executive Committee," ibid.

25 USBE, *Government Policies Involving the Schools in Wartime*, Teachers' Leaflet no. 3, April 1918, pp. 1–2.

26 Quoted in USBE, *Report of the Commissioner of Education, 1919*, p. 17.

27 USBE, *Biennial Survey of the Education, 1918–1920*, p. 37.

28 *Bulletin of the AAUP*, February–March, 1918, pp. 6–7.

29 U.S. Department of War, *Committee on Education and Special Training: A Review of Its Work during 1918* (Washington, D.C., 1919), p. 9.

30 Noble, *America by Design*, pp. 207–9, found that the specific techniques employed by the CCP had been developed by Walter Dill Scott. Scott was an industrial psychologist at the Bureau of Salesmanship Research, Carnegie Institute of Technology. Cf. Loren Baritz, *The Servants of Power* (Middletown, Conn.: Wesleyan University Press, 1960), pp. 42–57, on the advance of industrial psychology, job specification, testing, and "sorting out" during World War I.

31 USDW, *Committee on Education and Special Training*, p. 10.

32 Ibid., pp. 10–11.

33 USDW, General Order 15, February 10, 1918, quoted ibid.

34 See Appendix A, ibid., pp. 55–56, for a copy of this letter.

35 Ibid., pp. 13–16.

36 *Report of the Proceedings of the Thirty-Eighth Annual Convention of the American Federation of Labor*, St. Paul, Minnesota, June 10–20, 1918, p. 315.

37 USBE, Higher Education Circular no. 4, p. 2.

38 USBE, Higher Education Circular no. 5, p. 11.

39 USBE, *The Work of American Colleges and Universities during the War: Contribution of Higher Institutions to the War and to Reconstruction*, Higher Education Circular no. 6, January 1918, p. 6.

40 USBE, *Report of the Commissioner of Education, 1890–1891*, pp. 626–31.

41 Ibid., pp. 625–26.

42 USBE, *Physical Education in American Colleges and Universities*, Bulletin 1927, no. 14 (Washington, D.C.: GPO, 1927), p. 15.

43 *New York Times*, April 14, 1916, p. 4; April 23, 1916, pt. 6, p. 3; September 26, 1916, p. 14.

44 Ibid., October 18, 1916, p. 3.
45 USBE, *Land-Grant College Education, 1910–1920*, Bulletin, 1924, no. 37 (Washington, D.C.: GPO, 1924), pt. 2, pp. 59, 61; USBE, *Report of the Commissioner of Education, 1919*, p. 6. There were 35,091 students enrolled in ROTC at 106 colleges by the end of 1916. Of these, 20,000 were enrolled at 52 land-grant colleges.
46 USBE, Higher Education Circular no. 5, pp. 8–9.
47 USBE, *Engineering Education after the War*, Bulletin, 1921, no. 50 (Washington, D.C.: GPO, 1921), pp. 1–2; USDW, *Committee on Education and Special Training*, p. 22, for a copy of the letter announcing SATC.
48 USDW, *Committee on Education and Special Training*, Appendix C, p. 59, for a copy of the memorandum authorizing the program. General Order 15, which established CEST, was amended by this authorization so that CEST's functions included the authority to "supervise and administer military training in all colleges and civil institutions; to supervise and administer the furlough or enrollment in the Enlisted Reserve Corps of Technical Students and Teachers in accordance with the provisions of section 151 of the Selective Service Regulations."
49 For a copy of *SATC, Special Regulations*, see ibid., pp. 65–73.
50 USBE, *Report of the Commissioner of Education, 1918*, p. 18.
51 Thwing, *American Colleges and Universities in the Great War*, p. 61.
52 COPI, *Official U.S. Bulletin* 2, no. 413 (September 16, 1918): 13.
53 USBE, *Report of the Commissioner of Education, 1918*, p. 15.
54 USDW, *Committee on Education and Special Training*, p. 26; Woodrow Wilson, General Order 79, as reproduced in USBE, *Report of the Commissioner of Education, 1919*, p. 7.
55 USDW, *Committee on Education and Special Training*, App. F, pp. 87–91, for a complete list of the collegiate sections. There were 554 universities, colleges, and technical institutes in the United States in 1918; see USBE, *Biennial Survey of Education, 1916–1918*.
56 USBE, *Land-Grant College Education, 1910–1920*, pt. 2, p. 61.
57 Dupree, *Science in the Federal Government*, p. 297.
58 Tobey, *American Ideology of National Science*, p. 20.
59 Daniel Bell, *The Coming of Post-Industrial Society* (New York: Basic Books, 1976), p. 20.
60 Richard R. Nelson, Merton J. Peck, and Edward D. Kalachek, *Technology, Economic Growth, and Public Policy* (Washington, D.C.: Brookings Institution, 1967), p. 41.
61 Dupree, *Science in the Federal Government*, p. 288.
62 Tobey, *American Ideology of National Science*, p. xi; Poulantzas, *State, Power, Socialism*, pp. 54–59.
63 Quoted in Dupree, *Science in the Federal Government*, p. 309.
64 Noble, *America by Design*, pp. 110–256.
65 Geiger, *To Advance Knowledge*, p. 97.
66 Dupree, *Science in the Federal Government*, pp. 309–12.
67 CND, *First Annual Report* (Washington, D.C.: GPO, 1917), p. 48.
68 Dupree, *Science in the Federal Government*, pp. 313–25.
69 Levine, *American College*, p. 32.
70 USBE, *Biennial Survey of Education, 1916–1918*, pp. 65–66.

71   USBE, *Report of the Commissioner of Education, 1918,* p. 15.
72   James Wechsler, *Revolt on the Campus* (Seattle: University of Washington Press, 1936), p. 15.
73   USBE, *Education in Patriotism: A Synopsis of the Agencies at Work,* Teachers' Leaflet no. 2, April 1918.
74   USBE, *Report of the Commissioner of Education, 1917,* p. 16.
75   USBE, *Opportunities for History Teachers: The Lessons of the Great War in the Classroom,* Teachers' Leaflet no. 1, 1917, quoted in ibid., p. 16.
76   It is probable that antiwar opposition and draft resistance to the war went much deeper into the social structure and was far more widespread than it was during America's involvement in Vietnam. Although most historians identify 1912 as the high point of Socialist party electoral strength (when Eugene Debs captured 6% of the popular vote), during its leadership of the antiwar movement, the party won much higher percentages in the local elections of 1918: e.g., NYC, 20%; Buffalo, 25%; Toledo, 33%; Chicago, 33%; Dayton, 45%. Similarly, New York City (mostly the Bronx) elected eighteen Socialist officials: ten state assemblymen, seven aldermen, and a municipal judge.
77   USBE, *Opportunities for History Teachers,* p. 2.
78   Ibid., p. 5.
79   *New York Times,* May 31, 1917, p. 12. Dr. Alexander Meiklejohn, president of Amherst College, was the one notable opponent to this movement within the academy. It hardly requires an epic imagination to recognize that the American ideology has changed little in the twentieth century except for the opponents.
80   See USBE, *Education in Patriotism.*
81   Ibid., p. 7.
82   USBE, *Biennial Survey of Education, 1916–1918,* p. 68.
83   USDW, *Committee on Education and Special Training,* p. 16.
84   Ibid., pp. 16, 29, 123–32.
85   Nicholas Murray Butler, "Education after the War," in *Proceedings of the Association of Colleges and Preparatory Schools of the Middle States and Maryland,* November 29, 1918.
86   *New York Times,* January 14, 1919, p. 11.
87   USBE, *The Work of American Colleges and Universities during the War: Effect of the War on Student Enrollment,* Higher Education circular no. 9, April 1918, p. 1.
88   USBE, *The Work of American Colleges and Universities during the War: Effect of the War on College Budgets,* Higher Education Circular no. 10, April 1918, pp. 2–3.
89   USBE, *Biennial Survey of Education, 1918–1920,* pp. 37–38.
90   It would be too unwieldy to list all the permanent courses introduced at various institutions as a consequence of the war. The USBE made one effort to catalogue these changes, in its "Higher Education Circular no. 6," which lists technical courses added at colleges in twenty-one states; also see COPI, *Official U.S. Bulletin* 2, no. 413 (September 16, 1918): 13.
91   USBE, *Report of the Commissioner of Education, 1919,* p. 8.
92   *New York Times,* March 27, 1920, p. 19.
93   USBE, *Biennial Survey of Education, 1918–1920,* pp. 18–19.
94   *New York Times,* May 9, 1920, pt. 6, p. 6.

95 Winthrop D. Lane, *Military Training in Schools and Colleges of the United States* (New York: Committee on Military Training, 1926), pp. 16–17.

96 Dupree, *Science in the Federal Government*, pp. 327–29; Tobey, *American Ideology of National Science*, pp. 49–61.

97 Geiger, *To Advance Knowledge*, pp. 97–105.

98 Tobey, *American Ideology of National Science*, pp. 181–229.

99 The president of the Carnegie Corporation, which funded many of the SSRC grants, later admitted that the organization had "improperly" forced the techniques of natural science on the social sciences and humanities. See Daniel J. Kevles, *The Physicists: The History of a Scientific Community in Modern America* (New York: Vintage Press, 1979), p. 246.

100 Quoted in Noble, *America by Design*, p. 229. The committee also worked with ACE, SPEE, and similar organizations to assist universities in creating job placement centers, providing them with advice on career training, job specifications, and labor markets that would help integrate their curriculum into professional and white-collar labor markets. Ibid., pp. 231–56.

101 Geiger, *To Advance Knowledge*, pp. 150–56.

102 USBE, *Report of the Commissioner of Education, 1918*, p. 19.

Chapter 6. Is Anything to Be Done?

1 Veblen, *Higher Learning*, p. 98.

2 Ernest Mandel, "The Industrial Cycle in Late Capitalism," *New Left Review* 90 (March–April 1975).

3 Samuel P. Capen, *Recent Movements in University Administration*, USBE Bulletin, 1916, no. 46 (Washington, D.C.: GPO, 1916), p. 32.

4 Raymond M. Hughes, "Study of Costs at Miami University, Ohio," in USBE, *Report of the Commissioner of Education, 1914*.

5 Ibid.

6 Capen, *Recent Movements in University Administration*, p. 32.

7 Ibid., p. 36.

8 Capen, *A Survey of Educational Institutions in the State of Washington; USBE, State Survey of Higher Educational Institutions of Iowa*.

9 USBE, *State Survey of Higher Educational Institutions of Iowa*, p. 118.

10 USBE, "Outline of Investigation of Higher Institutions in Connection with Educational Survey of Alabama," pp. 5–6, Historical File no. 501, Box 103, NA.

11 Ibid., p. 1.

12 A. Lawrence Lowell, "The Physiology of Politics," *American Political Science Review* 4 (February 1910): 1–15.

13 Leonard V. Koos, *The Adjustment of a Teaching Load at a University*, USBE Bulletin, 1919, no. 15 (Washington, D.C.: GPO, 1919).

14 J. D. Heilman, "Methods of Reporting the College Teacher's Load and Administrative Efficiency," *Educational Administration and Supervision* 11 (March 1925): 176.

15 The term *economic status* is used here as a conceptual reference for real standards of living, i.e, real income, as opposed to *class* which refers to intellectuals' relation to the means of mental production. Economic status is

empirically related to class situation insofar as it involves "the typical chance for a supply of goods, external living conditions, and personal life experiences" that is "determined by the amount of power, or lack of such, to dispose of goods or skills for the sake of income in a given economic order." Weber, "Class, Status, Party," in *From Max Weber*, pp. 181–83.

16   Arthur O. Lovejoy, "Annual Message of the President of the AAUP," *Bulletin of the AAUP* 5 (November–December 1919): 14.

17   Ralph G. Hurlin, "The Salaries of College Teachers in 1920," *School and Society* 12 (October 30, 1920): 412–14.

18   Beardsley Ruml and Sidney Tickton, *Teaching Salaries Then and Now: A Fifty-Year Comparison with Other Occupations and Industries* (New York: Fund for the Advancement of Education, 1955), pp. 54–56.

19   USBE, *Increases in Salaries of College Teachers*, Higher Education Circular no. 15, July 1919, pp. 1–5.

20   Lovejoy, "Annual Message of the President," p. 14.

21   Paul H. Douglas, "Incomes and Living Costs of a University Faculty," *Bulletin of the AAUP* 15 (May 1929): 350.

22   Ruml and Tickton, *Teaching Salaries*, pp. 54–56.

23   *Social status* designates "every typical component of the life fate of men that is determined by a specific, positive, or negative, social estimation of honor." Weber, "Class, Status, Party," in *From Max Weber*, pp. 186–87. As Weber notes, property ownership "is not always recognized as a status qualification, but in the long run it is, and with extraordinary regularity." This is particularly true of capitalist societies, in which property and income are generally accepted measures of talent, competence, and prestige. Veysey, *Emergence of the American University*, p. 391, finds that professors saw their salary "as a symbol of comparison with one's rivals or as a means of living according to a respectable code."

24   USBE, *Land-Grant Colleges, 1926*, Bulletin, 1927, no. 37 (Washington, D.C.: GPO, 1927), p. 20.

25   Claude Charleton Bowman, *The College Professor in America* (New York: Arno Press, 1977), p. 39.

26   Hurlin, "Salaries of College Teachers."

27   Ruml and Tickton, *Teaching Salaries*, p. 60.

28   Rodney H. True, "Salary Scales of Trained Men and Women," *Bulletin of the AAUP* 15 (December 1929): 538–40.

29   Ruml and Tickton, *Teaching Salaries*, p. 65.

30   An American Professor, "The Status of the American Professor," p. 419.

31   Quoted in *New York Times*, August 20, 1919, p. 26.

32   USBE, *Report of the Commissioner of Education*, 1920, p. 10.

33   U.S. Bureau of Labor Statistics, *Union Scale of Wages and Hours of Labor*, Bulletin no. 431, May 15, 1926.

34   Hofstadter and Metzger, *Development of Academic Freedom*, pp. 465–66.

35   Will, "A Menace to Freedom," pp. 251–54.

36   Witmer, *The Nearing Case*, pp. 25–30.

37   University of Pennsylvania, "The Professors' Union," *Alumni Register*, February 1914.

38   Stevenson, "Status of American College Professors," p. 123; Lawton, "Decay

of Academic Courage," p. 398; H. B. Alexander, "The Professor and the Institution," *Science* 40 (January 9, 1914): 62.

39 Joseph J. Jastrow, "Academic Aspects of Administration," *Popular Science Monthly,* 73 (October 1908), p. 326. James McKeen Cattell, *University Control* (New York: Science Press, 1913) is a collection of these essays.

40 I am, of course, referring to Plato's *Republic,* trans. Francis MacDonald Cornford (Oxford: Oxford University Press, 1941), pp. 106–7.

41 An American Professor, "The Status of the American Professor," pp. 423, 430.

42 In some proposals, the senate was a radically democratic body open to all faculty members regardless of rank. In others, it retained the structure of a medieval guild in which full citizenship was restricted to tenured faculty who had completed seven years as apprentices (i.e., as graduate students) and seven more years as journeymen (i.e., as assistant professors).

43 Cf. John Dewey, "Academic Freedom," *Educational Review,* January 1902, pp. 1–14.

44 Cattell, *University Control,* pp. 19–30.

45 "Preliminary Report of the Joint Committee on Academic Freedom and Academic Tenure," *American Political Science Review* 9 (May 1915): 374–81.

46 Ibid., pp. 376–77.

47 "General Report on Academic Freedom and Academic Tenure," *Bulletin of the AAUP* 1 (December 1915): 490–507.

48 Leighton, "Report of Committee T."

49 Witmer, *The Nearing Case;* Nearing, "Who's Who among College Trustees?"; Colorado College, *Report on College and University Administration,* General Series, no. 94 (Colorado Springs: Colorado College Publications, 1917).

50 Leighton, "Report of Committee T," pp. 19–20, 25–26, 34–35; italics mine.

51 Ibid., p. 27.

52 Ibid., p. 35.

53 Ibid, pp. 26–29.

54 Ibid., pp. 39–43.

55 Ibid., p. 47.

56 Veysey, *Emergence of the American University,* p. 388.

57 Cattell, "Concerning the American University," pp. 180–82.

58 John Dewey, "The Need of an Industrial Education in an Industrial Democracy," *Proceedings of the Second Pan-American Scientific Congress,* Washington, D.C., December 27, 1915–January 8, 1916, 4: 222–25.

59 Thorstein Veblen, *The Instinct of Workmanship; and the state of the industrial arts* (New York: B. W. Huebsch, 1912).

60 Veblen, *Higher Learning,* p. 57.

61 Sinclair, *Goose-Step,* pp. 455–56.

62 Ibid., pp. 457–58.

63 Kirkpatrick, *American College and Its Rulers,* p. 8.

64 Ibid.

65 For a brief theoretical discussion of the concept of the "working-class intellectual" framed with specific reference to American history, see George Bernard Cotkin, "Working-Class Intellectuals and Evolutionary Thought in America, 1870–1915" (Ph.D. diss., Ohio State University, 1978), pp. 1–3.

66 Sinclair, *Goose-Step,* p. 465; Jack London, "Revolution," *Contemporary Review*

93 (January 1908): 2–31. London agreed with Sinclair that "the so-called great middle class is a growing anomaly in the social struggle. It is a perishing class (wily statisticians to the contrary), and its historic mission of buffer between the capitalist and working classes has just about been fulfilled" (p. 21).

67   Cf. Lewis Feuer, *The Conflict of Generations* (New York: Basic Books, 1969), p. 341; Seymour Martin Lipset, *Rebellion in the University* (London: Routledge and Kegan Paul, 1972), pp. 148–51.

68   Daniel Bell, *Marxian Socialism in the United States* (New York: Princeton University Press, 1972), pp. 50–97.

69   Sinclair, *Goose-Step*, pp. 230, 236.

70   Figures derived from information in Max Horn, *The Intercollegiate Socialist Society, 1905–1921* (Boulder: Westview Press, 1979), pp. 238–39.

71   Hofstadter, *Age of Reform*, pp. 150–52.

72   William Edward Eaton, *The American Federation of Teachers, 1916–1961: A History of the Movement* (Carbondale: Southern Illinois University Press, 1975), p. 31.

73   *New York Times*, December 10, 1919, p. 7.

74   Sinclair, *Goose-Step*, p. 459.

75   *New York Times*, December 9, 1919, p. 7.

76   Sinclair, *Goose-Step*, p. 459.

77   Samuel Gompers, "College Men and the American Labor Movement," *American Federationist*, March 1922, pp. 212–15; A similar position was articulated by Max Nordan, "White-Collar Slaves," *Railway Carmen's Journal*, January 1923, p. 57. James McKeen Cattell, "The Organization of Scientific Men," *Bulletin of the AAUP* 8 (October, 1922): 52, argued that scientists "add billions of dollars a year to the wealth of the world. . . . Why cannot scientific men learn how to retain even one percent of such wealth?" A contemporary effort to measure this value added is Fritz Machlup, *The Production and Distribution of Knowledge in the United States* (Princeton: Princeton University Press, 1962).

78   *Report of the Proceedings of the Fortieth Annual Convention of the American Federation of Labor*, Montreal, June 7–19, 1920, p. 471.

79   For the address, see Lovejoy, "Annual Message of the President of the AAUP," pp. 22–27.

80   Eliot R. Clark et al., "Report of the Missouri Local Branch of the AAUP," *Bulletin of the AAUP* 6 (April 1920): 16.

81   Lovejoy, *Bulletin of the AAUP*, April 1920, p. 18.

82   Eaton, *American Federation of Teachers*, p. 32.

83   Quoted in Jeanette Ann Lester, "The AFT in Higher Education: A History of Union Organization of Faculty Members in Colleges and Universities, 1916–1966" (Ph.D. diss., University of Toledo, 1968), p. 60.

84   Quoted ibid., p. 75.

85   "The Point of View," *Scribner's Magazine* 42 (1907): 122–24, was written by a professor who noted that farmers in legislatures or on boards of trustees think "the professor has an easy job and a princely salary, although [they respect] his learning" (p. 123).

86   Eaton, *American Federation of Teachers*, p. 33.

Chapter 7. Discipline and Punish

1 John Stuart Mill, "On Liberty," in *Three Essays* (Oxford: Oxford University Press, 1975), pp. 22–68.

2 Bertell Ollman, "Academic Freedom in America Today: A Marxist View," *Monthly Review,* March 1984, pp. 1–12.

3 Veysey, *Emergence of the American University,* p. 410.

4 John R. Commons, *Institutional Economics: Its Place in Political Economy* (New York: Macmillan, 1934).

5 Richard T. Ely, "Statement of Dr. Richard T. Ely," *Publications of the American Economic Association* 1 (1887): 19; Ely, "Discussion of the Farmers' Movement," *Proceedings of the Fifth Annual Meeting of the American Economic Association,* Chautauqua, N.Y., August 23–26, 1892, pp. 64–65, 67–69.

6 Allan G. Bogue and Robert Taylor, eds., *The University of Wisconsin: One Hundred and Twenty-Five Years* (Madison: University of Wisconsin Press, 1975), p. 22. For a more detailed description of the Ely case, see Furner, *Advocacy and Objectivity,* pp. 146–62; also, Merle Curti and Vernon Carstensen, *The University of Wisconsin: A History, 1848–1925,* 2 vols. (Madison: University of Wisconsin Press, 1949), 1: 508–21.

7 Furner, *Advocacy and Objectivity,* p. 163.

8 "The Freedom of Teaching," *Dial* 18 (September 1, 1894): 103–5, 110, 149.

9 His statement is reprinted as Richard T. Ely, "Fundamental Beliefs in My Social Philosophy," *Forum* 18 (1894): 173–83.

10 Quoted in Bogue and Taylor, *University of Wisconsin,* p. 23. The most prominent American scholars of the 1890s and early 1900s took the idea of academic freedom for granted, since most had received a graduate education in Germany; see Jurgen Herbst, *The German Historical School in American Scholarship: A Study in the Transfer of Culture* (Port Washington, N.Y.: Kennikat Press, 1972), and Charles F. Thwing, *The American and German University* (New York: Macmillan, 1928).

11 Sinclair, *Goose-Step,* pp. 230–36; Veysey, *Emergence of the American University,* p. 416.

12 Furner, *Advocacy and Objectivity,* pp. 162–63.

13 Edward W. Beemis, "The Discontent of the Farmers," *Proceedings of the American Economic Association, 1892,* pp. 75–76.

14 Harold E. Berquist, Jr., "The Edward W. Beemis Controversy at the University of Chicago," *Bulletin of the AAUP* 58 (December 1972): 384–93; Metzger, *Academic Freedom in the Age of the University,* p. 152; Furner, *Advocacy and Objectivity,* pp. 164–98.

15 Howard C. Warren, "Academic Freedom," *Atlantic Monthly* 114 (November 1914), p. 693.

16 Sinclair, *Goose-Step,* pp. 243–45.

17 Furner, *Advocacy and Objectivity,* pp. 196–98.

18 Manley, *Centennial History of the University of Nebraska,* 1:150; Furner, *Advocacy and Objectivity,* pp. 206–22.

19 "The Aggressions of American Wealth," *The Spectator,* July 31, 1897, pp. 135–36; E. D. Mead, "Editor's Table," *New England Magazine* (September 1897): 119–28; V. S. Yarreo, "Freedom of Teaching in America," *Westminster Review* January 1898, pp. 8–16.

20 See the examples in Will, "A Menace to Freedom," pp. 251–52.
21 Manley, *Centennial History of the University of Nebraska,* 1:150.
22 On the Ross case, see Orrin Leslie Elliot, *Stanford University: The First Twenty-five Years* (Stanford: Stanford University Press, 1937), pp. 326–78; Furner, *Advocacy and Objectivity,* pp. 229–259.
23 Furner, *Advocacy and Objectivity,* pp. 198–203.
24 Thomas C. McClintock, "J. Allen Smith: A Pacific Northwest Progressive," *Pacific Northwest Quarterly,* April 1962, pp. 49–59.
25 Colwell, "The Populist Image of Vernon Louis Parrington," pp. 52–66.
26 Butler, *Scholarship and Service,* p. 64.
27 Ibid., p. 116.
28 Ibid., pp. 65, 89–90, 158–59, 179–80.
29 Ibid., pp. 179–80.
30 Hyde, "Academic Freedom in America," pp. 2–9.
31 Butler, *Scholarship and Service,* p. 115.
32 Hyde, "Academic Freedom in America," pp. 2–3.
33 Arthur T. Hadley, "Academic Freedom in Theory and Practice," in Metzger, *The American Concept of Academic Freedom,* pp. 152, 343.
34 Furner, *Advocacy and Objectivity,* p. 183. The contemporary institutionalization of a "left academy" is the object of Jacoby's recent critique; see *The Last Intellectuals.* Cf. Bertell Ollman and Edward Vernoff, *The Left Academy: Marxist Scholarship on American Campuses* (New York: McGraw-Hill, 1982).
35 Anarchism and later Communism were always regarded as unacceptable on campus.
36 Furner, *Advocacy and Objectivity,* p. 181.
37 Geiger, *University of the Northern Plains,* pp. 169–70.
38 Ibid., p. 170.
39 Ibid., pp. 278–79.
40 Bogue and Taylor, *The University of Wisconsin,* p. 33. On Van Hise's own economic views, see Charles R. Van Hise, *Concentration and Control: A Solution of the Trust Problem in the United States* (New York: Macmillan, 1912).
41 Veysey, *Emergence of the American University,* p. 303.
42 Charles Beard, "A Statement," *New Republic,* December 29, 1917, p. 249.
43 On Cattell and Columbia, see "Columbia University vs. Professor Cattell," *Bulletin of the AAUP* (November 1922): 21–41.
44 Warren, "Academic Freedom," pp. 693–94.
45 USBE, *Recent Movements in University Administration,* pp. 57–58; "Academic Freedom," *Science,* March 21, 1913, p. 450; "The Academic Situation," *Popular Science Monthly,* March 1913, p. 307–8.
46 Warren, "Academic Freedom," pp. 693–94.
47 "The Academic Situation," p. 307.
48 Warren, "Academic Freedom," p. 693.
49 Ibid. For instance, Francis A. Walker, a political economist and president of MIT, declared that the Populist movement, when combined with an empirical political economy imported from Germany, had "swept away" the "bounds of tradition" and "the barriers of authority" which supported "the arbitrary and unreal" assumptions of laissez-faire economics; see Walker, "The Tide of Economic Thought: Presidential Address to the American Economic Association," *Proceedings of the Fourth Annual Meeting of the American Economic*

Association, December 26–30, 1890, pp. 15–21. Likewise, W. W. Folwell, president of the University of Minnesota, claimed that "the object of economic investigation is . . . the actual behavior of human society . . . posited at the economic standpoint, in historical review; not the possible behavior of abstract economic atoms acting under supposed conditions. . . . There is no longer any concern about 'the economic man.'" Folwell, "The New Economics: Address of the Acting President of the American Economic Association," *Proceedings of the American Economic Association,* 1893, p. 23. Cf. Richard Ashcraft, "German Historicism and the History of Political Theory," *History of Political Thought* 8 (Summer 1987): 289–302.

50   USBE, *Report of the Commissioner of Education, 1915,* pp. 158, 160.

51   Ibid., pp.157–58.

52   Ibid., p. 158; Rev. W. A. Lambert, "Liberty in Teaching," *The Nation* 97 (July 3, 1913).

53   USBE, *Report of the Commissioner of Education, 1915,* pp. 158–59.

54   Warren, "Academic Freedom," pp. 695–96.

55   Quoted in USBE, *Report of the Commissioner of Education,* 1915, p. 159.

56   Ibid.

57   "Academic Freedom," p. 450.

58   Quoted in USBE, *Report of the Commissioner of Education, 1915,* pp. 160–61; E.R.A. Seligman et al., "Preliminary Report of the Joint Committee on Academic Freedom and Academic Tenure," *American Political Science Review* 9 (May 1915): 374–81.

59   Veysey, *Emergence of the American University,* p. 387.

60   Warren, "Academic Freedom," pp. 696–98

61   "Call for the Meeting for Organization of a National Association of University Professors," *Bulletin of the AAUP,* March 1916, p. 11.

62   Quoted in USBE, *Report of the Commissioner of Education, 1915,* p. 161.

63   See the list in the *Bulletin of the AAUP,* December 1915.

64   Quoted in USBE, *Report of the Commissioner of Education,* 1915, p. 163; also see "Academic Freedom in Utah," *New Republic* 4 (October 16, 1915): 274–75.

65   Quoted in USBE, *Report of the Commissioner of Education, 1915,* p. 165.

66   Ibid., p. 163.

67   Ibid., pp. 163–65.

68   "Report on Charges of Violation of Academic Freedom at the University of Colorado and at Wesleyan University," *Bulletin of the AAUP* (1915).

69   Sinclair, *Goose-Step,* pp. 192–93.

70   USBE, *Report of the Commissioner of Education, 1915,* p. 165.

71   See Witmer, *The Nearing Case,* for an extensive treatment of the case. Also see Scott Nearing, *The Making of a Radical: A Political Autobiography* (New York: Harper and Row, 1972), pp. 83–94, and Stephen J. Whitfield, *Scott Nearing: Apostle of American Radicalism* (New York: Columbia University Press, 1974), pp. 25–52.

72   Edward Potts Cheyney, *History of the University of Pennsylvania, 1740–1940* (Philadelphia: University of Pennsylvania Press, 1940), pp. 367–68.

73   Ibid.

74   Ibid., p. 383.

75   Quoted in Witmer, *The Nearing Case,* pp. 68–69; also see USBE, *Report of the Commissioner of Education, 1915,* p. 167.

76 Quoted in USBE, *Report of the Commissioner of Education*, 1915, p. 166.
77 Cheyney, *University of Pennsylvania*, p. 370.
78 Witmer, *The Nearing Case*, p. xiv.
79 Quoted ibid., p. 33.
80 Quoted in USBE, *Report of the Commissioner of Education, 1915,* p. 166.
81 Ibid., p. 141.
82 "Academic Freedom: Changes in the Status of the Teaching Body of the University of Pennsylvania—A Pleasant Sequel to the Scott Nearing Case," *The Nation*, December 23, 1915, pp. 745–46.
83 Ibid.
84 USBE, *Recent Movements in University Administration*, p. 60.
85 "Academic Freedom," p. 746.
86 "General Report of the Committee on Academic Freedom and Tenure," in USBE, *Report of the Commissioner of Education, 1916*, p. 138.
87 Ibid., p. 139.
88 Ibid.
89 Ibid., p. 181.
90 Frank Thilly, "Report of the President," *Bulletin of the AAUP* 3 (November, 1917): p. 15. Also see J. H. Wigmore, "President's Report for 1916," *Bulletin of the AAUP* 2 (November, 1916): 15.
91 "Report of the Committee of Inquiry Concerning Charges of Violation of Academic Freedom at the University of Colorado," *Bulletin of the AAUP* 2 (April 1916): 3. USBE, *Report of the Commissioner of Education*, 1916, p. 138.
92 "Editorial Announcement," *Bulletin of the AAUP* 2 (March 1916): 6.
93 "Report of the Committee of Inquiry on the Colorado School of Mines," *Bulletin of the AAUP* 6 (May 1920): 27–37.

Chapter 8. Twilight of the Idols

1 Curti and Carstensen, *University of Wisconsin*, 2:56.
2 Sinclair, *Goose-Step,* pp. 45–49.
3 Beard, "A Statement," p. 249.
4 Ibid.
5 Edward S. Corwin, review of *Economic Interpretation of the Constitution of the United States* by Charles A. Beard, *History Teachers' Magazine*, 5 (February 1914): 65–66; Henry Cabot Lodge, "The Constitution and Its Makers," *North American Review* 196 (July 1912): 22.
6 Cf. Clyde W. Barrow, "Charles A. Beard's Social Democracy: A Critique of the Populist-Progressive Style in American Political Thought," *Polity* 21 (Winter 1988): 23–38; and Ellen Nore, *Charles A. Beard: An Intellectual Biography* (Carbondale: Southern Illinois University Press, 1983), pp. 28–29, 51–52, 94.
7 Freeman, *An American Testament*, pp. 106–7.
8 Beard, "A Statement," p. 249.
9 Ibid., pp. 249–50. Horace Coon, *Columbia: Colossus on the Hudson* (New York: E. P. Dutton and Co., 1947), p. 126, tells essentially the same story.
10 Quoted in the *New York Times*, March 6, 1917, p. 2.
11 "Disloyalists at School," *New York Times*, March 9, 1917, p. 6.
12 *New York Times*, March 24, 1917, p. 10; Henry D. May, *The Discontent of the Intellectuals* (Chicago: Rand McNally, 1963), p. 14.

13 *New York Times*, October 2, 1917, p. 1.
14 Freeman, *An American Testament*, p. 105.
15 *New York Times*, October 9, 1917, p. 1.
16 Freeman, *An American Testament*, pp. 107–9.
17 *New York Times*, October 11, 1917, p. 24; October 13, 1917, p. 13, col. 6; October 18, 1917, p. 5.
18 Ibid., December 4, 1917, p. 22.
19 Beard, "A Statement," p. 250.
20 Quoted in the *New York Times*, December 3, 1917, p. 11.
21 *New York Times*, March 2, 1918, p. 11.
22 Wechsler, *Revolt on the Campus*, p. 17; Freeman, *An American Testament*, p. 109.
23 James Gray, *The University of Minnesota, 1851–1951* (Minneapolis: University of Minnesota Press, 1951), pp. 246–47.
24 Quoted in Wechsler, *Revolt on Campus*, pp. 16–17.
25 Ibid., p. 17.
26 Frank Thilly, "Annual Report of the President," *Bulletin of the AAUP* 3 (November, 1917): 19–20. Thilly was an anti-Marxian, antisocialist progressive. As a philosopher, he derived his political opposition to socialism from a principled hostility to the perceived moral effects of philosophical "materialism"; see Frank Thilly, "The Characteristics of the Present Age," *Hibbert Journal* 10 (October 1911): 253–66.
27 Arthur O. Lovejoy, "Report on Academic Freedom in Wartime," *Bulletin of the AAUP* 4 (February–March, 1918): 37.
28 Ibid., pp. 16–21.
29 Quoted in the *New York Times*, May 27, 1917, p. 9. Also see ibid., June 24, 1917, sec. 6, pp. 8–9; June 2, 1917, p. 1, September 10, 1917, p. 5.
30 Horn, *Intercollegiate Socialist Society*, p. 162.
31 Gray, *University of Minnesota*, p. 256.
32 Ibid., p. 257.
33 Horn, *Intercollegiate Socialist Society*, pp. 165–69.
34 U.S. Senate Subcommittee on the Judiciary, *Report and Hearings: Brewing and Liquor Interests and German and Bolshevik Propaganda*, U.S. Senate Document no. 62, 66th Cong., 1st sess., (Washington, D.C.: GPO, 1919), 2:2184–87, 2478–85; ibid., 3:13; *New York Times*, January 9, 1919, p. 9: cols. 1–2.
35 *New York Times*, January 28, 1919, p. 8.
36 New York Joint Legislative Committee Investigating Seditious Activities, *Revolutionary Radicalism: Its History, Purposes, and Tactics, with an Exposition and Discussion of the Steps Being Taken and Required to Curb It*, 4 vols. (Albany: J. B. Lyon Co., 1920).
37 Cf. David M. Schneider, *The Workers' (Communist) Party and American Trade Unions* (Baltimore: Johns Hopkins Press, 1928). On specific unions, see William Z. Foster, "The Work of the Trade Union Educational League," in *American Trade Unionism* (New York: International Publishers, 1947); McAlister Coleman, *Men and Coal* (New York: Arno Press, 1969), pp. 105–14; Joel Seidman, *The Needle Trades* (New York: Farrar and Rinehart, 1942), pp. 153–85; Walter Galenson, *The United Brotherhood of Carpenters* (Cambridge: Harvard University Press, 1983), pp. 215–20; Mark Perlman, *The Machinists* (Cambridge: Harvard University Press, 1961), pp. 64–65; Philip Foner, *The Industrial Workers of the World* (New York: International Publishers, 1965).

38 Joint Legislative Committee, *Revolutionary Radicalism*, pp. 2035–75, 2084. Cf. Eldridge Foster Dowell, "A History of Criminal Syndicalism Legislation in the United States," *Studies in Historical and Political Science*, Series 57, no. 1, (Baltimore: Johns Hopkins Press, 1939), pp. 3–176.

39 "Local and Chapter Notes," *Bulletin of the AAUP* 11 (October 1925): 309–10.

40 Joint Legislative Committee, *Revolutionary Radicalism*, p. 4225. Cf. James O. Morris, *Conflict within the AFL: A Study of Craft versus Industrial Unionism, 1901–1938* (Ithaca: Cornell University Press, 1958).

41 Ibid., pp. 3346–4164.

42 See Robert W. Iverson, *The Communists and the Schools* (New York: Harcourt, Brace, 1959), and Eaton, *American Federation of Teachers*, pp. 90–93.

43 Horn, *Intercollegiate Socialist Society*, p. 184.

44 Ibid., p. 183.

45 *New York Times*, December 30, 1922, p.1.

46 Ibid., January 29, 1923, p. 8.

47 Quoted in ibid., March 5, 1923, p. 7.

48 Wechsler, *Revolt on Campus*, p. 26.

49 Alice Payne Hackett, *Wellesley: Part of the American Story* (New York, 1949), p. 222.

50 Quoted in "Intercollegiate Liberal League," *Bulletin of the AAUP* 7 (October, 1921): 8.

51 *New York Times*, April 3, 1921, p. 21; April 4, 1921, p. 3.

52 Ibid., April 5, 1921, p. 18; April 7, 1921, p. 8.

53 Ibid., July 14, 1922, p. 15. The names of individual professors, radical organizations, and so-called disloyal campuses were apparently well known at the highest levels of federal officialdom. A quite serious example of this surveillance is Calvin Coolidge, "Enemies of the Republic: Are the 'Reds' Stalking Our College Women?" *The Delineator*, June 1921, pp. 4–5, 65–66.

54 Graham Wallas, "The 'New Virility' in the United States," *New Statesman*, January 31, 1920, pp. 487–88; Russell Scott, "The 'New Virility' in America," February 28, 1920, pp. 613–14.

55 *New York Times*, April 10, 1921, p. 1.

56 Frank Hiscock, "Radicalism in Universities," *Bulletin of the AAUP* 9 (February, 1923): 33.

57 *New York Times*, May 30, 1926, sec. 4 p. 18.

58 "Report on the University of Montana—The Levine Case," *Bulletin of the AAUP*, May 1919, pp. 13–25; "Report on Washburn College," ibid. 7 (January–February, 1921); "Report on Middlebury College," ibid., (May 1921); "Report on the University of Montana," ibid. 10 (March, 1924); "Report on the University of Arizona," ibid., November 1924.

59 "Annual Meeting," *Bulletin of the AAUP* 7 (January–February, 1921): 8–9.

60 "Report of Committee A," *Bulletin of the AAUP*, February 1924, p. 71.

61 Arthur Livingston, "Academic Freedom," *New Republic*, (November 17, 1917), pp. 69–71.

62 "A Professional Fiasco," *New Republic*, May 28, 1924, p. 6.

63 *New York Times*, June 15, 1923, p. 1.

64 Ibid., June 16, 1923, p. 2. Cf. Alexander Meiklejohn, *The Liberal College* (Boston: Marshall Jones Co., 1920), and idem, *The Experimental College* (Cabin John, Md.: Seven Locks Press, 1981).

65 Quoted in the *New York Times,* June 16, 1923, p. 2.

66 Ibid.

67 Ibid., June 17, 1923, p. 1; June 18, 1923, p. 3.

68 Ibid., June 20, 1923, pp. 1 and 18.

69 Quoted ibid., June 21, 1923, p. 1.

70 Ibid., June 25, 1923, p. 1; June 30, 1923, p. 1; July 16, 1923, p. 22.

71 McVey and Hughes, *College and University Administration,* p. 54.

72 Wechsler, *Revolt on Campus,* p. 31.

73 "Report of Committee A," *Bulletin of the AAUP,* February 1925, p. 84.

74 Ibid., p. 86.

75 "Report of the Conference on Academic Freedom and Tenure," *Bulletin of the AAUP,* February 1925, p. 99.

76 H. R. Fairclough, "Academic Freedom and Academic Tenure," *Bulletin of the AAUP* 15 (February, 1929): 99.

77 See ibid., pp. 100–101, for a copy.

78 Ibid., p. 101.

Chapter 9. Hegemony and Autonomy

1 Barrow, "Intellectuals in Contemporary Social Theory," pp. 415–30.

2 Talcott Parsons and Gerald M. Platt, *The American University* (Cambridge: Harvard University Press, 1973); Parsons, "Considerations on the American Academic System," pp. 497–510; Lewis S. Feuer, *Ideology and the Ideologists* (New York: Harper and Row, 1975); Lewis S. Feuer, "What is an Intellectual?" in Aleksander Gella, ed., *The Intelligentsia and the Intellectuals: Theory, Method, and Case Study* (Beverly Hills: Sage Publications, 1976).

3 There is considerable disagreement among Marxists as to exactly what class or classes to assign the intellectuals. Various authors have designated them as bourgeois, petit bourgeois, proletarian, part of a new working class, one component in a professional-managerial class, as well as an objectively contradictory class location as a result of their incomplete proletarianization. See Herbert Aptheker, "Academic Freedom in the United States," *Political Affairs,* July 1965, pp. 53–60; Nicos Poulantzas, *Classes in Contemporary Capitalism* (London: New Left Books, 1975), pp. 224–99; Francesca Friedman, "The Internal Structure of the American Proletariat: A Marxist Analysis," Socialist Revolution 26 (October–December 1975): 41–83; Andre Gorz, "Technical Intelligence and the Capitalist Division of Labor," *Telos* 12 (Summer 1972): 27–41; Barbara Ehrenreich and John Ehrenreich, "The Professional Managerial Class," *Radical America* 11 (March–April 1977): 7–31; and Erik Olin Wright, "Intellectuals and the Working Class," *Insurgent Sociologist* 8 (Winter 1978): 5–18.

4 Wilbert E. Moore, *The Professions: Roles and Rules* (New York: Russell Sage Foundation, 1970); Shils, *The Constitution of Society,* p. 191; Draper, "Intellectuals in American Politics," pp. 15–42; Coser, *Men of Ideas,* and Howe, "Intellectuals, Dissent, and Bureaucrats," 303–8.

5 Poulantzas, *Political Power and Social Classes,* pp. 84–94.

6 Mannheim, *Ideology and Utopia,* pp. 153–64.

7 For example, *Irving Louis Horowitz, The Use and Abuse of Social Science* (New York: Transaction Books, 1971); idem, *The Rise and Fall of Project Camelot*

(Cambridge: MIT Press, 1967); Robert Nisbet, "Project Camelot: An Autopsy," in Rieff, *On Intellectuals*, pp. 307–39.

8   Gouldner, *Future of Intellectuals*, pp. 60–70; Baritz, *Servants of Power*; Noam Chomsky, *American Power and the New Mandarins* (New York: Pantheon Books, 1969); idem, "Objectivity and Liberal Scholarship," in O'Brien and Vanech, *Power and Consciousness*, pp. 43–136; idem, *Problems of Knowledge and Freedom*.

9   Miliband, *State in Capitalist Society*, p. 182.

10 Craig Kaplan and Ellen Schrecker, *Regulating the Intellectuals* (New York: Praeger Press, 1983).

11 See the essays in Paul Seabury, ed., *Bureaucrats and Brainpower* (San Francisco: Institute for Contemporary Studies, 1979); Piccard, *Science and Policy Issues*; and Finn, *Scholars, Dollars, and Bureaucrats*.

12 Michael Mann, "The Ideology of Intellectuals and Other People in the Development of Capitalism," in Leon Lindberg, ed., *Stress and Contradiction in Modern Capitalism* (Lexington, Mass.: D. C. Heath, 1975).

13 Ollman, "Academic Freedom in America Today."

14 Mannheim, *Ideology and Utopia*, pp. 157–59.

15 Ibid., pp. 282–84.

16 Ibid., p. 155.

17 George Rude, *Ideology and Popular Protest* (New York: Pantheon Books, 1979); Oberschall, *Social Conflict and Social Movements*.

18 Seymour Melman, *The Permanent War Economy* (New York: Simon and Schuster, 1974).

19 Ollman and Vernoff, *The Left Academy*.

20 Jacoby, *Last Intellectuals*.

Sources Consulted

BOOKS, ARTICLES, AND DISSERTATIONS

Abrams, Philip. 1982. *Historical Sociology*. Ithaca: Cornell University Press.

"Academic Freedom." *Science*, March 21, 1913, p. 450.

"Academic Freedom: Changes in the Status of the Teaching Body of the University of Pennsylvania—A Pleasant Sequel to the Scott Nearing Case." *The Nation*, December 23, 1915, pp. 745-46.

"Academic Freedom in Utah." *New Republic*, October 16, 1915, pp. 274-75.

"The Academic Situation." *Popular Science Monthly*, March 1913, pp. 307-8.

Adams, Henry. 1931. *The Education of Henry Adams*. New York: Modern Library.

"The Aggressions of American Wealth." *The Spectator*, July 31, 1897, pp. 135-36.

Alexander, H. B. 1914. "The Professor and the Institution." *Science* 40 (July 10): 60-62.

Althusser, Louis. 1971. "Ideology and Ideological State Apparatuses: Notes Toward an Investigation." In *Lenin and Philosophy and Other Essays*. New York: Monthly Review Press.

Althusser, Louis, and Balibar, Etienne. 1977. *Reading Capital*. London: New Left Books.

An American Professor. 1898. "The Status of the American Professor." *Educational Review*, December.

Anderson, James G. 1968. *Bureaucracy in Education*. Baltimore: Johns Hopkins Press.

Andreano, Ralph C. 1973. *Superconcentration/Supercorporation*. Andover: Warner Modular Publications.

"Annual Meeting." *Bulletin of the AAUP* 7 (January–February 1921): 3-10.

Apple, Michael W. 1979. *Ideology and Curriculum*. London: Routledge and Kegan Paul.

Apple, Michael W. 1982. *Education and Power*. London: Routledge and Kegan Paul.

Apple, Michael W. 1983. *Ideology and Practice in Schooling*. Philadelphia: Temple University Press.

Aptheker, Bettina. 1966. *Big Business and the Universities*. New York: Institute for Marxist Studies.

Aptheker, Herbert. 1965. "Academic Freedom in the United States." *Political Affairs*, July, pp. 53-60.

Armytage, W.H.G. 1965. *The Rise of the Technocrats: A Social History*. London: Routledge and Kegan Paul.

Ashcraft, Richard. 1987. "German Historicism and the History of Political Theory." *History of Political Thought* 8 (Summer) 289–324.

Baran, Paul A., and Sweezy, Paul M. 1966. *Monopoly Capital: An Essay on the American Economic and Social Order.* New York: Monthly Review Press.

Baritz, Loren. 1960. *The Servants of Power: A History of the Use of Social Science in American Industry.* Middletown: Wesleyan University Press.

Barnard, Chester. 1956. *The Functions of the Executive.* Cambridge: Harvard University Press.

Barnard, John. 1969. *From Evangelicalism to Progressivism at Oberlin College, 1866–1917.* Columbus: Ohio State University Press.

Barrow, Clyde W. 1987. "Intellectuals in Contemporary Social Theory: A Radical Critique." *Sociological Inquiry* 57 (Fall): 415–30.

Barrow, Clyde W. 1988. "Charles A. Beard's Social Democracy: A Critique of the Populist-Progressive Style in American Political Thought." *Polity* 21 (Winter): 253–276.

Beard, Charles. 1917. "A Statement." *New Republic* December 29.

Beard, Charles A., and Beard, Mary R. 1930. *The Rise of American Civilization,* 2 vols. New York: Macmillan Co.

Beck, Hubert Park. 1947. *Men Who Control Our Universities: The Economic and Social Composition of Governing Boards of Thirty Leading American Universities.* New York: King's Crown Press.

Beemis, Edward W. 1892. "The Discontent of the Farmers." *Proceedings of the Fifth Annual Meeting of the American Economic Association,* Chautauqua, N.Y., August 23–26.

Bell, Daniel. 1972. *Marxian Socialism in the United States.* Princeton: Princeton University Press.

Bell, Daniel. 1976. *The Coming of Post-Industrial Society.* New York: Basic Books.

Benet, James. 1972. "California's Regents: Window on the Ruling Class." *Change,* February.

Bensel, Richard Franklin. 1984. *Sectionalism and American Political Development.* Madison: University of Wisconsin Press.

Bernstein, Basil. 1975. *Toward a Theory of Educational Transmissions.* Vol. 3 of *Class, Codes, and Control.* London: Routledge and Kegan Paul.

Berquist, Harold E. 1972. "The Edward W. Beemis Controversy at the University of Chicago." *Bulletin of the AAUP* 58 (December): 384–93.

Bledstein, Burton J. 1976. *The Culture of Professionalism: The Middle Class and the Development of Higher Education in America.* New York: W. W. Norton and Co.

Block, Fred L. 1977. "The Ruling-Class Does Not Rule: Notes on the Marxist Theory of the State." *Socialist Revolution* 7, no. 3:6–28.

Bloom, Allan. 1987. *The Closing of the American Mind.* New York: Simon and Schuster.

Bogue, Allan G. , and Taylor, Robert, eds. 1975. *The University of Wisconsin: One Hundred and Twenty-Five Years.* Madison: University of Wisconsin Press.

Bond, Jesse A. 1927. "Results of School Surveys." M.A. thesis, University of Southern California.

Bowles, Samuel. 1972. "Unequal Education and the Reproduction of the Social Division of Labor." In Martin Carnoy, ed., *Schooling in a Corporate Society: The Political Economy of Education in America,* pp. 38–66. New York: McKay.

Bowles, Samuel, and Gintis, Herbert. 1969. *Schooling in Capitalist America: Educational Reform and the Contradictions of Economic Life.* New York: Basic Books.

Bowles, Samuel, and Gintis, Herbert. 1986. *Democracy and Capitalism.* New York: Basic Books.

Bowman, Claude Charleton. 1977. *The College Professor in America.* New York: Arno Press.

Brennan, J. Fletcher. 1879. *A Biographical Cyclopedia and Portrait Gallery of Distinguished Men, With an Historical Sketch of the State of Ohio.* Cincinnati: John C. Yorston and Co.

Brown, Elmer E. 1909. *Government by Influence and Other Essays.* London: Longmans, Green, and Co.

Brubacher, James S., and Rudy, Willis. 1976. *Higher Education in Transition.* New York: Harper and Row Publishers.

Bryan, Enoch Albert. 1928. *Historical Sketch of the State College of Washington.* Spokane: Inland American Printing Co.

Burns, James MacGregor. 1978. *Leadership.* New York: Harper and Row Publishers.

Butler, Nicholas Murray. 1918. "Education after the War." *Proceedings of the Association of Colleges and Preparatory Schools of the Middle States and Maryland,* November 29.

Butler, Nicholas Murray. 1921. *Scholarship and Service.* New York: Charles Scribner's Sons.

Cabaniss, Allen. 1971. *The University of Mississippi: Its First Hundred Years.* Hattiesburg: University and College Press of Mississippi.

"Call for the Meeting for Organization of a National Association of University Professors." *Bulletin of the AAUP* 2 (March 1916): 11–13.

Capen, Samuel P. 1911. "The Supervision of College Teaching." *Pedagogical Seminary* 18 (December): 543–50.

Capen, Samuel P. 1919. "The Colleges in a Nationalized Educational Scheme." *School and Society* 9 (March 24): 613–18.

Capen, Samuel P. 1953. *The Management of Universities.* Buffalo: Foster and Stewart Publishing Corp.

Carey, James C. 1977. *Kansas State University: The Quest for Identity.* Lawrence: Regents Press of Kansas.

"The Carnegie Pension." *Journal of Education,* April 28, 1910.

Carnoy, Martin, ed. 1977. *Schooling in a Corporate Society: The Political Economy of Education in America.* New York: McKay.

Carnoy, Martin. 1982. "Education, Economy, and the State." In Michael W. Apple, ed., *Cultural and Economic Reproduction in Education: Essays on Class, Ideology, and the State,* pp. 79–126. London: Routledge and Kegan Paul.

Carnoy, Martin. 1984. *The State and Political Theory.* Princeton: Princeton University Press.

Cary, Harold Whiting. 1962. *The University of Massachusetts: A History of One Hundred Years.* Amherst: University of Massachusetts Press.

Cattell, James McKeen. 1902. "Concerning the American University." *Popular Science Monthly* 61 (June): 170–82.

Cattell, James McKeen. 1909. "The Carnegie Foundation for the Advancement of Teaching." *Science* 29 (April 2): 532–39.

Cattell, James McKeen, ed. 1913. *University Control.* New York: Science Press.

Cattell, James McKeen, ed. 1919. *Carnegie Pensions*. New York: Science Press.

Cattell, James McKeen. 1922. "The Organization of Scientific Men." *Bulletin of the AAUP* 8 (October): 50–52.

Chandler, Alfred D. 1962. *Strategy and Structure: Chapters in the History of the American Industrial Enterprise*. Cambridge: MIT Press.

Chandler, Alfred D. , and Redlich, Fritz. 1961. "Recent Developments in American Business Administration and Their Conceptualization." *Business History Review,* Spring, pp. 103–28.

Cheyney, Edward Potts. 1940. *History of the University of Pennsylvania, 1740–1940*. Philadelphia: University of Pennsylvania Press.

Chomsky, Noam. 1969. *American Power and the New Mandarins*. New York: Pantheon Books.

Chomsky, Noam. 1969. "Objectivity and Liberal Scholarship." In Conor Cruise O'Brien and William Dean Vanech, eds., *Power and Consciousness*, pp. 43–116. New York: New York University Press.

Chomsky, Noam. 1971. *Problems of Knowledge and Freedom*. New York: Pantheon Books.

Churchill, Thomas W. 1914. "Carnegie Foundation." *Journal of Education*, September 3.

Clark, Eliot R., et al. 1920. "Report of the Missouri Local Branch of the AAUP." *Bulletin of the AAUP* 6 (April): 14–18.

Cleaver, Harry. 1979. *Reading Capital Politically*. Austin: University of Texas Press.

Cleaver, Harry, and Bell, Peter. 1982. "Marx's Crisis Theory as a Theory of Class Relations." *Research in Political Economy,* no. 5.

Clough, Wilson O. 1965. *A History of the University of Wyoming, 1887–1964*. Laramie: University of Wyoming Press.

Cochran, Thomas C. 1972. *Business in American Life: A History*. New York: McGraw-Hill Book Co.

Cohen, Jean L. 1982. "Between Crisis Management and Social Movements: The Place of Institutional Reform." *Telos* 52 (Summer): 21–40.

Coleman, McAlister. 1969. *Men and Coal*. New York: Arno Press.

Collins, Varnum Lansing. 1914. *Princeton*. New York: Oxford University Press.

Colorado College. 1917. *Report on College and University Administration*. General Series, no. 94. Colorado Springs: Colorado College Publications.

"Columbia University vs. Professor Cattell." *Bulletin of the AAUP* 8 (November 1922): 21–41.

Colwell, James L. 1962. "The Populist Image of Vernon Louis Parrington." *Mississippi Valley Historical Review* 49 (June): 52–66.

Commons, John R. 1934. *Institutional Economics: Its Place in Political Economy*. New York: Macmillan Co.

Coolidge, Calvin. 1921. "Enemies of the Republic: Are the 'Reds ' Stalking Our College Women?" *The Delineator,* June, pp. 4–5, 65–66.

Coon, Horace. 1947. *Columbia: Colossus on the Hudson*. New York: E. P. Dutton and Co.

Corey, Lewis. 1930. *House of Morgan: A Social Biography of the Masters of Money*. New York: G. H. Wyatt.

Corwin, Edwin S. 1914. Review of *Economic Interpretation of the Constitution of the United States*, by Charles A. Beard. History Teachers' Magazine 5 (February): 65–66.

Coser, Lewis A. 1965. *Men of Ideas: A Sociologist's View.* New York: Free Press.

Cotkin, George Bernard. 1978. "Working-Class Intellectuals and Evolutionary Thought in America, 1870–1915." Ph.D. diss., Ohio State University.

Crane, R. T. 1909. *The Utility of All Kinds of Higher Learning.* Chicago.

Creamer, Daniel; Dobrovolski, Sergei P.; and Borenstein, Israel. 1960. *Capital in Manufacturing and Mining.* Princeton: Princeton University Press.

Croly, Herbert. 1909. *The Promise of American Life.* New York: Macmillan Co.

Curti, Merle, and Carstensen, Vernon. 1949. *The University of Wisconsin: A History, 1848–1925.* 2 vols. Madison: University of Wisconsin Press.

Curti, Merle, and Nash, Roderick. 1965. *Philanthropy in the Shaping of American Higher Education.* New Brunswick: Rutgers University Press.

Dahl, Robert. 1971. *Polyarchy: Participation and Opposition.* New Haven: Yale University Press.

Dahl, Robert. 1985. *A Preface to Economic Democracy.* Berkeley and Los Angeles: University of California Press.

Dale, Roger. 1982. "Education and the Capitalist State: Contributions and Contradictions." In Michael W. Apple, ed., *Cultural and Economic Reproduction in Education: Essays on Class, Ideology, and the State,* pp. 127–61. London: Routledge and Kegan Paul.

Davis, Mike. 1986. *Prisoners of the American Dream: Politics and Economy in the History of the U.S. Working Class.* London: Verso Books.

Demarest, William H.S. 1924. *A History of Rutgers College, 1776–1924.* New Brunswick: Rutgers University Press.

Dewey, John. 1902. "Academic Freedom." *Educational Review,* January, pp. 1–14.

Dewey, John. 1916. "The Need of an Industrial Education in an Industrial Democracy." *Proceedings of the Second Pan-American Scientific Congress.* Washington, D.C. December 27, 1915 to January 8, 1916. Vol. 4.

Domhoff, G. William. 1967. *Who Rules America?* Englewood Cliffs, N.J.: Prentice-Hall.

Domhoff, G. William. 1970. *The Higher Circles: The Governing Class in America.* New York: Random House.

Doten, Samuel Bradford. 1924. *An Illustrated History of the University of Nevada.* Reno: University of Nevada Press.

Douglas, Paul H. 1929. "Incomes and Living Costs of a University Faculty." *Bulletin of the AAUP* 15 (May): 350–55.

Dowd, Douglas. 1974. *The Twisted Dream: Capitalist Development in the United States since 1776.* Cambridge: Winthrop Publishers.

Dowell, Eldridge Foster. 1939. "A History of Criminal Syndicalism Legislation in the United States." *Studies in Historical and Political Science.* Series 57, no. 1. Baltimore: Johns Hopkins Press.

Draper, Theodore. 1984. "Intellectuals in American Politics: Past and Present." In Nissan Oren, ed., *Intellectuals in Politics,* pp. 15–42. Jerusalem: Magnes Press.

Dunaway, Wayland Fuller. 1946. *History of the Pennsylvania State College.* Lancaster: Pennsylvania State College.

Dupree, A. Hunter. 1957. *Science in the Federal Government: A History of Policies and Activities to 1940.* Cambridge: Harvard University Press.

Durham, N. W. 1912. *History of the City of Spokane and Spokane County, Washington.* 3 vols. Chicago: S. J. Clarke Publishing Co.

Duster, Troy. N.d. *The Aims of Higher Learning and the Control of the Universities.* Berkeley pamphlet.

Easterby, J. H. 1935. *A History of the College of Charleston, Founded 1770*. Charleston: Scribner Press.

Eaton, William Edward. 1975. *The American Federation of Teachers, 1916–1961: A History of the Movement*. Carbondale: Southern Illinois University Press.

Eddy, Edward Danforth, Jr. 1956. *Colleges for Our Land and Time: The Land-Grant Idea in American Education*. Westport, Conn.: Greenwood Press.

"Editorial Announcement." *Bulletin of the AAUP* 2 (March 1916): 6.

Ehrenreich, Barbara, and Ehrenreich, John. 1977. "The Professional Managerial Class." *Radical America* 11 (March–April) 7–31.

Eliot, Charles. 1907. "Academic Freedom." In Walter P. Metzger, ed., *The American Concept of Academic Freedom in Formation*, pp. 1–12. New York: Arno Press, 1977.

Eliot, Charles. 1908. *University Administration*. Boston: Houghton-Mifflin Co.

Elkin, Stephen L. 1987. *City and Regime in the American Republic*. Chicago: University of Chicago Press.

Elliot, Orrin Leslie. 1937. *Stanford University: The First Twenty-Five Years*. Stanford: Stanford University Press.

Ely, Richard T. 1887. "Statement of Dr. Richard T. Ely." *Publications of the American Economic Association*. Vol. 1.

Ely, Richard T. 1892. "Discussion of the Farmers' Movement." *Report of the Proceedings of the Fifth Annual Meeting of the American Economic Association*, Chautauqua, N.Y., August 23–26.

Ely, Richard T. 1894. "Fundamental Beliefs in My Social Philosophy." *Forum* 18: 173–83.

Fairclough, H. R. 1929. "Academic Freedom and Academic Tenure." *Bulletin of the AAUP* 15 (February): 99–101.

Feuer, Lewis S. 1969. *The Conflict of Generations: The Character and Significance of Student Movements*. New York: Basic Books.

Feuer, Lewis S. 1975. *Ideology and the Ideologists*. New York: Harper and Row Publishers.

Feuer, Lewis S. 1976. "What Is an Intellectual?" In Aleksander Gella, ed., *The Intelligentsia and the Intellectuals: Theory, Method, and Case Study*, pp. 47–58. Beverly Hills: Sage Publications.

Fine, Ben. 1975. *Marx's Capital*. London: Macmillan Co.

Finn, Chester E. 1978. *Scholars, Dollars, and Bureaucrats*. Washington, D.C.: Brookings Institution.

Fleming, Walter L. 1936. *Louisiana State University*. Baton Rouge: Louisiana State University Press.

Flexner, Abraham. 1940. *I Remember*. New York: Simon and Schuster.

Folwell, W. W. 1893. "The New Economics: Address of the Acting President of the American Economic Association." *Report of the Proceedings of the American Economic Association* .

Foner, Philip. 1965. *The Industrial Workers of the World*. New York: International Publishers.

Fosdick, Raymond B. 1962. *Adventure in Giving: The Story of the General Education Board, a Foundation Established by John D. Rockefeller*. New York: Harper and Row Publishers.

Foster, William Z. 1947. *American Trade Unionism: Principles and Organization, Strategy and Tactics*. New York: International Publishers.

"The Freedom of Teaching." *Dial* 18 (September 1, 1894): 103–5.

Freeman, Joseph. 1973. *An American Testament: A Narrative of Rebels and Romantics.* New York: Octagon Books.

Friedman, Francesca. 1975. "The Internal Structure of the American Proletariat: A Marxist Analysis." *Socialist Revolution* 5 (October–December): 41–83.

Furner, Mary O. 1975. *Advocacy and Objectivity: A Crisis in the Professionalization of American Social Science, 1865–1905.* Lexington: University Press of Kentucky.

Galenson, Walter. 1983. *The United Brotherhood of Carpenters: The First Hundred Years.* Cambridge: Harvard University Press.

Gates, Charles Marvin. 1961. *The First Century at the University of Washington, 1861–1961.* Seattle: University of Washington Press.

Geiger, Louis M. 1958. *University of the Northern Plains: A History of the University of North Dakota, 1883–1958.* Grand Forks: University of North Dakota Press.

Geiger, Roger L. 1986. *To Advance Knowledge: The Growth of American Research Universities, 1900–1940.* New York: Oxford University Press.

"General Report of the Committee on Academic Freedom and Academic Tenure." *Bulletin of the AAUP* 8 (December 1922): 4–21.

"General Report on Academic Freedom and Academic Tenure." *Bulletin of the AAUP* 1 (December 1915): 490–507.

Gerstenberger, Heide. 1978. "Class Conflict, Competition, and State Functions." In John Holloway and Sol Picciotto, eds., *State and Capital: A Marxist Debate,* pp. 148–59. Austin: University of Texas Press.

Gilbreth, Frank. 1912. *A Primer of Scientific Management.* New York: D. Van Nostrand Co.

Gilman, Daniel Coit. 1898. *University Problems in the United States.* New York: Century Co.

Goldman, Eric F. 1944. "J. Allen Smith: The Reformer and His Dilemma." *Pacific Northwest Quarterly,* July, pp. 195–214.

Gompers, Samuel. 1922. "College Men and the American Labor Movement." *American Federationist,* March, pp. 212–15.

Gompers, Samuel. 1922. "For Higher Universal Education." *American Federationist,* November, pp. 843–44.

Goodnow, Frank J. 1900. *Politics and Administration.* New York: Macmillan Co.

Goodspeed, Thomas Wakefield. 1922. *The University of Chicago Biographical Sketches.* 2 vols. Chicago: University of Chicago Press.

Goodspeed, Thomas Wakefield. 1933. *The Story of the University of Chicago, 1890–1925.* Chicago: University of Chicago Press.

Gorz, Andre. 1972. "Technical Intelligence and the Capitalist Division of Labor." *Telos* 12 (Summer): 27–41.

Gould, Jay M. 1966. *The Technical Elite.* New York: Augustus M. Kelley Publishers.

Gouldner, Alvin W. 1979. *The Future of Intellectuals and the Rise of the New Class.* New York: Continuum Publishing Corp.

Gramsci, Antonio. 1971. *Selections from the Prison Notebooks.* New York: International Publishers.

Grantham, Dewey W. 1983. *Southern Progressivism: The Reconciliation of Progress and Tradition.* Knoxville: University of Tennessee Press.

Graves, Frank P. 1902. "The Need of Training for the College Presidency." *Forum* 32: 680–85.

Gray, James. 1951. *The University of Minnesota, 1851–1951.* Minneapolis: University of Minnesota Press.

Griffin, Clifford S. 1974. *The University of Kansas: A History.* Lawrence: University of Kansas Press.

Haber, Samuel. 1964. *Efficiency and Uplift: Scientific Management in the Progressive Era, 1890–1920.* Chicago: University of Chicago Press.

Habermas, Jurgen. 1975. *Legitimation Crisis.* Boston: Beacon Press.

Hacker, Louis. 1940. *The Triumph of American Capitalism: The Development of Forces in American History to the End of the Nineteenth Century.* New York: Columbia University Press.

Hackett, Alice Payne. 1949. *Wellesley: Part of the American Story.* New York: E. P. Dutton and Co.

Hadley, Arthur T. 1977. "Academic Freedom in Theory and Practice." In Walter P. Metzger, ed., *The American Concept of Academic Freedom in Formation.* New York: Arno Press.

Hanford, Cornelius H. 1924. *Seattle and Environs.* Seattle: Pioneer Historical Publishing Co.

Harvard University. 1937. *Historical Register of Harvard University, 1636–1936.* Cambridge: Harvard University Press.

Haskell, Thomas L. 1977. *The Emergence of Professional Social Science: The American Social Science Association and the Nineteenth-Century Crisis of Authority.* Urbana: University of Illinois Press.

Hays, Samuel P. 1957. *The Response to Industrialism, 1885–1914.* Chicago: University of Chicago Press.

Hays, Samuel P. 1959. *Conservation and the Gospel of Efficiency: The Progressive Conservation Movement, 1890–1920.* Cambridge: Harvard University Press.

Hays, Samuel P. 1960. *Municipal Reform in the Progressive Era: Whose Class Interest?* Boston: New England Free Press.

Heilman, J. D. 1925. "Methods of Reporting the College Teachers' Load and Administrative Efficiency." *Educational Administration and Supervision* 11 (March): 167–87.

Herbst, Jurgen. 1972. *The German Historical School in American Scholarship: A Study in the Transfer of Culture.* Port Washington, N.Y.: Kennikat Press.

Herman, Stanley M. 1968. *The People Specialists: An Examination of Realities and Fantasies in the Corporation's View of People.* New York: Alfred A. Knopf.

Hewett, Waterman Thomas. 1905. *Cornell University: A History.* 2 vols. New York: University Publishing Society.

Heyl, Charles C. 1910. "The Carnegie Foundation and Some American Educational Problems." *Journal of Education,* May 26.

Hilferding, Franz. 1981. *Finance Capital: A Study of the Latest Phase of Capitalist Development.* Boston: Routledge and Kegan Paul.

Hirsch, E. D. 1987. *Cultural Literacy.* Boston: Houghton-Mifflin Co.

Hirsch, Joachim. 1978. "The State Apparatus and Social Reproduction: Elements of a Theory of the Bourgeois State." In John Holloway and Sol Picciotto, eds., *State and Capital: A Marxist Debate,* pp. 57–107. Austin: University of Texas Press.

Hiscock, Frank. 1923. "Radicalism in Universities." *Bulletin of the AAUP* 9 (February): 33.

Hobsbawm, Eric. 1976. "The Crisis of Capitalism in Historical Perspective." *Socialist Revolution* 6 (October–December): 77–96.

Hofstadter, Richard. 1955. *The Age of Reform: From Bryan to F.D.R.* New York: Vintage Books.

Hofstadter, Richard. 1963. *Anti-Intellectualism in American Life*. New York: Vintage Books.

Hofstadter, Richard, and Metzger, Walter P. 1955. *The Development of Academic Freedom in the United States*. New York: Columbia University Press.

Hollis, Daniel Walker. 1956. *University of South Carolina*. Columbia: University of South Carolina Press.

Hollis, Ernest Victor. 1938. *Philanthropic Foundations and Higher Education*. New York: Columbia University Press.

Horn, Max. 1979. *The Intercollegiate Socialist Society, 1905–1921*. Boulder: Westview Press.

Horowitz, Irving Louis. 1967. *The Rise and Fall of Project Camelot: Studies in the Relationship between Social Science and Practical Politics*. Cambridge: MIT Press.

Horowitz, Irving Louis. 1971. *The Use and Abuse of Social Science*. New York: Transaction Books.

Howe, Irving. 1984. "Intellectuals, Dissent, and Bureaucrats." *Dissent* 31 (Summer): 303–8.

Hunt, Herbert. *Tacoma: Its History and Its Builders*. 3 vols. Chicago: S. J. Clarke Publishing Co.

Hurlin, Ralph G. 1920. "The Salaries of College Teachers in 1920." *School and Society* 12 (October 30): 412–14.

Hyde, William Dewitt. 1977. "Academic Freedom in America." In Walter P. Metzger, ed., *The American Concept of Academic Freedom in Formation*. New York: Arno Press.

Hymer, Stephen. 1978. "The Evolution of the Corporation." In Richard C. Edwards, ed., *The Capitalist System: A Radical Analysis of American Society*, pp. 120–25. 2nd ed. Englewood Cliffs, N.J.: Prentice-Hall.

Indiana Survey Commission. 1926. *Report of a Survey of the State Institutions of Higher Learning*. Indianapolis: William Buford.

"Intercollegiate Liberal League." *Bulletin of the AAUP* 7 (October 1921): 8.

Iverson, Robert W. 1959. *The Communists and the Schools*. New York: Harcourt, Brace, and Co.

Jacoby, Russell. 1987. *The Last Intellectuals: American Culture in the Age of Academe*. New York: Basic Books.

Jastrow, Joseph J. 1906. "The Academic Career as Affected by Administration." *Science* 23: 561–74.

Jastrow, Joseph J. 1908. "Academic Aspects of Administration." *Popular Science Monthly* 73 (October): 326–29.

Jessop, Bob. 1982. *The Capitalist State*. New York: New York University Press.

Johns Hopkins University. 1926. *Johns Hopkins Half Century Directory, 1876–1926*. Baltimore: Johns Hopkins Press.

Johnston, Thomas R., and Hand, Helen. 1940. *The Trustees and the Officers of Purdue University*. Lafayette: Purdue University.

Kadushin, Charles. 1974. *The American Intellectual Elite*. Boston: Little, Brown, and Co.

Kaplan, Craig, and Schrecker, Ellen. *Regulating the Intellectuals: Perspectives on Academic Freedom in the 1980s*. New York: Praeger Press.

Karabel, Jerome, ed. 1977. *Power and Ideology in Education*. Oxford: Oxford University Press.

Karabel, Jerome. 1981. *Trends in the Racial, Sexual, and Class Inequalities in Access to American Higher Education*. Cambridge, Mass.: Huron Institute.

Kevles, Daniel J. 1979. *The Physicists: The History of a Scientific Community in Modern America*. New York: Vintage Press.

Kirkland, Moses. 1895. *History of Chicago*. 2 vols. Chicago: Munsell and Co.

Kirkpatrick, James E. 1926. *The American College and Its Rulers*. New York: New Republic Press.

Kolko, Gabriel. 1977. *The Triumph of Conservatism: A Reinterpretation of American History, 1900–1916*. New York: Free Press.

Kotz, David M. 1978. "Finance Capital and Corporate Control." In Richard C. Edwards, ed., *The Capitalist System: A Radical Analysis of American Society*, pp. 147–58. 2nd ed. Englewood Cliffs, N.J.: Prentice-Hall.

Ladd, Everett Carl, and Lipset, Seymour Martin. 1975. *The Divided Academy: Professors and Politics*. New York: W. W. Norton and Co.

Lambert, W. A. 1913. "Liberty in Teaching." *The Nation* 97 (July 3): 11.

Lampman, Robert J. 1962. *The Share of Top Wealth-Holders in National Wealth*. Princeton: Princeton University Press.

Lane, Winthrop D. 1926. *Military Training in Schools and Colleges of the United States*. New York: Committee on Military Training.

Larson, Margali Sarfatti. 1977. *The Rise of Professionalism: A Sociological Analysis*. Berkeley and Los Angeles: University of California Press.

Lawton, William Cranston. 1906. "The Decay of Academic Courage." *Educational Review* 32 (November): 395–404.

Lefort, Claude. 1986. "What Is Bureaucracy?" In *The Political Forms of Modern Society: Bureaucracy, Democracy, Totalitarianism*, pp. 89–121. Cambridge: MIT Press.

Leighton, J. A. 1920. "Report of Committee T on the Place and Function of Faculties in University Government and Administration." *Bulletin of the AAUP* 6 (March): 17–47.

Lester, Jeanette Ann. 1968. "The AFT in Higher Education: A History of Union Organization of Faculty Members in Colleges and Universities, 1916–1966." Ph.D. diss., University of Toledo.

Levine, David O. 1986. *The American College and the Culture of Aspiration, 1915–1940*. Ithaca: Cornell University Press.

Lindblom, Charles. 1977. *Politics and Markets*. New York: Basic Books.

Lindeman, Eduard C. 1936. *Wealth and Culture: A Study of One Hundred Foundations and Community Trusts and Their Operations during the Decade 1921–1930*. New York: Harcourt, Brace, and World.

Lintner, John. 1969. "The Financing of Corporations." In Edward Mason, ed., *The Corporation in Modern Society*. New York: Atheneum Press.

Lipset, Seymour Martin. 1972. *Rebellion in the University: A History of Student Activism in America*. London: Routledge and Kegan Paul.

Livingston, Arthur. 1917. "Academic Freedom." *New Republic*, November 17, pp. 69–71.

"Local and Chapter Notes." 1925. *Bulletin of the AAUP* 11 (October): 309–10.

Lockmiller, David A. 1939. *History of the North Carolina State College of Agriculture and Engineering, 1889–1939*. Raleigh: Edwards and Broughton Co.

Lodge, Henry Cabot. 1912. "The Constitution and Its Makers." *North American Review* 196 (July): 20–51.

London, Jack. 1908. "Revolution." *Contemporary Review* 93 (January): 2–31.

Lovejoy, Arthur O. 1918. "Report on Academic Freedom in Wartime." *Bulletin of the AAUP* 4 (February–March): 29–47.

Lovejoy, Arthur O. 1919. "Annual Message of the President of the AAUP." *Bulletin of the AAUP* 5 (November–December): 10–40.

Lowell, A. Lawrence. 1910. "The Physiology of Politics." *American Political Science Review* 4 (February): 1–15.

Lukes, Steven. 1974. *Power: A Radical View.* London: Macmillan.

McCarthy, Charles. 1912. *The Wisconsin Idea.* New York: Macmillan Co.

McClintock, Thomas C. 1962. "J. Allen Smith: A Pacific Northwest Progressive." *Pacific Northwest Quarterly*, April, pp. 49–59.

McCracken, John Henry. 1920. *College and Commonwealth.* New York: Century Co.

MacDonald, Edward D., and Hinton, Edward M. 1942. *Drexel Institute of Technology, 1891–1941: A Memorial History.* Philadelphia: Drexel Institute of Technology.

McGrath, Earl J. 1936. "The Control of Higher Education in America." *Educational Record* 17 (April): 259–72.

Machlup, Fritz. 1962. *The Production and Distribution of Knowledge in the United States.* Princeton: Princeton University Press.

McVey, Frank L., and Hughes, Raymond M. 1952. *College and University Administration.* Ames: Iowa State University Press.

Mandel, Ernest. 1975. "The Industrial Cycle in Late Capitalism." *New Left Review* 90 (March–April): 3–25.

Mandel, Ernest. 1980. *Long Waves of Capitalist Development: The Marxist Interpretation.* Cambridge: Cambridge University Press.

Manley, Robert N. 1967. *Centennial History of the University of Nebraska.* 2 vols. Lincoln: University of Nebraska Press.

Mann, Michael. 1975. "The Ideology of Intellectuals and Other People in the Development of Capitalism." In Leon Lindberg, ed., *Stress and Contradiction in Modern Capitalism: Public Policy and the Theory of the State*, pp. 275–307. Lexington, Mass.: D. C. Heath.

Mannheim, Karl. 1936. *Ideology and Utopia.* New York: Harcourt, Brace, Jovanovich.

Marx, Karl, and Engels, Friedrich. 1970. *The German Ideology.* New York: International Publishers.

May, Henry. 1963. *The Discontent of the Intellectuals: A Problem of the Twenties.* Chicago: Rand-McNally and Co.

Mead, E. D. 1897. "Editor's Table." *New England Magazine*, September, pp. 119–28.

Means, Gardiner C. 1939. *The Structure of the American Economy.* Washington, D.C.: GPO.

Means, Gardiner C. 1972. "Business Concentration in the American Economy." In Richard C. Edwards, ed., *The Capitalist System: A Radical Analysis of American Society*, pp. 145–56. Englewood Cliffs, N.J.: Prentice-Hall.

Meiklejohn, Alexander. 1920. *The Liberal College.* Boston: Marshall Jones Co.

Meiklejohn, Alexander. 1981. *The Experimental College.* Cabin John, Md.: Seven Locks Press.

Melman, Seymour. 1974. *The Permanent War Economy: American Capitalism in Decline.* New York: Simon and Schuster.

Merton, Robert. 1972. *Social Theory and Social Structure.* Chicago: University of Chicago Press.

Merwin, C. L. 1942. "American Studies of the Distribution of Wealth and Income by Size." *Studies in Income and Wealth.* New York: Columbia University Press.

Miliband, Ralph. 1969. *The State in Capitalist Society: An Analysis of the Western System of Power.* New York: Basic Books.

Mill, John Stuart. 1975. "On Liberty." In *Three Essays*, pp. 5–141. Oxford: Oxford University Press.

"Mr. Rockefeller's Educational Trust." *Current Literature* 42 (March 1907): 253–54.

Moore, Wilbert E. 1970. *The Professions: Roles and Rules*. New York: Russell Sage Foundation.

Morris, James O. 1958. *Conflict within the AFL: A Study of Craft versus Industrial Unionism, 1901–1938*. Ithaca: Cornell University Press.

Morton, J. Sterling. 1905. *Illustrated History of Nebraska*. 2 vols. Lincoln: Jacob North and Co.

Myers, Burton Dorr. 1951. *Officers of Indiana University, 1820–1950*. Bloomington: Indiana University Press.

Nearing, Scott. 1917. "Who's Who among College Trustees?" *School and Society* 6 (September 8): 297–99.

Nearing, Scott. 1972. *The Making of a Radical: A Political Autobiography*. New York: Harper and Row Publishers.

Nelson, Daniel. 1980. *Frederick Taylor and the Rise of Scientific Management*. Madison: University of Wisconsin Press.

Nelson, Ralph L. 1959. *Merger Movements in American Industry, 1895–1956*. Princeton: Princeton University Press.

Nelson, Richard R.; Peck, Merton J.; and Kalachek, Edward D. 1967. *Technology, Economic Growth, and Public Policy*. Washington, D.C.: Brookings Institution.

Nisbet, Robert. 1970. "Project Camelot: An Autopsy." In Philip Rieff, ed., *On Intellectuals*, pp. 307–39. Garden City: Doubleday and Co.

Noble, David. 1977. *America by Design: Science, Technology, and the Rise of Corporate Capitalism*. New York: Alfred A. Knopf.

Nordan, Max. 1923. "White-Collar Slaves." *Railway Carmen's Journal*, January, p. 57.

Nore, Ellen. 1983. *Charles A. Beard: An Intellectual Biography*. Carbondale: Southern Illinois University Press.

Norton, Theodore N., and Ollman, Bertell, eds. 1979. *Studies in Socialist Pedagogy*. New York: Monthly Review Press.

Oberschall, Anthony. 1973. *Social Conflict and Social Movements*. Englewood Cliffs, N.J.: Prentice-Hall.

O'Brien, Conor Cruise, and Vanech, William Dean, eds. 1969. *Power and Consciousness*. New York: New York University Press.

O'Connor, James. 1973. *The Fiscal Crisis of the State*. New York: St. Martin's Press.

O'Connor, James. 1987. *The Meaning of Crisis: A Theoretical Introduction*. London: Basil Blackwell.

Offe, Claus. 1984. *Contradictions of the Welfare State*. Cambridge: MIT Press.

Okun, Arthur. 1975. *Equality and Efficiency: The Big Trade-Off*. Washington, D.C.: Brookings Institution.

Ollman, Bertell. 1984. "Academic Freedom in America Today: A Marxist View." *Monthly Review*, March, pp. 1–12.

Ollman, Bertell, and Vernoff, Edward. 1982. *The Left Academy: Marxist Scholarship on American Campuses*. New York: McGraw-Hill Book Co.

Parsons, Talcott. 1970. "The Intellectual: A Social Role Category." In Philip Rieff, ed., *On Intellectuals*. Garden City, N.Y.: Doubleday and Co.

Parsons, Talcott. 1977. "Considerations on the American Academic System." In Walter P. Metzger, ed., *Reader on the Sociology of the Academic Profession*, pp. 497–510. New York: Arno Press.

Parsons, Talcott, and Platt, Gerald M. 1973. *The American University.* Cambridge: Harvard University Press.

Perlman, Mark. 1961. *The Machinists: A New Study in American Trade Unionism.* Cambridge: Harvard University Press.

Perry, George Sessions. 1951. *The Story of Texas A&M.* New York: McGraw-Hill Co.

Petersen, William J. 1952. *The Story of Iowa.* 4 vols. New York: Lewis Historical Publishing Co.

Peterson, George E. 1964. *The New England College in the Age of the University.* Amherst: Amherst College Press.

Piccard, Paul J., ed. 1969. *Science and Policy Issues.* Itasca, Ill.: F. E. Peacock Publishers.

"The Point of View." *Scribner's Magazine* 42 (1907): 122–24.

Polanyi, Karl. 1944. *The Great Transformation.* Boston: Beacon Press.

"Political Revolt in the Northwest, III: Making the Schools an Issue." *New Republic,* November 17, 1917, pp. 71–73.

Pollard, James E. 1952. *History of the Ohio State University: The Story of Its First Seventy-Five Years, 1873–1948.* Columbus: Ohio State University Press.

Poulantzas, Nicos. 1973. *Political Power and Social Classes.* London: New Left Books.

Poulantzas, Nicos. 1978. *Classes in Contemporary Capitalism.* London: New Left Books.

Poulantzas, Nicos. 1980. *State, Power, Socialism.* London: New Left Books.

Powers, William H. 1931. *A History of South Dakota State College.* Brookings: South Dakota State College.

Presthus, Robert. 1962. *The Organizational Society.* New York: Alfred A. Knopf.

Price, Geoffrey. 1984–1985. "Universities Today: Between the Corporate State and the Market." *Culture, Education, and Society* 39 (Winter): 43–58.

Pritchett, Henry S. 1905. "Shall the University Become a Business Corporation?" *Atlantic Monthly* 96 (September): 289–99.

Pritchett, Henry S. 1906. "Policy of the Carnegie Foundation." *Educational Review* 32 (June): 83–93.

Pritchett, Henry S. 1908. "Organization of Higher Education." *Atlantic Monthly* 102 (December): 783–89.

Pritchett, Henry S. 1908. "Scope and Practical Workings of the Carnegie Foundation for the Advancement of Teaching." *Journal of Education,* December 17, pp. 656–57.

"A Professional Fiasco." *New Republic,* May 28, 1924, p. 6.

Ratner, Sidney. 1942. *American Taxation: Its History as a Social Force in Democracy.* New York: W. W. Norton and Co.

Raugh, Morton A. 1968. *The Trusteeship of Colleges and Universities.* New York: McGraw-Hill Book Co.

Reeves, Floyd W. 1933. *Organization and Administration.* Chicago: University of Chicago Press.

Reich, Michael. 1972. "The Evolution of the United States Labor Force." In Richard C. Edwards, ed., *The Capitalist System.* Englewood Cliffs, N.J.: Prentice-Hall.

"Report of the Committee of Inquiry Concerning Charges of Violation of Academic Freedom at the University of Colorado." *Bulletin of the AAUP* 2 (April 1916): 3–71.

"Report of the Committee of Inquiry on the Colorado School of Mines." *Bulletin of the AAUP* 6 (May 1920): 9–40.

Report of the Proceedings of the Thirty-Eighth Annual Convention of the American Federation of Labor, St. Paul, Minn., June 10–20, 1918.

"Report on Charges of Violation of Academic Freedom at the University of Colorado and at Wesleyan University." *Bulletin of the AAUP* (1915).

"Report on Middlebury College." *Bulletin of the AAUP* 7 (May 1921): 28–37.

"Report on the University of Arizona." *Bulletin of the AAUP* 10 (November 1924): 18–35.

"Report on the University of Montana." *Bulletin of the AAUP* 10 (March 1924): 50–58.

"Report on the University of Montana—The Levine Case." *Bulletin of the AAUP* (May 1919): 13–25.

"Report on Washburn College." *Bulletin of the AAUP* 7 (January–February 1921): 66–137.

Reynolds, John Hugh, and Thomas, David Yancey. 1910. *History of the University of Arkansas*. Fayetteville: University of Arkansas Press.

Ross, Earle D. 1942. *A History of the Iowa State College of Agriculture and Mechanic Arts*. Ames: Iowa State College Press.

Rowland, Dunbar. 1925. *History of Mississippi: The Heart of the South*. Jackson: S. J. Clarke Publishing Co.

Rude, George. 1979. *Ideology and Popular Protest*. New York: Pantheon Books.

Rudolph, Frederick. 1962. *The American College and University: A History*. New York: Alfred A. Knopf.

Ruml, Beardsley, and Tickton, Sidney. 1955. *Teaching Salaries Then and Now: A Fifty-Year Comparison with Other Occupations and Industries*. New York: Fund for the Advancement of Education.

Sanders, Elizabeth. 1987. "Industrial Concentration, Sectional Competition, and Antitrust Politics in America, 1880–1980." *Studies in American Political Development* 1: 142–214.

Sargeant, Ide G. 1915. "Vermont and the Carnegie Survey." *Journal of Education* 81 (May 13): 508–11.

Sartre, Jean-Paul. 1974. *Between Existentialism and Marxism*. New York: Pantheon Books.

Scase, Richard, ed. 1980. *The State in Western Europe*. London: St. Martin's Press.

Schneider, David. 1928. *The Workers' (Communist) Party and American Trade Unions*. Baltimore: Johns Hopkins Press.

Scott, Russell. 1920. "The 'New Virility' in America." *New Statesman*, February 28, pp. 613–14.

Seabury, Paul, ed. 1979. *Bureaucrats and Brainpower*. San Francisco: Institute for Contemporary Studies.

Seidman, Joel. 1942. *The Needle Trades*. New York: Farrar and Rinehart.

Seligman, E.R.A., et al. 1915. "Preliminary Report of the Joint Committee on Academic Freedom." *American Political Science Review* 9 (May): 374–81.

Sellers, Charles Coleman. 1973. Dickinson College: A History. Middletown, Conn.: Wesleyan University Press.

"A Serious Situation." *Journal of Education*, February 15, 1915.

Shibley, G. H. 1900. "The University and Social Questions." *Arena* 23: 294–96.

Shils, Edward. 1972. *The Intellectuals and the Powers*. Chicago: University of Chicago Press.

Shils, Edward. 1972. *The Constitution of Society*. Chicago: University of Chicago Press.

Shor, Ira. 1980. *Critical Teaching and Everyday Life*. Boston: South End Press.

Shor, Ira. 1987. *A Pedagogy for Liberation*. South Hadley, Mass.: Bergin and Garvey Publishers.

Shugg, Robert W. 1939. *Origins of Class Struggle in Louisiana: A Social History of White Farmers and Laborers during Slavery and After, 1840–1875.* Baton Rouge: Louisiana State University Press.

Sinclair, Upton. 1923. *The Goose-Step: A Study of American Education.* Rev. ed. Pasadena: Privately Printed.

Skillman, David B. 1932. *The Biography of a College: Being the History of the First Century of the Life of Lafayette College.* 2 vols. Easton, Pa.: Lafayette College.

Skocpol, Theda. 1979. *States and Revolution.* Cambridge: Cambridge University Press.

Skocpol, Theda. 1980. "Political Response to Capitalist Crisis: Neo-Marxist Theories of the State and the Case of the New Deal." *Politics and Society* 10:155–201.

Skowronek, Stephen. 1982. *Building a New American State: The Expansion of National Administrative Capacities, 1877–1920.* Cambridge: Cambridge University Press.

Smith, Adam. 1965. *An Inquiry into the Nature and Causes of the Wealth of Nations.* New York: Modern Library.

Smith, David N. 1974. *Who Rules the Universities? An Essay in Class Analysis.* New York: Monthly Review Press.

Smith, Durrell Hevenor. 1923. *The Bureau of Education: Its History, Activities, and Organization.* Baltimore: Johns Hopkins Press.

Snowden, Clinton A. 1909. *History of Washington.* 4 vols. New York: Century History Co.

Solberg, Winton U. 1968. *The University of Illinois, 1867–1894: An Intellectual and Cultural History.* Chicago: University of Illinois Press.

Spring, Joel H. 1972. *Education and the Rise of the Corporate State.* Boston: Beacon Press.

Spring, Joel H. 1980. *Educating the Worker-Citizen.* New York: Longman.

Stadtman, Verne A. 1968. *The Centennial Record of the University of California, 1868–1968.* Berkeley and Los Angeles: University of California Press.

Stevenson, John J. 1904. "The Status of American College Professors." *Popular Science Monthly* 66 (December): 122–30.

Story, Ronald. 1980. *The Forging of an Aristocracy: Harvard and the Boston Upper Class, 1800–1870.* Middletown, Conn.: Wesleyan University Press.

"A Survey of the Vermont Survey." *Journal of Education* 79 (March 26, 1914): 350–51.

Taylor, Frederick. 1911. *The Principles of Scientific Management.* New York: Harper and Bros.

Taylor, James Monroe, and Haight, Elizabeth Hazelton. 1915. *Vassar.* New York: Oxford University Press.

Thilly, Frank. 1911. "The Characteristics of the Present Age." *Hibbert Journal* 10 (October): 253–66.

Thilly, Frank. 1917. "Annual Report of the President." *Bulletin of the AAUP* 3 (November): 11–24.

Thompson, Edward P. 1963. *The Making of the English Working Class.* London: Gollancz.

Thwing, Charles. 1920. *The American College and Universities in the Great War, 1914–1919.* New York: Macmillan Co.

Thwing, Charles. 1928. *The American and German University: One Hundred Years of History.* New York: Macmillan Co.

Tilly, Charles. 1975. *The Formation of National States in Western Europe.* Princeton: Princeton University Press.

Tilly, Charles. 1978. *From Mobilization to Revolution.* New York: Random House.

Tobey, Ronald C. 1971. *The American Ideology of National Science, 1919–1930.* Pittsburgh: University of Pittsburgh Press.

Touraine, Alain. 1974. *The Academic System in American Society.* New York: McGraw-Hill Book Co.

Trombley, Kenneth E. 1954. *The Life and Times of a Happy Liberal: A Biography of Morris Llewellyn Cooke.* New York: Harper and Brothers.

True, Rodney H. 1929. "Salary Scales of Trained Men and Women." *Bulletin of the AAUP* 15 (December): 538–40.

University of Mississippi. 1910. *Historical Catalogue of the University of Mississippi, 1849–1909.* Nashville: Marshall and Bruce Co.

University of Pennsylvania. 1914. "The Professors' Union." *Alumni Register,* February.

Vanderlip, Frank A. 1907. *Business and Education.* New York: Duffield and Co.

Van Hise, Charles R. 1912. *Concentration and Control: A Solution of the Trust Problem in the United States.* New York: Macmillan Co.

Veblen, Thorstein. 1912. *The Instinct of Workmanship and the State of the Industrial Arts.* New York: B. W. Huebsch.

Veblen, Thorstein. 1957. *The Higher Learning in America: A Memorandum on the Conduct of Universities by Businessmen.* New York: Sagamore Press.

Veysey, Laurence R. 1965. *The Emergence of the American University.* Chicago: University of Chicago Press.

Wakeby, Arthur C. 1917. *Omaha: The Gate City and Douglas County, Nebraska.* 2 vols. Chicago: S. J. Clarke Publishing Co.

Walker, Francis A. 1890. "The Tide of Economic Thought: Presidential Address to the American Economic Association." *Report of the Proceedings of the Fourth Annual Meeting of the American Economic Association,* December 26–30, pp. 15–21.

Wallas, Graham. 1920. "The 'New Virility' in America." *New Statesman,* January 31, pp. 487–88.

Warren, Howard C. 1914. "Academic Freedom." *Atlantic Monthly* 114 (November): 689–99.

Weber, Max. 1949. *The Methodology of the Social Sciences.* New York: Free Press.

Weber, Max. 1977. *From Max Weber: Essays in Sociology.* Ed. Hans H. Gerth and C. Wright Mills. New York: Oxford University Press.

Wechsler, James. 1936. *Revolt on the Campus.* Seattle: University of Washington Press.

Weinstein, James. 1968. *The Corporate Ideal in the Liberal State, 1900–1918.* Boston: Beacon Press.

Whitfield, Stephen J. 1974. *Scott Nearing: Apostle of American Radicalism.* New York: Columbia University Press.

Who Rules Columbia? New York: North American Congress on Latin America, 1968.

Wiebe, Robert. 1962. *Businessmen and Reform: A Study of the Progressive Movement.* Cambridge: Harvard University Press.

Wiebe, Robert. 1967. *The Search for Order, 1877–1920.* New York: Hill and Wang.

Wigmore, J. H. 1916. "President's Report for 1916." *Bulletin of the AAUP* 2 (November): 9–52.

Will, Thomas Elmer. 1901. "A Menace to Freedom: The College Trust." *Arena* 26 (September): 244–57.

Willard, Julius Terras. 1940. *History of the Kansas State College of Agriculture and Applied Science.* Manhattan, Kans.: Kansas State College Press.

Williams, William Appleman. 1972. "A Profile of the Corporate Elite." In Ronald Radosh and Murray N. Rothbard, eds., *A New History of Leviathan*, pp. 1–6. New York: E. P. Dutton.

Wills, Elbert Vaughn. 1936. *The Growth of American Higher Education*. Philadelphia: Dorrance and Co.

Witmer, Lightner. 1915. *The Nearing Case*. New York: B. W. Huebsch.

Wolfe, Alan. 1978. *The Limits of Legitimacy: Political Contradictions of Contemporary Capitalism*. New York: Free Press.

Wolff, Robert Paul. 1969. *The Ideal of the University*. Boston: Beacon Press.

Wright, Erik Olin. 1978. "Intellectuals and the Working Class." *Insurgent Sociologist* 8 (Winter): 5–18.

Yarreo, V. S. 1898. "Freedom of Teaching in America." *Westminster Review*, January, pp. 8–16.

Zimmerman, Ekhart. 1985. "The 1930s World Economic Crisis in Six European Countries: A First Report on Causes of Political Instability and Reactions to Crisis." In Paul M. Johnson and William R. Thompson, eds., *Rhythms in Politics and Economics*. New York: Praeger Press.

GOVERNMENT DOCUMENTS

All printed documents published in Washington, D.C., by the Government Printing Office, unless otherwise noted.

U.S. Bureau of Education: Published Documents

Annual Report of the Commissioner of Education, 1870–1914.

Biennial Survey of Education, 1916–30.

Capen, Samuel P. 1916. *A Survey of Educational Institutions in the State of Washington*. Bulletin, 1916, no. 26.

Educational Surveys. Bulletin, 1928, no. 11.

Education in Patriotism: A Synopsis of the Agencies at Work. Teachers' Leaflet no. 2. April 1918.

Ellis, A. Coswell. *The Money Value of Education*. Bulletin, 1917, no. 22.

Engineering Education after the War. Bulletin, 1921, no. 50.

Government Policies Involving the Schools in Wartime. Teachers' Leaflet no. 3. April 1918.

Increases in Salaries of College Teachers. Higher Education Circular no. 15. July 1919.

Koos, Leonard V. *The Adjustment of a Teaching Load at a University*. Bulletin, 1919, no. 15.

Land-Grant College Education, 1910–1920. Bulletin, 1924, no. 30.

Land-Grant Colleges, 1926. Bulletin, 1927, no. 37.

National Crisis in Education: An Appeal to the People. Bulletin, 1920, no. 29.

Opportunities for History Teachers: The Lessons of the Great War in the Classroom. Teachers' Leaflet no. 1. December 1917.

Physical Education in American Colleges and Universities. Bulletin, 1927, no. 14.

Recent Movements in University Administration. Bulletin, 1916, no. 46.

Sears, Jesse B. *Philanthropy in American Higher Education*. Bulletin, 1922, no. 26.

State Survey of Higher Educational Institutions of Iowa. Bulletin, 1916. no. 19.

Survey of Negro Colleges and Universities. Bulletin, 1928, no. 7.

The Work of American Colleges and Universities during the War: A Report of the Work of the Education Section of the Committee on Engineering and Education of the Advisory Commission of the Council of National Defense. Higher Education Circular no. 2. June 8, 1917.

The Work of American Colleges and Universities during the War: Contribution of Higher Institutions to the War and to Reconstruction. Higher Education Circular no. 4. August 30, 1917.

The Work of American Colleges and Universities during the War: A Report of the Work of the Education Section of the Committee on Engineering and Education of the Advisory Commission of the Council of National Defense. Higher Education Circular no. 5. December 15, 1917.

The Work of American Colleges and Universities during the War: Contribution of Higher Institutions to the War and to Reconstruction. Higher Education Circular no. 6. January 1918.

Work of American Colleges and Universities during the War: Effect of the War on College Budgets. Higher Education Circular no. 10. April 1918.

Work of American Colleges and Universities during the War: Effect of the War on Student Enrollment. Higher Education Circular no. 9. April 1918.

U.S. Bureau of Education: Unpublished Documents

All of the following documents are located in the National Archives, Washington, D.C., Record Group 12. Listings are in chronological order.

Documents from Press Copies of Letters Sent, 1870–1908: "O" Series, M635.
Commissioner of Education to the Secretary of the Interior, January 8, 1903.
Elmer E. Brown, Commissioner of Education, to Henry S. Pritchett, President of the Carnegie Foundation, August 13, 1906.
Lovich Pierce, Acting Commissioner of Education, to A. Le F. Derby, Assistant Secretary of the Carnegie Foundation, October 3, 1906.
Commissioner of Education to Secretary of the Interior, December 12, 1906.
Elmer E. Brown, Commissioner of Education, to Dr. Samuel A. Green, Massachusetts Historical Society, April 18, 1907.
Indexes to Letters Received.
Documents from Historical File no. 100: Organization of the Office, vol. 2.
Brown, E. E. "Partial Program for the Development of the Bureau of Education in the Near Future." Undated.
Gulick, L. "A Brief for the Extension Plans of the United States Bureau of Education." Undated.
James A. Tawney, Chairman, Committee on Appropriations, House of Representatives to Hon. Elmer E. Brown, Commissioner of Education, June 10, 1908.
Report Prepared by L. A. Kalbach, Acting Commissioner of Education, and Submitted to Secretary of Interior Bollinger for use by Senator Bourne, Jr., Chairman, Committee on Public Expenditures, August 20, 1909.
Gulick, L. "What the Bureau of Education Should Be and Do to Further Education in America." October 1909.
Memorandum of Conference at Luncheon at the Hotel Willard, Washington, D.C., Saturday, March 26, 1910.

Memorandum of Meeting Held at the Ebbitt House, Washington, D.C., March 27, 1910.

Memorandum by Elmer Elsworth Brown. Undated.

Report on the Campaign in Behalf of the United States Bureau of Education. Undated.

Henry S. Pritchett to Hon. Walter L. Fisher, Secretary of the Interior, May 29, 1911.

P. P. Claxton to the Secretary of the Interior, August 10, 1911.

Assistant Attorney General for the Department of the Interior to the Secretary of the Interior, August 20, 1911.

Acting Secretary of the Interior to P. P. Claxton, August 28, 1911.

Assistant Attorney General for the Department of the Interior to the Secretary of the Interior, November 9, 1911.

P. P. Claxton to Hon. Franklin K. Lane, Secretary of the Interior, January 13, 1917.

Documents from Historical File no. 106, vol. 8.

Loose handwritten note, signed JDW. Undated.

Loose handwritten note, signed J.C.B. Undated.

Loose handwritten note, signed F.B.D. Undated.

Loose handwritten note, signed Kle. B. Undated.

Loose handwritten note, signed A.S. Undated.

Miss Elsa Denison, Bureau of Municipal Research, to P. P. Claxton, Commissioner of Education, January 31, 1912.

P. P. Claxton to Miss Elsa Denison, February 3, 1912.

Chief Clerk of the Bureau of Education to Miss Elsa Denison, March 2, 1912.

P. P. Claxton, Commissioner of Education to Hon. James K. Baker, Secretary of the Interior, August 7, 1914.

Chief Clerk of the Bureau of Education to Mr. Basil M. Manly, January 20, 1915.

Documents from Historical File: Commissioner's File no. 107, War Articles, P. P. Claxton.

"Bureau of Education: Suggestions for War Service."

"P. P. Claxton, Activities in Connection with War Work."

Capen, Samuel P. "Report of the Division of Higher Education to the Executive Committee."

Woodrow Wilson to Franklin K. Lane, July 20, 1917.

Minutes of 3:30 P.M. to 5:15 P.M. Conference, Thursday, January 31, 1918.

Minutes of Conference, Friday, February 1, 1918.

"Scientific and Industrial Training in the War Emergency," June 28, 1918.

Commissioner P. P. Claxton to College Officers and Teachers, August 16, 1918.

Documents from School Survey Materials: Historical File no. 501.

E. A. Bryan to S. P. Capen, March 8, 1915. Box no. 106.

P. P. Claxton to Hollis Godfrey, February 23, 1916. Box no. 105.

S. P. Capen to P. P. Claxton, May 17, 1916. Box no. 104.

"Outline of Investigation of Higher Institutions in Connection with Educational Survey of Alabama." Undated.

"Information about Surveys Compiled for Use by Appropriations Committee." January 2, 1922.

"Higher Educational Surveys since 1921." January 5, 1926.

Jesse A. Bond to P. P. Claxton, January 29, 1927.

"Results of Educational Surveys Conducted by the U.S. Bureau of Education." September, 1928.

U.S. Secretary of the Interior

"General Education Board Annual Report," 1903–14. Secretary's Central File, National Archives, Record Group 48.

Letters from the Commissioner of Education to the Secretary of the Interior. Secretary's Central File, sec. 6, boxes 1526 and 1538, National Archives, Record Group 48.

U.S. House and Senate Documents

Report of the Committee Appointed Pursuant to H.R. 429 and 574 to Investigate the Concentration of Money and Credit by the U.S. House Banking and Currency Committee. 62nd Congress, 2nd Session. 1913.

Report of the U.S. Senate Subcommittee on the Judiciary: Brewing and Liquor Interests and German and Bolshevik Propaganda. U.S. Senate Documents, no. 61. 66th Congress, 1st Session. 1919.

Report and Hearings of the U.S. Senate Subcommittee on the Judiciary: Brewing and Liquor Interests and German and Bolshevik Propaganda. U.S. Senate Documents, no. 62. 66th Congress, 1st Session. Vols. 2–3. 1919.

Miscellaneous Government Documents

Bureau of the Census. 1975. *Historical Statistics of the United States: Colonial Times to 1970.* 2 vols.

Bureau of Labor Statistics. 1926. *Union Scale of Wages and Hours of Labor.* Bulletin no. 431. May 15.

Capen, Samuel P. 1915. *Report of a Survey of the University of Oregon.* University of Oregon Bulletin, n.s., vol. 13, no. 4. Salem: State Printing Department.

Capen, Samuel P. 1916. *A Report on the Colleges of North Carolina.* Raleigh: Office of the State Superintendent of Public Instruction.

Committee on Public Information. 1918. *Official U.S. Bulletin.* Vol. 2, no. 413. September 16.

Department of Health, Education, and Welfare. 1979. *Digest of Education Statistics.*

Department of the Navy. 1918. "Schools and Colleges with Naval Units." *Report of the Secretary of the Navy.*

Department of War. 1919. *Committee on Education and Special Training: A Review of Its Work during 1918.*

New York Joint Legislative Committee Investigating Seditious Activities. 1920. *Revolutionary Radicalism: Its History, Purposes, and Tactics, with an Exposition and Discussion of the Steps Being Taken and Required to Curb it.* 4 vols. Albany: J. B. Lyon Co., Printers.

Temporary National Economic Committee. 1941. *Investigation of Concentration of Economic Power: The Structure of Industry.*

Temporary National Economic Committee. 1941. *Investigation of Concentration of Economic Power: Final Report.*

PUBLICATIONS OF PRIVATE EDUCATIONAL FOUNDATIONS

Carnegie Foundation for the Advancement of Teaching

Admission of State Institutions to the System of Retiring Allowances of the Carnegie Foundation. Bulletin no. 1. New York, 1907.

Annual Report. New York, 1907–30.

Cooke, Morris L. 1910. *Academic and Industrial Efficiency: A Report.* Bulletin no. 5. Boston: Merrymount Press.

Financial Status of the Professor in America and Germany. Bulletin no. 2. New York: G. P. Putnam's Sons, 1917.

Mann, Charles R. 1918. *Study of Engineering Education.* Bulletin no. 11. New York.

Standard Forms for Financial Reports of Colleges, Universities, and Technical Schools. Bulletin no. 3. New York, 1910.

Study of Education in Vermont. Bulletin no. 7. Montpelier, 1914.

General Education Board

Annual Report of the General Education Board, 1915/16–1929/30.

General Education Board: An Account of Its Activities, 1902–1914. 1915.

Flexner, Abraham, and Bachman, Frank P. 1915. *Public Education in Maryland.*

MISCELLANEOUS MANUSCRIPTS

Capen, Samuel P. Letters from Samuel P. Capen to Mrs. Samuel P. Capen, 1914–19. Capen Papers, boxes 7–10, University Archives, State University of New York at Buffalo.

Capen, Samuel P. "The Status of the Land-Grant College as Outlined in Reports of Surveys Recently Made by the United States Bureau of Education." 1919. Capen Speeches, University Archives, State University of New York at Buffalo.

Index

Academic freedom: material limits to, 12, 13, 198; and political movements, 183–84, 188; western islands of, 188, 199; institutional organization of, 202–3; and academic tenure, 209–10, 214; during WWI, 221–31; psychology of, 231, 235–36; and Red Scare, 231–36; decline in violations of, 246–47
—concept of: defined, 186; German, 188, 194, 220, 291*n*10; managerial, 194–200, 244–45;
—cases: Richard T. Ely, 187–89; Edward W. Beemis, 189–90; E. Benjamin Andrews, 190–91; Edward A. Ross, 191–92; John R. Commons, 192–93; I. A. Hourwich, 193; James Allen Smith, 193; Frank Parsons, 193–94; Vernon L. Parrington, 194; John Lewinsohn, 201; Charles E. Carpenter, 201; Professor X, 204; James McKeen Cattell, 204, 225; A. E. Morse, 205; University of Iowa, 205; Willard C. Fisher, 205, 208–9; John M. Mecklin, 206–7; University of Utah, 211–12; James H. Brewster, 213; Scott Nearing, 214–17, 220; Charles O. Fest, 220; John C. Bailar, 220; Benjamin Kendrick, 222, 224; Leon Fraser, 222, 224; Charles Beard, 222–23, 225–26; H. W. L. Dana, 225; Ellery C. Stowell, 227; William Schaper, 227–28, 230–31; Allan Eaton, 228; Lyford Edwards, 228; Patten, 228; William E. Waltz, 228; Arthur Fisher, 241; Herriot C. Palmer, 241; James G. Stevens, 241; Louis Levine, 241; University of Arizona, 241; W. H. Lawrence, 241; evolution cases, 241–42; Alexander Meiklejohn, 243–46. *See also* American Association of University Professors; New York Joint Legislative Committee Investigating Seditious Activities

Academy of Political Science, 144
Adelphi College: faculty union at, 181; mentioned, 80
Agriculture, Department of. *See* United States Government
Alabama, University of, 119, 157
American Association for the Advancement of Science, 164
American Association of University Professors: on faculty salaries, 163; committee T on Place and Function of Faculties, 171–73; unionization rejected by, 182–84, 212; Committee on Academic Freedom and Academic Tenure, 210–13, 217, 219–20, 220, 241–42, 247–48, 249; accommodationist strategy of, 212–13, 247–48, 255; statement on academic freedom and academic tenure, 218–19, 229, 258; Committee on Academic Freedom in Wartime, 229; and criminal syndicalism laws, 234; proceduralism of, 241–42; mentioned, 130. *See also* Academic freedom
American Association of University Women, 248
American Council on Education: manpower training promoted by, 147–48; Conference on Academic Freedom, 248–49; mentioned, 255
American Economic Association: committee on academic freedom and academic tenure, 170–71, 208–9, 210; and Populism, 189, 192, 208; mentioned, 187
American Federation of Labor: and WWI, 125, 133–34; faculty unionization supported by, 182; mentioned, 186, 191, 235, 247

American Federation of Teachers, 180–82, 255
American Historical Association, 160
American Philosophical Association: statement on academic freedom and academic tenure 206–8
American Political Science Association: committee on academic freedom and academic tenure, 170, 208–9, 210; mentioned, 160
American Psychological Association, 206–8
American Socialist Party, 113, 143, 178, 214, 225, 230, 232, 238
American Sociological Society, 170–71, 208–9, 210
American Telephone and Telegraph, 148, 149
American University, 167
Amherst College: Meiklejohn case at, 243–46; mentioned, 190
Anarchism: Ely accused of, 187–88; and academic freedom, 196, 231, 234, 292n35
Andrews, E. Benjamin: academic freedom case, 190–91; appoints Edward A. Ross to University of Nebraska, 192; mentioned, 167, 187, 243
Angell, James R., 117, 137
Anna T. Jeannes Fund, 53, 64
Arizona, University of: survey of, 119; academic freedom case at, 241
Arnett, Trevor, 77
Association of American Agricultural Colleges, 127
Association of American Colleges, 248
Association of American Universities, 127, 248
Association of Governing Boards, 248
Association of Land-Grant Colleges, 248
Association of Urban Universities, 130, 248
Aydelotte, Frank, 145

Babcock, Kendrick C., 107, 111, 117
Bailey, Liberty Hyde, 117
Beard, Charles A.: on Professor X case, 204; flag incident, 222–23; resigns from Columbia University, 225–27; and League for Industrial Democracy, 236
Beck, Hubert Park: on university trustees, 41–42, 58, 271n12; mentioned, 258
Beemis, Edward W.: academic freedom

case, 189–90, 199; mentioned, 187, 189, 193, 194
Boards of Trustees. See Governing boards
Bowdoin College, 135
Boyd, Paul, 146
Boykin, J. C., 106
Brown, Elmer E.: and educational foundations, 102; mobilizes education lobby, 104; on government by influence, 107; described by Capen, 297n35; mentioned, 114
Brown University: Andrews case at, 190–91; mentioned, 167
Bryan, Enoch Albert, 116–17, 281n84
Bryan, William Jennings, 93, 190
Bureau of Education. See United States Government
Bureau of Labor Statistics. See United States Government
Bureau of Municipal Research, 105–6
Butler, Nicholas Murray: and CFAT, 61; on liberal education, 84; and Vermont survey, 98; and Henry Suzzalo, 114, 281n73; and national preparedness, 125; on impact of WWI, 146; on academic freedom, 195–204 passim, 221–27 passim; on educational progress, 273n18; mentioned, 240
Buttrick, Wallace, 62, 85

California, University of: survey of, 122; mentioned, 95–96, 178
Calvin, Henrietta, 117
Capen, Samuel P.: and Abraham Flexner, 111; and Hollis Godfrey, 111, 112; North Carolina survey, 111–12; and Washington Survey, 112, 116–17; and Raymond M. Hughes, 112, 117; and Iowa survey, 117; and WWI, 126, 129–30, 137; and American Council on Education, 147, 248; and National Research Council, 150; on USBE routine, 279n28; on E. E. Brown, 279n35; on P. P. Claxton, 279n35; on E. A. Bryan, 281n84; mentioned, 119, 160
Capitalism: and political development, 3–14 passim; and universities, 8–14, passim, 118–19, 148; and culture of aspiration, 8; and long-waves of economic development, 14–16; and uneven development, 26–29; and problem of academic freedom, 186, 237; accumulation crises of, 268n25; and

85–86, 98; endowment, 86; and strategy of perpendicular development, 86–87, 282*n105*; criticisms of, 88–89; and local politics, 94; and U.S. Bureau of Education, 103–9 *passim,* 112; group dynamics of, 272–73*n8*; mentioned, 61, 103. *See also* Financial groups; Educational surveys

General Electric, 149

Giddings, Franklin H., 210

Gillette, John M., 200–201

Gilman, Daniel Coit, 82

Godfrey, Hollis: and Frederick Taylor, 109; and Morris L. Cooke, 109; surveys Drexel Institute of Technology, 109–10; and Samuel P. Capen, 111, 112; chairs Committee on Engineering and Education, 126–27; on faculty productivity, 156–57; mentioned, 130

Goldman, Emma, 202, 234

Gompers, Samuel: and intellectuals, 181–82; Lusk committee on, 234, 235; mentioned 96, 151

Goodyear, 148

Governing boards: proprietary rights of, 13, 34; clergy on, 35, 39, 46; lawyers on, 39, 46; functions of, 43–44, 59, 67–68; attitudes of, 46, 78, 246; public officials on, 49–50, 51; agriculturalists on, 51–58 *passim;* labor and, 58

—social composition of: general, 32–35, 77–78; at major private universities and technical institutes in the Northeast, 35–46; at private liberal arts and denominational colleges, 46–50; at public universities in the South, 50–53; at state universities in the Midwest and West, 54–55; at land-grant colleges, 56–58, 272*n37*. *See also* Financial groups; Employment-at-Will Doctrine

Graves, Frank P., 76

Hadley, Arthur T.: on academic freedom, 198; mentioned, 117, 281*n90*

Hale, George Ellery, 139–141 *passim,* 149

Hampton Institute, 53

Harper, William Rainey, 189–90

Harrison, Charles C., 61

Harvard University, 42, 86, 89, 122, 135, 141, 178, 210, 238

Herron, George D.: and Christian Socialist movement, 192; dismissed from Iowa College, 194

Hofstadter, Richard, 24–25, 46

Hollis, Ernest Victor, 65, 87, 93

Howard University, 53, 181, 185

Hughes, Raymond M.: surveys Miami University, 110, 155–56; and Samuel P. Capen, 112; Iowa survey, 117, 281*n89*; on governing boards, 246

Humphreys, Alexander C., 61–62

Hunter College, 181

Hyde, William Dewitt: on business trustees, 77; university defined by, 197–98

Ideological Leadership: defined, 74–75, 274*n43*; exerted through surveys, 119; mentioned, 107

Ideological Power: defined, 14, 268*n12*; as a hegemonic project, 274–75*n46*; information and, 279*n37*; mentioned, 256

Ideological State Apparatus: universities as the polycentric core of, 7, 122–23; historical analysis of, 10; American ideology promoted by, 142–46; and academic freedom, 203; as a regulatory structure, 251–55

Illinois, University of: faculty union at, 180, 185; academic freedom at during WWI, 228; and students' class background, 277*n5*; mentioned, 95–96, 122, 190

Illinois State Normal School, 181, 185

Indiana University: and Commons case, 192–93; and students' class background, 277*n5*

Industrial Workers of the World, 113, 181, 231, 234

Intellectuals: and corporate-liberal state, 7–8; ideology of, 10, 171, 255–56; economic conditioning of, 12; businessmen critical of, 46; and strategy of survival, 200, 231

—autonomy of: 7, 256–57; limits to, 13–14, 198–200

—organic: clergy as, 39; engineers as, 39; lawyers as, 39; corporate, 61, 74–75; defined, 271*n11*, 297*n3*; working class, 178–80, 237–38, 255

Intercollegiate Liberal League, 238–40

Intercollegiate Socialist Society: described, 177–80; during WWI, 230–31; U.S. Senate investigates, 232; and Lusk Committee, 235; mentioned, 247, 255

International Harvester, 19

Index

329

alumni, 198, 214–216 *passim*, 243–44; instrumental order of defined, 265*n25*; expressive order of defined, 265*n26*. *See also* Colleges; Governing Boards; names of individual colleges and universities
Utah, University of, 211–12

Vail, Theodore N., 98, 99
Vanderlip, Frank A., 62, 82, 273*n18*
Van Hise, Charles, 196, 201–2, 203, 221
Veblen, Thorstein: origins of critical genre, 10; university defined by, 12; on governing boards, 32, 43, 45–46; on corporate ideal, 97, 154; social democratic ideal, 176; mentioned, 199
Vermont, University of, 98, 100
Vermont Agricultural College, 98, 100
Vincent, George E., 146, 149

War, Department of. *See* United States Government
Warner-Swasey, 149
Warren, Howard C.: on academic freedom, 205–6; and AAUP, 211
Washburn College: faculty union at, 181, 182, 185; Kirkpatrick case at, 241

Washington, University of: and Populist Party, 58, 113; and intellectual dissent, 92–93, 113; mentioned, 95–96
Weatherly, Ulysses G., 170, 208
Wechsler, James: on Columbia massacre, 227; mentioned, 258
Wentworth Institute, 145
Wesleyan University, 205, 208–9
Will, Thomas E., 89, 91, 92, 115, 190, 277*n108*
Williams College, 135
Wilson, Woodrow: and national preparedness, 125, 131; on applied science in the war, 127; National Research Council sanctioned by, 140, 141, 149
Wisconsin, University of: and intellectual dissent, 92–93, 192; survey of, 122; wartime research at, 142; union drive at, 185; academic freedom at, 188, 196, 200, 201–2, 221; mentioned, 79, 95–96, 210

Yale University: faculty salaries at, 163; faculty union at, 181; mentioned, 86, 122, 135, 167, 178, 210
Yerkes, Robert, 150